Health Care and Public Policy

Also by David Reisman

Adam Smith's Sociological Economics
Alfred Marshall: Progress and Politics
Alfred Marshall's Mission
Anthony Crosland: The Mixed Economy
Conservative Capitalism: The Social Economy
Crosland's Future: Opportunity and Outcome
Democracy and Exchange: Schumpeter, Galbraith, T.H. Marshall, Titmuss and
  Adam Smith
The Economics of Alfred Marshall
Galbraith and Market Capitalism
The Institutional Economy: Demand and Supply
Market and Health
The Political Economy of Health Care
The Political Economy of James Buchanan
Richard Titmuss: Welfare and Society
Schumpeter's Market: Enterprise and Evolution
State and Welfare: Tawney, Galbraith and Adam Smith
Theories of Collective Action: Downs, Olson and Hirsch

Health Care and Public Policy

David Reisman

Edward Elgar
Cheltenham, UK • Northampton, MA, USA

Published by
Edward Elgar Publishing Limited
Glensanda House
Montpellier Parade
Cheltenham
Glos GL50 1UA
UK

Edward Elgar Publishing, Inc.
William Pratt House
9 Dewey Court
Northampton
Massachusetts 01060
USA

A catalogue record for this book
is available from the British Library

Library of Congress Cataloguing in Publication Data
Reisman, David A.
   Health care and public policy / by David Reisman.
      p. cm.
   Includes bibliographical references and index.
   1. Medical policy. 2. Medical policy—Economic aspects. I. Title.

   RA393.R445 2007
   362.1—dc22

                                              2007001396

ISBN 978 1 84542 924 9

Typeset by Manton Typesetters, Louth, Lincolnshire, UK
Printed and bound in Great Britain by MPG Books Ltd, Bodmin, Cornwall

Contents

1. Introduction: a thing apart?

Adam Smith was in favour of pecuniary self-interest, rational choice and the invisible hand of supply and demand. The consumer and the shopper, he said, could be relied upon to produce the well-being of nations. The unique individual knows where the shoe pinches. The gain-seeking salesman knows whom he has to satisfy in order to live well: 'By pursuing his own interest he frequently promotes that of the society more effectually than when he really intends to promote it. I have never known much good done by those who affected to trade for the public good' (Smith, 1961 [1776]: I, 448).

Adam Smith looked to goal-orientated exchange to maximise people's welfare, self-perceived. Taken literally, his defence of devolution and factoring-down would suggest that health care is not a topic in public policy at all. The body-holder in need of a recommendation or a procedure buys in the intervention of the specialist even as the butcher buys in beer from the brewer and the brewer buys in bread from the baker. The doctor, the nurse and the anaesthetist serve us not out of benevolence but with a view to their own profit, but at least they do serve us. Supply and demand are enough. Public policy is not needed. The State is not wanted. Shepherds and nannies need not apply.

This book takes a more pragmatic view. It argues that the free market is a good mechanism for allocating most goods and services but that the market for health has unusual properties that set it apart. This book explores the nature of those special characteristics. It argues that other commodities may have some of the unique properties but that health care is at the margins and the extremes in the extent to which it deviates from textbook supply and demand. The book asks if those properties mean that there is a role for social regulation and management. Apples and oranges can be left to the buyers and the sellers. But health care is different.

Chapter 2, *Health Status and Health Care*, says that health care is different because it is so difficult to define the inputs, list the outcomes or specify the production-function. All of human life is there. The inputs include not just the jabs and the plasters but the ban on cigarette advertising that paternalistically buffers the impressionable, the role-models who are defiantly not anorexic, alcoholic or on drugs, the subcultural peer pressures that encourage the couch potato to register for keep-fit. The outcomes are not just the sneeze arrested or the organ transplanted but the comfort of palliative care where there is no cure,

1

the warmth of human contact where the doctor just listens to the friendless, the reintegration of the marginalised where the community nurse informs the house-bound that there are welfare benefits for which they can apply. Health status is mortality and morbidity. Health care leads to amelioration and improvement. It is hard, however, to identify the stream that fills up the lake. It is even harder to know the precise relationship between the tool and the task that it is being expected to perform.

A needle and not a shovel is the appropriate instrument to sew on a button. People, valuing life and fearing death, are convinced that health care is itself the indispensable link in the chain that extends from symptom to cure. People have a strong resistance to pain, disease, depression, impairment of faculties, permanent disability, premature death. They believe that health care is the wonder drug that will turn the tables on misfortune and drive the Grim Reaper from the door. To that extent the doctrine is self-perpetuating. As we believe in God, so we believe in the medicine man, the shaman who can make miracles happen. The appeal is emotive and non-rational. No one likes to think that his life hangs by a shoestring or that there is no way to arrest his tremors.

Such wishful thinking is a fundamental psychological constant. Even though doctors themselves are uncertain and cannot therefore guarantee their results, nonetheless people follow the leader because the alternative is to have no lead at all. People demand health. Health is not for sale. Health *care* is the derived demand. It is the nearest the health-seeking can come to a nebulous core that no one knows how to make into an economic tradeable. Health care is different. It is different because people like to think that someone, somewhere knows what to do.

Chapter 3, *Needs and Wants*, says that health care is different because the consumer is ignorant, the future unknowable, and information asymmetry an invitation to abuse. The liberal economics of Smith, Mill and Pareto makes the assumption that the individual is the best judge of his own well-being. The argument for tolerance and patient sovereignty is called into question by the assertion that the shopper is not in a position to distinguish his wants from his needs or to protect himself against the supplier-induced demand of medical doctors with a for-profit goal-function of their own. Consumers are at the mercy of producers. Consumers do not know if they have an asymptomatic defect or what tests they require or where to go for good-quality service. They cannot decide if their demand curve is elastic or inelastic. They do not know what to do in unfamiliar territory where treatments are alternatives, markets are segmented, practitioners are differentiated and finance makes the world go round. Health care is instantaneous: the individual consumes the operation in the real time that the surgeon produces it. Health care is active: the patient must supply some input into making himself well. Health care, most of all, is unbalanced. The doctor knows best. Every patient knows that.

The temptation to palm off a 'lemon' is a fact of life. Yet the doctor at the same time has a professional ethic which pulls him in the opposite direction. Asymmetrical information may in that sense be a greater threat when the consumer is buying a car or trying to decide if a chicken is fresh. The doctor's role as a carer makes him see himself as the agent of a purposive teleology that is more than crass money-making alone. Like an emergency clinic, he will not turn away a desperate client since his ultimate maximand is survival and health. He is often accredited to a non-profit supplier, either a private clinic or a British-type National Health Service. He works in highly regulated markets that circumscribe what he can and cannot do. Morality restricts flexibility and licensing filters entry. Competitive pricing, commercial advertising and entrepreneurial innovation can get a professional struck off. The butcher may have an instinct of workmanship but no one would say he had sworn a Hippocratic Oath that complements the law of contract. Health care, however, is different.

Society, meanwhile, has values and objectives of its own which it wishes to impose upon the dyad of market exchange. Health care involves other people. Other people want contagious externalities and third-party spillovers to be contained by collective action. As well as You and Me, there is also an Us which has a vision, a consensus and a baseline that is a common bond. Other people want absolute values like social justice, collective responsibility and respect for persons to complement the economist's maximand of input–output efficiency. Our common value system is what makes us fellow citizens, team-mates and integrated cooperators rather than isolated perfect competitors whose only purpose is to turn a penny whenever a gull is to be twisted. The market is about wants. Health care is about wants *and* about needs. Health care, in other words, is not the same.

Chapter 4, *Payment for Health*, says that health care is different because where people are insured it is other people who share the cost. Uncertainty is endemic: just as businesses do not know how fellow strategists will react and forecasters cannot be certain of the weather next Wimbledon, so consumers do not know what health care they will require, or when, or what it will cost. To reduce their vulnerability out-of-pocket to the unknown and the unanticipated, consumers often buy an entry ticket and share their risks as a club. There are no free riders where the baker sells bread to the butcher. All the costs and benefits are internalised in their swap. Insured health care, however, is exposed to a buffet syndrome. The socialism by consent is greater even than in other kinds of insurance. Fire or theft are unambiguous negativities that allow for little discretion or judgment. Health care, on the other hand, is an open-ended spectrum of alternative treatments and differing amenities. Not only can the diner eat as much as he likes, he can ask for different dishes, more expensive dishes to be served up.

Where health insurance is a fringe benefit, it has spillover effects on employment, cost of production, economic growth and the mobility of labour. Where
health insurance is subsidised by the nation, its integration into the tax/spend
budgetary matrix makes it a public concern. Sometimes the subsidy is paid to
the service: then the sense of citizenship is reinforced when black and white,
rich and poor lie side by side in a common ward. Sometimes the subsidy is paid
to the needy: then the deprived are means-tested up into a medical minimum
and guaranteed a basic floor below which no human being will be allowed to
sink. Sometimes the sponsorship is simply directed to the sick: all insurance is
pooling and all pooling is cross-subsidisation. Nobody but a beggar expects
such a hand-out when he walks into a bakery or a pub. Health care, however, is
different.

Chapter 5, *The Value of Life*, continues the discussion of the patient, the
practitioner and the public. It asks when enough is enough and the patient's life
is no longer worth the cost. Millions spent on Jack is millions not spent on Jill.
The nation cannot bury its head in the sand and pretend that a choice does not
have to be made. The patient reveals his hidden trade-offs when he buys a cheap
appliance that might give him an electrical shock or accepts danger-money to
work at heights without a belt or harness. The practitioner gets involved when
he says that clinical freedom means service to people and that professionals do
not need the advice of dismal cost-effectiveness to tell them what to do about a
life. Society takes a view when it says that it wants the limited supply of organs
to be transplanted into productive high-flyers and not into retired has-beens who
are no longer adding value for their tribe. Social expectations need not be more
merciful than the market. For some thoroughly decent men they will be the ugly
short-cut to the knacker's yard. The same must be said for some thoroughly
decent women. This book uses 'he' and 'his' as a convenient shorthand to denote
humankind as a whole. The language may be gendered but the argument is
not.

Laissez-faire as a doctrine teaches that the butcher, the brewer and the baker
should be trusted to buy and sell their own life-years. Where the patient is ill-
informed, however, where the agent advising his principal does not understand
that his duty to Jack is at variance with his duty to Jill, there the market for a
human life may be said to perform less well than when it is allocating meat to
the highest bidder or beer to the thirsty shopper just willing to make the greatest
sacrifice. Where, moreover, society is not satisfied with the market outcomes
and wants to impose its own rankings on the passengers allowed first into the
lifeboats, the market may be said to fail because it fails to satisfy the reasonable
expectations of all the signatories to the social contract. The pressure of all upon
each and the *sui generis* of mutual constraint has inexorably nationalised the
scarce kidneys. The collectivity as a whole has said that it wants to make its
voice heard.

Chapter 6, *Efficiency*, says that health care is different because different doctors do different things and because randomised controlled trials seldom pick up the long-run consequences. That being the case, it is confusing to design a league-table of cost-effective treatments or to discount future earnings-streams saved over the expected life span of the representative bodyholder.

Health care is different as well because cost-effectiveness and cost-benefit analysis are seldom employed by the unique automaton. These techniques are more frequently used by an aggregate such as a nation to get value for money from a given endowment or to ensure that the internal rate of return matches society's next-best payoff from an identical outlay. Few individuals think of a hip transplant in terms of a three per cent payoff on human capital juxtaposed to an opportunity cost of five per cent from a Treasury bill. All governments, however, are expected to do so. Meat, beer and bread are not discounted by the nation when it decides whether to authorise the expense. But health care is different.

Chapter 7, *Utility*, is a reminder that cost-effectiveness and cost-benefit analysis are topics in economic psychology. Health care is desired not for its own sake but for the subjective satisfaction that the intervention will produce. That satisfaction in turn is both an end in itself (such as the pleasure of being able to walk unassisted) and a means to other ends (such as the self-respect that comes from being able to earn a living). It is difficult to know how to evaluate a status that is at once both an input and an outcome. No less is it difficult to gain a purchase on other people's invisible mind, or to add up all the images they are storing somewhere in their perception-base. Nor can the observer be confident that the evidence collected at great cost is free from irrational bias. Tradition, stereotyping, inertia, ideology, knee-jerk reflex are all psychological reasons why the probabilities might be distorted by the heuristic. So might an emotive response to the unknown. Risk-lovers enjoy taking a chance. Risk-averters feel that their hopes fall short of their fears. It is not easy to decide which member of a highly mixed community is the dead-centre representative who speaks with the voice of the whole.

Questionnaires try to find out the ordinal and the cardinal values that people put upon different procedures carrying different risks. Induction from revealed willingness to pay gives an insight into the intervals that separate the alternatives when people quantify their preferences through the money they spend. The bodyholder consulted, there is an argument that the practitioner and the public must be consulted as well if a robust measure of 'the good life' is to be constructed bottom-up by investigating the intuitions that most people most strongly hold. It would be bad economics to ask the butcher how much extra happiness he thinks the brewer obtains from one more slice of bread: interpersonal comparisons cannot reliably be made. In the area of health, however, such comparisons are, exceptionally, being made all the time. Health care is different.

Chapter 8, *Equity and Equality*, considers the relationship between fairness and levelling. No one wants equal access to cinema-tickets, motorcars or pins. Access to doctors and nurses is, however, widely seen as a different breed of dog. Society feels strongly that it is only fair for all citizens to be guaranteed at least a basic package irrespective of their ability to pay. Perhaps this is because sickness and health, life and death are believed to be big issues that transcend the shopkeeper's calculus and the achievement-based reward. Health services are not the only basic goods (housing, education and food are also targeted for social support) but they are generally assigned a high ranking within the bundle. Health care is simultaneously a good thing in itself and the means to the attainment of other good things. Not everyone agrees on precisely what is just or on the frontier that separates the needs from the wants, the essential from the peripheral. Even so, there is near universal consensus that something should be done to level up the life-chances. The moral imperative casts a long shadow before.

Most of all does it do this in societies with religious values that preach compassion, altruism and solidarity, with historical traditions that are imbued with sharing, overlap and common culture. Even, however, in cultures that have invested heavily in meritocratic recognition and rising living standards, there is a surprisingly high level of commitment to equitable access and the infrastructure of health. T.H. Green on the State that levels up is alive and well in the clinics and the hospitals. Freedom is not just freedom *from* the State. It is the freedom *to* develop, to unfold, to become truly and fully oneself.

Chapter 9, *Equality and Health*, says that mortality and morbidity are not random but patterned. Disparities in outcomes are correlated with occupational hierarchy and geographical location. Low incomes make it more difficult for the deprived to pay for nutritious food, medical insurance and medical care. Subcultural *mores* mean that some strata are socialised into deferred gratification while others smoke heavily because they live for the day. Occupational differences are the reason why roofers have more falls from heights and lower-grade civil servants suffer more heart attacks. Medical attention, finally, is not available to all on the non-discriminatory basis of equal care for equal need.

The social failure suggests that there is scope for social intervention. Low incomes can be supplemented through housing allowances and child benefits. Subcultural conventions can be challenged through uninhibited mixing and health education. Occupational differences can be narrowed through works clinics and health and safety legislation. Medical care can be brought within each citizen's reach through community rating, non-exclusionary contracts, a National Health Service – and economic growth itself which makes all of us better able to afford the good things in life.

Chapter 10, *Cost*, issues a reminder that the cost of care is rising, both per unit of care consumed and as a share of the national product. A richer society spends more on meals out and luxury kitchens than does a poorer one. But health care is different. Hospitals in many areas are the regional multiplier that creates health-related jobs and keeps local people in work. Medical services in rust-belt countries are the sunrise sector that will make the nation an exporter and a hub. Producers as well as consumers have a vested interest in the health of health. The consequence is escalation. One dollar in every seven spent in the United States is being spent on formal care. This is more than in virtually any other nation. It was one dollar in every twenty in 1960. What is being spent on the doctors is not being spent on the warships. Crowding out is on the horizon.

Chapter 11, *Containing the Cost*, concludes the book by suggesting public policies that can limit cost while not threatening health. Third-party payment, rising expectations, new technology, an ageing population all have contributed to a sector-specific rise that is well in excess of the rate of general inflation. So have supply-side imperfections such as professional bodies, local monopolies, the entry barrier of protracted training, the high capital cost of opening a new hospital, State intervention which limits the treatment centres in an attempt to keep down the cost of excess capacity, State subsidies which channel the treatments into areas that the market would have ignored. The market for care is not as competitive as the textbook ideal; but there are solutions which can be found to bend back the bent rod. The free market way forward would be to encourage entry and rivalry while doing away with counterproductive restrictions. The political way forward would be a greater reliance on charges, pecuniary incentives, waiting times, utilisation review to countervail the supplier's power to exploit, nationalisation of supply to reduce wasteful duplication, allocation by social criteria rather than by payment-led priorities lest effective demand starve the social organism of higher-valued utilities. Meat, beer and bread do not present so great a challenge as to necessitate a collective and a coordinated response. But health care is different. It is a thing apart.

2. Health status and health care

Everyone wants health. Along with vodka, cigarettes, hang gliding, high-fat grease, serial promiscuity and fast cars, it is one of the good things in life that people want. This chapter is about health. It says that robust definitions are not easy to come by and that the endstates are a mix. It attempts nonetheless to shed some light on what is meant by a satisfactory health status. It attempts to put a name to the health care inputs that keep us well. Health and health care are elusive concepts. Few, however, are so highly valued or figure so often in the eye of debate.

Section 1 examines the mortality and the morbidity statistics. Section 2 discusses the actors and the instruments. Section 3 is about health capital in the sense of Grossman. Section 4 is about the correlation between health status and economic growth. The message of the chapter is in line with the assessment that 'one man's *explicandum* is another man's *conundrum*'; that 'a market for health ... must also be a market for ideas' (Reisman, 1993: 240). It therefore recommends that doctors, economists, policymakers and politicians should all have an open mind when exploring the intellectual maze of optimal health and care.

2.1. HEALTH STATUS

The World Health Organization has made it all clear. Good health, it says, means 'a state of complete physical, mental and social well-being and not merely the absence of disease or infirmity' (World Health Organization, 1962 [1946]: 1). Physical well-being is the body. Mental well-being is the spirit. Social well-being is the role. The definition specifies that health to be ideal must be complete. Anyone whose mouth is dry, or who is feeling a bit anxious, or who suspects that his co-workers want him to move on, may be said to be a person whose health status is less than 100 per cent.

Titmuss, as always, could see that there was something wrong: 'To me this statement is meaningless as a working definition; it is a statement of an unattainable perfection of body, mind and soul. There is even something unhealthy about the perfection of the absolute.... In scientific terms, we do not know where health begins and disease ends. The lines that we draw are arbitrary ones and largely fashioned by the culture in which we live' (Titmuss, n.d.). What Titmuss is saying is that *completeness* itself might be a sign of illness, a symptom of obsessive-compulsive perfectionism, an exaggerated fastidiousness which suggests that the healthy themselves might be well on the way to the padded cell. What he is implying is that most people define good health as something less than a single priceless possession of which the importance transcends any other end and is insensitive to financial cost. Most people define good health not as the *complete* but as the *acceptable*, the *tolerable* and the *satisfactory*: 'The majority of people do not have totally healthy or unhealthy lifestyles: most are mixed' (Blaxter, 1990: 144). What most people want is a balanced portfolio. Good health is one of the many good things that they would like to have.

Mildred Blaxter recognises that the WHO definition is in the tradition of nirvana-like ideals such as 'the classical Platonic model of health as harmony among the body's processes, or the Galenian concept of disease as disturbance of equilibrium' that give only limited guidance to the doctor or policymaker: 'Trying to operationalize such a wide concept of health has the danger of subsuming all human life and happiness under this label' (Blaxter, 1990: 3). Nevertheless she does think that the refusal to treat health policy as illness policy is a step in the right direction: 'It does draw attention to the fact that positive aspects of healthiness ought to be considered, and not only the negative aspects of pathology. It may be that it is as important to distinguish the factors which differentiate health which is above average and that which is merely average, as it is to look at those which cause the average to become "bad"'(Blaxter, 1990: 3). To attempt too much is to render one's holism toothless. To attempt too little, however, is to conflate freedom *from* constraining illness with freedom *to* squeeze the most from one's scarce endowment of body and mind.

2.1.1. Mortality

Health itself is invisible. There is no single index of health status. There is no known unit in which it could be measured. Just as economists estimate felt satisfaction in non-observable 'utils', so policymakers could quantify health in hypothetical 'hells'. It will not serve any practical purpose. Like it or not, they will have to formulate policy on the basis of indicators like the tail, the tusks or the trunk. A mix of these indicators might be enough for recording and targeting without requiring the reconstruction of the elephant as a whole: 'We take it as self-evident that the choice of indicator is governed by the purposes for which it is intended to be used' (Culyer, Lavers and Williams, 1972: 94). Different indicators will be used for different purposes. Different weights will reflect different priorities. The ideal index will be an index of good health. In practice, virtually all the indices describe the things that can go wrong.

One indicator which is particularly useful is the death rate. At least it is relatively straightforward. Although there is the problem of saying whether it must be the brain or the heart that has ceased its activity, and although not everyone agrees when a foetus becomes an independent life that it would be murder to abort, most people would probably accept that they understand what it means to be dead. Illness is more difficult to quantify.

Data on deaths, moreover, are collected centrally. Not self-reported (and open to subjective miscalibration), not pluralistic (and at risk from under-reporting or double counting), data on deaths, like the throughput of births and marriages, are assembled by a single national agency. In the UK, for example, the Registrar General is charged with the task of producing a historical record that is comprehensive, reliable and accurate.

Data on deaths are attractive because they can be presented in a variety of ways. Mortality rates per 1000 women, or blacks, or dwellers in forgotten slums, or workers in particular occupations can be picked out to make useful comparisons. Mortality can also be cross-correlated with age group (weighted by life expectancy) so as to measure future earnings foregone on the part of the nation as a whole. Disaggregated data can be presented as perinatal mortality (immediately before or after birth), neonatal mortality (in the first 27 days of life), infant mortality (from day 28 to the end of the first year of life), childhood mortality (in the first 14 years of life), adult mortality, mortality in the retirement years. The phrase 'life-expectancy at ...' is a reminder of just how adaptable the information is for a researcher wishing to elucidate particular stages in the life cycle. It is also a reminder that comparisons must be age-standardised. Otherwise regions or countries with younger people will be mistaken for areas where the government has been especially astute in introducing the best-possible policies.

Data on deaths is in a limited sense data on illnesses as well. The reason is that the death certificate gives the proximate cause. Admittedly the proximate cause is not the full medical history. A death will be put down to bronchitis or lung cancer, not to smoking; and the full length or painfulness of the final illness will not appear. Often death is caused not by a single disease but by a complex sequence or mix. Diagnostic criteria may themselves be variable. There is no measure of the quality of life or even the reduction of suffering that is brought about by care. Mortality in many cases occurs without morbidity (homicide or a car accident, for example). Morbidity, for that matter, can occur without mortality: illustrations would be arthritis, rheumatism, asthma and diabetes. Often, however, the two go together. Where they do, the fatalities can then shed light on the illnesses and disabilities which preceded the demise.

2.1.2. Morbidity

Illness is more difficult to measure. First and foremost, there is the lack of a single data-collecting agency. Vital statistics are registered centrally. A database on symptoms and diagnoses must be built up from a variety of discrete sources. Doctors and hospitals will often reveal what they know: while computerisation will make the keyboard database comprehensive, still conventions on privacy and confidentiality will be an impediment to detailed disclosure. Inputs may already be over-stretched: bed disability days are an underestimate where local hospitals have no beds available. Insurance companies can be approached for information on contingency estimates and payouts: they may not, however, be able to distinguish three persons with one cold each from one person with three or to correlate incidence of restricted activity with average days lost per sufferer. Health-related questions will sometimes be included in the national census, or surveys such as the British General Household Survey and Family Expenditure Survey: a cross-section of the population as a whole, such coverage, unlike data from the treatment centres, picks up the non-presenting as well as the certified ill.

Investigators sometimes conduct surveys and medical assessments of their own. These are subject to the usual constraints of sample size and representativeness but do produce fresh data, sometimes enriched by clinical opinions on the probable evolution of a disorder and, indeed, the likelihood of death as a result. An indication will often come from compulsory blanket examinations of children at school, workers in particular industries, applicants for health and life insurance, conscripts about to do national service. Such screening picks up asymptomatic pathologies of which the subjects themselves would not otherwise have been aware.

Individual ministries publish data on specific areas of concern such as road accidents, salmonella in food, notifiable diseases such as cholera. Recorded days off work give some measure of crude malfunctions per year; the data is, however, not the same as days of illness actually experienced, not the same as bed disability days and not the same (unless a medical certificate is required) as incapacity certified into a diagnostic category by a qualified professional. Additional information can be obtained through social insurance on those registered as permanently disabled. A picture emerges, but it is incomplete. Much illness is simply not reported, either because the patient grits his teeth since the day's work has to be done, or because cocaine use while pregnant is something one prefers not to disclose, or because mental illness is a source of stigma and shame, or because the sufferer doesn't have the money to approach a practitioner about non-emergency anxieties like listlessness, lack of energy or feelings of isolation. Under-presenting and under-reporting is the norm. Only a minority of diseases (usually those with acute public health implications) are notifiable in law. Even, moreover, if adequate raw data could be collected, there is no index that picks up the aggregate. It is not obvious how to add together the heart attacks, the headaches, the hay fever and the mild rash. There is no common denominator. There is no composite 'unit of disease', of pain, of impeded function, of length of disease as opposed to simple occurrence. In contrast to mortality, morbidity is an overgrown administrative thicket.

No less problematic than the collection of data is, however, the conceptualisation of disability. Statisticians speak of acute morbidity with light symptoms (minor discomfort in the joints and the inconvenience of postponing a morning run), acute morbidity with more serious symptoms (unrelenting lumbar pain necessitating time off work), chronic morbidity with modest symptoms (the muscle aches and sleep problems associated with chronic fatigue syndrome) and chronic morbidity with severe symptoms (pulmonary or kidney disease which may in the limit lead to death). It is, however, hard to know where to draw the line. Different people have different perceptions of abnormality and malfunction. They do not all see the doctor for the same complaints. Not do they assign the same importance to the symptoms. Nor do their expectations and attitudes remain constant over time.

Besides that, there can be a trade-off between the characteristics of a substandard state: 'A successful treatment is *not only* one which reduces intensity and duration but could also be one that reduces intensity without affecting duration, or vice versa; or even that increases one at the expense of the other, providing the net outcome is to *reduce* the index number (a product of intensity *and* duration)' (Culyer, Lavers and Williams, 1972: 105; original emphasis). The substandard state must be recorded using a weighted average of the characteristics. Otherwise the picture will be incomplete and one-dimensional. One week is not the same as another week. One person is not the same as another person. The practical difficulties are immense.

Symptoms give a clue as to the illness. Temperature, pulse rate, weight gain, weight loss, insomnia, hypersomnia, swollen digits, a coughing fit, a rash, indigestion, uncontrollable aggression, serious delusion, hot flushes, nausea, all suggest that something out of the usual may be happening. Incontinence, amnesia, confusion, inability to walk, eat, shop, hear, see, do up buttons, climb stairs or wash unaided are all indicators of substandard health. Symptoms, however, are not an illness. It is the function of the trained practitioner to certify the sick role by putting it into a recognised medical category or classification. At that point it acquires a name and the stamp of authority. An ache in the joints becomes rheumatoid arthritis. A pain in the chest becomes coronary thrombosis. High blood pressure becomes an accident waiting to happen. The statistician, thanks to the doctor's definitions, is able to record a familiar kind of problem.

Yet the legitimation of the professional does not include the subjective meaning that the sufferer attaches to it. There is no quantification of the distress or inconvenience that it causes. There is no investigation into the hidden problem that made the patient whom the doctor dismisses as a hypochondriac actually present for treatment. Each patient is unique. It is in any case difficult to find a universal metric for something like a headache that is non-observable and non-articulable. The throbbing and the pressure cannot be put into words.

Partly this will be so because of socialised expectations. Being ill and feeling ill are not the same thing. Medical opinion and public opinion might not take the same symptoms to be a malfunction. Not all people have the same reactions to pain or fatigue. There are social subcultures where everyone is tired. The doctor, in imposing his own perception of normalcy, is in fact imputing the sick role to a patient whose peer group is telling him that he is average. There are social subcultures where everyone is on psychedelics. The doctor, in refusing to prescribe narcotics, is telling the poets and the painters that they may not expand their consciousness in this way. It can even be argued that middle class labelling actually boosts the stock of illness in the community. It underestimates the amount of cultural heterogeneity, the plurality of perceptions in the nation. Societies have at various times labelled criminals, homosexuals and political dissidents as ill. Such deviants have been handed over to doctors for a cure. Such labelling is problematic. It reinforces the contention that good health cannot accurately be observed.

Socialisation has functional as well as attitudinal connotations. Restriction of activity must be evaluated not just by severity and days but by the use that people usually make of their faculties. A teenager playing football would regard a sprained ankle as an interference with his lifeplan and lifestyle; a civil servant preparing for an evening's light television might regard it simply as a minor nuisance. Health for each of them is doing what they want to do when they want to do it. What is said about leisure must be said *a fortiori* about work. Different occupations demand different capacities and different standards of fitness. A person who works from home with a computer and a telephone can afford to be bedridden; a coalminer or a busdriver cannot. A retired person has different expectations from a breadwinner with a young family. A housewife in the Third World is expected to bear children. Infertility for her calls into question her very *raison d'être*. Her handicap is many times more significant in her peasant context than it would be in an urban culture where lack of houseroom and a guaranteed old age pension alter the targets and the imperatives. Interpersonal comparisons are always a guess. Cross-cultural and cross-national comparisons are fraught with difficulty. In some countries it is common to 'hear voices'. In other countries people who 'hear voices' go into the statistics as mentally ill.

Role performance is social, contingent upon 'the activities which the community would expect individuals of that age and sex to be able to carry out' (Williams, 1974: 365). This too conditions the definition of the sick role. Some pain and some anxiety are normal and functional: without them people would not survive. The question is at what point such states become morbid, at what point the individual finds it impossible to carry out his normal functions. Objective measures to some extent can be used: a condition can be called pathological where the person cannot lift himself into bed or is experiencing double vision. In other cases the evaluation will be that of other people. The doctor says that she is ill and needs a tablet. Her neighbours say that she is letting herself go: she should not demand sympathy when the rest of the street feels precisely as she does. Subculture and subgroup convert occasional dizziness and lower back pain into neurotic hypochondria. Is the doctor right or are the peers? Should the statistician record an episode of illness or should he write down 'business as usual'?

The subjective dimension makes the specification of health not just a social but an individual problem. Morbidity is partly a mechanical malfunction but partly the healthholder's perception that his body is not meeting his expectations. Such an assessment is intensely personal. Different people want different standards of wellness. Different people assign different degrees of disutility to the same symptom or shortfall. Simple enumeration does not pick up the diversity in the qualitative disamenity where what is normal to one discrete human being is pathological to another.

It is clearly necessary to differentiate the cold data in terms of the individual's own perceptions if a correct measure of the stock of illness is to be derived. It is, however, not easy to do this precisely because there is no observable statistic that gets at the internal states. The market mechanism to the textbook liberal at least has the attraction of proportioning cost to benefit, fee to consultation. Information asymmetry, inflexible pricing and unequal incomes cast some doubt upon this method as a way of streaming symptoms for the purpose of weighted records. Surveys of consumer opinion are an alternative. Here at least the client is invited to say in words what illness is, and to rank different scenarios in terms of factored-down expectations.

Thus data, self-reported, should be obtained on ordinal utility. Most people would probably prefer life to death. Less certain, however, is whether they would prefer the disease to the drugs where the drugs have a price and the complaint will go by itself given time. The cure often has side-effects which the patient might regard as worse than the disease. Life with a handicap might be regarded as inferior in one's own eyes to not being alive at all: 'Some argue that medicine is sustaining people who have a very poor quality of life, for whom the benefits of a longer life are not very great. This phenomenon has been termed the "failure of success"' (Cutler, 2004: 6). The ranking scheme must be tabulated if the patient's own self-assessment of healthy life is to be known.

Cardinal utility amplifies ordinal utility in that it quantifies the intervals between the preferences. The scale is useful if professionals are to maximise the subjective well-being that is secured by a bundle of interventions. Quality-adjusted life-years, built up from raw perceptual data as estimated by cross-sectional sampling, give an insight into felt welfare as estimated by individuals themselves. If people reveal that a year with a given disability is worth only (affords a quality-of-life, QoL, of only) 80 per cent of a year without the disability, then a year that would otherwise be worth $100 000 must be assigned a value of only $80 000: 'Conversely, avoiding the impairment for a year would be worth $20,000. This approach can also be used to value acute morbidities. Suppose that someone has an acute condition for seven days which if experienced for a year would correspond to a QoL of 0.8, the cost of the acute morbidity would be $384 ($20,000 multiplied by 7/365)' (Abelson, 2003: S3–S4).

Quality-adjusted life-years will be discussed in more detail in chapter 7. That chapter will also explain that the *social* value of life-years can be quantified using the same techniques but with a broad cross-section. Quality-adjustment need not be personal, exclusive and individual. As chapter 7 will also show, however, the information generated does not necessarily say what the policymaker needs to know about the intensity of want or need. A sample must be found that is sufficiently representative of the policymaker's population. Age, gender, race, occupation must all be assigned their proper proportions. Besides that, a view must be taken on preexistent and probable conditions that are likely to influence the replies of the respondents. The veil of ignorance might make it easier for a person to give an impartial assessment of prostate cancer or pneumoconiosis or sickle-cell anaemia. The knowledge that one is oneself suffering from delirium tremens or is the parent of a child in a persistent vegetative state makes such an assessment more problematic. A choice must be made between a detached evaluation and a passionate response.

For the purpose of preparing statistics on illness and health, it is not clear which subset would give the more appropriate response. What is clear nonetheless is that the statistic must be derived. In rich countries people demand not just longevity but enjoyment from life. A statistic on deaths does not pick up their felt well-being, self-perceived. A simple tabulation of the inputs used up or the medical expenses *ex post* incurred contributes even less to an accurate measurement of health and illness in a community.

2.2.   HEALTH CARE

Health is an area of life where outcomes are often conceptualised as inputs. In few other areas of social life is there a greater willingness to assume that increased spending is a good proxy for realised success. Perhaps it is wishful thinking that makes people assume that more means more; but still it is a common assumption in the field of health. This also makes resourcing a sacred cow. To sacrifice health inputs for transportation inputs at the margin is to condemn the population to an increase in coughs and sneezes.

2.2.1. Medical Care

Any list of inputs into the health care production-function will usefully begin with medical care, narrowly defined. The candidates on the side of personnel will be the general practitioners, hospital doctors, radiographers, physiotherapists, pharmacists, hospital nurses, district nurses, health visitors, dentists and other health care professionals. To this must be added capital stock such as hospital beds, diagnostic equipment, therapeutic facilities, medical supplies stored up (drugs, clean sheets, surgical gloves), medical complements on offer (wheelchairs, dentures, walking-frames). The figures are normally expressed as a ratio ('per 100 000 of population') so as to obtain an indication of their significance. Often they are disaggregated by area, region or other subgrouping lest national data conceal local disparities. Occasionally they will be presented not as simple numbers (say, of ambulances or of scanners) but as an economic measure. The measure might be the cost of technology in a general practitioner's clinic or the market value of the referrals made to a top-notch specialist.

Utilisation is important as well as brute availability. Thus data should be collected on patient consultations and outpatient visits, medical tests performed and vaccinations administered, prescriptions written and dressings changed. In the case of hospitals, relevant statistics would be patient throughput, treatments delivered, the bed occupancy census. Such data identify the flow. A built bed is a piece of rusting metal that gathers dust. It is not a medical input until it is filled. A doctor watching television is not very different from anyone else. Doctor hours committed to patient care would be a better statistic.

To obtain a consistent series, the numbers should reflect comparable standards. Statisticians should ensure that treatments are quality-constant. Otherwise quality might have been sacrificed in order to contain the cost. The task of adjustment is not an easy one. Quality is difficult to define. Not everyone agrees on what quality really means. It is more difficult still to measure. There is no central agency that collects and processes the data: 'We have no mandatory national system and few local systems to track the quality of care delivered to the American people. More information is available on the quality of airlines, restaurants, cars, and VCRs than on the quality of health care' (Schuster, McGlynn and Brook, 1998: 517–8). Despite the lack of consensus, policy-relevant proxies must nonetheless be found. There are three approaches that can be employed in the reconstruction of information that is not accessible to the naked eye.

One approach is to use input as a measure of standards. Relevant indicators would include capital equipment per staffed bed, staff member's time per patient visit, doctor/patient or nurse/patient ratios, vintage of capital, specialists on the hospital's panel, computerised record-keeping. Other indicators will have an educational element. An inference of investment in high-level proficiency may be drawn from involvement in research, decennial recertification, in-service training per hospital professional, 'conspicuous production' in the form of staff educated in the high-prestige 'ivy league'. Other statistics will concentrate on the thrust of the encounter. Group practices might be used as a quality indicator since they allow general practitioners to fine-tune and focus their skills. Preventive medicine might be taken to suggest that the doctor is improving the stock of health through introducing the patient to exercise, weight loss and a nutritious diet.

Another approach is to use goal attainment to track the attributes of the service. The proof of the pudding is in the eating. If the patients return speedily to work, experience less-than-average cross-infection, do not report an allergic reaction or an addiction, do not come back with complications or a relapse, express satisfaction with the product supplied, enjoy longer life-expectancy because the disease is gone, one inference might be that the quality of the attention provided was high. Quality in such a case is being shadowed by the outcomes. If the diagnosis is accurate and the treatment works, the quality must be good. If the outcome is above-average, the quality must be very good. If the patient is given the wrong operation or dies of an unexpected reaction, the quality must be a cause of concern: 'One study estimates that 50,000 to 100,000 people die every year of medical mistakes in hospitals, making hospital errors a leading cause of death.... Only one-quarter of people with hypertension have their blood pressure successfully controlled, despite a wealth of effective medications.... What we do not prevent, we wind up treating later, frequently at higher cost' (Cutler, 2004: xi).

A final approach is to fall back upon authority and experience. Good quality will here be defined as the quality that the wise and the certified have declared to be good. Such care will be care that has been validated by the doctors who are deemed to know best. Good-quality care is what the experts say it is. It is the benchmark that they impose and the expectation that they entertain. Too little would not be good quality: underuse of inputs deprives the patient of his chance to get well. Too much would not be good quality either: unnecessary tests or procedures expose the patient to discomfort, anxiety, risk, without adding anything to the patient's health. In each case, 'good' means 'appropriate' and 'appropriate' means 'competence in line with professional standards'. Women aged 40 and above should have a mammogram every one to two years. Middle-aged men should be screened for cholesterol at least once every five years. An above-average number of Caesarians performed on the Friday before a public holiday should be regarded with some suspicion. Quality is conformity to the protocol. Randomised controlled trials, international comparisons and tried-and-tested heuristics all focus the mind.

Quantifying the inputs, there are two interrelated ratios which attract disproportionate attention. These are the share of health care in the government's budget and the share of health care in the gross national product. Rightly or wrongly, incumbents and oppositions win and lose elections by pointing to the amount of money they are investing in health. They look for confirmation to the comparative experience of nations facing similar challenges and constrained by a similar resource-base.

The statistics are themselves a mixed bag. Private sector health care will be valued at the market price (including profit) billed to the final consumer. Public sector health care will be valued at the historic cost of the factor inputs. That cost in turn will often be no more than an administered value. Lacking the subjective assessment of supply and demand, it might simply be an accounting number proclaimed *ex cathedra* by civil servants. One sector is chalk. The other sector is cheese. The information conveyed by the sum of the two is less valuable than it would be if the figures were derived in the same way.

Total cost, moreover, is a statistical catch-all. The figure includes the fishtank as well as the pills, the prints on the wall as well as the open hearts. Not all expenditures are equally relevant to good health itself. A hospital has a postroom and a garden. Attractive as they are, hotel services like these are not directly relevant to the specifically *medical* nature of the institution. Also, the share of care in the national product is actually boosted by inefficiency. Above-average cost per case, unwarranted diagnostic tests, protracted inpatient convalescence, all produce the statistic that the nation is doing more to help the sick. Unquestioned, they sound like flu arrested and gangrene turned round. Unpacked, they turn out to be fishtanks and prints. Good surroundings unquestionably add something to the felt utility of the experience. It is, however, misleading to call them necessary stages on the road to good health.

Intertemporal comparisons often fail to pick up the changes in the nature of the medical encounter. Better educated patients might spend more time with the doctor and ask more questions. Urbanisation ameliorates the disparities in geographical access. The capital component (tests, drugs, lasers, scans) might be rising as a percentage of the whole. Generics might be taking the place of brand names or vice versa. Shorter stays might be making hospital beds service a greater patient turnover. The chlorination and filtering of drinking water might be substituting public prevention for private cure. Long-stay homes might be taking the place of family nursing. Care 'in the community' might be taking the place of psychiatric beds. New equipment, new techniques, lengthier certification, radical specialisms not previously on offer might mean a rise in quality and not just in cost. They could also mean high-tech glamour not justified by the cures.

Intercountry comparisons are beset with problems of their own. Not only are exchange rates subject to fluctuation and the national accounts compiled using different schemata, the medical care bundle is not always the same. Spas, sanatoria, optical care, a medical library, fringe medicine, a works infirmary, pharmacist-only drugs, medical research, are illustrations of elements that are included in some countries but excluded in others. Western definitions do not always correspond to non-Western practice. Although patients in the Orient have recourse to herbalists and acupuncturists, traditional Chinese medicine (TCM) even in the Orient is sometimes included and sometimes not. This heterogeneity makes it difficult to say that one country is spending significantly more or less on health care than another.

Nor should it be forgotten that other things do not remain equal. A study of doctors' advice to stop smoking that does not take into account education, income, pollution and uncertainty will be partial and incomplete. Causality cannot be established unless multivariate analysis is used to separate out the interdependent influences. Whole cultures must be studied if the inputs and the outcomes are properly to be understood. Doctors' advice may be one influence but peer pressure is another. Smoking depends not just on price and information but on the role-model of the young adolescents' parents and the good opinion of their close friends and associates.

2.2.2. Care beyond Medicine

A list that is too long becomes unwieldy and even ridiculous. There are few goods or activities that are not related in some way to health. Yet a list that is too short falls victim to the same charge. Critics will say that too unimaginative a list will be measuring *medical* inputs but not the sum total of the health-influencing inputs that make morbidity and mortality what they are.

Consider household spending on health-related inputs. Consumers put money into health. The fee that they pay to a doctor is included in health care spending. Their fares, travelling times and earnings lost through waits are treated as if for a trip to the supermarket. It is rather one-sided. A restful holiday can be as beneficial as a prescription tranquilliser. The drug makes its way into the statistics. The beach resort does not.

Non-prescription drugs such as an aspirin are health-related. So are surgical stockings bought in a High Street shop and a bracing game of cricket played on the Green. The whole of the pharmaceutical industry from research to patents is health-related. Internet searches are health-related if that is how the patient checks up on poor peripheral circulation. Explanatory manuals are health-related if that is where the patient goes for a gluten-free diet. The statistics seldom include the non-traditional therapies of hypnotists, homeopathists, faith healers and colour therapists. It is an omission decided upon by the experts which is at variance with the revealed preference of the beneficiary who has picked them as promising and paid for them out-of-pocket. The consumer says that they are health-related. Willingness to pay says that they are health-related. Talking economics, therefore, they are health-related and ought to be recorded as health-related in the data.

An apple a day keeps the doctor away. A morning swim tones up the heart and lungs. Prunes and muesli keep the colon up to scratch. Early nights and sound breakfasts protect the body from wear-and-tear. Flossing and brushing put the root canal job to rout. Higher rents buy access to less polluted suburbs. A son or daughter looks after an Alzheimer's parent. As the list gets longer, so it becomes clearer that there is more to spending than the doctors and nurses alone. Households contribute to health when they buy organic vegetables and use fewer pesticides. Regular exercise and limited sunbathing are difficult to measure. That does not mean that they are of no relevance to health.

The simple fact of being married is itself an argument in the production-function. Married adults are healthier than unmarried adults, other things held constant. In Britain, Gardner and Oswald, controlling for the individual's health at the start of the period through the use of longitudinal data from the Household Panel Survey, found that marriage has a greater effect on the length of a middle-aged or elderly person's life than income does. Married men (the figure is adjusted for initial health status) were 6.3 per cent less likely to die in the decade 1993–2001 than were unmarried men. For married over unmarried women the figure was 3.4 per cent. The coefficient of preservation in the case of men is so great that it effectively cancels out the 5 per cent excess mortality that is the negative consequence of smoking (Gardner and Oswald, 2004: 1191, 1204).

In Norway, Kravdal discovered that never-married people (both men and women) were 15 per cent less likely to survive 12 common forms of cancer than were married people (Kravdal, 2001: 359). In Israel Manor and his associates, narrowing their study to women, found that the mortality rate of the married was lower than that for the unmarried (Manor, Eisenbach, Israeli and Friedlander, 2000: 1183). They recognised that their data did not allow them to distinguish between the 'selection effect' (that less healthy people might be less inclined to marry: a correction must therefore be made between the never-married and those rendered single through divorce or widowhood) and the 'protection effect' (that marriage has a beneficial effect in terms of material resources, a stable lifestyle, a reduced propensity to drink and smoke, less stress-related disease and greater informal care in time of illness). They pointed nonetheless to the strong statistical correlation. Even widowed women have a lower mortality rate than do never-married women. This was especially the case for women with children: it is not clear if the reason was biological or if it was the wider network of contacts. The effects of marriage at any rate are apparently long lasting. The coefficient of preservation survives the death of the spouse.

Households can protect. So can firms. Masks and visors are supplied to employees exposed to viruses or sparks. Good freezers work against food poisoning. An on-site clinic provides first-aid to the victim of an industrial accident. Both in environmental and in occupational health, the firm incurs a cost to supply a service. Were that service not supplied, the inevitable treatment would be a financial drain on the medical budget, narrowly defined.

The State too can get involved. Infrastructure is one contribution that it can make. Refuse collection and clean drinking water are conducive to good health, just as inadequate sewers and polluted rivers are the breeding grounds for dysentery and dengue. Secure stores provide a dumping ground for radioactive waste. Subsidised research improves treatment of disease. Ranging more widely, rising average incomes, an adequate supply of jobs and the *embourgeoisement* of dangerous manual labour will have a beneficial effect on health. Sound economic policies mean rising incomes. More money makes possible nutritious food, heating in winter, hygienic accommodation, medical insurance, out-of-pocket top-ups.

Besides that, economic growth generates the resources that pay for the National Health Service. In that way the invisible and the visible hand can complement one another and make each other viable. A rise in taxes beyond a point stifles the initiative that generates the value-added. Growing affluence encounters no such buffer. Economic growth creates the national dividend that, as Crosland has emphasised, makes fiscally possible a move towards more equality and more welfare: 'Rapid growth is an essential condition of any significant re-allocation of resources ... I do assert dogmatically that in a democracy low or zero growth wholly excludes the possibility' (Crosland, 1974 [1971]: 74, 75).

However long the list becomes, insurance, it should be observed, should not be included as a health care input. The reason is that compensation (including financial support from the welfare State) is only a transfer. Where the patient pays the doctor and the insurer reimburses the cost, it would be double counting to include the payment and the treatment when in truth they are two measures of the same circular flow. One could, of course, argue that the very fact of insurance promotes good health to the extent that it protects the patient against anxiety-related illness. Peace of mind is favourable to good health. Stress and agitation can be a threat to the heart and the psyche. By that argument a Sunday sermon should be counted as if the equivalent of a preventive injection to ward off tetanus or polio. A list that brings in all the world is not much more help than a list that stops short at the doctors and the nurses who clearly constitute only a part of the census.

2.2.3. Regulation

Laws that force households to pay for additive-free cereals and make it compulsory for firms to install smoke filters that limit the belching gases are laws that create a private cost. That cost is none the less private for having been imposed by legislation and not by the free choice of the market. The inference is clearly that State regulation is itself an argument in the production-function of health.

Thus the State may insist on the date-stamping of food products. It may impose a mandatory speed limit on the roads. Alcohol may be heavily taxed lest cheap spirits poison the kidneys. Motorcycle helmets may be made compulsory lest weakness of will sentence the lazy to death. Seat belts and airbags may not be left to the consumer who knows best. Prescription drugs may not be advertised between the television soaps. Guns may be controlled. Marijuana may be banned. It may be State paternalism but it is also beneficent authority that delivers better health. Regulation is a health care input like any other. Like any other input, moreover, someone has to pay. A speed limit on the roads cuts morbidity and mortality but also lengthens the turnover-times in shipping and retailing. Time is money. The pensioners and the needy have to spend more on their meat and vegetables or tighten their belts.

Tawney contends that 'the mother of liberty has, in fact, been law' (Tawney, 1966: 169). Child safety seats are an illustration. Evans and Graham studied the impact of protective legislation in selected American states. They found that lives had been saved as surely as if the government had built a new hospital or well-baby clinic: 'The mean number of infant and toddler fatalities is reduced by 39 per cent and 30 per cent respectively in states with mandatory restraint laws' (Evans and Graham, 1990: 140). In 1986 alone, Evans and Graham calculated, the lives of 161 children had been saved because their parents' incentive structure had been politically modified.

In some cases (as with substance abuse) there is an element of ignorance: the consumer has to be protected from himself because he hasn't a clue. In other cases (as with voluntary overwork) the individual is torn between two options: here the State must intervene to prevent weak-willed Ulysses from destroying himself on the sirens' rock. In the former case the State is a teacher who assists the all-at-sea to do what they would have done anyway had they known that psittacosis is only a beak-bite away. In the latter case the State is a nanny who assists the short-horizoned not to sacrifice their health capital because an evanescent fix bulks larger in their imagination than an irreversible narcosis. Excessive drink, like well-serviced brakes and prescription-only sedatives, is a case in point where self-inflicted morbidity is avoided because a wise and thinking lawmaker has made himself an input in the nation's good health production-function.

The minimum drinking age and the unexpected breathalyser contribute to preventive health. So do excise duties. After all, as Phelps explains, the risk of being involved in a fatal car crash is 100 times greater for drivers under 22 who have drunk six beers than it is for their counterparts who have drunk no beers at all. The high price-elasticity of −2.3 is for that reason on the side of good health where a sensible interventionist uses the power to tax as the power to protect: 'A tax of approximately 35 per cent of the retail price of beer eliminates half of the alcohol-related fatalities arising from youthful drinkers, and a 50 per cent tax eliminates approximately three-quarters of alcohol-related deaths' (Phelps, 1988: 12). Alcohol is addictive. Habits developed as a child are difficult to break as an adult. Health capital destroyed as a child may be difficult or impossible to rebuild. It is useful to study elasticity not just in terms of total quantity but in respect of the age-profile of the individuals who enter, imitate or give up.

Chaloupka, studying cigarettes, obtained a less price-sensitive response. He discovered that the long-run elasticity of demand for cigarettes was not –2.3 but only –0.36 to –0.27: 'These estimates suggest that doubling the federal excise tax on cigarettes to 32¢ (proposed as part of a deficit reduction package), resulting in an increase of approximately 15 percent in price (assuming a competitive market), would lead, in the long run, to about a 6 percent fall in average cigarette consumption' (Chaloupka, 1991: 735–6). Young people as a subgroup may be especially inelastic. Peer pressures keep the marginal benefits high. Adolescents are vulnerable in this respect: 'If peer influences are the major determinant of youth smoking, then the demand for cigarettes can be viewed as derived from the demand for peer acceptance' (De Cicca, Kenkel and Mathios, 2002: 166).

Younger people and less educated people are more myopic, less inclined to plan for the future. Even so, being on lower incomes, a tax remains a deterrent, and a burdensome tax most of all. The United States Treasury Department estimates that for a ten per cent rise in the price of cigarettes, seven per cent fewer young people (under 25) will smoke. Using a cross-section of twelfth-graders, De Cicca, Kenkel and Mathios established a not very different price-elasticity of –0.72 (De Cicca, Kenkel and Mathios, 2002: 164). Religion confers similar benefits. Mormons in Utah, who do not drink or smoke, live longer than do non-Mormons in Nevada whose lifestyle is more unsettled.

Wasserman and his colleagues found once again that cigarette consumption was a function of price. They found that a four-fold increase in the intensity of restrictive legislation would lead to a 5.9 per cent decrease in smoking and that a 10 per cent increase in excise duty would lead to a 2.3 per cent fall (Wasserman, Manning, Newhouse and Winkler, 1991: 56–7). Evans and Ringel confirmed that Pigovian taxes would improve the outcomes. Not only would the smokers themselves be spared the heart disease and the malignant neoplasms but expectant mothers (17 per cent of whom smoke), when forced by price to cut back, would then give birth to more robust babies: 'Pregnant women are responsive to changes in cigarette tax rates. The smoking participation price elasticity is roughly –0.50.... Increases in cigarette tax rates have a beneficial impact on mean birth weight.... A one-cent increase in the state tax rate on cigarettes increases average birth weight by 0.16g' (Evans and Ringel, 1999: 148, 150, 152). Smoking doubles the risk. It accounts for about 20 per cent of all low birth weight babies in the United States. The cost is self-inflicted. Including maternal smoking, the external (social) cost is 45 cents per packet. An excise duty of 45 cents would internalise the spillover. The buyer and the seller would cover the externality. The rest of the community would not have to bear the inefficiencies of the market failure.

The nation as a whole reaps the benefit from the tax. Not only do days off work go down but citizens with skills live longer and cost the collectivity less: 'Smoking, the most important preventable cause of disease in the United States, leads to an estimated 430,000 premature deaths annually from increased risk of cancer, coronary heart disease, stroke, respiratory illness and other ailments' (Ruhm, 2005: 344). There is less passive smoking and fewer smoking-related fires. Less smoking means less disease. Less disease means less of a burden on health insurance and the medical services. Otherwise, when there is overproduction of the bads, the consequence is that other people pay.

Healthy people cross-subsidise the self-destructive. Sturm studied the impact of drinking, smoking, being overweight, being obese. He found that obesity did the most harm: it had the same effect on 17 chronic conditions as 20 years of natural ageing. In terms of physical health-related quality of life, the figure was 30 years. He also quantified the financial implications for medical care. Obesity was associated with an average increase in medical expenditures among adults aged 18 to 65 of $395 a year. The equivalent figure for smoking (current or in the past) was $230. For problem drinking it was only $150 (Sturm, 2002).

From 1976 to 2001 the rate of obesity among United States adults increased from 7.9 per cent to 20.4 per cent. In Britain the percentage is 23.6 per cent for the men, 23.8 per cent for the women. The percentages in 1993 were only 13.2 per cent and 16.4 per cent respectively. Britain now has the highest rate of adult obesity in Europe. It is well ahead of Spain (13.1 per cent), Germany (12.9 per cent), France (9.4 per cent) and Italy (8.4 per cent). Including the overweight with the obese, two-thirds of British men and about 60 per cent of British women are carrying more corporation than is good for their health. Alarmingly, 23.7 per cent of British boys aged 11 to 15 and 26.2 per cent of British girls already count as obese (Department of Health, 2006: 26). Children who are obese aged 11 to 15 are twice as likely to die before they are 50. Health promotion and health education have some way to go.

Obesity is a private problem: witness the implications for diabetes and hypertension, avoidable blindness or the loss of a limb. Yet it is a social problem as well: insurance pooling and publicly-funded medicine make it a spillover concern for all. Eating too much imposes a heavy burden on the nation's scarce resource: 'Obesity is the second leading cause of preventable death and a major risk factor for hypertension, type-2 diabetes, coronary heart disease, stroke, gallbladder disease, respiratory problems and several types of cancer ... 300,000 deaths annually are attributed to excess weight and its economic cost was estimated at US$117 billion in 2000' (Ruhm, 2005: 345). It is only sound economics for the State to subsidise weight loss clinics that reduce the incidence of sleep apnea and to educate young people not to binge despite the example of their friends. A tax on food to discourage the amount consumed is not, however, a realistic proposition: 'It is difficult to tax only excess calories; a blanket food tax affects even socially beneficial calorie intake' (Lakdawalla and Philipson, 2006: 79)

Pollution too can damage health. Schwartz and Dockery, in their study in Philadelphia, discovered that a rise in air pollution of 100 micrograms per cubic metre was associated with a rise in mortality of over 7 per cent in the general population and about 10 per cent in the over-65s (Schwartz and Dockery, 1992: 600). Selling licences to pollute, like rationing the right to smoke, would reduce the chronic pulmonary disease, the episodes of pneumonia, the cardiovascular disease and the avoidable deaths even more successfully than would an increment of doctors and nurses. It is interesting to compare the evidence on laws preventing smoking in public places and on taxes that price out the addictive luxury with the more modest results reported by Auster, Leveson and Sarachek when they studied medical care: 'A 1 per cent increase in the quantity of medical services is associated with a reduction in mortality of about 0.1 per cent' (Auster, Leveson and Sarachek, 1969: 430). In Delhi a policy to cut by a quarter the volume of total suspended particulates (TSP) in the air would save percentagewise more lives than that: 'The percentage decrease in deaths corresponding to a 100-microgram reduction in TSP is 2.3%.... Weighing each of the 1,385 lives lost by remaining life expectancy implies a loss of 51,403 life-years' (Cropper, Simon, Alberini, Arora and Sharma, 1997: 1625, 1628). Protection of the environment is in that sense a health care input.

Auster, Leveson and Sarachek found that the impact of education on mortality rates was twice as favourable as that of medical care (Auster, Leveson and Sarachek, 1969: 434). Education, they said, made it more likely that symptoms would be recognised and treatment sought in time. Education was also a cause of preventive action and of a health-furthering lifestyle. Education disseminated information and instilled disciplined attitudes. Formal schooling made it possible to continue informal learning, both on the job and through the media. These causal variables were favourable to good health. Grossman established that the pattern was the same on an intergenerational basis when he correlated children's morbidity with mother's schooling (Grossman, 1982: 192).

Education (both general and health-related), and not just the doctors and the nurses, should evidently be counted as a health care input. Better educated people can produce good body maintenance more cheaply. Earning more, they also have a stronger motive to demand better health. Falling cost of production and rising next-best foregone are both on the side of health. Reality, however, can let the economic theories down. An evocative illustration of how little educated people actually know is given by Phelps. He asked 50 university undergraduates about the extra risk associated with driving under the influence of at least six beers. His sample underestimated the statistical probability by a factor of ten (Phelps, 1988: 12). These, moreover, were *university students*.

Disinformation should be reduced even as dependable information should become more widely available. Saffer's seventeen-nation study of broadcast advertising shows precisely what the State can do by way of prohibition: 'The regressions indicate that countries with bans on spirits advertising have about 16 per cent lower alcohol consumption than countries with no bans and that countries with bans on beer and wine advertising have about 11 per cent lower alcohol consumption than countries with bans only on spirits advertising. The regressions also indicate that countries with bans on spirits advertising have about 10 per cent lower motor vehicle fatality rates than countries with no bans and that countries with bans on beer and wine advertising have about 23 per cent lower motor vehicles fatality rates than countries with bans only on spirits advertising' (Saffer, 1991: 77).

Doctors and nurses, hospital beds and prescription drugs are all inputs in the health care production-function. They treat cirrhosis of the liver and try to prevent drink-related deaths. Just as much an input is, however, the elimination of manipulative commercialism that makes rowdy drunkenness seem attractive. Want-creation draws the impressionable and the malleable down a road that leads directly to Accident and Emergency if not to something worse. Policemen are health care because they deter violent crime. Sunscreen is health care because it keeps out the rays. Reliable information is health care because it makes possible a rational choice. Health care inputs are a broad church. They are more than medical attention alone.

2.3.   HEALTH CAPITAL

The consumer has a limited endowment of income and time. The allocation has to be budgeted. One of the goods in the choice set is medical care. It is not the only option. Health and health care are good things in utility space, but so are excitement and family life. There are an infinite number of points on a nation's utility surface. Most people will settle somewhere between the extremes of all-health and all-beer. Not all will settle at the same compromise point. Not all will want the same balance between immediate well-being and deferred but greater gratification.

Health is a final utility. It is also a capital good. Michael Grossman (1972) has argued that the demand for health and care is simultaneously a demand for a here-and-now consumable and a demand for a long-lived asset that will deliver more and better healthy days over time. His theory of human capital treats investment in health as if the expenditure were, like formal education and on-the-job training, an investment in a machine that increases the average productivity of the worker and the shopper over the life span of the input. Both market and non-market activity are included in the benefits stream. The demand is a derived demand. People demand the status, not per se the medical attention or even the therapeutic steam-room that opens the pores. Yet it is a durable that must be costed and priced as if it were any other means to an end.

Health capital is an unusual commodity. As Grossman shows, healthy days are a thing that the healthholder (and/or his family) not only purchases but produces as well. The healthholder must accept the constants that he cannot change. These are his family history, a congenital defect, an acquired handicap, a random unpredictable. He accumulates his health capital within the tramlines of the inherited, the chronic and the given. Yet there remains much that can and will be self-determined. Active as well as passive, the bodyholder must make a choice of the income and leisure lost that he believes will deliver his return-maximising portfolio. In doing this, the investor must take into account the multiperiod nature of the machine, the insurer's part-payment, the rate of depreciation to which the flesh is heir, the restoration and repair on the part of the medical mechanics, the compound interest that is the opportunity cost. He must also make an allowance for the complementary inputs like health club memberships and formal schooling that he must buy in order to complete his production plans.

The bodyholder sacrifices some income, some leisure, some cigarettes and some alcohol in the short-run. His aim is to have more productivity, more pay, more working-days, more non-work recreation later on. Planning for the whole of his life cycle, the bodyholder also hopes to reap more life-years at the end: death itself is to some extent a self-selected endogeneity. Higher-paid workers will have a greater incentive to insure their future through an investment in healthy days. Illness-free days will probably more than compensate them for the higher opportunity cost of sinking time into care. Unhealthy workers have lower incomes. Yet they too have an economic reason to invest in an earnings-stream that does not fall short of its potential. They invest in better health. Their investment becomes a virtuous circle.

The investor buys a stock in order to acquire a flow. He pays for a cooker now in order to enjoy home-cooked meals spaced out over future time. It is not the cooker that he wants but rather the service-stream that the cooker makes possible. He makes his choice in the light of his tastes and preferences. Health care in the sense of Grossman is such a durable. Yet there is a difference. A cooker has resale value. Health status does not. Once bought, the asset can never be transferred: 'The stock of health capital, like the stock of knowledge capital, cannot be sold because it is imbedded in the investor' (Grossman, 1990: 356).

The investor cannot know the precise relationship between marginal inputs, planned outcomes and incremental earnings. The causal variables which are most likely to impact upon his decision will be age, income, income-elasticity, marital status, current health status and (as a proxy for the investor's technical efficiency in the production of good health) level of education. Much, however, is hidden: 'A utility maximizing diabetic faces a trade-off when choosing optimal health capital investment…. The costs are borne today while the benefits are uncertain and are received in the future' (Kahn, 1998: 880). The unhealthy pleasures are here-and-now. Future disutilities will be addressed later, if and when they arise. Diminishing marginal utility means that beyond some point people might feel that they do not want to be much healthier than they are.

Not everyone puts a high value on the future. The investment might not pay off. No one knows when he will die; or at what rate the deterioration in health status will accelerate in old age; or how much investment will be required to retard the inevitable run down in a piece of human capital; or beyond what point a further investment in health capital (an example being one more test or screen) will become uneconomically low-return. Optimisation is a minefield of ambiguities. The trade-off is not once-for-all but step-by-step. Information is incomplete. Pecuniary incentives are not the only incentives. People are not always rational. At least the proclivity to take a chance seems to have a logic that can be modelled and anticipated in advance.

2.4. PROSPERITY AND PROGRESS

Both in absolute terms and as a share of the national income, medical care inputs in virtually all countries tend to rise over time. What is less clear is whether the rise in that composite delivers a proportionate improvement in health. Perhaps, some critical level of affluence once attained, neither the aggregate nor its parts delivers any further improvement at all. There is a remarkable degree of consensus among the experts that beyond some critical point the impact of marginal inputs on status outcomes becomes exceedingly small. Diminishing marginal productivity does its worst. The curve relating the incremental inputs to the health status improved becomes flat. The additional outlay ceases to represent value for morbidity or mortality or both: 'I am aware of no data suggesting that Swedes are healthier than Norwegians or Finns, or that Canadians are healthier than residents of the United Kingdom or Australia, despite much higher spending on medical care in Sweden and Canada' (Newhouse, 1977: 121–2).

Fuchs is one of many observers who question the incremental effectiveness of additional treatments. He has this to say about the assumption that more money will normally, necessarily buy better health: 'The marginal contribution of medical care to health in developed countries is very small…. Medical intervention has a significant effect on outcome in only a small fraction of the cases seen by the average physician' (Fuchs, 1974a: 64). Some illnesses such as the common cold will cure themselves given time. Other conditions such as motor neurone disease remain incurable no matter what the doctor does. Medical intervention in cases like these will not make a great difference to the final outcome. Cochrane says that he regards such instances as the rule. They are not the exception: 'One should ... be delightfully surprised when any treatment at all is effective, and always assume that a treatment is ineffective unless there is evidence to the contrary' (Cochrane, 1972: 8).

2.4.1. Mortality

Cochrane, like Fuchs a sceptic, calls it a 'myth' to assume that therapy is the same as improvement. Jointly with others, he conducted a study of health service inputs and mortality outcomes in 18 developed countries. His findings challenge the 'layman's uncritical belief' (Cochrane, 1972: 8) that the doctor makes the difference between life and death: 'None of the health service factors were consistently negatively related to mortality.... Health service factors are relatively unimportant in explaining the differences between our 18 developed countries' (Cochrane, St Leger and Moore, 1978: 202, 204).

The causal variable with the greatest explanatory significance in Cochrane's study was not a personal care variable at all but rather the gross national product per capita. Good living standards, education and common sense seem to be the principal causes of the health of nations. It is a conclusion which is echoed by McKeown, convinced as he is that much doctoring is unneeded, much hospital attention 'palliative or unproved': 'Most of those who are born well will remain well, apart from minor morbidity, at least until late life, if they have enough to eat, if they are not exposed to serious hazards, and if they do not injure themselves by unwise behaviour' (McKeown, 1979: 137, 194). Some conditions are self-correcting. Some diseases are incurable. Medical care can sometimes make a difference. Very often it will not. Newhouse and Friedlander, explaining healthy gums, found that education was a better predictor than was the availability of dentists (Newhouse and Friedlander, 1980: 201).

Newhouse and Friedlander tabulated the relationships between care inputs and health outcomes. Their results suggested that McKeown was right: 'The physiological measures were little affected by additional medical resources. The results are consistent with the view that what the individual does (or does not) do for himself affects health more than do additional medical resources' (Newhouse and Friedlander, 1980: 200). An apple a day should do the trick. Good parents will help. The RAND Health Insurance Experiment (Newhouse and the Insurance Experiment Group 1993), as will be seen in chapter 11, found little or no relationship between health insurance, health care and health status despite the fact that the fully insured consumed 40 per cent more care than the uninsured. The production-function of better health seemed insensitive to differences in payment and delivery. Maxwell, studying ten countries, was forced to admit that 'there is no consistent correlation between high levels of spending and low mortality rates': 'Although nations like Sweden and the Netherlands spend highly and enjoy excellent health status, West Germany and the United States spend equally highly and have a relatively low standard of health by these measures' (Maxwell, 1981: 51).

West Germany in Maxwell's league table was first out of ten on the basis of health care spending as a percentage of gross national product. It was tenth out of ten when ranked by the rate both of mortality and of morbidity. Britain was tenth out of ten on the input measure but fourth out of ten by its outcomes. The rankings for the United States were second and ninth respectively. If Maxwell and others are right, then money spent and outcomes achieved are not to be regarded as fixed coefficients. Fuchs sums up the state of knowledge in the following words: 'Today ... differences in health levels between the United States and other developed countries or among populations in the United States are not primarily related to differences in the quantity or quality of health care. Rather, they are attributable to genetic and environmental factors and to personal behavior' (Fuchs, 1974a: 6).

The World Health Organization ranks health systems in 191 countries. Mainly influenced by expert opinion, the WHO does not, however, interview clients to determine their own personal level of satisfaction. Robert Blendon has filled the gap. His comparison of survey data with the WHO's performance indicators for a subset of 17 industrialised nations has revealed that there is 'little relationship' between the league table and the feelings on the ground: 'Italy is ranked second by WHO. But only 20 percent of its citizens say they are satisfied with their health care system.... Denmark is ranked sixteenth in the WHO overall performance measure, yet 91 percent of Danish citizens say they are satisfied with their health system. Once again, those who live in the country have a different perception than the WHO experts have' (Blendon, Kim and Benson, 2001: 15). Spain was third on the WHO scale but thirteenth in the currency of citizen satisfaction. (It was, coincidentally, thirteenth also in per capita resourcing.) Finland (12th out of 17 by per capita health expenditure) was fifteenth but second respectively. The United States (first out of 17 by per capita spending) came seventeenth and fourteenth. France, ranked best by the WHO (and occupying third place in health expenditure per capita), fell to sixth place when assessed by its own people. Fuchs and Maxwell are closer to the WHO measures than they are to the views of the general public who have waited in the queues, experienced the lack of respect, fought with inefficient bureaucrats over scarce services wastefully scheduled. Blendon takes the view that the health care production function should take grassroots responsiveness into account as well.

Fuchs is a moderate. He believes that the impact on health status outcomes of incremental medical inputs will be very small but seldom actually negative.

Ivan Illich is more pessimistic. Illich says that the relationship is not health-neutral and flat-of-the-curve but rather forward-falling and insidious. Seeing a doctor is detrimental to the patient's health: 'A professional and physician-based health care system that has grown beyond critical bounds ... must produce clinical damage that outweighs its potential benefits' (Illich, 1977: 16).

Thus a stay in hospital can result in cross-infection from other patients and side-effects from anaesthetics and drugs. Surgery can go wrong: the knife can slip, the oxygen can stop, the wrong leg can be amputated. Rubella vaccinations of young girls can make it more rather than less likely that they will suffer from severe arthritis or contract the rubella virus later in life (Chantler, Tingle and Petty, 1985: 1117). Doctors can be lazy or tired. Platelets in the bloodstream can acquire a will of their own. One's health can suffer once one falls into the hands of the professionals. Cochrane and his colleagues found a positive association between the numbers of doctors and the age-specific mortality rates (most of all those for infants) save for the 45–64 age cohort (Cochrane, St Leger and Moore, 1978: 204). The correlation between cigarette smoking and death rates was positive as well.

Illich is concerned with physical iatrogenesis. Here he may be exaggerating the doctor-induced disasters while underestimating the great majority of treatment episodes that end satisfactorily. Self-diagnosis can be problematic (asymptomatic diabetes in its early stages, for example). Self-treatment can be hazardous (consider the home-induced abortion). Illich is exaggerating the case for independence when he throws out the baby because he believes that the bathwater has lost its function.

Illich is concerned with psychic dependency as well. This too he regards as counterproductive and pathological. Illich feels that care that is no more than the relief of suffering is of negative marginal benefit: medicalisation reduces the capacity of the individual to face up to the great inevitabilities of illness and death. He would not have much time for the view of the patients that the tranquillisers, the anti-depressants and the painkillers, the support, the social workers and the counselling, all help them to cope that much more easily with the realities of migraine, cancer and discomfort around them. People wear glasses. People go to dentists. Illich's critics would object that professionals represent more than just a listening ear. Sometimes they do supply non-judgmental sympathy but sometimes they also help the patient to get back on his feet.

2.4.2. Morbidity

The hypothesis that care is of low or even negative value has normally been tested against national data on deaths. Morbidity instead of mortality might, however, paint a more optimistic picture.

Thus doctors raise felt well-being by treating complaints such as thyroid disorders which are unlikely to prove fatal. Hip replacements make it possible to walk without pain. Immunisations against tetanus reduce the likelihood of future disability. Not all observers, moreover, would agree with Illich that patients should cope stoically with suffering when drugs are an alterative that would improve their quality of life. Even if there is no cure for their schizophrenia or their multiple sclerosis, having someone to talk to can lighten the burden of worry and despair. Death is not all that counts. Success rates should incorporate data on sickness and reassurance as well.

Besides that, patients' expectations are being upgraded. They do not see the nexus exclusively in terms of mortality postponed or morbidity reversed. They increasingly expect the kind of personal interaction that in an organic community would be provided by the extended family and the parish priest. One can complain that the relationship with the doctor ought to be a clinical one, not at all the surrogate for kinship and belonging. Even so, history is taking its course. Geographical mobility, secularisation, smaller families, divorce, all undermine the traditional support systems. The pastoral role is becoming more important as the alternatives to the doctor become more vestigial.

Time spent discussing possible futures with a stroke victim, a battered housewife, an on-the-edge executive, a child terminally ill with AIDS, is not time likely to have a payoff in the sense of a reduction in the mortality rate. A hip or knee replacement will not contribute to longevity even if it does improve function and alleviate discomfort. Severe migraine treated with drugs allows the patient the freedom to get on with work and play. An additional test might marginally improve the accuracy of a diagnosis. Eyeglasses and contact lenses give people the chance to read and drive. Cochlear implants improve hearing. Bunker, Frazier and Mosteller say that it would be good for the medical nihilists to use their common sense: 'The miseries of depression, shortness of breath, angina, creaky and painful joints, severe pain, disabling headaches, major indigestion, urinary difficulties, toothache and sore gums, fuzzy vision, faulty hearing, paralysis, and broken bones would add up to a national disaster without the relief we are able to document' (Bunker, Frazier and Mosteller, 1994: 242).

Well-being is not calendar years. Care is not cure. Yet it is hard for all that to call it flat-of-the-curve and write it out of the equation. Medicine is not just about death and not just about science. Increasingly, as Fuchs writes, medicine is about helping ordinary people to get through the day: 'Paediatricians, for example, know that calming nervous mothers is often more time-consuming than treating their children. Obstetricians must deal with expectant fathers as well as their pregnant spouses. Relieving anxiety is a large part of almost every physician's stock-in-trade' (Fuchs, 1974a: 65). Clearly, as a society becomes more affluent, one concomitant of upgraded self-image is likely to be a greater emphasis on person-centred care. Statistics on morbidity, self-perceived, are likely to become even more important over time.

2.4.3. Increments and Totals

Whether the curve that links the cause of care to the effect of status is rather flat, or forward-falling, or upward sloped, is a matter for debate. What is not in question is the need to adopt the marginal approach. Newhouse, himself somewhat of a sceptic, is careful to insist that totals must not be confused with increments. All policy must start with the status quo: 'Eliminating medical care services altogether could lead to a marked increase in mortality and morbidity rates, even though a further increase in medical services would show little effect' (Newhouse, 1978: 81). We start from here. Our choices are not of averages but of small changes built atop the existing base. It is the small changes, not the totals, that the society would want to arrest if it chose to divert money from health care to other public projects like defence or education which it deemed to be of greater urgency. Health status itself could even go up if resources were to be channelled away from new hospitals and towards subsidies for lead-free petrol or scientific research.

Newhouse is trying to make a distinction between *any at all* on the one hand, a *small increment or decrement* on the other. The example he gives is cardiovascular disease. Where care is not widely available, he says, it is likely that the medically underdeveloped countries will be able to cut their mortality rates through an expansion in health care interventions. This was the experience of the United States in the 1960s and 1970s, where 'improved emergency services and greater control of high blood pressure ... probably played a role in reducing the toll from heart disease' (Newhouse, 1978: 80–81). The great benefits arose when the base was small. As society grows medically better provided, the incremental benefits are likely to be much less dramatic. Diminishing returns make the gains in areas such as cardiovascular disease, road accidents and malignant neoplasms more modest over time: 'It is problematic whether further extension of medical care services can reduce mortality from any of these causes substantially' (Newhouse, 1978: 81). The gains were real at a lower point on the curve. They are unlikely be very significant starting from here. That means that the rate of growth of medical services in an adequately provided area of care cannot meaningfully be taken as an indicator of progress and advance. Once it could. Since then, history has moved on.

That is why medical activity in the past cannot be taken as a good guide to medical requirements in the future. Cultural attitudes change. New technologies will do different things. What happened in history will not point to a single unambiguous spot where today's more-advanced or even today's less-developed countries ought to be now. Yet historians do study the historical correlation between life-expectancy and medical intervention. Their results, which are history and no more, often do surprise.

Thomas McKeown has examined the historical association between medical care and health in England and Wales since about 1750. His conclusion is not very supportive. Medical care, though useful, he writes, has been 'often less effective than has been thought': 'The predominant influences which led to the improvement in health in the past three centuries were nutritional, environmental (particularly control of water and food), and behavioural; the last through the change in reproductive practices which limited population growth.... The contribution of personal medical measures remains tertiary in relation to the predominant behavioural and environmental influences' (McKeown, 1979: vii, 9). The single most important cause of the fall in infant and adult mortality (used as an indicator of overall good health) has been, McKeown writes, the improvement in nutrition. Rotation, mechanisation, manuring, winter feeding, have all raised agricultural productivity. Improvements in transportation on canals, rivers and roads have meant that food sold to the consumer is fresher and less expensive. International trade, the relaxation of tariffs, the invention of refrigeration have globalised the supply and demand of primary produce. Above all else there has been the rise in incomes which has given the impoverished and the undernourished access to a balanced diet which has enabled them to fight off germs and infections.

McKeown adds that public investment in health infrastructure has had a contribution of its own to make. Szreter and Woolcock have amplified this insight in their analysis of Joseph Chamberlain's 'gas and water socialism' in mid-Victorian Birmingham: 'The provision of sufficient clean water and sewerage systems to preserve human health in such rapidly expanding residential centres required the effective mobilization of political will in order to solve a classic collective action problem.... Science and technology, alone, is not enough' (Szreter and Woolcock, 2004: 658–9). Hygiene is important and not just nutrition. Nutrients cannot be absorbed where a child is sickly and weak.

The purification of drinking water and the sanitary disposal of sewage have reduced the threat from waterborne diseases such as cholera, dysentery and typhoid. Public goods with spillovers such as these are commonly made a charge upon the State. They are financed publicly by the collectivity through taxes and, in poor countries, foreign aid. Vaccination can contain the spread of measles, polio and pertussis. Spraying and fogging can keep down mosquitoes in residential districts. Health education can improve the outcomes by teaching people what to do. Increasingly, people have learned to wash their hands with soap before handling food; to limit and space their pregnancies in order to protect the mother's health; to take reasonable exercise because fresh air is good for the body; to limit high-risk sexual activity because sexually transmitted diseases are far worse than sensible precautions. Health workers, trained at public expense, have spread the message into the villages. Behaviour and attitudes thus reinforce income, nutrition and environment in helping to raise the average level of health.

The argument for the political lead should not be pressed too far. Mosquito nets and water filters can privatise at least a part of the cost. Airborne contagions such as tuberculosis, bronchitis and pneumonia become less of a threat when more affluent people trade up from Dickensian overcrowding into better ventilated units. Preventive health in short has been ensured not just by good sewers and public housing but by money-driven ambition and the profit motive which supplies in order to sell.

Medical care in all of this has had very much the character of a footnote. Some estimates suggest that as little as 10 per cent of the decline in preventable (premature) deaths in the twentieth century actually occurred in the era of the biotechnological take-off. *Post festum* was not *propter festum*. Simply, 'when the tide is receding from the beach it is easy to have the illusion that one can empty the ocean by removing water with a pail' (Dubos, 1959: 23). McKinlay and McKinlay, documenting the American experience from 1900 to 1973, showed that about 92 per cent of the marked decline in (age-adjusted) mortality from measles, scarlet fever, tuberculosis, pneumonia, diphtheria and typhoid had already occurred *before* the expensive new techniques and vaccines came into general use in the late 1940s. Only deaths from influenza, poliomyelitis and whooping cough showed declines of 25 per cent or more (the association need not be the cause) after the date when the appropriate medical breakthroughs were made commercially available (McKinlay and McKinlay, 1977: 414, 420). The authors conclude that modern medicine was not the reason why the great killer contagions had receded into history: '*At most 3.5 per cent of the total decline in mortality since 1900 could be ascribed to medical measures introduced for the diseases considered here*' (McKinlay and McKinlay, 1977: 425; original emphasis).

McKeown confirmed the result for England and Wales: 'Immunization is relatively ineffective even today, and therapeutic measures of some value were not employed until about 1950, by which time the number of deaths had fallen to a low level' (McKeown, 1979: 54). Improvements in antibiotics, blood, anaesthetics and obstetrics have had a role to play. Joints can be replaced and coronary arteries unblocked. Hypertension can be treated through drugs and diabetes managed with insulin. The net effect has not been very great: 'Today the life expectancy of a 40-year-old suffering end-stage renal disease is 8.8 years, that of a 59-year-old, 4.2 years, ... advances that have added an estimated two to three months to the life expectancy of the population' (Bunker, Frazier and Mosteller, 1994: 234). McKeown's point is that the aggregate expenditures do not produce much of an overall improvement. Individuals gain in years. The national figures go up by months. A woman successfully treated for cancer of the cervix achieves a further twenty-one years of life. Her nation, statistically speaking, improves its life expectancy by two weeks (with the potential for one more). Critics who say that two weeks is not very much should concentrate instead on the twenty-one years.

Bunker, Frazier and Mosteller warn that the benefits from curative and preventive medicine must not be written off. There are the antenatal clinics. There are the hernia repairs. There are the playground accidents patched up. The end-stage renal disease and the cancer of the cervix are discouraging illustrations which, however, fall at the low end of the scale. All told, the authors say, the figures suggest 'an estimated current gain in life expectancy of about five years and a potential for adding one and a half or two more years, all derived from therapies already known to be efficacious' (Bunker, Frazier and Mosteller, 1994: 238). Medical care is extending the length of life. Lifestyle, however, is contributing even more. McKeown's thesis, supported by other historians, is that the contribution of penicillin and blood transfusion to the fall in deaths is as nothing compared to the far greater impact of better diet and hygiene: 'The appraisal of influences on health in the past three centuries suggested that we owe the improvement, not to what happens when we are ill, but to the fact that we do not so often become ill; and we remain well, not because of specific measures such as vaccination and immunization, but because we enjoy a higher standard of nutrition and live in a healthier atmosphere' (McKeown, 1979: 79).

The lesson for today's less-developed countries could not be more striking. Avoid the medical mystique. *Enrichissez-vous.* Improve the daily calorific intake. Invest in public health. Invest in education. Improve the conditions of life. In the words of Pritchett and Summers: 'Wealthier nations are healthier nations.... The estimated income elasticity of infant and child mortality is between –0.2 and –0.4.... Raising per capita incomes will be an important component of any country's health strategy. The estimates imply that if income were 1 percent higher in the developing countries, as many as 33,000 infant and 53,000 child deaths would be averted annually' (Pritchett and Summers, 1996: 841, 844). The positive relationship between income and health (where health is proxied by death) is causal and not merely associative. At least in the poorer countries, rising incomes prevent ill health. Prevention is better than cure. Flat-of-the-curve is an uneconomic misuse of scarce resources.

National data are not, however, the only data. Evidence such as that presented by McKeown relates to the average. Evidence documenting the specific procedures, the races, the genders, the age-cohorts suggests that there is less reason for complacency. The curve is not always flat when the macro-picture is broken down into its component parts. It is this distinction between the sweeping overview and the areas of neglect that led Wennberg and Cooper to say that health care does matter even if throwing more money at some global aggregate does not: 'There is little evidence that greater spending brings better health.... More spending does not result in less underservice. In other words, the "cure" for underservice ... appears to be better management of resources, not more spending' (Wennberg and Cooper, 1999: 238). Waste and inefficiency should be reduced. Targeting should be more precise. Spending is a good thing that can make a big difference to some. That is why it should be concentrated more studiously on the programmes and the beneficiaries who stand to make the greatest gains. We are not *all* flat-of-the-curve.

Reallocation could take place in such a way as to favour undersupplied services. Medical guidelines specify an annual faecal occult blood test for colorectal cancer and an annual retinal eye examination for diabetics. These services despite the medical benchmarks are supplied to only 12 per cent and 45.3 per cent of Medicare enrollees respectively (Wennberg and Cooper, 1999: 214, 215). Social groupings have been neglected as well. Currie and Gruber discovered that an extension of Medicaid eligibility to uninsured women on very low incomes would be able to save a non-flat-of-the-curve number of newborn children's lives: 'A 30-percentage-point increase in targeted eligibility would have been associated with an 11.5 percent decline in infant mortality' (Currie and Gruber, 1996: 1278).

The cost of $840 000 per infant life saved may suggest that the rescued lives were not cost-effective. The same sum would have paid for 206 child years of primary and secondary schooling or 247 family years of income maintenance. Value-of-life studies do, however, indicate that $840 000 is cheap at the price. Child-resistant cigarette lighters cost $3.15 million per child life saved, child-restraint systems in cars $5.5 million, improvements in school bus safety in excess of $10 million, on the assumption of a child's life-expectancy of 75 years. The present point is not, however, the cost-effectiveness but specifically the crude census. Concentrating the resources on the margin that most stands to gain is not flat-of-the-curve but a high-powered strategy that will improve the data on deaths. Reaganomic monetarism in the 1980s was in that sense microeconomic even as it declared itself to be impartially across-the-board. Strict budgeting starved the needy of their prenatal and neonatal care: 'The cutbacks coincide with a slowing in the decline of mortality rates, especially for blacks. For instance, from 1981 to 1982, the black neonatal mortality rate fell by 2.2 percent, and the white rate fell by 4.2 percent' (Corman, Joyce and Grossman, 1987: 340). McKeown's averages are more typical of the whole than they are of the women, the poor, the blacks and the low birth weight babies who without the incubators never stood a chance.

McKeown's focus is on death rates and life-expectancy. He would have been the first to say that the Samaritan role is of importance too. The comfort of the patient, even if the dying patient, cannot be written off because it is a consumption good and not an investment. It may be that modern medicine should rely on a multiplicity of success-indicators and that sympathetic interaction might be regarded as one of its most valuable inputs. This would be the view of Cochrane who, reflecting on what he believes to be the 'relative unimportance of therapy in comparison with the recuperative power of the human body', states unequivocally that near flat-of-the-curve in no way means a total rejection of the medical input: 'I believe that cure is rare while the need for care is widespread, and that the pursuit of cure at all costs may restrict the supply of care' (Cochrane, 1972: 5, 7).

3. Needs and wants

Consumer sovereignty means that the shopper is the best judge of his own interest. Liberal democracy means that the citizen and not the dictator determines the mix that will be supplied. The markets and the voters speak with a single voice in support of factoring down and of bottom-up precisely because only the patient can say where it hurts: 'Underlying most arguments against the free market is a lack of belief in freedom itself' (Friedman, 1962: 15).

The freedom to choose is the freedom to translate wants into facts. Needs, however, are a different matter. Wants are perceptions: a person who is mentally ill is not mentally ill if he says he is sane. Needs are absolutes: 'Whales were not fishes merely because people thought they were for centuries' (Daniels, 1985: 29–30). Wants are fleeting: they are whims that can be disregarded without irreparable damage to the bedrock essence. Needs are imperatives. They carry the implication 'that the entity asserted to be needed is actually necessary'. They convey the message that 'this needed entity ought to be received' (Culyer, 2005: 227).

Wants are preferences: the consumer alone knows if his marginal utility is just worth the marginal expense. Needs are structures: 'Fiddlers need fiddles; photographers need cameras' (Braybrooke, 1987: 33). Needs are objective: the benefit has an identity of its own that has form and substance even when it is not seen, felt or heard. Wants are subjective: the assessment, all in the individual's mind, vanishes when the ostrich buries its sensory faculties in the sand.

Wants are *de gustibus non est disputandum*. Needs are *ne plus ultra* and *sine qua non*. Needs are uncompromisingly linked to the human condition. They are the irreducible constraints that remain behind once the froth of inclination has been scraped aside: 'People have a need for exercise regardless of what they wish, prefer, want otherwise, or choose. They have the need even if they do not much care to live or be healthy' (Braybrooke, 1987: 32). Needs are species-constants. They are validated by natural law. They derive from the definition of what it means to be a *human* being: 'An imperfect satisfaction of needs leads to the stunting of our nature. Failure to satisfy them brings about our destruction. But to satisfy our needs is to live and prosper' (Menger, 1976 [1871]: 77). To live and prosper is a constitution precondition. It is not a higgledy-piggledy of the piecemeal and the *ad hoc*. Needs cannot reasonably be swapped at the margin by traders in the bazaar.

Jack wants alcohol and cigarettes. Jill wants chocolates and cholesterol. Their wants are quintessentially their own. Yet, since they are alive and human, their needs cry out with a single voice that they will regret their decision if they continue to chip away at their healthy life-years: 'You can need what you want, and want or not want what you need. What you cannot consistently do is not need what is required in order to avoid serious harm – whatever you may want' (Doyal and Gough, 1991: 42). In the final analysis, the needs take precedence over the preferences. If the needs were not satisfied, serious harm would result. Serious harm means that the process of want-satisfaction would lose its momentum until eventually it ground to a halt.

The subject of this chapter is needs and wants. It argues that decision-making in the field of health is a triangle of forces and a combination of constituencies. Section 1, The Patient, identifies the bodyholder as the first participant and the initiating source of demand. Non-judgmental individualists will like it that way: 'Only the slave has needs; the free man has demands' (Boulding, 1966: 202). Section 2, The Practitioner, says that health care is too important and too specialised to be delegated to the under-informed bodyholder who is ill-equipped to decide: 'Only the doctor knows what good doctoring is' (Lord Horder, quoted in Johnson, 1977: 74). Section 3, The Public, says that society as a whole situates the consumer and the provider in a seamless web of cultural norms, standard-size roles and interdependent interests which only the deviant and the psychopathic will have any wish to disregard: 'Needs arise by virtue of the kind of society to which individuals belong. Society imposes expectations, through its occupational, educational, economic, and other systems, and it also creates wants, through its organization and customs' (Townsend, 1979: 50). I am I because We are We. Health care is a social fact. The sick role is a matter of time and place. The neighbours are watching and commenting every time the patient sees the doctor and says he thinks that he is ill.

3.1.   THE PATIENT

The patient tends to be the first mover in the medical sequence. There are exceptions. An accident victim might be unconscious on arrival. A schizophrenic might believe that the voices in his head are real. An insurance company or an employer might insist on a full annual check-up. A proactive doctor might call in all at-risk women for a smear. A school clinic might check all children for vision and growth. A works clinic might screen all employees for lung cancer from pollutants. Sometimes supply comes first and the individual fits in. More often than not it is the individual who makes the contact because he thinks he is ill.

The problem is that the patient may not be certain that he is ill. His visit to the doctor will often be heralded with the personal apology of 'I don't think it's serious but …'. The visit costs time and money. The patient cannot know in advance that the diagnosis will throw up an abnormality or that a cure for the malfunction has actually been found. All that the patient can do is to invest in a precautionary consultation and breathe a sigh of relief when he is reassured that his stomach ache is not a peptic ulcer after all. The patient is not an expert. He is not fully the master of rational choice. He does not know that he is pre-diabetic or that his blood glucose is impaired. He cannot be very confident that he is investing his resources in a way that will give him a sound payoff.

3.1.1. Knowledge and Ignorance

Most people have acquired some background information about health. There are biology lessons at school. There are television documentaries. There are articles on body maintenance in the quality press. Many people, moreover, are curious about health and want to find out more. Their knowledge is the unintended outcome of their hobby. It will stand them in good stead if the complaints with which they are familiar come up in their examination. The probability that general reading will be cost-effective cannot, however, be called very high.

Some bodies of knowledge are more likely to be called upon than others. Children are offered immunisation against mumps, measles and rubella. A young couple will need to know about contraception and childbirth. An older woman should expect the menopause. An older man has a high probability of a prostate problem. A worker in the chemicals industry will have a personal stake in finding out about lead. Life cycle or occupational, in cases like these the consumer is not entirely hidden behind a veil of unknowledge. Where the ambit is narrow, the need to know jumps off the page. More usually, however, it does not. In most cases the position is that it would be irrational and uneconomic to collect information on disease A if the likelihood is more or less the same that one will be struck down by disease B, C or D instead.

Once the malady has actually been diagnosed, the position is then somewhat different. The affliction having been identified, information collected on it will be targeted and finely tuned. At that stage the patient might conceivably have more to contribute to the competitive sift. Even so, he might nonetheless make a personal decision to remain in the dark. The patient might be so emotional that he does not feel able impartially to weigh the evidence he is accumulating. He might not want to amass information at all if all that it will do is to reiterate that there is no cure. He might prefer to remain in the dark if thinking about his condition is itself a source of unhappiness and anxiety. He might have insurance. If he does, then he has no financial incentive to discover the most cost-effective way out of his maze.

Besides that, there is the doctor. Once the medical practitioner has moved in and taken charge, the bodyholder might feel that he can afford to go passive.

He can depend on his hired agent for the good advice that puts balanced conjecture into the market mechanism. There is no need to be fully informed if the prices, quantities, qualities and technical relationships can be delegated to a representative. These things change all the time. The cost of being up to date is too high to attempt the impossible on one's own, or at all. As Culyer writes: 'If information about one's health is costly to collect, it may be irrational to dispel all ignorance; i.e. it is perfect information, rather than ignorance, that is *a priori* more likely to be inconsistent with the postulates of welfare economics' (Culyer, 1971: 192).

Given the inconvenience and the cost, the patient might feel that it is enough to buy in the counsel and opinion of the specialist. The problem is that the patient does not usually know what it is he is being asked to select: 'The value of information is frequently not known in any meaningful sense to the buyer; if, indeed, he knew enough to measure the value of information, he would know the information itself. But information, in the form of skilled care, is precisely what is being bought from most physicians, and, indeed, from most professionals. The elusive character of information as a commodity suggests that it departs considerably from the usual marketability assumptions about commodities' (Arrow, 1973 [1963]: 18). In the case of a normal consumable, the consumer will often have learned from experience. He will have some idea of what quality of service to expect. In the case of information, the consumer by definition is asking for what he does not know. Because he does not know it, he will not know if the diagnosis he has been given is full and fair.

In routine and repetitive cases the patient is able to learn by trial and error. A dental patient can see the difference between one filling and the next. A woman who has more than one delivery can compare the obstetricians pregnancy by pregnancy. A long-term sufferer from chronic mood swings will recognise when new psychiatrists are trying new compounds. Personal contacts and self-help groups make expectations less fanciful. Family and friends describe the nursing homes on the web. Health maintenance organisations are selected not in a medical emergency but in a moment of calm. Pauly, taking experience and networks into account, estimates that about one-third of personal health care decisions can be regarded as reasonably informed (Pauly, 1988: 45). Two-thirds are not.

In some cases there is learning by doing. In many cases, however, the procedure will be once-for-all. The patient will have no memory capital on which to draw. An appendectomy, a hysterectomy or a gall bladder operation is not an apple that is purchased regularly every day. Nor is it a replumbed pipe that by inspection can be seen to let the water through. Major disasters will come to light and will be the stuff of a malpractice suit. The patient will know soon enough if the wrong leg has been amputated, if 0.25 mg was inadvertently misread as 25, if full-body bruising indicates that he was dropped in theatre. Inconspicuous mistakes, on the other hand, are unlikely to be noticed. Slovenly stitching or even an abandoned clip will probably not be detected. Practice variation, moreover, is the essence of medicine. Not all doctors replicate the same procedures. A patient about to complain that he was given a more expensive drug than his neighbour or that discretionary tissue was removed to play safe will be met with the reply 'but that's what I *always* do'.

People who see doctors are, besides that, abnormally trusting. They do not want to contemplate the possibility that something might have gone wrong. Psychologically, they are not keen to think that the assessment was mistaken and the service negligent. Their optimism, their anxiety, their fear of mutilation, their sensitivity to cross-infection, have the same effect as their ignorance. Medical services cannot be returned if they fail to satisfy. There is always the possibility of unavoidable failure and even unpreventable death. The market is a learning process. There are commodities where the lessons can prove fatal to a layman who tries to build up the knowledge-stock on his own.

Wishful thinking boosts the relative power of the supplier who is believed to know best. So does inertia and a non-calculative propensity to misread the evidence. Even when people are given full information they will tend to make relatively limited use of the facts. The following survey data suggest that consumers' choices can badly let the free market down: 'The results show that quality ratings had very little impact on consumer choice of hospitals. A hospital that had twice the expected death rate had less than one fewer discharge per week in the first year, and only 116 fewer discharges over nine years. In contrast, if there is a press report of a single, unexpected death, there is a 9 percent reduction in admissions for the next year' (Rice, 2001: 27). If individuals were as casual about their tomatoes as they are about their appendectomies, the enemies of consumer sovereignty would say that the invisible hand could not be trusted to maximise anyone's welfare save that of the teachers of economics alone.

3.1.2. Information Asymmetry

Unequal knowledge, 'information impactedness' (Williamson, 1975: 14), leaves the patient susceptible and dependent. The supplier has superior knowledge and the consumer is weak. The medical contract is not the only instance of the imbalance. The motorist must rely on the mechanic for unbiased intelligence. The lawyer can demand unneeded documentation purely in order to garner extra fees. The greengrocer knows more about the freshness of his fruit. The rancher knows more about the hormones in his beef. Unequal knowledge is not *obiter dictum* but the essence of supply and demand. Anaesthetics and scalpels, however, make the individual abnormally aware that he is exposed. It is an odd assumption. The mechanic who does a slovenly job with the brakes or the rancher who injects dangerous chemicals into his herd can do just as much harm. Fear is notoriously irrational.

The patient lacks knowledge about medicine. The patient does not know which drug will make him more talented or more energetic. Yet the doctor lacks knowledge about the patient. The doctor does not know that the patient sees his big nose as a shameful deformity or needs his anabolic steroids for his one big chance in life. The ignorance is on both sides and not only on one. The doctor is in touch with the latest thinking on diseases and cures. He knows how to set a broken bone, to recognise the presenting symptoms of septicaemia, to assign a statistical probability to a lump or a faint. What he does not know is the subjective meaning of the contingency for the patient himself. Patients are unique. Their well-being, self-perceived, is not just an objective tabulation of facts.

Only the purchaser can decide if the riskiness of a motorbike compensates for the cost of a car. Only the consumer can know if the discomfort of new fashions exceeds the status purchased by the ostentation. Medicine is more of the same. The patient alone is in a position to compare the pain of the metastases with the side-effects of the bicalutamide; or if the danger of complications from a blood transfusion is greater than the anticipated benefit from the procedure; or if home convalescence is preferable to a less stressful but more costly hospital stay. The patient alone is in a position to assess the value to him of income foregone when he closes his shop or of debt incurred to finance a last-ditch intervention. The patient alone knows what he regards as 'full recovery' and what he sees as his maximum tolerable standard of disability. The patient alone has an idea, however loose, of the weighting scheme. The doctor does not. Yet the knowledge is vital. An architect does not ask a house whether it wants to face south. A veterinarian does not ask a cat if it is planning to go for a family. People, however, have preferences. These preferences affect the amount of benefit that the patient believes he is deriving from his cure.

Daniels observes that 'normal species functioning', so easy to reify into the constancy of a need, is in fact surprisingly plastic. It is a function of the single discrete individual's unique way of life. Different people might have different goals. Different communities inculcate different traditions. Different objectives presuppose different bundles of health. Besides that, things change: 'For many of us, some of our goals, perhaps even those we feel are most important to us, are not necessarily undermined by failing health or disability. Moreover, we can often adjust our goals, and presumably our levels of satisfaction, to fit better with our dysfunction or disability' (Daniels, 1985: 27). Much depends on the social role that the individual wishes to play. A black man who wants to be a white woman might be reacting against the social pecking-order and not simply expressing a free-floating predilection. Gender reassignment is a medical answer. Public policy to replace discrimination with tolerance (combined with equal access to training and skills) is the socio-political equivalent.

Much depends as well on the refinement or redefinition of that role as life cycle personal evolution takes its course. A married person who wants children has a different sense of self from a single person who (while still young enough to function as a parent) at least in the short-run does not. Life chances must be matched up to life plans. There is no point in giving people a way in that they do not want or cannot use. There is a sense in which it would be true to say that new social opportunities can trigger new needs for healthcare. Assuming it could be cured by brain surgery, Daniels writes, 'dyslexia may be less important to treat in an illiterate society than in a literate one.... The social importance of particular diseases is a notion which we ought to view as socially relative' (Daniels, 1985: 34).

Indeed it is; but that is not to deny that it is personal as well. Emphysema prevents a worker from continuing as a building labourer but it leaves open the chance of a new career in artificial flowers. Only the individual can say if the costs and benefits are such that treatment (which can be unpleasant) will make possible a life-path which for him is significantly more pleasurable. Normal functioning seen in that light is at least as much a topic in kaleidoscopic satisfaction-seeking as it is a fact of essential humanness that cannot be denied: 'When people's preferences run contrary to their needs, perhaps the project of meeting their needs will have to be suspended' (Braybrooke, 1987: 6).

People are reflective and self-aware. They have a *need* to defend their space. That being the case, the medical practitioner ought ideally to consult the patient even as the patient consults his guide. The most sensitive agency relationship will be one where the agent decides precisely as the principal would have done if only the principal had possessed the agent's stock of sector-specific expertise. Medicine then becomes a two-way street. The doctor does not decide *for* the patient but rather *with* the patient. The objective and the subjective inputs collaborate. The symbiosis ensures that the joint decisions will be personally tailored and made to measure. How can the doctors return a mental patient to his community if they do not know how he gets on with his children or whether he would prefer to be sleeping rough?

The movement away from producer's sovereignty is an acknowledgement that economic man likes to be asked what he wants. Yet it is not an unmixed blessing. Telling the whole truth is open-ended and time-consuming. Resources used for discussion with insiders are resources not being used to bring outsiders into the fold. The ill-informed and the inconsistent might not be the best judge of their welfare. A patient who is clinically depressed might not be in a fit state to debate the side-effects of electroconvulsive therapy. A patient unaccustomed to the language of probability might not understand that the treatment-sequence he is being quoted is only a large-sample estimate. Social externalities are not likely to figure prominently in doctor–patient consultation. Democracy, in short, has an opportunity cost. Depth is gained. Breadth is lost. The seminar-like exchange of views might not make scarce social resources go far enough. It is a reason why some doctors will say that they prefer throughput instead. Where one is added crudely to one, it is numbers that will maximise the sum of utilitarian gain.

Differentiation itself is uneconomic. There is not much point in asking people what they want if the system is determined to offer them a standard service. If, however, different patients are promised different things, then administrative costs are incurred and economies of scale are sacrificed. A distinction should also be made between effectiveness and comfort. If the clinical outcomes are the same, it might be deemed rather unkind to put extra money into amenity so long as other patients are not getting the basic service that they need. Collective rather than decentralised feedback might in the circumstances be more appropriate. It might be better to determine if there is a *majority* opinion in favour of a specific option than to ask Jim Jones if he, Jim alone, would prefer a private room.

Consultation need not be popular. Not everyone feels a need to be perfectly informed. Many will be especially reluctant to be involved when they are ill and afraid: 'It is not surprising that the consumer becomes reliant upon the supplier. In fact if the anxiety costs become too high the consumer may be unwilling to participate in the choice process and default on making decisions, in which case the doctor/supplier takes over this decision-making role' (McGuire, Henderson and Mooney, 1988: 156). Consumers who want the doctor to decide will feel nervous and apprehensive when asked to speak up proudly for themselves. Perhaps they will not want to bear the responsibility and the guilt if something goes wrong. Richard Thaler explains the utility of choosing not to choose in the following way: 'Why do consumers want the first dollar coverage? I believe the reasons involve regret. Most consumers find decisions involving trade-offs between health care and money very distasteful. This is especially true when the decision is made for someone else, like a child' (Thaler, 1991: 16–17). Psychic costs such as remorse are avoided if the health cover is fully prepaid and if it is the doctor who decides what to do. Devolution of the mandate will be especially sensitive 'if the physician knows the patient well (and can thus do a good job of reflecting the patient's preferences)' (Thaler, 1991: 17). Where the relationship is womb to tomb, the family doctor can make a good guess. He does not need to ask.

Bounded rationality means the choice of a heuristic. For many people, delegation to an agent is the best decision-making rule they can find. If patients do not want to select their own in-period pathways, if consumers have instructed their agent to vote their proxy on their behalf, it is clearly a violation of their sovereignty to insist that the full menu should be disclosed and informed consent continuously be sought. Freedom in such a scenario is not the freedom to choose so much as it is the freedom to choose the choosers. Besides that, the clients, if informed, might simply rubber stamp whatever the doctor has told them. It is a waste of resources to consult the rank and file if they themselves see no need to express a view that is different from sage old Sir who knows best.

The problem seems to be that some patients will value consultation while others will want to be left alone. Not all patients are equally curious, equally independent, equally intelligent. Not all are equally determined to read their notes, to ask supplementary questions, to be told the worst. If consultation is to make all patients feel better off in their own estimation, then it would have to take the form of an invitation but not an obligation. It is, in other words, not only the demand for care but the demand for consultation about care that must form an important part of patient-led medicine.

The possibility that the pushy will as a consequence get more of the doctor's time than the self-effacing is a real one. It is the eternal predicament of any system that encourages participation but also allows the nervous to abstain. Even more of a dilemma is how the doctor is to know which patient would like to be involved and which would prefer sage old Sir to tick the box. Perhaps they should put their preferences on record when they first register with their practitioner or are admitted into a ward.

3.1.3. Objective and Subjective

Aristotelians take issue with utilitarians because individualists undervalue the solid foundation even of the unseen. Their criticism of patient-led medicine would be that it puts too much emphasis on tastes and not enough on what it means to develop fully into oneself. Freedom is not just the freedom to shop. It is also the freedom to unfold an essence without which the atom will feel empty, isolated, dissatisfied with life: 'Real guilt comes from not being true to yourself, to your own fate in life, to your own intrinsic nature' (Maslow, 1968 [1962]: 121). Liberal marketeers take little interest in 'the good life' as a value-free philosophical construct that exists independently of the unique decision-maker. Their normative standard is quintessentially microscopic, self-consciously perceptual. Aristotelians are more concerned with the basic capabilities that distinguish a human being from a rock or a tree. An Aristotelian would say that a need for health is not a need for *health* at all. Rather, it is the means to the ultimate end of personal growth. An Aristotelian would therefore look to wise leaders to educate people in such a way as to give them access to the single and virtuous road up.

I am what I am but also what I have the capacity to be. In the words of Amartya Sen: 'Development consists of the removal of various types of unfreedoms that leave people with little choice and little opportunity of exercising their reasoned agency. The removal of substantial unfreedoms.... is *constitutive* of development' (Sen, 1999: xii). In supporting good health through health care, society is facilitating personal liberation from the material road-blocks which stunt and destroy. Death is incompatible with life. Policies to preserve life are by definition in keeping with the generic essence of a human being: 'The substantive freedoms include elementary capabilities like being able to avoid such deprivations as starvation, undernourishment, escapable morbidity and premature mortality' (Sen, 1999: 36).

Maslow writes that the body is subject to developmental laws and that the psyche is no different: 'We have, each of us, an essential biologically based inner nature, which is to some degree "natural", intrinsic, given, and in a certain limited sense, unchangeable' (Maslow, 1968 [1962]: 3). The species-being cannot be reduced to effective demand revealed in the supermarket or mall. Maslow sees needs as absolute and universal rather than as relative to the individual or even to the culture which shapes the malleable wax in its mould. His hierarchy ascends through five levels of predetermined fulfilment.

It is Maslow's diagnosis that the lower needs must be satisfied first. Human beings must satisfy their animal needs for food, housing, sleep, the opportunity to reproduce. One dimension of this fundamental first stage would be the need to be free of disease. People should not be enfeebled by malnutrition nor too poor to afford life-saving surgery.

The body fed and watered, human beings then have a need to move up to safety, security and the containment of anxiety. In terms of health policy this second stage might mean regulations to prevent accidents at work. It might also mean market-shaping laws to protect mental health put at risk through ruthless dismissals.

The third step upward will be the need for integration, fellowship, inclusion, organicism, community, social acceptance, common roots: 'The atomistic way of thinking is a form of mild psychopathology, or is at least one aspect of the syndrome of cognitive immaturity. The holistic way of thinking and seeing seems to come quite naturally and automatically to healthier, self-actualizing people' (Maslow, 1970 [1954]: xi). Applied to health, this might be an argument for a National Health Service which makes all citizens aware that they are joint tenants in a common experience. National military service might unlock the same hidden need to belong to a team.

Blood donation is an illustration of the stage-three sense of shared attachment. Commercial donors have a pecuniary incentive to sell contaminated blood. Their myopic monetarism can cost the recipient his life. Community donors give away good blood. They do so because they are aware that the stranger gift is the biological precondition for their own psychic fulfilment: 'To "love" themselves they recognized the need to "love" strangers' (Titmuss, 1970: 239). Institutions matter. Social channels must be the appropriate ones for the satisfaction of psychological and emotional needs and not just for the bodily imperatives. Unrestrained individualism and single-minded marketeering can damage the health of the donor and of the recipient alike.

The fourth level of need-satisfaction is the need for self-esteem and self-respect. Frustration, shame and self-loathing boost the roster of the suicides and the coronaries. Dignity and acceptance keep the ulcers at bay. If means testing inflicts stigma and if stigma leads to illness, then one inference might be a social need for a free-on-demand health service. The open door would protect fellow citizens from the social sanctions that are heaped upon the misfits who have failed.

The fifth and highest level is self-actualisation. It is the stage which seeks to liberate potential through creativity, maturity and service. *Homo faber* is different from a satiated pig. Doctors and nurses find an outlet for their purposiveness in the meaningful work they do to alleviate the suffering of strangers. Their sense of a vocation is intrinsic motivation that does not stop short at their cash incentive. Maslow would say that other people too should be given the same opportunity to protect their health through meaningful gratification of the higher need for workmanlike and other-orientated accomplishment. It is a sensation that people straitjacketed into the more egotistic, the more economic satisfactions will never be able to experience.

Needs, Maslow argues, are a mountain. Individuals who have not climbed the mountain might not be able to imagine the view that awaits them from the top. A health system, like social policy in general, must nonetheless be designed in such a way as to liberate the not-yet-enlightened from their own self-shackling narrowness: '*Being* a human being – in the sense of being born to the human species – must be defined also in terms of *becoming* a human being' (Maslow, 1970 [1954]: xviii; original emphasis). People might know who they are. They are less likely to know what they have the capability to become. Leaderly empowerment is the only way to release the butterfly from the cocoon. It is the duty of medical attention narrowly defined and of the health care system as a whole to give them the true need-satisfaction of which in their blinkered underdevelopment they are not yet aware.

If self-esteem is a need, just as good health is a need, then some self-determination is implied. There must be at least a grain of truth in the market economist's propensity to log buried needs through the wants that are expressed. Individual preferences must be treated with respect. Most self-conscious people want to have a say. In that respect, speaking up, they are revealing that they are mature adults for whom a father figure or a mother figure can no longer be trusted to rule with absolute sway. Marmot's Whitehall studies showed clearly that cardiovascular disease can result where people have a low degree of control over their lives: 'Disease rates are powerfully affected by the social environment' (Marmot and Bobak, 2000: 1128). It is possible therefore to reach a compromise between the objectivists and the subjectivists in this way. The *cognoscenti* might chart the course but still the ordinary passenger might be given face on the choice of his bunk and of his meals.

The individual has to rely on the doctor to tell him why his joints are painful and stiff. The doctor, however, has to rely on the patient for a personal reaction to the spectrum of treatments that may or may not unfreeze the paralysis. Even an Aristotelian can accept that in certain circumstances the 'good life' must imply a dialogue and an affirmation of voice. Even an Aristotelian can accept that human autonomy can be a core element in the human essence that a sensitive leadership sets out to ring-fence. Mortality and physiology are constraints that philosophy cannot argue away. The quality of life, on the other hand, is better suited to an exchange of views. As Martha Nussbaum writes: 'This is how the Aristotelian approach works – hanging on to a general (and open-ended) picture of human life, its needs and possibilities, but at every stage immersing itself in the concrete circumstances of history and culture.... Thus the Aristotelian virtue-based morality can capture a great deal of what the relativist is after, and still make a claim to objectivity' (Nussbaum, 1993: 259).

3.2.   THE PRACTITIONER

Rawls writes as follows about the doctor who makes an interpersonal comparison of a dish that the diner had never ordered: 'On birthdays we give things that we know are wanted, or that will please, to express affection; our gifts are chosen in the light of intimate knowledge and shared experiences. But doctors are expected to assess the situation of their patients, and teachers to judge their students, on an entirely different basis.... Doctors consider their patients' medical needs, what is required to restore them to good health and how urgent their treatment is' (Rawls, 1982: 172). On birthdays we go by wants. Social utility is then determined by personal preferences. Surgery depends, however, on need. What is desired is not the same as a requirement that must be met if the function or the role is to survive. Doctors in this perspective have a clear image in their mind of the requirement that must be met. They are not playing God or stating their own view. Rather, they are actualising an ideal that is the free gift of nature and of circumstance alone: 'The idea of professional need always rests on some definition of homeostasis or state maintenance of the client, his property or his environment. The professional defines a certain state of his client and his related systems as a state of "health" which he has a professional interest in maintaining' (Boulding, 1966: 204).

Moral autonomy is not under attack. The ultimate criterion, Rawls would say, must be the benchmark of the individual's own wants and preferences. The slippage arises where the patient's choice is a non-rational one, not very likely to produce the pleasure that the patient himself intends. The patient does not know best. In the words of Harsanyi: 'All we have to do is to distinguish between a person's manifest preferences and his true preferences. His manifest preferences are his actual preferences as manifested by his observed behaviour, including preferences possibly based on erroneous factual beliefs or on careless logical analysis, or on strong emotions that at the moment greatly hinder rational choice. In contrast, a person's true preferences are the preferences he *would* have if he had all the relevant factual information, always reasoned with the greatest possible care, and were in a state of mind most conducive to rational choice…. In my opinion, social utility must be defined in terms of people's true preferences' (Harsanyi, 1982 [1977]: 55).

The patient does not know enough to know what deep down he would really have preferred. That is a fact of life: 'One does not know what visiting the Taj Mahal is going to be like' (Mirrlees, 1982: 69). Individualism is not always the best road home where floundering subjects approach the crossroads without a map. Mirrlees says what this lack of overview must mean for the opinion-polls, the cigarette-smoking and the danger differentials: 'People sometimes have mistaken conceptions of their well-being. At least the conception must somehow be purified of obvious errors of foresight or memory. More, one ought to be willing to entertain the possibility that some experiences are not usually correctly valued by the individual: that, in certain respects, people do not know what is good for them' (Mirrlees, 1982: 64). It is the doctor's role to mediate between the whole truth and the semi-deluded gut reaction. Whether it would also be the doctor's role to impose order on people who have access to the facts but still make choices that are random, knee-jerk, impulsive or intransitive is a separate matter. Revealing the truth is not the same as imposing a Procrustean off-the-peg. Unless the doctor has been expressly briefed by strong Ulysses to prevent weak Ulysses from running his craft on to a rock, it is difficult to justify coercion to a divided self who says he is perfectly happy to make and then to break his New Year's resolutions.

If one accepts the liberal interpretation that the individual knows best, then one would have to agree that the ideal agent is the principal's perfectly enlightened clone. The ideal doctor can access both the scientific truth about the illness and the subjective preferences of the patient. He marries up the evidence and does so without any trace of himself. Paternalism is different: here the doctor is convinced that the expert and not the bodyholder is the better judge of *what ought to be*. Commercialism is different yet again: the doctor who takes on the role of seller and buyer is determined to maximise his cash flow despite any conflict of loyalties. At least to a liberal, however, the ideal is clear enough. The doctor is *as if* the patient. It is therefore the patient who through the doctor actually speaks.

Reality falls short of the ideal. It must do so since the doctor cannot see the conscious trade-offs, the conflicting time-preferences and the subconscious biases of a sick person who hasn't a clue. In the real world the doctor has no choice but to show initiative and to influence demand: 'Thus, the medical service market cannot be simply dichotomized into demand side and supply side, with price serving as the only nexus between the two; rather we must allow for shifts in the demand curve itself in response to supplier behaviour' (Evans, 1974: 163–4). Prices are determined by supply and demand. Supply, however, stands behind demand and advises it on how to vote. That is precisely what the doctor–patient relationship is all about. Even if the principal is not up to date and logical his agent will ideally do the economising on his behalf. No one would expect a doctor to conceal a malignant carcinoma merely because the patient did not spot it first.

The doctor assesses a want and decides if it is a need. Specialist knowledge puts the educated and the experienced in a position to know if the resources committed may reasonably be expected to secure the improvement intended. For there to be a medical need, there must also be a capacity to benefit.

A need, medically speaking, can only be whole and uncompromising. It is 'the expenditure required to effect the maximum possible health improvement or, equivalently, the expenditure required to reduce the individual's capacity to benefit to zero' (Culyer and Wagstaff, 1993: 436). Economics, inevitably, muddies the clarity of the definition. Economics can suggest that a need is not a real need until competing claims have been weighed at the margin and the *general* equilibrium established. The 'maximum possible' might have to be compressed into the 'minimum that is adequate' if the need for new bridges and ports is also to be acknowledged or the neighbourhood costs of burgeoning care kept within limits. It is hard to believe that a responsible society would encourage the medical profession to validate 'maximum possible' health at the expense of all other social goals. An infinite commitment of money is arguably as bad as no commitment at all. Diminishing returns on the road to a technical maximum suggest that marginal productivity beyond a point might not be worth the sacrifice that it costs.

Be that as it may, this section is concerned with medical effectiveness as interpreted by the well-drilled practitioner. Medical need in the context of *multiple* needs will be examined in the final section on the public stake. Only then, as Culyer and Wagstaff point out, will a full picture of the means–ends nexus emerge: 'The moral force of the word "need" when applied to health care stems from the moral force of the goals associated with health itself' (Culyer and Wagstaff, 1993: 435).

3.2.1. Payment for Care

The doctor's duty is 'to help the sick'. Yet doctors are human too. Apart from their professional ethic, they also pursue private and personal objectives which bring them closer to the economic everyday of their bill-paying, tax-paying fellow citizens. Among their goals might be job satisfaction, income and prestige. It is their private objectives which are the most closely correlated with the three modes of payment for care.

Not one of the three is outcome-based. Doctors are not paid by results. It would be costly and perhaps impossible to determine if a professional had done his best: 'How successful is a treatment that saves a person's life but renders him permanently disabled? How does one measure a treatment that relieves, but does not eliminate, a particular set of symptoms? How successful is a treatment that prolongs a life for two months, or three, or four?' (Culyer, 1971: 197).The principal must pay the agent even if his illness gets worse. His estate must settle his debt even if he dies without a cure. Only proof of negligence or fraud will excuse the principal from his contractual obligation to pay.

The first mode of payment is *fee for service*. In this case the doctor is paid by piecework. The personal incentive is therefore to expand his supply in order to maximise his income. This need not mean that the practitioner necessarily performs redundant surgery knee-jerk because he wants the cash. Cost (including time-cost) may exceed the benefit. What it can mean, however, is that at the margin the doctor increases the tests he conducts; or sells additional medication from his in-house reserve; or performs unfamiliar operations himself when he could refer the patient to a more experienced colleague; or shortens his consultations in order to force through his peak paying turnover.

Patients themselves may be to blame. If they demand comfort medicines or home-visit follow-up, it would be unkind to call a doctor greedy merely because he supplied higher quality and put their mind at rest. Yet the temptation is there. Asymmetric information can lead to the removal of a healthy appendix. It does not do a lot for the patient's confidence to know that the doctor might be cost-benefiting him as an asset to be used.

Schuster has estimated the proportion of medical services in the United States that should, professionally speaking, not have been delivered at all. He found that the figure might be as high as 30 per cent for acute care, 20 per cent for chronic (Schuster, McGlynn and Brook, 1998: 521). Cutler, concentrating on surgery, came up with further evidence that some Americans were getting too much: 'About one in ten people undergoing a major operation does not meet the clinical criteria for that operation' (Cutler, 2004: xi). As there is no robust statistic on overuse or underuse, the precise values cannot be known. Nor can it be known if doctors are cynically milking the cow for all they can get. All that can be said is that fee for service makes it easier for a gain-seeking businessman to take the money and run.

The second is *salary*. Where the doctor is employed by an institution such as a hospital, he is not an independent contractor but a cog on a scale. His remuneration is not a function either of the patients he sees or of the outcomes he delivers. He has the certainty of knowing what he will be paid. The institution has the convenience of budgeting for the cost. Different institutions can pay different salaries. Flexible payment in that way attracts scarce professionals into under-doctored areas while not departing from the core principle of a fixed monthly wage.

Salary scales normally make provision for annual reviews, promotion exercises and bonus payments. Hurdles like these build in a performance-related component that complements the non-discretionary guarantee. On-the-job updating is made that much more attractive by virtue of the fact that the doctor loses no fees while he is attending refresher courses. Administrators can fine-tune their criteria in order to balance their budget or, more optimistically, to raise the standard of health. Doctors on salary can, for example, be given incentive payments for additional screening or health education. In ways such as these, targeted achievement can increase the baseline amount.

The disadvantages are clear enough. Where pay is not proportioned to work, there is no economic incentive to supply discretionary service, to answer e-mail inquiries, to monitor patients' medication or to volunteer for after-hours work. Even the appropriate service might not be provided in full. Nor is there any financial stake in satisfying the patient. So long as poor bedside manner does not lead to a formal complaint or a legal action, the doctor can afford to be abrupt, rude or slipshod without any threat to his remuneration. Salary does little to encourage the below-average performer. The time-server can do the minimum. So long as he is just adequate, he will not put his income on the line.

Incentive payments themselves have their disadvantages. Age-related scales make seniority a proxy for productivity: merit increments upset traditional hierarchies. Hospital criteria might rank publicity above care: where appraisals focus on reduced waiting times and rapid circulation through beds, the doctor might have to turn down a chronic patient or spend less time with a frightened child who wants to talk. Minimax might boost the cost to the institution: a doctor being monitored for the recoveries he has managed might prescribe marginal procedures and expensive tomography out of fear that one bad mistake will scupper his promotion. He can afford to do this so long as there is no personalised print-out of his prescriptions and treatments. Itemised billing and continuous reporting would at least pick up who in the institution was standing out from the norm. Complemented by comprehensive patient feedback, it might help to reduce the unnecessary expense that can be incurred where the doctor himself falls victim to anxiety and concern.

The third and last mode of payment is the *capitation fee*. In this case the doctor, an independent contractor, receives an annual fee from the patient or the patient's insurer. In exchange for this single payment the generalist undertakes to meet the patient's specified needs for the period in question. These needs can be primary or they can be global. The practice budget is global. It requires a fundholding general practitioner to use his allocated resources to purchase all outpatient and hospital services for all the clients on his list.

The doctor on capitation has no financial incentive to supply additional services. In contrast to fee per service, he has good time-and-effort grounds to deliver as little as he can. As for his total remuneration, his economic incentive will be such that he will want to maximise his registrations. Each new name brings in a further payment. That in turn means that he will want to select young, healthy patients. They will seek fewer consultations and (important for a fund-holder) will require fewer referrals. The doctor on capitation would be much less keen to register the anorexic, the autistic, the leukaemia hard cases and the myelitis incurables. They are more likely to impose an above-average burden on his diary and budget.

The insuring agency can use economics to correct this bias. It can do this by offering higher (needs-based) capitations where the patient is chronic, terminal, old, or in a high-risk industry. Where the insurer is the State, it might also address geographical inequalities through the promise of higher payments in neglected rural areas or run-down urban slums. Transparency is always a help. A doctor who is known to undersupply quality services must expect in the long-run to lose patients to his competitors.

As with salary, capitation systems can offer top-up payments for named extra services. The doctors might be given piece-rate remuneration for minor surgery, child health, precautionary screening, contraceptive advice, night visits. They might be paid lump-sums for going on courses. Negatively speaking, the rules might specify that no list can exceed a ceiling number of patients. Such a restriction would protect the public against whirlwind examinations and the practitioners themselves against voluntary overwork.

Where the patient is expected to remain for an extended period on the list, the doctor will have a non-medical reason to practise preventive medicine. Stress management and hepatitis injections mean extra work and marginal cost in the here-and-now. Such services, on the other hand, are an investment which will pay off through fewer presentations and interventions over the life span of the relationship. Discounting is, of course, rational. The patient might not re-register with the same doctor. Illness prevented or health status assured might become a cost or a benefit to a rival firm.

The three modes of payment, conceptually speaking, are separate. Reality is more complex. In some cases a doctor can be paid partly by one method and partly by another. Productivity payments can be made for prompt access and electronic record-keeping. Special bonuses can be offered for longer consultations where the depressed or the bereaved are in need of 'talking therapy'. Cuts in the income of the lazy and the insensitive are the counterpart technique. Such cuts will run up against the strong opposition of the medical professionals. Even if patient feedback is below the benchmark and psychotropics with side-effects are too frequently prescribed, only a very determined funding agency will be able to free up income for the successful and the assiduous by imposing financial penalties on the long-term benchwarmers who are not trying very hard.

People respond to incentives. Croxson, Propper and Perkins have shown that even in welfarist Britain some doctors at least have been scheming and

Machiavellian: 'Fundholders raise those admissions over which they have most control and which determine their budgets in the year before they become fundholders and lower them immediately afterwards.... The changes in admissions resulting from fundholding might have benefited family doctors who were fundholders, or their patients or both, but probably did so at the expense of other patients' (Croxson, Propper and Perkins, 2001: 377, 392–3). Financial incentives alter treatment practices even in the National Health Service.

Medicine in Denmark is no less sensitive to *turpe lucrum*. General practitioners in Denmark receive two-thirds of their income from fee for service and one-third from capitation. Doctors, because of the mixed system, are able to earn fees from additional services such as prescriptions, tests and night visits. Services that attract additional fees have expanded. At the same time there are fewer referrals to specialists and hospitals. Doctors have exercised their discretion (fee for service) but there is also continuity of care and multiperiod commitment (capitation). One advantage is the even spread: 'The part-per-capitation funding makes such geographical dispersion of GPs more possible.... This would certainly be more difficult with a "fuller" fee-for-service (FFS) system which would more likely lead to concentration of GPs in the major population centres' (Mooney, 2002: 166–7). Mixed payment alters the package. Since different doctors have different maximands, one conclusion might be that the biases will cancel each other out. It is not the only conclusion.

3.2.2. Supplier-Induced Demand

Bias can be of omission or commission. Doctors can supply too little. Doctors can supply too much. Medical excellence means that no condition should be left untreated because the doctor failed to conduct an examination. Profit and loss means that the nation should not be surcharged for interventions that are not needed and that it cannot afford. Supplier-induced demand is a layer of fat. It is a level of care greater than that which the patients would have demanded had they been perfectly informed.

Supplier-induced demand is, in Pauly's definition, a bundle of pathologies and aberrations. It is a dog's breakfast of 'alterations in the quantity or quality of services consumers demand as physicians change the accuracy of the information they provide in response to economic incentives' (Pauly, 1994a: 370). It is therefore not to be confused with supplier-*shaped* demand. Disinterested advice, without exaggeration, without overstatement, is precisely the commodity that the layman demands when he employs an expert in order to lead him to the right choice. The consumer's preferences are not intrinsic. They are learned from a teacher in whom the pupil places his trust. Trust and trustworthiness are *sine qua non* in an area where know-what is as unequal as know-how and where, as in surgery, unanticipated complications necessitate extra-contractual discretion. Health care is not an ordinary consumable. Decisions are often delegated to the seller. Information asymmetry gives the seller the freedom to test the limits of the fiduciary bond.

The starting point is Milton Roemer. He found a positive correlation between (short-term, general) hospital beds and hospital days/stays per 1000 of population. More beds meant more admissions. A built bed was a filled bed: 'The level at which need is recognized is heavily influenced by the supply of beds available for its satisfaction.... The number and type of hospital beds materially influenced the practice of medicine' (Roemer, 1961: 37, 41). Roemer's Law is the Parkinson's Law, the Say's Law of inpatient attention. Fuchs, studying surgery, found that it too seemed to be a case where supply creates its own demand. Surgery faces an inelastic demand curve. As prices go up, however, so do utilisation and total expenditure. The demand curve must have been subject to a rightward displacement that in commerce could have been brought about by unprincipled huckstering. The displacers were the suppliers because otherwise their incomes would fall.

Fuchs compared different areas within the United States. Interpreting his cross-section, he found that the demand for surgery seemed to slope upwards to the right: 'Where surgeons are more numerous, the demand for operations increases. Other things being equal, a 10 per cent higher surgeon/population ratio results in about a 3 per cent increase in the number of operations and an *increase* in price. Thus, the average surgeon's work load decreases by 7 per cent, but income per surgeon decreases by much less' (Fuchs, 1986 [1978]: 147). What Fuchs found was that an increase in quantity was associated with an increase and not a decrease in the price that was charged. He believed that the discretion and the power of surgeons over patients was the reason for the association. He also believed that the impact was if anything greater than he had estimated: 'The ability of surgeons to shift the demand for outpatient services is probably greater than for operations. Thus the total impact of supply on demand may be larger' (Fuchs, 1986 [1978]: 147).

Fuchs suggests that under-employed specialists might at the margin have manipulated the public into paying more for more. The implication is that unutilised hospital beds were available in the local area (or, for rural demand, the nearest urban hub) and that doctors were willing to compromise at the margin on the integrity of the agency relationship. Demand is not independent of supply. That is Fuchs's explanation of the fact that per capita surgery rates in the United States have been rising more rapidly than can convincingly be explained in terms of additional variables like the rising percentage of elderly persons in the community.

Cromwell and Mitchell reported that Fuchs had been correct about the direction but had overestimated the response: 'A 10 percent increase in surgeons per capita (around the mean of 0.3) results in a 0.9 percent increase in overall surgery per capita and 1.3 percent increase in elective surgery.... More discretionary surgical procedures are performed in areas of high surgeon concentration' (Cromwell and Mitchell, 1986: 304). Cromwell and Mitchell suggested from their study that the elasticities were only one-third of those estimated by Fuchs. They were in no doubt, however, as to the 'strong, positive influence': 'A 10 percent increase in surgeon density results in a fee inducement of 9 percent per operation.... This would imply only a marginal decline in net incomes from surgery with increased competition' (Cromwell and Mitchell, 1986: 305).

Significant expansion in the manpower pool will evidently do little to keep the price of surgery down. Nguyen and Derrick, agreeing, found that a reduction in Medicare fees had been the very reason why doctors had decided to inflate the supply of services per case: 'For every dollar cut in their fees, physicians recoup approximately 40 cents by increasing volume' (Nguyen and Derrick, 1997: 283). Yip discovered that they had recouped even more. A cut in Medicare reimbursement rates, Yip said, had led doctors to restore and overtake their former income levels through a rise in the volume of coronary artery bypass grafting that they performed (Yip, 1998: 695). Gruber and Owings established that the 13.5 per cent fall in fertility between 1970 and 1982 had encouraged American obstetricians and gynaecologists to substitute better-reimbursed Caesarean section for lower-paid normal childbirth: 'A 10% decline in the fertility rate is associated with a .97 percentage point increase in the cesarean delivery rate.... Financial incentives did play an important role .... Physicians overused cesarean delivery relative to the level that would be chosen by a financially disinterested medical provider' (Gruber and Owings, 1996: 100, 120). Price controls could be snookered by an expansion in volume. The demand curve could not be assumed to be stable or fixed.

Free telephone consultations could be abandoned in favour of paid office visits. Repeat prescriptions could be made contingent on a repeat examination. More blood tests and treadmill assessments could be required. Shorter but more frequent appointments could become the norm. The opportunity is there to create new demand: 'In Quebec, a doubling of fees for home visits was followed by rapid increases in the number of home visits ... despite a general decline in home visits by community-based doctors generally' (Culyer, 1989: 30). Doctors who own pharmacies prescribe more drugs than do doctors without a shop. Doctors with diagnostic equipment test more frequently than doctors who must refer.

Yip, like Culyer, found that the doctors had taken advantage. Grytten and Sørensen, on the other hand, found that they had not. Doctors in Norway, they said, had not fallen back on demand inducement to compensate for a fall in incomes. The increased availability of doctors had gone up. The number of patients per doctor had gone down. The intensity of service per patient had not changed noticeably in response: 'In municipalities with a high physician density, there is high competition for patients. Contract physicians in these municipalities did not increase provision of services in order to maintain their income…. Even though contract physicians have the possibility to induce demand for their services, they do not behave in that way' (Grytten and Sørensen, 2001: 387). Financial incentives are important. They are not, however, the only incentives.

If want creation does exist, it is necessary to explain why it occurs when it does. Presumably the doctors in the studies did not induce demand before their numbers increased because they were then producing at full capacity. It is surprising that they did not discover the maximisation of income until new entry and competition in their local area had undermined their status quo workload and with it their target income. No less odd is the fact that they seem not to have cut their fees in response to the rise in their numbers. A price cut would have been the logical first step where the demand curve was unchanged and slack was introduced into the system. Oddest of all is the implication that doctors can induce whatever they want until, in the limit, the patient's entire income is going to his surgeon. Doctors can try. Whether they succeed depends, however, on the plasticity of demand, the time-cost of seeking more advice and the willingness of the consumer to let himself be led. Consumers are incompletely informed. To say, however, that they have no informed demand at all is pushing a plausible hypothesis too far.

The problem is that the facts do not speak for themselves. Perfectly informed patients do not exist: the benchmark decision patterns are therefore as unobservable as a perfect vacuum. People who need more care should get more care: it is no defence of fewer interventions to say that stoic acceptance and premature death keep the demand curve in its place. Patients who demand more care will get more care: the doctor alone is not to be blamed if patients insist that something should be done. Under-served areas will have a backlog to make good: more doctors mean more doctoring because, there at least, long waits and the high costs of travel will have caused excess demand to be stored up and neglected. Also, if Bunker and Brown's results are typical, doctors and their families are actually more exposed than the rest of us. In California, they write, 'the appendectomy rate for physicians remains nearly twice as great as the national rate from age 25 to 40' (Bunker and Brown, 1974: 1053). Whatever this statistic might mean, it is unlikely to suggest that knowledgeable professionals are prescribing superfluous treatment to their subjects merely because asymmetric information gives them the power to persuade.

It is a source of reassurance to know that, while most consumers are underinformed, there are a small number of experts in the market who know which therapies are likely to be effective and which of their fellows is *prima facie* over-filling his private trough. A small number of marginal consumers with extraordinary knowledge might be enough to police prices, sample quantities and keep standards up. They are a critical mass on which the uninformed and the in-the-dark are able to travel free. Even car-mechanics buy cars. Even estate-agents buy houses. The sellers of cars and houses know this. They are reluctant to supply 'lemons' to any segment of their market because they are aware that an unidentifiable in-group is able to detect the abuse. If anything, doctors feel frustrated because their clients' wants fall short even of the recommended responses that their medical needs would suggest. Doctors, Kenkel writes, seem to be convinced that their clients 'systematically underestimate the marginal product of medical care': 'All individuals use less medical care than experts believe is appropriate.... Apparently, physicians cannot even convince people to buy enough care, much less induce them to buy more than enough' (Kenkel, 1990: 594).

It is a difficult task to identify the autonomous, exogenous pressure of the specialist. It is more difficult still to ascertain if the influence was a violation of the ideal principal/agent nexus. Interests might converge and not diverge even where the doctor commits the patient to a discretionary purchase. It is hard to believe that the patient derives no utility at all from elective procedures such as hernia repair, varicose sclerotherapy, tonsillectomy or haemorrhoidectomy merely because the initiative for cold surgery came from the physician. If, however, the patient's welfare, self-perceived, goes up, then it would be wrong to speak of supplier-induced demand. The suppliers may have unearthed the never-articulated demand but the hardcore preference – normal demand, latent demand, authentic demand – was there all along. A positive medical outcome is not required: success is not the same as aspiration. Every *ex ante* choice is vulnerable *ex post* to regret. All that matters is that the consumer be satisfied that *ex ante* the doctor did what the consumer if calculative and informed would himself have wanted to do.

Personal gain is a good thing and not an aberration where the butcher, the brewer, the baker and the doctor in the end raise us to a higher level of personal well-being. Consumer sovereignty has not given way to control where the counsellor only recommends what the sick would themselves have preferred. Not all tests, services and follow-ups that make people feel well can be described as the sour fruit of embellishment and mendacity. Where the need-satisfaction is known to have gone up at the same time as the fees, it is inappropriate to say that the medical professionals have crassly exploited the information gap or ridden roughshod over the best interests of their cash cow. Where the need-satisfaction is seen to be negligible, however, then it is possible that scarce resources are being wasted on interventions billed because the supplier needs the money for a car.

It is never easy to falsify a hypothesis where the data that are required are all in the mind. Questionnaires and structured interviews are unlikely to elicit an admission of unadulterated guilt: many doctors probably rationalise their management of demand as going the extra mile to meet a genuine need. Nor will deviation from the statistical median be proof positive by itself that an abuse has occurred: the word 'necessary' in medicine is a range and not a point. Ideally, the debate between demand-led supply and supply-led demand should be settled by empirical evidence. As hard facts are hard to find, it is often settled instead by an appeal to *a prioris* and ideologies. The inferences can surprise. Logic augmented by experience does not necessarily suggest that the doctors are having things all their own way.

Supplier-induced demand, for one thing, may operate disproportionately at the margins. It need not inevitably be an either/or: 'Increased intensity can take the form of more ancillary services per bypass procedure.... Intensity can also take the form of a more intensive bypass procedure (i.e., bypassing more vessels)' (Yip, 1998: 692). Yip cautions that medical need is not a routine matter of transporting a familiar jug in order to fill up a standard-size mug: 'There are circumstances of clinical uncertainty in which individual judgment is necessary. It is under those circumstances that financial incentives would play a role in clinical decision making' (Yip, 1998: 692). A cardiologist might be led by financial interest to err on the side of a few grafts more. What is less likely is that he will bypass entirely healthy vessels merely because his integrity has fallen victim to his income.

Much depends on how the suppliers are paid. Doctors indemnified by a fee for service will have a financial incentive to go gung-ho on their interventions. Doctors contracted for salary or capitation will, in contrast, find it in their economic self-interest to supply only what the patient explicitly requests. Need in both cases gives way to pecuniary interest. Yet it is not the same bias and not the same distortion. Overutilisation is the counterweight to underutilisation. Supplier-induced extravagance is cheek-by-jowl with supplier-reduced frugality. A Health Maintenance Organisation (HMO) that gives a bonus to skilled procrastinators who postpone and patch will be different from a corrupt fee-splitter who gets a percentage kickback on specialist referrals. Cost-sharing, unlike free-on-demand, will make the patient more cautious about unnecessary interventions that will hurt, cost money and perhaps even fail. Reforming the mode of payment might at least reverse the sign on the imperfection. So might publicity. Independent agencies, computer websites, newspapers and magazines diffuse information on the alternatives. They make league-tables and plan-ratings a public good.

It should not, moreover, be assumed that all doctors are avaricious merchants, always on the look-out for a lucrative trade. Economic models assume that producers are profit-maximisers whose first duty is to their bank balance. While some doctors undoubtedly correspond to the neoclassical norm, others will have been attracted into medicine because of a felt desire to help the sick. Their first duty is to their patient. Such people will suffer from a guilty conscience and spoiled self-image if they violate the normative code into which they were socialised. Like judges and teachers, doctors enjoy standing in the community because they are believed to be impartial, trustworthy and professional. The Hippocratic Oath corrects a market failure that the commercial goal-function leaves untreated. Adam Smith said that every sensitive person, striving for 'not only praise, but praise-worthiness', will make every effort to be 'that thing which, though it should be praised by nobody, is, however, the natural and proper object of praise' (Smith, 1966 [1759]: 166). The sensitive doctor is no exception to the rule that psychic income is a part of the payment package.

The patient's utility is the doctor's utility since the doctor has a heart. Maximisation and demand-creation make the supplier feel bad about himself. Feeling bad is the moral cost of inducing demand. Unless the extra remuneration is so great as to be obscene, a caring human being will not want to pay the price. To say that the doctor is able to manipulate demand for financial gain is not the same as to say that he will be willing to do so. In the case of an insured patient, the doctor might arguably take the more commercial view that that inducement is effectively a private tax upon a giant corporation that can well afford to pay. His first duty may or may not be to the company that puts food on his table. Where, however, the patient is poor, sick and paying out-of-pocket, the moral position will be seen as different. The doctor might price-discriminate or even supply *pro bono* because he genuinely wants to help.

Besides that, the doctor is a member of a professional community and subject as such to its sanctions. Peer pressures may be as informal as ostracism and rudeness. They may be as institutional as exclusion from a professional body with a monopoly charter. A doctor whose ethics are suspect may be denied malpractice insurance by his cooperative. He may be blocked out of hospital admitting privileges because managers (who do not receive the windfall profits from oversupply) do not want the hospital's reputation to be tarnished. Certification, litigation, re-licensing, second opinions, regulatory controls that cap the numbers of doctors and hospitals, all give the ignorant some protection from the venal. Less-than-free entry is a supply-side imperfection. It has the function of countervailing a demand-side darkness.

Professional codes can be rigid and unimaginative. They can discourage much-needed innovation. They can protect monopoly power by restricting advertising and competitive undercutting. In terms of supplier-induced demand, however, they can also put the lid on cost. Familiar drills and habituated self-regulation can arguably keep opportunistic overtreatment within bounds.

When the velvet glove fails, there is always the law. The police might become involved where a practitioner with his own retail outlet repeatedly prescribes medicines that are discredited, useless, addictive or dangerous. The malpractice suit might itself stop the less-than-professional supplier in his tracks. The patient will not find it easy to obtain financial compensation for over-imaginative discretion. He is more likely to be paid damages if he can show that the knife slipped because the surgeon was drunk. Even so, the mere spectre of legal action might keep down the flagrantly unnecessary element in supplier-induced demand. The professional has no wish to deplete his scarce reputational capital.

Repeat business and word of mouth have the same trimming effect on superfluity. Often the medical relationship will be continuing: doctors learn over time what the client expects while the client keeps a running balance of the services he is given. A one-off walk-in is not an ongoing sequence. Knowing that people consume an appendectomy only once, the doctor cannot invest in a return visit from a satisfied customer. Even then, however, personal recommendations give him a shopkeeper's stake in standards. Where the service is known to be differentiated, the ailing approach their friends and acquaintances for a name they can trust. A brand signalling veracity and competence is a sound business asset in a market where there are many merchants, where personal services are slightly differentiated, where search is costly and where 'self-interest seeking with guile' (Williamson, 1975: 9) is known to be a real possibility: 'Reputations based on the quality of services provided in the past can serve as signals of the quality of services that will be produced in the future. Thus consumers may be able to learn about sellers' reputations without directly observing their price or quality' (Haas-Wilson, 1990: 322). Haas-Wilson believed she had found that perceived goodwill was the antidote to information asymmetry. Her evidence related to the price-premium in the market for private-practice psychotherapists in Massachusetts.

Networks, as Granovetter has said, embed choices in a matrix of interdependent contacts (Granovetter, 1985). They protect the consumers from a profit-seeking supplier who does not deserve their trust. They are also a cause of price dispersion. Competition is less intense since the consumer will lose the support of the network if, making demand elastic, he responds to a price incentive and moves on to something new.

Further protection is provided by medical referrals. Even if the pool of clients is self-renewing and evanescent, the family doctor goes on and on. That is why it makes sense for the patient to begin the sequence with primary care. It is cost-effective to leave it to the generalist to recommend a specialist who will not abuse the client's ignorance. The use of an adviser who is not the supplier protects the supplier from conflict of interest and weakness of will. The power of the surgeon to sell low-quality services at high-quality prices is less where it is the task of the referring doctor to make the initial diagnosis and check up on the recovery. A patient who goes directly to a surgeon is more likely to stumble upon a fly-by-night wit-matcher who knows that no one is watching. Clearly, the specialist will lose the trust of his primary contact if he shows that the confidence was not well placed.

Supplier-induced demand is not a free good. This too limits the power of the doctors and the hospitals. Marketing costs must be incurred as monopolistic

competitors strive to promote a non-standard product. Time must be invested
in persuading the consumers to demand a service in which they had expressed
no interest. Besides that, salesmanship can be counterproductive. Business may
be lost where regular customers, alarmed by the hype, lose confidence in a doctor they had come to trust. No doctor can assume that he is a pure monopolist
or that consumers will forever give him a blank cheque. Capitalism supplies its
own correctives. One of these is the cost-benefit relationship between seller's
expense and the targeted response.

Finally, there is insurance. The paying agency has a financial interest of its
own in keeping down provision and charges. These eat into its profits. Insurers
audit bills, query supernormal claims, standardise practice, conduct preoperative
examinations. They compare the prices charged by different suppliers and shop
around for their client. They know that the doctor is exposed to moral hazard
when he reasons that an insured patient is a patient who can be charged more
for more. They also know that it is the function of the third-party not to reimburse for superfluity or waste. Prospective payment is one expedient that they
adopt. Where the fee is agreed in advance, the surgeon or hospital can supply
the overhang if it wishes but it cannot bill for an additional charge. In some
cases the insurers even impose a volume control of their own. If the doctor can
have an impact on the perception of need, then so can the insurers who exert
countervailing power and keep supplier inducement in check.

3.3.   THE PUBLIC

Individualism maintains that the patient knows best what is right for his mind
and body. Professionalism insists that the doctor must have clinical freedom
since the clinician alone can recognise the need. Then there is We. Society,
Durkheim said, is an entity *sui generis*. Its *mores*, laws and conventions eman-
cipate the Spencerian atom from meaningless egotism. Transcending detachment,
they force the integrated being into a state of interdependence with his fellows:
'We may say that what is moral is everything that is a source of solidarity, everything that forces man to take account of other people' (Durkheim, 1984
[1893]: 331). Where there is a social mind, the patient and the doctor are not
free to choose. Where there is a social need, a third-party must sit in judgment
whenever the buyer and the seller meet to contract into a cure. T.H. Marshall
reminded his readers that even in the liberal democracy constraint is all around:
'Your body is part of the national capital, and must be looked after, and sickness
causes a loss of national income, in addition to being liable to spread' (Marshall,
1981 [1965]: 91). Your body belongs to us and not just to you. Your cigarettes
and alcohol are our value-added foregone. You should pay your tax. You should
do your homework. You should eat an apple a day.

You should also consume 'merit goods'. These are an area of social life where wise and thinking paternalists have imposed good criteria. Musgrave says that merit goods have a 'social stamp' and that leaderly guidance must override the individual's whim. In this area, even in a free market economy, 'interference is not accidental': 'The existence of merit goods thus defined may be taken to suggest that our society, which considers itself democratic, retains elements of autocracy, which permit the elite (however defined) to impose their preferences. Or, it may be interpreted as adherence to community interests and values by which individual preferences are overridden. Either explanation contravenes free consumer choice, the otherwise accepted principle of resource use' (Musgrave and Musgrave, 1980: 85). Normal economic goods are an individual choice. Merit goods are supra-economic goods which the isolated individual does not have the right to refuse.

3.3.1. Social Values

Citizens who share their imperatives will be prone to support some departures and to stigmatise others. Their choices are their own but they are also shared. Even preferences revealed in markets are not self-forming but are the cumulative product of a historical sequence. *De gustibus* is thee and me. It is not, Kenneth Boulding says, just another name for a normative Immaculate Conception: 'Even personal tastes are learned, in the matrix of a culture or a subculture in which we grow up, by very much the same kind of process by which we learn our common values' (Boulding, 1969: 1). Even High Street purchases are the self-magnifying absolutes of people who pray with greater conviction when they pray in concert as a church. As Durkheim writes: 'Society ... is not a mere juxtaposition of individuals who, upon entering into it, bring with them an intrinsic morality. Man is only a moral being because he lives in society, since morality consists in solidarity with the group, and varies according to that solidarity. Cause all social life to vanish, and moral life would vanish at the same time, having no object to cling to' (Durkheim, 1984 [1893]: 331).

Values can validate consumer sovereignty, calculative rationality, hedonistic materialism and utility-seeking atomism: 'Purely personal tastes, indeed, can only survive in a culture which tolerates them, that is, which has a common value that private tastes of certain kinds should be allowed' (Boulding, 1969: 1). In such a case the representative citizen would want decision-making in medicine to be as decentralised as possible. Values can also suggest that it is the doctors who must lead: here it will be the expressed wish of all the democrats that training and experience should have the final say. Values can favour political *laissez-faire* and a private market for health. Values can demand the State and one-standard provision paid for through tax. There are many payment and delivery mechanisms. Values single out some. Values declare that others are out of keeping with the kind of people that we are.

Values separate the needs from the wants. They decree that the ecstatic trance of the drug addict is neither a real need nor even a valid want. They in that way go against the revealed preference of the shopper himself that his craving for cocaine is as much a need for him as is his basic need for food. Values also specify when one need must be denied additional support in order that the scarce social margin can be transferred to another and different need. Not everything that contributes to collective well-being can be funded by a society that has more than one need. Beliefs and attitudes spotlight the increments that ought to be satisfied first. Two miners trapped underground have an urgent need. A thousand children requiring an anti-flu vaccine also have an urgent need. Neither need has the lexicographic first place. Neither need is a cast-iron claim simply because it is rooted in the imperative to survive. Both needs are contingent. Both needs depend on social validation. Adopting the perspective of agreement and values can mean that the miners – or the children – would be well-advised to draw up their will. Social values compare the costs and the benefits. Social values thereupon pull the plug.

Individual needs, in short, are necessary but not sufficient. It is not enough to say that 'N needs x in order to y'. An economic choice must also be made as to whether the endstate is really *worth* the time and money that it will cost the All: 'Nothing that cannot be fitted into the relational formula can be regarded as a need' (Braybrooke, 1987: 30). A professor 'needs larger house-room, more quiet, lighter and more digestible food, and perhaps more change of scene and other comforts than will suffice for maintaining the efficiency of unskilled work' (Marshall, 1966 [1907]: 324–5). Maybe he does. But do we as a society really want to vote him the money for a holiday in order that he can continue robustly to profess?

Just as values can identify the structures, so they can spotlight the priorities. Inputs are limited. Choices have to be made. Values can help to minimise the resentment, frustration and felt exclusion by ensuring that consensual rankings are respected and that the outliers are treated last. There will, of course, be a problem if values conflict. There can also be a subcultural clash between the public and the professionals. Even if the public speaks with a single voice, the medical professionals might want to allocate scarce organs or procedures using best-practice criteria from which they would feel ashamed to deviate.

Popular preferences are encoded in the 'social welfare function' (Bergson, 1938). Such a function maximises the felt well-being that the society can derive from its productive possibilities. The welfare function is social and specific through and through. It is the property of a 'reference population', a 'self-governing linguistic subset', a nation, a State (Braybrooke, 1987: 62). Individuals are the agency that converts social values into market prices. Still, however, their choices have a home in time and space: 'The communitarian would argue for individuals being valuers as long as these individuals are allowed to reflect their history and their community…. Values, in other words, are context specific' (Mooney, 1991: 51).

Some societies will put economic growth first. They will find it correct for resources to be skewed towards high-flyers with a good education who are the most likely to contribute to national advance. Other societies will be especially concerned about deprivation and unrelieved distress. They will want to see a generous supply of geriatric beds, HIV hospices and village clinics. Most societies will probably opt for a mix: they will say that no need, however highly-ranked in itself, can automatically be satisfied without regard to the incremental cost. Many people would agree with Alan Williams that the ethical entitlement is not unlimited life but a 'fair innings' of normal quality and length: 'Those who get less than this are entitled to feel unfairly treated, whereas those who get more than this have no cause to complain on equity grounds when they eventually die' (Williams and Cookson, 2000: 1876). Yet many people will also feel that the crippled or the old should not be abandoned without even a doctor's visit. Rising expectations and widening reference groups mean that even the past-it cannot be left without a colour television, tasty food and necessary antibiotics if their blood becomes infected and their tongue goes black. Most societies will want to diversify their maximand. Time and place will, of course, determine the precise specifications of the mix. There is no continent so vast as the middle ground.

Society is likely to express particularly strong views on the beginning and the end of life. Stem-cell research, embryonic cloning, artificial insemination, the preselection of a child's gender, abortion, surrogacy, the morning-after pill, the prescription of contraceptives to underage women, are all areas in which the public interest is engaged and public opinion demands to be given a voice. Economics and not just emotion will often play a role. The failure to abort a severely disabled child is the decision to impose a lifetime burden on the National Health Service. Early replacement of disappointing genes can make the ultimate contribution to the containment of medical cost. A ban on contraception can lead to surplus labour, mass unemployment and rampant AIDS. Politicisation can damage both your wealth and your health where society dictates who should be born and how many.

Again, in respect of death, people express attitudes about organ sales, euthanasia on demand, the 'do not resuscitate' label, the switching off of the life-support machine where the patient has no reasonable hope of an early recovery or a decent quality of life. The bodyholder might feel that he has no wish to go on. His fellow citizens might feel that they do not want him to live but they are not prepared to let him die. Some will find the *vox populi* distastefully priggish and self-righteous when it gets involved in decisions such as these. Mill spoke for all such sceptics when he told his neighbours that his liver belonged to himself alone: 'The only purpose for which power can be rightfully exercised over any member of a civilized community, against his will, is to prevent harm to others. His own good, either physical or moral, is not a sufficient warrant.... Over himself, over his own body and mind, the individual is sovereign' (Mill, 1974 [1859]: 68–9).

Mill's principle can be made into a strong defence of suicide on the National Health Service. Each adult is the best judge of his own well-being. The reply will, however, be that the majority knows best; and that minorities in a democracy cannot expect to call every tune. Government by groundswell can lead to a massive breach of medical confidentiality where the doctor has by law to notify diseases that the Hippocratic Oath dictates ought to be kept a secret and where a freedom fighter shot in an ambush is immediately reported to the police. That is inevitable when the public makes the choice that the privacy of the confessional cannot be made a sanctuary from the rest of the club. No one seriously believes that consensus is always the same as unanimity. In agreeing to play the democratic game, what the citizens are indicating is that they want to live by the operational rules that were the product of their decision-making accord. People have attitudes. Values become laws. What we call needs take the place of what Jim Jones calls wants. Emigration is all that remains for a discontented outsider who only wants to die.

3.3.2.   Externalities

Pigou was an economist who saw that there could be a discrepancy between marginal private cost (or benefit) and marginal social cost (or benefit). His argument was that social efficiency is not attained when the traveller buys a ticket from the conductor so long as the unpriced transfer of sparks from the train continues to set a neighbouring farmer's crop ablaze (Pigou, 1932 [1920]). His discussion is expressed in the language of wheat destroyed. The internalisation of the externalities could just as easily have been put into the framework of Hobbesian aggression and the unauthorised entry of a bully who never contributes and never consults. Consumer sovereignty, market competition and producer's profit do not exhaust the costs and benefits. The bystanders who neither buy nor sell have the moral right to complain about the noise.

Third-party spillovers are a topic in values. It is values alone that determine if the side-effects are costs or benefits, good or bad. External costs might be noxious effluent dumped into the creek or value-creating, tax-creating days lost through illness. External benefits might be medical research into cystic fibrosis or the widespread satisfaction that results when income support is paid to the disabled. Costs or benefits, values make us aware that there is more to a contract than supply, demand and the equilibrium price. Embedding the dyad, there is the social interest as well. The socially optimal level cannot safely be entrusted to *laissez-faire*.

Consider first the material diswelfare. A contagious disease affects non-contracting individuals who have not given their consent. Epidemics and communicable germs, in the sense of Mill, are a violation of their personal integrity. The consequence is that innocent bystanders ask their government to put right the market failure. The government's response is to act directly on the quantity or to get at the quantity by means of the price. Education is used to warn against stagnant water in plant-pots where mosquitoes breed. Examination means that a chest X-ray is made compulsory for all new immigrants. Prevention takes the form of fume cupboards for unscrubbed chemicals and the comprehensive destruction of infected fowl. Regulation is instanced by the tolerant apartheid of the tobacco-free zone that protects the health-conscious against passive smoking. Infrastructure ensures that the squatter colonies give way to council estates and the malarial swamps are thoroughly drained. Privileges such as priority in the choice of public housing are granted to sterilised parents who have exploded a Malthusian bad. Taxes internalise the spillovers from drink and discourage the use of leaded fuel. Subsidies support isolation wards so that diphtheria or cholera will not spread. Interdictions limit gun culture and stamp out speeding on the roads. Stratagems such as these can be employed by the up-and-doing State to safeguard the neighbourhood interest. They reduce the economic slippage that would otherwise be the result when one person's fist collides uninvited with another person's nose.

Consider now the sentimental disutility. It not just disease but unhappiness that keeps the Good Samaritan awake when he tallies up his balance sheet for the day. As Culyer writes: 'One individual is not affected merely by the possibility of another passing some disease on to him ... but also, and much more importantly, by the state of health of the other in itself. Individuals are affected by others' health status for the simple reason that *most of them care*' (Culyer, 1976: 8, 9). Culyer argues that socialised individuals tend to take a genuine interest in their fellow citizens' medical well-being: 'If this were not the case, who other than the very poor would ever advocate subsidising the health care of the very poor? The remarkable fact is that almost the only people who do not actively advocate such subsidies are the poor themselves' (Culyer, 1982: 40).

Privatisation, Culyer concluded, was likely to breed economic inefficiency in the sense of Pigou for the very reason that the private market makes no allowance for the caring externality: 'It immediately follows that the market will *undersupply* health (and/or health care) by failing to allow for the additional value placed upon it by people other than the direct consumer' (Culyer, 1982: 40; original emphasis). The National Health Service makes the requisite adjustment. It incorporates a collective valuation that is both morally and materially superior to effective demand. It is also as functional to the survival of the group as the watching deer who sounds the alarm but attracts the predator to himself. Evolution is on the side of fairness. Without altruism there would be no one left to study their Hobbes. In the words of Alfred Marshall: 'The struggle for existence causes in the long run those races of men to survive in which the individual is most willing to sacrifice himself for the benefit of those around him' (Marshall, 1949 [1890]: 202).

The citizen experiences personal distress at the thought that fellow human beings, in his own country or abroad, are suffering from preventable blindness or treatable cancers. Their unhappiness has become an argument in his own happiness function. He reaps gains from trade as a result of helping them to realise their essence. Interest labours alongside compassion, making it difficult to separate the egoism from the altruism. Either way, redistribution through the stranger gift is the consequence. The social individual decides that he wants to pay money to a charity or a public agency in order to eliminate the disturbing pollutant of scabies which reduces the quality of his personal and psychic environment. Utilities are interdependent. The humanitarian spillover is the response to need.

Nowadays we are all social-ists. We respect each other as being in possession of equal rights. Nowadays we are often pro-statists as well. We know that much of the nation's health stock is a pure 'public good' (Samuelson, 1954). Non-excludable, non-rivalrous in consumption, desired even by rational free riders who see no reason to contribute to the cost, there may be general agreement that if we as a community do not empower our leadership to do what we want, the health stock on which we have set our hearts will be under-provided and deficient. Where the good is a public good, the private bargain will fail to satisfy the far-reaching need. Optimisation is tough where the spillovers stubbornly lie where they fall.

3.3.3.   Path Dependence

We start from here. Our institutions are in place. A country being created *ab initio* can mould and shape at will. A green field already encumbered does not have the same freedom to design. In that sense the values that produce the institutions are trend-dominated and history-driven. Once upon a time it was values that led the nation to choose the market or opt for the State. That was then. The institutions once in place, momentum takes over. The past convinces the present that today wants what yesterday has left behind for it to use. People see what they expect to see. Without the heuristic of tradition they would certainly go mad.

Thus a society which believed in independence, self-reliance, choice and achievement will once have put in place a market-orientated health care system which relies on private insurance and private doctoring. Such a society will have decided to do without a free-on-demand National Health Service that refuses to means-test or exclude. The decision once made, the institutions become self-perpetuating. People learn by living. Adult socialisation and not just spot rationality conditions public opinion to say, with Milton Friedman, that I am my own man and that you may not tread on me: 'The characteristic feature of action through political channels is that it tends to require or enforce substantial conformity. The great advantage of the market, on the other hand, is that it permits wide diversity' (Friedman, 1962: 15). People who are accustomed to a social order in which every citizen can buy the product of his choice will have a bias in favour of the variety and diversity to which they are accustomed. The snowball effect leads them to demand more of the same.

Different will be people who have grown up in a society which treats individuals not as free-floating isolates, self-sufficient and self-creating, but as team-players, as parts of a whole. Titmuss believed that the British National Blood Transfusion System was not just about blood but about good citizenship as well: 'If the bonds of community giving are broken the result is not a state of value neutralism. The vacuum is likely to be filled by hostility and social conflict' (Titmuss, 1970: 199). Initially there was nature, man's 'biological need to help' (Titmuss, 1970: 198). Then there was interdependence, 'society's will to survive as an organic whole' (Titmuss, 1963: 39). Finally there was nurture, the tendency of the British National Health Service to do away with any 'allocation of resources which could create a sense of separateness between people' (Titmuss, 1970: 238). The end result was a collectivist delivery system which bred and fostered the social values of fellowship, compassion, community, empathy and generosity upon which a collectivist delivery system must depend. Citizens become accustomed to classlessness and the common state. They grow to like the overlap and the solidarity which shared wards and non-discriminatory services represent to them. They learn to love the new social climate which Bevan describes in the following terms: 'Society becomes more wholesome, more serene, and spiritually healthier, if it knows that its citizens have at the back of their consciousness the knowledge that not only themselves, but all their fellows, have access, when ill, to the best that medical skill can provide' (Bevan, 1961 [1952]: 100).

People know no thing but the done thing. Their need for clothing is a need to perpetuate a social ritual: 'Custom ... has rendered leather shoes a necessary of life in England. The poorest creditable person of either sex would be ashamed to appear in public without them' (Smith, 1961 [1776]: II, 399–400). Their need for food is a need to do what their culture instructs: 'A Masai drinks the blood of cattle; an Eskimo eats blubber; a Buddhist monk needs a bowl of rice with some vegetables' (Braybrooke, 1987: 12). Their need for institutions is no less convention-driven. People have grown up under free enterprise or under collectivism. Personal dissatisfaction and intellectual appraisal can make them

question the status quo. Even so, they are what they are: 'Human beings naturally live by conventions; so they must be said to have a natural need for some
minimum familiarity with the conventions of the society in which they find
themselves' (Braybrooke, 1987: 92). Stamped identity reinforced by remembered iteration has them in its grip.

3.3.4. Public Choice

Politics, Braybrooke says, is the art of combining structure with decoration:
'We are certainly not licensed to disregard one another's preferences; but needs
make a claim on us more compelling than mere preferences do.... The most
fundamental issues of politics arise as aspects of the general social task of rec-
onciling attention to needs with attention to preferences' (Braybrooke, 1987: 7,
8). Society wants to satisfy its wants. Society also needs to satisfy its needs.
Politics is the art of identifying the basics and ensuring the mix.

(a) Consensus

Titmuss uses the language of agreement and consensus. All collectively provided
services, he writes, are manifestations 'of the expressed wish of all the people
to assist the survival of some people' (Titmuss, 1963: 39). *All the people* describes an unshakeable coalition. If *all* agree, then *no one* does not.

The consensus model is the vision of Rousseau on the general will and of
Bergson on social welfare. It is the logic of Wicksell on the primacy of unanimity precisely because the disutility of the tails may far exceed the satisfaction
of the median. It is even the reasoning behind Pigou on the frictionless equation
of the marginal social costs and benefits. *Gesellschaft* is about agreement even
if *Gemeinschaft* is about the decentralised swap. The consensus model assumes
that we all want the same. The problem is how to measure the common mind.

Elections sample opinions on salient issues. Politicians probe their constituents at grassroots meetings. Questionnaires provide feedback and so do users'
councils. Complaints mechanisms are an ever-present deterrent to deviance. The
media publicise practices on which the reporters feel the public has a view. Attitudes and predilections emerge, but there is no guarantee that they are the
consensus. The future does not have a vote: does this mean that personal medical
care will be oversupplied relative to prevention that would save a greater number
of lives? The creaking hinge gets the oil: who speaks for the silent and the self-
effacing? Majorities are not totalities: Titmuss's 'all' means what it says. A
fragment is not a manifesto: no survey can collect data on more than a subset
of the policy issues. Consensus makes each of us feel good about our national
family. Pluralism makes us wonder how it all adds up.

Pluralism assigns considerable power to politicians. It is they who must reconcile the different opinions and modulate the conflicting pressures. Ideally they

will promise a mixed portfolio in which there will be something for everyone. They have to attempt to please the electorate. Their legitimacy is tested by the vote mechanism. Winning an election does not mean Titmuss's 'all'. It does, however, mean the democratic compromise of 'most'. Politicians follow the people. If they do not follow the people, they will not be politicians for long. As Tullock writes: 'The market operates by providing a structure in which individuals who simply want to make money end up by producing motor cars that people want. Similarly, democracy operates so that politicians who simply want to hold public office end up by doing things the people want.... There is no reason why we should be disturbed by this phenomenon' (Tullock, 1976: 25).

(b) Leadership
Tullock's phrase 'the things the people want' is a reminder that some political thinkers put the citizen's revealed preferences first. Their politics is their economics and their economics is consumer choice. Other thinkers, more paternalistic, assign primary importance to basic needs. They feel that the government is in office *in loco parentis*. They see it as the task of leadership to ensure that individual and collective imperatives are satisfactorily met.

At the base there are the physical needs: 'Human beings need vitamins, and did so before they had any notion of vitamins' (Braybrooke, 1987: 91). Built upon the animal needs there are the cultural ones: 'By necessaries I understand, not only the commodities which are indispensably necessary for the support of life, but whatever the custom of the country renders it indecent for creditable people, even of the lowest order, to be without' (Smith, 1961 [1776]: II, 399). It is never easy to know precisely what is a physical need (for nutrition), what is a cultural need (for nutrition from blubber), what is a psychological need (for self-affirmation through social ritual) and what is merely a wild assertion. Psychosomatic illness caused by the repression of the human need for creativity, appreciation and challenge at work is an illustration of what happens when the list of needs is not long enough.

A long list is a more comprehensive census. Yet it is also an invitation to the war of each against all: 'If the means of meeting everybody's needs are absent, needs may engender desperate, bitter struggles among human beings' (Braybrooke, 1987: 237). Once only the upper classes wore leather shoes. Now everyone does so. Once a television, a computer, a telephone, a mobile telephone satisfied an individual want. Now each is targeted at a conventional need since each is essential to survive in a social role. The minimum standard of decency has gone up. What was a luxury once is a necessity now. It is a bottomless pit.

A need that is conventional rather than natural may be said to enjoy the lower lexicographic ordering: 'If a need derives from an existing social arrangement and thus depends on conventions, it loses some of its ineluctability' (Braybrooke, 1987: 189). Water will not be traded for education in the desert.

Psychotherapy, stress-management clinics, second opinions, single-occupancy rooms for privacy and comfort are more exposed. Politicians cannot apply the marginal standard when they authorise the polio jab. Conventional needs are easier to trim. As the list of way-of-life needs becomes longer, so the politicians become more and more aware that they might have to refuse. Leadership does not always mean doing what will win applause. Leadership can well cost them popularity and support.

Just as the politicians can refuse to satisfy felt needs, so they can devote their attention to satisfying hidden absolutes that the citizens have not unearthed. People have a want: they want to smoke. People have a need: they need not to smoke. People have a want: they want women to stay at home. People have a need: they need skilled labour and an educated citizenry. People have a want: they want to be left alone. People have a need: they need fraternal fellow-feeling and common, collectivised provision. In cases like these the politicians will have to take the initiative. They will have to educate the electorate to want what they need. Reconditioning takes time. Long before the intellectual engineering – the brainwashing – has begun to bear fruit, the paternalists who put needs before wants may well be voted out by an electorate that simply does not want to live on soya beans and a nice glass of milk. Democracy is always a problem. Majorities have to be satisfied. Preferences have to be satisfied. Invisible needs and unseen imperatives can condemn the social visionary to the back benches where the journalists never go.

(c) The economics of politics

Anthony Downs has formulated a theory of democracy which makes election and re-election the sole maximand. In Downs's economic model, the politician is in competition with other politicians for the mandate that gives him the five good things he craves: power, prestige, income, conflictual strategy, access to the Parliamentary game (Downs, 1957). In the sense of Tullock, this vote motive is a guarantee that the majority at least will get what it wants. One problem is that unseen minorities tend to stay under-protected. In the case of health, this would mean that research would not be conducted on sickle cell anaemia and conditions would be no more than basic in long-stay mental wards. A related problem is that special-interest groups might sway the political market because it is in the nature of redistributive coalitions that they focus time and resources on the single issue which for them will pay. Medical associations and hospital federations lobby hard to make the partial interest look like the well-being of all. Farmers' representatives persuade the parliamentarians that domestic agriculture must be protected against cheap imported food. The interest groups are insiders and they have specialist knowledge. Some put in campaign contributions as well as dispensing free advice. The politicians are generalists who are obliged to listen and learn. Neither an efficient nor an equitable outcome can be said to be guaranteed where information is so unequal. The government in correcting a market failure creates new political failings of its own.

There is a further shortcoming. It cannot be assumed that politicians themselves are faceless automatons who passively make public opinion into the public interest. Downs and Tullock do not treat world-views and ideals as something that would make the politician, a follower and not a leader, into a natural fanatic. Buchanan is more open to the idea of politician-induced demand. Downs's five motives, he suggests, are necessary but not sufficient. He cannot imagine why a person would choose politics and not business if the candidate for office did not have a vision of the 'good life': 'Within what he treats as his feasible set, the politician will choose that alternative or option which maximizes his own, not his constituents', utility. This opportunity offers one of the primary motivations to politicians. In a meaningful sense, this is "political income", and it must be reckoned as a part of the total rewards of office' (Buchanan, 1975: 157). What Buchanan is implying is that the need for health might not bubble up from consensus. Instead it might be identified at the top by self-styled shepherds who think that they, not the patient, not the doctor, not the public, really know best.

The politician can have a private interest which he wishes to impose upon the whole. The bureaucrat too can have organisational objectives which, as in the large corporation, are the goals of staff on a salary rather than of the taxpayers who support them. Buchanan writes as follows of a small clique that comes to wield disproportionate influence: 'As students of political economy have long recognized, producer interests tend to dominate consumer interests, and the producer interests of government employees are no different from those of any other group in society' (Buchanan, 1975: 160). Downs notes that some bureaucrats will have a bias towards inertia even when innovative intervention is urgently required; while other bureaucrats will be zealots and obsessives who trample balanced argument under foot in their determination to push through their own favoured cause. He points with some trepidation to the well-known human propensity to play up what fits in with one's own vested interest and to play down what is embarrassingly inconvenient.

The danger is that people with a stranglehold on specialised information will always make a biased selection of the facts that best suit their prejudices and will conceal results that damage their own promotion-prospects. Niskanen adds empire-building to the list of good things. Reputation, salary, fringe benefits, power, are all, he writes, 'a positive monotonic function of the total *budget* of the bureau' (Niskanen, 1971: 41; original emphasis). Occupational objectives such as these may or may not be a positive monotonic function of some underlying social need. There is no way to know.

4. Payment for health

Medical care costs scarce resources. The mode of payment influences the quantity that changes hands and the price that the demanders can afford to pay. It also has an impact on the extent of sharing and redistribution in society. The mode of payment is a topic in *who* and not just in *what*. Effective demand is social interaction. It is not just the theory of price.

Effective demand always marches out in front. Money makes the market go round. True in all exchanges, the proposition is twice as true in the market for health. The reason is that the market for health is very frequently not single but twinned. The final market is care: the patient pays the doctor to make him well. The intermediate market is protection: a third-party is prepaid to share the risk.

This chapter examines the contribution of the insuring agency to the purchase of care. The first section addresses the principles of pooling. The second and third sections explore the private and then the public alternatives. The final section, on payment beyond insurance, is a reminder that health care can be affordable even if there is no third-party to share the risk.

4.1. THE LOGIC OF INSURANCE

The future is unknown and the cost is uncertain. People are fearful both that their good health will go and that they will be exposed to financial burdens which will exhaust their wealth. Few other areas of social life cause more sleepless nights than do the possibility of illness and the costliness of care. Wishing to purchase peace of mind, people therefore pay a known sum in advance in order to protect themselves against the greater unknown of an unanticipated calamity which may or may not occur. Insurance is an unusual arrangement in that few people really want ever to enjoy the doctoring and the surgery on which they have a lien.

4.1.1. Uncertainty and Risk

Insurance is purchased because of ignorance. People do not know if or when ever-lurking ill health will strike. They do not know how much the recommended future treatment will cost. If the insurers and their clients had perfect knowledge of the date and the amount, those certain to be afflicted would not buy insurance at all. They would put the earmarked sum in an interest-bearing account with a fixed date of maturity. It would not be rational for them to buy prepayment through an insurance fund for an annual check-up or for a repeat prescription that will permanently be a known, predictable monthly drain. Deducting surplus and overheads, the policy, charging premiums that reflect its reimbursements, would give them back less than they put in.

Unknowledge is the rock on which the industry is built. Those certain that illness will pass them by will have no reason to buy insurance. It would be a waste of money to cross-subsidise a club from which they themselves would never derive any benefit. Those certain that catastrophic illness is already here or about to descend will, on the other hand, have a strong incentive to buy insurance. Their problem is that no gain-seeking agency will offer them the contract. No rational bookkeeper can afford to accept bets from well-informed insiders who know in advance the outcome of a takeover bid or which boxer has been bribed to take a fall. No insuring fund that wishes to remain solvent can by the same token promise reimbursement in excess of the premium to omniscient loss-makers who know today precisely what they will want to take out. Predictable outlays will have to be settled out-of-pocket or out of savings. The intermediary can take deposits and invest money on account. What it cannot do is to quote odds on a race that has been run.

Insurance exists because the future is situated behind a veil. It exists because foreknowledge is imperfect. Even so, the intermediary is not entirely without a compass. Whereas the one-off cannot know that he will be attacked by a burglar this Friday evening at 10, the insurer can take advantage of the law of large numbers. The insurer can extrapolate the probabilities from recent frequencies that are expected to recur. Relevant variables must be taken into account: break-ins will be weighted by the postal code, von Willebrand's Disease predicted from the parents' dominant gene. Circumstances might change; and each subscriber has more than a single risk-related characteristic. Even so, the insurer generalising for an established pool cannot be compared to a gambler who picks random numbers out of the air. Uncertainty means 'I haven't a clue'. Risk means 'I know the probable outcome'. Insurance is a system which converts radical uncertainty into actuarial risk.

The ideal premium for the applicant would be a value corresponding to the mean of the probability distribution. It is not a price which the insurer will be able to accept. Insurers must cover transaction costs such as marketing, claims-processing and (as part of cost containment) their utilisation review. A commercial insurer will in addition be expected to return a profit. For that reason, all insurance has a built-in deterrent. The premium is always and everywhere above the actuarial mean. The risk-indifferent will see no reason to pay this supplement; and risk-lovers by temperament will never insure at all. It is only the risk-averse who will regard it as economic to subscribe to the loading. The logic is the diminishing marginal utility of income. As so many in the tradition of Bernoulli have hypothesised, the distress caused by income lost is greater than the pleasure that would have accrued to an equivalent gain (Friedman and Savage, 1948: 303). The same people who buy insurance also buy lottery tickets. Making speculative investments, they are revealing a willingness to spend a small amount for the small chance of a big win. Buying health cover, they are in the same way revealing a preference for low-cost protection against the small but non-negligible probability of a disproportionate loss.

Discouraged by the surcharge but frightened nonetheless by what it means to be on their own, the most the risk-averse will do is to pay their subscription but to economise on the content. They might choose a budget policy with an exclusion clause for low-likelihood 'acts of God'. They might self-insure through a high-deductible plan that requires them to pay the first tranche themselves. They might reserve health insurance for medical catastrophes while buying inexpensive aspirins and plasters on their own. Thresholds and selectivity would keep their premiums more affordable. Yet there will always be some people who will nonetheless opt for comprehensive policies and the first-dollar umbrella. They will pay what it costs irrespective of the expected loss. Worry affects people in different ways. Subjective salience is not the same as the statistical frequency. A widely-reported plane crash causes people to play safe and travel by car. The chance of a fatal accident on the roads is many times more.

Worry is disutility but so is payment. The result is a downward-sloping curve. If the price of insurance goes down, the quantity demanded of protection will rise. Holmer, testing the willingness to pay for health insurance in the United States, found that the price elasticity was –0.16 and the income elasticity 0.01 (Holmer, 1984: 217). The relatively low price elasticity suggests that removing the tax subsidy or increasing the co-payment rate would make a rather limited contribution to cost containment. The very low income elasticity confirms that risk-averseness is a positive function of prosperity but that beyond some point consumer satiety sets in. Holmer's very low 0.01 may also reflect the institutional arrangements. Much of American health cover is employer-sponsored. Perhaps American workers prefer to take increased compensation not in more generous health policies but in other fringe benefits or simply in cash.

4.1.2. Risk-Rating

Insurance is redistributive. This is true by definition. If all the members pay their premiums but only the unfortunate few ever claim on a rainy day, it is clear that there will be a transfer of pooled resources from the healthy to the ill. Henry Aaron's statistic for the US dramatically illustrates the extent of the bunching and therewith the bias of the transfer: 'Each year a small proportion of the population accounts for the majority of health care outlays.... Five percent of the population accounts for more than half of all health care outlays in any given year. One percent of the population spends more than one-fourth of all health care outlays' (Aaron, 1991: 51). Redistribution and risk pooling go hand in hand. The promise of mutual aid is the very reason why the anxious sacrifice a certainty for a probability and pay premiums for a contingency that might never arise.

The carrier is itself at risk. On the one hand its premiums must be in line with its responsibilities. On the other hand it must keep its package attractive and its prices keen. The result is that the insuring agency is compelled by the logic of market competition to choose the right pond. It is uneconomic to water the wine with bad risks like chronic alcoholics and Ebola victims. It is far more lucrative to mix gold with gold in the form of young graduates who eat healthily and get plenty of sleep. The good risks will be creamed off into low-premium policies. They may even decide that they do not need insurance at all. The known losers will have to band together in high-premium pools. There the drowning buoy up the drowning and there is no strong swimmer to cross-subsidise the rest. Premiums rise and services are restricted as Gresham's Law drives out all but the desperate. In the end the high-risk pools will become economically unviable. The rejects and the residuals will not be able to afford the premiums. They will have to manage on their own.

The insurer is led by economic self-interest to segregate the pools. It knows that it has no choice but to select and target. The problem is how to risk-rate the applicants. Anyone who applies for insurance must be suspected of knowing that he is already ill or that his lifestyle makes him a ticking time-bomb. The sickly applicant faces a conflict of interest in that he will be denied the product if he tells the truth. Moral thou-shalt-nots give way to competing moral absolutes if a mother knows that her baby has a hole in the heart.

Adverse selection is the tendency of the worst to crowd in first. It is the reason, as described by Akerlof, why it is that only the 'lemons' will survive in the market for insurance. No one would sell a top-notch sedan at a common price that factors in the substandard wrecks (Akerlof, 1970). The insurer must compete to differentiate its pool. Unknowledge makes rational filtering a business game of bluff and probe. The duplicity of the sick means that natural selection will in the long-run discourage the good risks from joining the club: 'The less healthy naturally prefer more generous insurance than the healthy.... Healthy people, in turn, will want to avoid those plans, to keep from subsidizing their less healthy brethren. If adverse selection is large, it may destroy the market for the generous insurance entirely' (Cutler and Reber, 1998: 434).

Unable to put its faith in honour-system self-declaration, the organisation will have to work out the expected gain and loss for itself. It may insist on a physical examination: expensive as it would be to see each applicant individually, a blood test, a DNA sample, a psychological profile, an electrocardiogram of the heart, an angiogram of the head and neck, an arm X-ray for bone disease will reveal many of the pathologies which the candidate will have a financial incentive to conceal (and of which he might not even be aware). The insurer may ask for a full medical history: this will throw into relief pre-existing conditions like diabetes, haemophilia, hypertension, arthritis, depression, anorexia, asthma, premature senility and incipient schizophrenia. It may approach the police to see if there is a record of drink-driving. It may interview a former employer to learn if a redundancy was caused by bad health, fist fights or careless accidents. It may demand information on parents and siblings as an indicator of what a healthy applicant is likely to cost. The discovery that all the males in the family experience heart failure in their early 40s will set alarm bells ringing when a male of 39 puts in an application to cover his heart.

Patients complain that the procedures and the paperwork are costly and humiliating. They say that their genes are confidential and that disclosure violates their civil rights. It is hard to know which side to take when an applicant rejected for a company plan is no longer able to keep secret from his employer that in-service training might not pay off since he is HIV-positive. Looking at the tests and the investigations from the perspective of the insurer, however, the position is more encouraging. At least the insurer will have a chance to inspect the goods. It will be able to find out for itself if the named body before it really is value for money.

Less accurate but less intrusive is risk-rating on the basis not of named individuals but of broad categories. Risk-profiling classifies the applicant in terms of key characteristics such as age, gender, marital status, ethnicity, education, occupation, lifestyle. A differential premium can be demanded from statistical outliers who smoke heavily, have a large family or indulge in extreme sports. Applicants deemed to be high-risk because they are homosexual, or have requested an HIV test, or have a history of violent crime may simply be excluded altogether. Occupational group may be used as an indicator of an above-average drain. Mercenary soldiers and heavyweight boxers are more exposed to head wounds than are shopkeepers or monks. Barmen are more likely to drink. Branch of industry picks up known workplace hazards such as those associated with asbestos, radioactivity, mercury and burning buildings. Place of residence can be stereotyped as a proxy on the assumption that everyone on an inner-city estate is equally deprived. Classification by characteristics is a blunt instrument compared with person-by-person assessment. It is, however, a more rational approach than to charge the same premium for all.

The insurance contract itself might be written in such a way as to induce the applicants to risk-rate themselves into multiple pools. Thus a no-claims bonus will tend *ceteris paribus* to attract applicants who are not anticipating a self-inflicted contingency. A policy that combines low premiums with high deductibles and high co-payments will, on the other hand, be a deterrent to applicants aware that undisclosed complaints are likely to require costly surgery and long-term prescriptions. A discount offered to the non-smoker or non-drinker both identifies the applicant less likely to make a claim and provides an economic incentive to the unhealthy to pull back from self-destruction. Insurance in this way has an active as well as a passive role to play.

Business is business. The insurance industry would prefer experience rating: it is attracted by differential premiums that track historical frequencies, identifiable categories and the current costs of treatment in a specified locality. The State, however, often insists on community rating: premiums are shaded by age and by treatment-costs in the locality but are not tailor-made for the individual or risk-related by any category. In the former case the above-average consumers pay higher premiums or are entitled to smaller packages. In the latter case the price and the entitlement are the same for every citizen or resident who boasts a pulse. The latter policy will be more popular with the coughs and the sneezes than it will with the health-conscious whose premiums will go up.

Pauly writes that risk-rating is seen differently depending on the kind of risk that is being underwritten: 'If we were discussing fire insurance – and the financial impact of a fire is surely many times larger than that of illness, even a serious illness – no one would object to the person with the higher expected loss paying the higher premium. But in health insurance, it may not seem fair that the diabetic should pay more than the non-diabetic and that the person with a stroke should pay the most' (Pauly, 1988: 52). Fairness-seeming is a strange animal. It does not seem fair for the chronic to pay more than the hale. Nor, however, does it seem fair for them not to do so. While it is never good to spin general theory from the devil-may-care when not every accident or cancer is Cain's stigma of fault, the objection nonetheless will be raised that it is rather hard on people who exercise and eat sensibly that they will have to pay more because the drug addicts are pulling the community average up.

Where the premium is across the board, the insurer still has the option of cherry-picking the healthiest specimens. To prevent the cream from being skimmed, the State will often complement community rating with an insistence on an open door. No applicant can then be turned away and (provided that the fee is paid) all coverage must be renewed. The law is not a cast-iron guarantee. The insurers can respond by restricting the services or raising the co-payments. They can in the limit withdraw altogether from health insurance business. There is not much the State can do to stop commercial cover from drying up. It is a possibility that must be taken into account in countries where the population is ageing rapidly. Medicare in the United States has been one response.

4.1.3. Moral Hazard

Once the applicants have joined the club, they no longer have the same incentive to avoid the risks. Economically speaking, the tendency is for them to become more accident prone. Where the seat belts and the vitamins cost money but the visit to the doctor is co-paid by the pool, the individual will have a financial incentive to economise on prevention. He will substitute wasteful medical care which privately will cost him less. Third-party payment can make the individual feel less responsible for himself. It can make the nation's health status fall.

The neglect is a tendency. It is not a prediction. Precisely because health is a Grossman-like good thing in its own right it would be premature to say that people will inevitably cut back merely because avoidable repairs have become more affordable. It is hard to believe that many more people will go out in the sun merely because their cancers will be treated free on the National Health Service. Yet the tendency is there. People might take fewer precautions or fail to shop around because they know that the liability will be a collective one.

It is hard to say what this means for overall well-being. People who drive fast are more likely to crash but will save money-making time that will increase their satisfying net worth. People who drink heavily are more likely to damage their liver and pancreas but will have had such convivial evenings in the pub. It is hard to sum up the pluses and the minuses. All that can be stated is that insurance can cause people to alter their behaviour patterns; and very often will do so. A sample calculation is that made by Manning and his colleagues. They asked what would happen if the American under-65s were to move to insurance policies with a zero co-payment. They found that the welfare loss due to moral hazard would lie between $37 billion and $60 billion. The total health care spend (in 1984) was $200 billion. The economic loss associated with excessive consumption would clearly represent a considerable strain upon the whole (Manning, Newhouse, Duan, Keeler, Leibowitz and Marquis, 1987: 270).

The doctor, like the patient, has a tendency to revise his clinical priorities once he appreciates that his principal is insurance-protected. Even if the doctor knows that a marginal intervention will almost certainly be flat-of-the-curve, he has the luxury of recommending further tests, referrals and prescriptions. He knows that the unique human being across the table from him will not have to make a direct pecuniary sacrifice. More venal doctors will take advantage of the position to garner extra fees for themselves. Supply will find it easier to induce its own demand where someone other than the beneficiary is settling the bills.

4.1.4. A Cause of Change

Insurance can shape events. It is more than knee-jerk reimbursement. It is not just a passive pass-through.

The wording of the insurance contract may itself lead to a reordering of the treatment options. There are policies where the insurer will pay for inpatient care but not for day-case surgery. There are policies where the insurer will pay for an appliance but not for a linctus. There are policies where the insurer imposes annual co-payment ceilings. They are a reason to concentrate postponable treatments in a single insurance year. In cases such as these the doctor may select the reimbursable alternative because it is cheaper for the patient or more lucrative for himself. He might ignore the greater burden that the prepaid option puts on the nation as a whole. One isolated treatment will not be much of a strain. The doctor and the patient are both subject to the tyranny of small decisions. It all adds up. In the long-run the costs and the premiums will rise.

Insurance protects the doctor's clinical freedom. It sets the professional free to do what his medical ethic dictates. The doctor has a Hippocratic Oath. He has a moral commitment to deliver an irreversible service even to a patient whose credit-worthiness is poor. On the other hand, the doctor is not a charity. He cannot afford to become the insurer of last resort by supplying the service free. In order to cushion himself against bad debt and default, the doctor might choose to raise his average charges: then it will be his paying customers who credit in the *pro bono* business. Insurance is the other option. It ensures that patients who cannot pay will not be turned away. It also ensures that the doctor himself will receive his fee.

Research and development follow the course set by effective demand. Insurance plays an active role in facilitating the demand for care. What this means is that if insurance is prepared to validate high-technology departures, the research laboratories and the commercial manufacturers will have an economic incentive to supply them. The cost per treatment episode rises. The amount of cover purchased then rises in response: 'Costly new surgical techniques such as organ transplants and artificial replacement parts spur the demand for insurance; low-cost vaccines diminish it' (Weisbrod, 1991: 534). It is a vicious circle. The treatments may be relatively ineffective and possibly very expensive. They must nonetheless be made a part of the promise. The insurer who fails to sell the most modern entitlements may lose out to the one who is believed to be state-of-the-art.

Insurers can make costs go up. They can also shape events through their need as businesses to keep the escalation down. Insurers collect comparative data on doctors and hospitals. They monitor waits, techniques, stays, inputs and recoveries. They refuse reimbursement for innovatory therapies until they are satisfied that the treatment is medically effective and economically efficient. They scrutinise large claims and query unexpected departures from the mean. They insist upon prospective rather than retrospective payment in order to force the treatment centre to share the risk of a cost-overrun. The self-interest of the insurer comes to countervail the self-interest of the provider. Value for money is the economical result.

4.1.5. Combinations and Permutations

Insurance is a kaleidoscope of possibilities. It is not a single commodity, always and everywhere the same. The differentiation in service maximises the non-median consumer's felt well-being. It appeals to the marginal who are seeking a choice.

Sometimes the insurer refunds the fee without specifying a ceiling limit. Sometimes there is a prearranged maximum: this can be per calendar year, per treatment episode or over the whole of the policyholder's life. Sometimes there is a deductible: this is a lump-sum excess or threshold which is at the patient's own charge. Sometimes there is a co-payment: this is a percentage of the reimbursable band that must be covered by the insured party himself. Sometimes the coinsurance requirement is never finally lifted: to prevent moral hazard the individual is never completely secure. Sometimes the coinsurance requirement cuts off at a preannounced limit: all marginal treatment becomes free at that point. Sometimes the insurer preannounces a fixed indemnity for each kind of medical care: the consumer must pay the difference if his demands exceed the scale. Sometimes the insurer has a closed panel. Sometimes the patient can select his own provider.

Sometimes the policies protect the individual alone. Sometimes they extend to the spouse, children and even parents as well. Sometimes the policies are automatically and permanently renewed. Sometimes the cover is restricted from the first renewal after a chronic diagnosis. Sometimes the premiums are age-related. Sometimes they are the same flat rate for all. Sometimes the policies impose a special-risks surcharge on the motorist, the sportsman, the drinker and the smoker. Sometimes the coverage is deliberately non-judgmental, avowedly indifferent to the policyholder's personal lifestyle.

Sometimes the contracts are restricted to major contingencies such as expensive hospitalisation. Sometimes the refund extends to walk-in clinics, routine check-ups and prescription drugs. Sometimes the insurer will pay for preventive health (such as immunisation and mammograms), body-maintenance fitness (such as an aerobics class) and rehabilitative care (such as support centres for drug abuse or alcohol). Some contracts exclude mental health. Some contracts exclude venereal disease. Some contracts exclude artificial insemination, pregnancy and antenatal care. Some contracts exclude blood, organ transplants, cosmetic surgery, gender reassignment, walking frames, dentistry or refraction.

In some cases the individual pays the full cost of the insurance. In other cases the employer pays, or the Exchequer matches the contributions, or the burden is shared. In some cases there is tax relief for premiums. In other cases the fiscal subsidy is limited to the lowest rate of income tax. In other cases the tax deduction cuts off at a ceiling maximum. Sometimes there is no fiscal welfare at all.

In some cases the patient is allowed to buy a top-up rider for better amenities, shorter waits, a very expensive drug, a named surgeon or the abrogation of co-payments. In other cases what is guaranteed is the standard package, no more and no less. Sometimes prescription brand names and not just generics are included on the list. Sometimes only essential and not comfort drugs will be refunded. Sometimes there is a monthly ceiling on the cost of pharmaceuticals. All contracts are insurance. Yet what is insured is not always the same.

4.1.6. A Single Package?

Insurance is a restaurant with many dishes. Options are attractive where people are different and one-size-fits-all fails to satisfy their infinite complexity. An apprehensive hypochondriac might put protection first. A self-reliant adventurer might prefer to make his own mistakes. A person with savings might want low premiums accompanied by a considerable excess. A person who is unemployed and ill might feel more comfortable with a free-on-demand regimen. The case against a uniform package is the liberal's defence of devolution, autonomy, personal choice and respect for persons. A system which values the autonomy of the individual, it is argued, ought to leave it to the individual to decide what he wants: 'Underlying most arguments against the free market is a lack of belief in freedom itself' (Friedman, 1962: 15).

Not only should people have the right to shape their protection, they should have the right to rethink their choice. It is not evidence of inconsistency and contradiction but of change and mutability that the same person might be a risk-lover when single but a risk-averter when a family member requires chronic care. The same consumer might find it rational to go for a low-cost, low-cover policy one year and for a high-cost, high-cover policy the next. A prudent, sensible economiser might even plan to concentrate his elective surgery in the comprehensive phase and to re-contract back to limited cover once there is nothing more to fix.

The case for planning ahead, for shopping around, for differentiating the purchase seems to be a persuasive one. As Fuchs writes, a single blanket for different people who put different values on different services will distort the relative utilities and the quantities consumed: 'Any system which attempts to force all people to buy the same amount of health services is likely to result in a significant misallocation of resources' (Fuchs, 1973 [1966]: 163). Pauly, similarly, is concerned about the felt well-being foregone when the cat is forced to eat the dog food and to pay for it as well: 'If individual demands for medical care differ, it is possible that the loss due to "excess" use under insurance may exceed the welfare gain from insurance for one individual but fall short of it for another individual. It follows that it may not be optimal policy to provide compulsory insurance against particular events for all individuals' (Pauly, 1968: 534). Tastes can differ. Where they differ, it is not really optimal to expect even the vegetarians to eat beef. It is insensitive and intolerant to require risk-lovers to join a club designed for risk-averters merely because wise paternalists have decreed that silly Dubb's revealed preferences are not very good.

The case for *laissez-faire* is the case for factored-down decision-making: 'No exchange will take place unless both parties do benefit from it. Co-operation is thereby achieved without coercion' (Friedman, 1962: 13). Persuasive as it is, the truth is that restricted choice knows some good tunes as well.

The first is economies of scale. It is sometimes suggested that administrative overheads can be spread and high-cost duplication cost-effectively minimised where there is a small number of oligopolistic giants. Some theorists of good husbandry have even argued in favour of a single State monopoly. Titmuss in the 1950s observed that in the United States the administration, marketing and commission costs of insurance companies were so high that 'the consumer now gets less than half his dollar back in medical care' (Titmuss, 1963: 258). He contrasted the bad example of private provision with the good experience of socialised supply in the British welfare State: 'The administrative costs of private Workmen's Compensation Insurance were of the order of 30 to 40 per cent of the premiums collected. Such figures can now be compared with the administrative costs of the Department of Health and Social Security in administering the present system of National Insurance against Industrial Injuries and Diseases. These costs are in the neighbourhood of 5 to 10 per cent. The private market was many times more costly in terms of administrative efficiency' (Titmuss, 1974: 82). Weberian bureaucrats spread the overheads. Textbook competitive profit-seekers reduce the quality of the product for all.

A second reason for a uniform package might be that most medical patients most of the time want more or less the same thing. The argument for wide-ranging choice might be entirely persuasive in the market for fruit but still not be equally strong in the market for health. People might prefer lower costs with standardisation to frivolous and marginal differentiation for which they would have to pay. They might, moreover, prefer not to have to search. The future is unknown, information is asymmetrical, and people might be happy to take the combinations that they are offered. They would not be so complacent if there were radical divisions in society. If, however, there is broad consensus – if most of the citizens most of the time open their umbrella when it starts to rain – then coercion by consent might seem to them the better choice.

The third reason is the citizenship commitment. This is the argument that it is desirable in the area of welfare not to supply a residual service for second-rate failures but to integrate all into a homogeneous set of overlapping experiences. A distinguished advocate of the welfare community because national cohesion makes us a We was Richard Henry Tawney. For Tawney it was clear that comprehensive schooling and shared experience made malleable men and women aware that they worshipped a single God: 'What a community requires, as the word itself suggests, is a common culture, because, without it, it would not be a community at all' (Tawney, 1964 [1931]: 43). Richard Titmuss, similarly, was inspired by the ideal of a National Health that was part and parcel of the *national* health: 'We want to see a health service developing which will not be separate and aloof from the life of the nation but an expression and reinforcement of national unity' (Titmuss, with Abel-Smith, Macdonald, Williams and Ward, 1964: 124). Tawney and Titmuss found little to admire in the loneliness and isolation of free enterprise that had no time for friends or fellows. They could see a case for a mandatory package and minimal choice precisely because the whole is an organism and the tribe must strengthen its bonds.

4.2.   PRIVATE HEALTH INSURANCE

Insurance contracts can take a variety of forms. Equally, they can be issued by a variety of agencies. This section is concerned with insuring agencies in the non-State sector. Not all are commercial and for-profit. Some are linked to private charities, professional associations, trade unions, consumer cooperatives. Some large employers even operate their own insurance funds in order to keep down the costs.

Individuals can secure private insurance either on their own or as a member of a group. These two ways of obtaining cover will be discussed in turn. The section concludes with the case-study of the prepaid plan.

4.2.1.   The Individual Plan

There are two reasons why the individual might turn to a private insurer. The first is complements and luxuries. In Britain the principal contingencies are covered by the National Health Service but cheap add-ons like holiday health insurance, a full-time home nurse or a live-in home help do something to make the collectivism more comfortable. The second is core protection. Where there is no National Health Service and no occupational plan, the discrete individual might recognise that he will have to pay for himself unless he approaches an insurance company and fills in a form.

The fact that an individual applies for insurance does not, however, mean that the agency will accept his business. An employee who does not apply through an occupational plan will be seen as a statistical black box. He will be a one-off and a mystery. The very fact that the applicant is self-selected might be a sign that he thinks he may make an above-average claim. A person who has made a calculated choice to spend money in the hand on an outcome in the bush is always regarded with suspicion. The insurer will wonder what he knows about himself that he is not revealing.

Individual plans are higher-cost plans due to the uncertainty of the unknown. They are higher-cost plans as well because of administrative overheads. Marketing, selling, correspondence, records, claims are less susceptible to economies of scale or quantity discounts. Fiscal arrangements also make a difference. In many countries business-sponsored health is counted as a productivity-enhancing fringe benefit. The group plan is set against the employer's tax. The individual plan, treated as a private consumable, is often excluded from this concession. The fact that the microscopic supplicant does not *de facto* enjoy the public subsidy makes the individual plan more expensive.

A side-effect of the inequality is unfairness. The rich executive enjoys a good and subsidised package. The unemployed and the elderly find it difficult to buy affordable cover at all. Assuming that the goal of policy is equitable treatment for equal citizens, there may be a case either for withdrawing tax concessions from the occupational plan or extending them to the individual contract.

4.2.2.   The Group Plan

In some countries, health cover is normally employer-sponsored. About 90 per cent of private health insurance in the United States is provided through employment. The employer either self-insures through running the insurance scheme in-house or registers its employees en bloc with an outside carrier.

Comprehensive registration is attractive to the insurer. The firm, blanketing in its entire workforce, is signalling that adverse selection has been eliminated. The pool it enrols is a representative cross-section of its good health status and bad. Prediction is improved still further by the availability of statistical data on the firm and the industry. This allows the carrier to set an experience-related premium.

The insurer for its own part must convince the sponsor that its cover, internal efficiency, profits and premiums are competitive. The sponsor is always on the look-out for a better bid. The rigidities of oligopolistic competition may cushion interdependent giants in the short-run. In the long-run, however, the profit motive will force the insurers as natural enemies to cheat.

As for the employee, the fact that the firm pays all or most of the contributions is a great advantage. Unions strive to make the employee's contribution, if any, as small as possible. Employers are especially prone to concede if they think they will be able to shift the incidence on to the final consumer in the form of higher prices. If there is a shortage of skill or if there is full employment, labour will be in a stronger position to bargain for better benefits. Search itself is a benefit. Because it is the employer who searches, screens and checks, the individual member is spared the labour of tracking down the best deal.

Professionalisation of intelligent decision-making means that fewer opportunities will be missed. Cost-effectiveness is too important to be left to the uninitiated. Personnel officers and vigilant unions, Paul Feldstein writes, 'develop the necessary expertise and information to evaluate alternative medical care delivery options available to their employees.... The greater selectivity of better-informed groups benefits the less-informed subscriber.... The competition among health plans for the better-informed purchasers, those who are more likely to switch plans if quality deteriorates, will help those who are less well informed' (Feldstein, 1988: 326). The suppliers will have an incentive to upgrade their product even if not all participants in the market are equally knowledgeable or equally prepared to make a change. A small number of active and cost-conscious choice-makers can be enough to ensure that the community as a whole will reap the spillover benefits of allocative and dynamic efficiency.

The insurer quotes lower premiums for a standardised contract; and this is likely to be the option that the employer selects. What is sauce for the median might not be sauce for the deviant. An unmarried member has no need for a policy that covers a non-existent spouse and child: such a member might want to exchange redundant clauses for a better dental package or the suppression of user-charges that he values more highly. The same would be true of a two-income couple where each is protected under both partners' plans: they might prefer an improvement in non-health benefits like pensions to duplicate health care cover which they cannot use. Unique one-offs do not like to be repressed. If the collective arrangements are such that they only indemnify and reimburse, the employees who prefer a capitated health maintenance organisation will feel that they have been left out in the cold.

Usually the package is a standard one. It offers a single set of benefits for all. Sometimes, however, the employee is given a range of choices within the framework of the group plan as a whole. In such a case the members have the freedom to pay more for more or to ask for a different menu. Price in economics is a primary selling point.

Strombom, Buchmueller and Feldstein studied price-conscious consumer choice at the time of the annual enrolment. Their finding was that some people responded to changes in relative premiums and some people did not: 'While

significant price effects are estimated for all groups, the elasticities for individuals presumed to face the lowest switching costs – younger, recently hired
employees who are in good health – are roughly four times larger than those
estimated for individuals for whom switching plans is likely to be more costly
– older, incumbent employees who have recently been hospitalized or diagnosed
with cancer' (Strombom, Buchmueller and Feldstein, 2002: 90). When a plan
raised its price, it lost some of its clients to other plans on offer within the group.
Its market share within the group went down. Price sensitivity decreased with
age: the elasticities for employees under 30 are twice the elasticities of the employees over 45. The result was adverse retention due to inertia. The young
moved to cheaper plans. Older members seized the default option. A change
means that information on the alternatives must be collected. Transactions costs
are incurred. Switching plans often means switching providers. Particularly if
they had been ill, members preferred to remain with a doctor they knew. In that
way they pushed up the mean age, the average risk and the fair price of their
plan.

A continuous curve assumes that individuals are able to make marginal adjustments. Where the employee is credited in by his firm, his choice is either/or
if indeed he has any choice at all. Although 90 per cent of insured Americans
under the age of 65 obtain their coverage from their employer, approximately
two-thirds of them do not have a choice of plan. The evidence produced by
Marquis and Long is therefore especially interesting. It is derived exclusively
from the decision to purchase cover made by *uninsured* working Americans
who do *not* have group plans. They do not enjoy the discounted loading or the
tax concessions. Marquis and Long estimated that the price elasticity for this
subgroup was –0.3 to –0.4 and that the income elasticity was 0.15. A 10 per
cent decrease in price would only lead to a 3 or 4 per cent increase in the number
of families who would decide to purchase insurance. The demand curve remains
inelastic: 'Our estimate of the price response raises doubts that even substantial
subsidies to the working uninsured would induce many of them to purchase
coverage voluntarily' (Marquis and Long, 1995: 47). A subsidy targeted on
low-income families would be ineffective. Most of it would go to low-income
families who were already buying health insurance and not to the low-income
uninsured who had made up their mind to spend their money on other goods
and services. For them at least, mandatory cover would reduce their own level
of well-being, self-perceived.

A fringe benefit that one is not going to use is not really a fringe *benefit* at
all. Diversity, however, puts up the average cost. It also makes it difficult for
employees to absorb and digest the information overload. Where the employee
is offered a selection of plans, the administrative overheads go up and less actual
care is provided per dollar paid in. Small firms, needless to say, are the least
likely to be able to afford the overhead: 'Among employers offering health

coverage, about 80 percent of employees who work for firms with a staff of 200 or more are offered a choice of plans. This is true, however, of only 10 percent in firms with 2–9 employees, 15 percent in firms with 10–24 employees, and 28 percent in firms with 25–199 employees' (Rice, 2001: 25). People who want freedom of choice in their plans should go to a larger firm.

Occupational plans are an impediment to occupational mobility. A job change can mean a new plan, perhaps a new annual excess, perhaps a waiting time, perhaps even a new general practitioner where the new insurer has a panel of its own and business-minded financiers assign little importance to continuity in the doctor–patient relationship (Madrian, 1994). Medical tests might have to be repeated (at an economic cost) and a new medical history taken. An existing complaint only diagnosed after the old plan became legally binding might be made the subject of a new exclusion clause: 'For type I diabetics, diagnosed early in the life cycle, job lock may be a very serious issue.... Having a preexistent condition may reduce the ability of young type I diabetics from switching firms to find their best employment match' (Kahn, 1998: 896). Premiums might be high. Cover might be denied. The fact that some firms offer especially attractive health packages in order to retain staff itself restricts the willingness of staff to move to better-paid jobs that do not offer the same benefits. Portable medical insurance would solve a number of these problems at a stroke. It would not, however, assist the employee who wants to switch to an adventurous new enterprise but knows that he is moving from a group plan to an unprotected young business where he will have to apply for a risk-related individual plan.

The nation as a whole wants the entrepreneurial to recruit the efficient and the economy to maximise its potential productivity. The employee, however, might simply be too afraid to shake off his golden handcuffs. About 30 per cent of Americans said in a survey that the loss of health insurance had prevented them or someone else in their household from changing jobs. Cooper and Monheit found that married men who stood to lose their health insurance were 23 per cent less likely than the uninsured to change jobs (Cooper and Monheit, 1993: 412). It was the young, the low paid and the unskilled who were the least afraid to try new things. Since the experienced and the educated are generally the bottleneck input, it would be fair to say that job lock is at variance with economic growth.

Occupational plans are a good reason not to indulge in voluntary unemployment. This is an economic loss where the quits followed by the search would ultimately lead to a better deployment of the nation's scarce manpower stock. Occupational plans also make dismissals more frightening. Unemployment means not just the loss of income but the exclusion of the whole family from job-related medical cover. Unemployment, transitional or long-term, is a bad time to fall ill. Historically, therefore, there has been popular pressure for legislation to fill the market void.

Regulation takes a variety of forms. Those between jobs are sometimes allowed to retain their previous group plan at their own expense, often for an
extended period. They are allowed to have easier access to an individual plan
where their previous job did not come to an end because of ill health. Employees
moving from one group plan to another are granted exemption from a new waiting period in respect of a previously-diagnosed condition. In ways such as these
the government contributes to the humanitarian spillover while unfreezing a
frozen labour market as well. Whether it is efficient or profitable for commercial
insurers to be required to offer these contracts is more debatable.

The retired by definition do not have occupational cover. Nor do dependants
left on their own by a divorce or the death of the breadwinner. Nor does the
part-timer, or the freelance, or the seasonally employed, or the self-employed
who work for a number of organisations. Nor do those quoted a waiting time:
minimum periods before cover becomes operative are little help to workers who
come and go. Employees of a firm which does not offer an occupational plan
will be vulnerable, not least where they are on low incomes (and cannot pay for
a private policy) or where they work in hazardous sweat-shops (which means
an insurer would insist on an expensive risk supplement). Small firms will be
exposed, as where the insurer states that the pool is not large enough for meaningful odds. It is likely that those without cover will be the young, the old, the
black, the female, the unskilled, who are suffering from other disadvantages as
well. A household carer such as a single mother will often not know where to
turn.

Occupational plans are a non-wage cost. As with all fringe benefits, they can
be seen as a tax on jobs. The incidence of the burden will be especially heavy
in labour intensive industries, or on the unskilled and the low paid for whom
the cost of cover will be a higher proportion of pay. As with the textbook minimum wage, there is a possibility that the overhead will mean reduced
employment opportunities. It would not if the benefit explicitly took the place
of higher pay foregone. It would if the employer felt compelled to mechanise
and shed labour because he could not afford to pay.

4.2.3. A Case-Study: Managed Care

Both the individual plan and the group plan can take the form of the prepaid
option. In the case of private insurance the practitioner treats and the insurer
reimburses. In the case of the prepaid plan the legal entity that supplies the
treatment is the legal entity that covers the bills. Risk-bearing and medical attention are not under the control of different bodies. Payment and provision are
not two things apart.

The best-known of the prepaid structures are the health maintenance organisations (HMOs) that have grown up, principally but not exclusively in the United

States. In 1988 73 per cent of American employees were enrolled in conventional (typically fee-for-service) plans and 27 per cent in managed care (Berk and Monheit, 2001: 11). By 2004 the 27 per cent had become 95 per cent: 'Traditional insurance is an anachronism' (Cutler, 2004: 87). The largest is Kaiser Permanente. Founded in 1945, by 2006 it had 8.3 million members and annual operating revenues of $22.5 billion.

In the prepaid system there are a number of competing organisations. They collect an annual fee from the applicant or, more commonly, from the enrollee's employer. In return they agree to meet all the health care needs named in the contract for the period in question. That is why the system is called 'managed care'. About four-fifths of the American HMOs expect co-payments. These contributions are almost always moderate and affordable.

In some cases (the 'staff model') the organisation has premises of its own such as a health centre and even a hospital. It employs its own doctors, pays them a salary, and requires them to see HMO patients only. Utilisation review and physician profiling are practised in-house to ensure that referrals correspond to norms and standards are maintained. Organisational guidelines minimise unnecessary practice-variation. In other cases (the 'group model') the doctors remain in outside practice. The HMO pays a capitation or even reimburses a (discounted) fee for service to the physician group. The primary care practice then distributes the money according to its own criteria. In other cases (the 'network model') the organisation will have a network of contracts with a selection of independent physicians and hospitals. None of them is closed-panel. Patients going outside the recommended suppliers in all three models might have to pay a higher coinsurance rate or compensate the non-HMO treatment centre out-of-pocket. To protect themselves, some HMOs actually take out commercial insurance to underwrite large losses. An earthquake or a flood in the area can destroy the financial reserves of an organisation with a regional catchment. Other organisations are so large and so national that they can act as their own insurer of last resort. They can diversify their risks.

Some HMOs are profit-seeking. Others price and market purely in order to cover their costs. Some give the medical professionals a share in the operating surplus: this is a cost containment measure which may also be seen as a tacit acknowledgement of the producer-cooperative principle. Others merely pay the doctors their capitations, salaries and fees: they do not believe there is any need for the doctor to be on profits as well. Clearly, the precise arrangements can vary. The principle, however, remains the same. Insurance is integrated with delivery.

The prepaid plan has an incentive to keep down the average cost per patient year. The reason is that the burden of inefficient delivery or unnecessary treatment falls on the HMO itself. One way in which excessive treatments are kept in check is through practice budgets: the family doctor put on budget cannot afford the luxuries as he must pay for all tests and hospital days out of his own per-patient resourcing. A second way in which costs are saved is by requiring the primary care doctor to act as the gatekeeper to more expensive consultant and hospital attention. A third way in which waste is kept down is to require the insurer's preauthorisation before a (non-emergency) hospital sequence is launched. Not only does the general practitioner have to validate the choice, so does the paying wing.

The HMO is led by the economics of commerce to economise on non-essential hospitalisation. Tests and simple procedures are performed in the doctor's office rather than in an inpatient setting. Referrals outside are kept to the minimum. Drugs are preferred to psychotherapy. Waiting times build in a delay. The unified structure ensures that resources will not be squandered on administration, billing, the taking of a medical history, the communication of information. Bed occupancy in HMO-owned hospitals must be kept high. Inpatient stays must be shortened. Equipment and operating theatres must not be left idle. Throughput is productivity. Productivity keeps the HMO lean.

Cost-consciousness extends to prevention as well as cure. By keeping the patient well through flu injections, educational input and early detection the organisation is making a saving on expensive treatments later on. A discount must, of course, be applied in recognition of the multiplicity of agents. The patient might in the long-run move on to a competitor. A National Health Service is not vulnerable to the same extent to an out-migration of its paying investments.

Competition too forces the HMO to keep costs keen. The prepaid system must bargain hard with its suppliers for cost-effective contracts. It must pass the gains on to its customers in the form of shorter waits and more attractive prices. It must promise convenient opening hours, well situated premises, a good package, appropriate access to specialists in order to retain patients when contracts are renewed. Transparency makes the HMOs apprehensive about an inferior track-record. Market capitalism, in short, forces the HMOs to satisfy their customers and to trim the fat. The evidence suggests that health outcomes in managed care are not very different from the survivals and recoveries in traditional insurance: 'Fears that HMOs uniformly lead to worse quality of care are not supported by the evidence.... Hopes that HMOs would improve overall quality also are not supported' (Miller and Luft, 1997: 8). Medical indicators are not much affected. Cost savings, however, appear to be reaped.

Less attractive is the manipulation, the salesmanship and the selling. Razzle-dazzle and consumer sovereignty do not go well together. Yet commercial markets have long disseminated factual information on prices and qualities; and in the majority of cases have done so without any suggestion that the crying of the wares had turned seriously malign. In the case of the prepaid plan, consumers normally enrol or re-enrol on an annual basis. The fact that they shop only once a year means that they have time to study performance scores and investigate alternative offerings. They have time for discussions with advisers, employers, brokers and friends. It might be difficult to be detached and calculative in the heat of a genuine emergency. Once a year, however, surrounded by prospectuses, articles and hard copy, it is not impossible that they will have the background and interest to make responsible use of their freedom of choice. Besides that, want creation will cut no ice with a company selecting an HMO in which to enrol its staff. Most American prepaid plans are marketed to the employer. Where the employer makes the choice, value for money rather than undignified touting for business is likely to sway the balance.

The prepaid plan has an effect on the doctor–patient relationship. The prediction, however, is not clear cut. On the one hand, in contrast to fee for service, the patient knows that the doctor has no financial incentive to over-treat. On the other hand, the paying wing putting pressure on the providing wing, confidence can be eroded by the economic temptation to treat too little. There is, in other words, a recognisable conflict of interest within the multiproduct HMO between its financial and its health-maximising objectives. The trade-off between profit and medicine, between volume of business and length of consultation, between economic returns and clinical freedom, will be especially acute where the doctors have a share in ownership or are promised a bonus if they rein in their services. They may even fear that their contract will not be renewed if they exercise their autonomy, exceed the norm or propose a treatment that the fund would prefer them to conceal. Deselection would interrupt the continuity of the doctor–patient relationship. The possibility of deselection is a reminder to the patient not to trust the doctor too far.

Provision is threatened not just by greed but by resourcing. A prepaid plan is dependent on premiums for the budget it can commit. It cannot spend more money than it has. Radical default will lead to litigation. Cutting corners and exercising discretion will probably pass unseen. Most contracts in any case have a ceiling limit. The HMO gives no undertaking to spend an infinite amount. Once the ceiling has been reached, all but life-saving treatment will be suspended. The contract runs for no more than a year. Waiting times and gatekeeper authorisations can be used to limit the take-up even of a package which on paper looks good. Unless there is a statutory obligation to renew, the organisation might simply delay inevitable surgery, postpone tests that will almost certainly detect an abnormality, or put off an expensive new drug until the patient goes off the books.

Potential loss-makers are not welcome. Falling into a high-risk category, irrespective of one's own health status, might be enough to invite a refusal. The advertising campaign of an HMO might sell an image of sport and athletics with which the sickly and the wheelchair-bound might find it difficult to identify. The nurses and doctors might make the very ill feel like unwelcome pariahs.

Prospectuses might be written in small type that old people cannot easily read. The practice might be situated on a high floor without a lift. The organisation might specialise in the kind of services which effectively screen out the drug addicts who cost more to treat and self-select the suburban professionals who will not take out very much: 'For example, a health care plan might recruit an outstanding pediatrics department, to encourage the enrollment of healthy young families, but offer a weak cardiology program, to discourage the enrollment of people with heart problems' (Enthoven, 1980: 120–21). Premises might be located in prosperous areas rather than in the slums in order to facilitate effective discrimination. The co-payments themselves might be moulded into a deterrent. A high cost-sharing ratio for insulin and syringes keeps the diabetics out.

Risk-segmentation is the rule. Low-severity patients are 'creamed'. High severity patients are 'skimped'. Very high severity patients are 'dumped' (Ellis, 1998: 538). The reason, Dowd and Feldman observe, is not the failure of the market so much as it is the ill-advised practice of imposing a standard charge: 'The true culprit in this theory is neither multiple competing health plans, nor even risk-based health plan choice.... Instead, it is the constraint, commonly imposed by both public and private purchasers, that health plans must charge the same premium to enrollees regardless of their health risk.... The problem could be solved, or at least attenuated, by allowing plans to risk-rate enrollees within a market' (Dowd and Feldman, 2006: 142). The market would become more efficient and there would be fewer uninsured rejects if the appropriate risk adjustments could be made. A fixed premium irrespective of the services provided can mean that the sum total of the coverage falls short of the social optimum. Price differentiation improves the sensitivity of the market. The downside is that beyond some trigger-price the least healthy will no longer be in a position to pay.

The membership is skewed. One inference might be that the American HMOs are abnormally cost-effective precisely because they concentrate on enrollees who are healthier than the average. The high-cost cases are dumped on the traditional insurers. They must then increase their charges in self-defence: 'Above some threshold level, the net effect of increased HMO activity is to raise traditional insurers' premiums' (Baker and Corts, 1996: 389). Baker and Corts, conducting a nationwide survey in the United States, found that adverse selection had made traditional insurance even less of a close substitute. Only in areas with less than 15 per cent HMO penetration was there any evidence of lower premiums being quoted by the traditional insurers in order to defend their market-share. As for the HMOs themselves, entry has been a mixed blessing. Competition has dented the returns of the incumbent organisations. The rate of profit declines (depending on the assumptions made) by 11.6–30.1 per cent if a new HMO enters and secures a 10 per cent market share (Pauly, Hillman, Kim and Brown, 2002: 198).

Competition protects the consumer interest. Still, however, things can go wrong. Services may converge on a standard product in order to capture the median consumer. Travelling times may reinforce the tendency towards demand-led homogeneity. Local monopoly may civilise the cutthroat rivalries. Local collusion may contain the supply of service. Pluralism is bounded. Supply continues to make its decision for demand.

At the best of times the range is limited. If the patient must select his family doctor from a closed panel, he does not have complete freedom of choice until the next annual renewal. Even, moreover, if he then migrates to a different panel, he will still only be going from one restricted subset to another. Consumer representation on the boards of the HMOs might ensure that 'voice' and not simply 'exit' is able to sensitise the organisations to the preferences of the rank-and-file. It is, however, more likely to be the case that the decisions are made by the medical professionals and the business-conscious administrators. User-opinion will be canvassed only indirectly through re-registrations, desertions, feedback and malpractice litigation.

4.3. THE STATE SECTOR

The State foregoes tax revenues when it exempts the company plan. It subsidises private hospitals where otherwise an unprofitable locality would be under-bedded and under-staffed. Most commodities in a market economy do not receive so much support. Private capitalists tend to supply the knitwear and the computer peripherals without a grant from the State. Government is not normally active in the market for car insurance or even for cover against flood. Health care, however, is different. It enjoys special treatment.

Taxes and subsidies are not thought to be enough where health care is believed to be a thing apart. The result is that the State sometimes insures and sometimes actually delivers as well. Unlike the commercial sector, it does this without regard to profit. Its shareholders are its members. Its members are its citizens. Its citizens are the club.

The first part of this section deals with the payment function. The second part examines the two-stage sequence of payment *and* provision.

4.3.1. Payment

National health insurance is widely provided by the government even where the doctors and the hospitals remain non-State and private. In some countries the word 'national' will mean what it says. Democracy will suggest the unitary command-structure of Westminster and Washington rather than cacophonous opinion-shouting of fringe and periphery. In other countries the 'national' element will be decentralised and devolved. Different provinces and different towns will be given every encouragement to put flesh on their different preferences. Always, however, it is State and not market that collects the subscriptions and reimburses the costs.

(a)   The self-funding system

Contributions to fully-funded insurance are hypothecated and earmarked. There is no Exchequer grant in aid. Although tripartism is excluded, bipartism is common. Here the employee and the employer each puts in a contribution, frequently identical. The employer's contribution, as always, cannot be regarded as a net increase in compensation: 'The "employer's share" of payment for a job-related fringe benefit eventually reduces worker money wages spendable on other things by approximately the amount of the payment' (Pauly, 1994b: 47). It may not be new money but at least it is high-powered money. It is diverted from general consumption and made sector-specific to health. The employer's contribution ceases when the worker retires or is made redundant. Children, housewives, the unemployed and the self-employed have no employer. They may be required to put in double contributions of their own in order to ensure that the other members of the fund are not short-changed.

Rigorously self-supporting, the fund is outside politics. Separate and transparent accounts ensure that politicians cannot redeploy funds meant for health into marginal constituencies or national defence. They cannot run a budget deficit to finance short-run consumables which in the long-run will be a charge on the future. The most they can do is to commit in perpetuity a 'sin-tax' such as a tobacco excise to the health care fund. Non-fungibility is a constitutional bulwark against discretion and piecemeal interference. What is political are the rules of the game. Will the cover be compulsory or optional? Which services will be eligible? Can the fund dispense with co-payments? Will top-ups be allowed to supplement the basic cover?

A pool that is regional or national is non-discriminatory and even-handed. The premiums follow the actuarial values on a basis that is (age-adjusted) strictly geographical. Contributions, averaged out across the whole, automatically reflect the cross-subsidy granted by the good risks to the infirm. They are representative precisely because the legislators normally select open enrolment with community rating in preference to selective enrolment experience-rated down to the level of the individual applicant. The anomaly that is thereby corrected is described by Cutler in the following words: 'At most one-quarter of the difference between high and low plan is due to differences in the generosity of the benefits. The remainder is due to the demographic and health status of the group being insured. Moving towards "community rating" – charging everyone the same rate or rates based only on age and location – is a feature of most reform proposals' (Cutler, 1994: 19).

Differentiation can be a function of age profile or non-average local costs. It can also be a consequence of differences in tastes and preferences. Some areas may decide to charge higher premiums for more comprehensive entitlements. Other areas may feel that a basic package is all that they need. Insurance in the State sector cannot afford to neglect the social implications of these choices. High premiums impose a disproportionate burden on the poor. The ability to put up subscriptions weakens the resistance to cost-care inflation. Democratic as it will be, the central government is obliged by its mandate to keep all the spillovers under review. A cap on the level or rate of change of premiums is one avenue that it might explore. The danger is that a ceiling might trigger a reduction in quantity and quality. Clients will not be satisfied if premiums have to be kept constant but availability must then be rationed.

Hypothecation could mean a uniform lump-sum. Like the dog licence or the congestion charge, such a fee is fixed per poll. The community rate interpreted as a per capita overhead does not vary with earnings any more than it does with health. This means that it is regressive. It is a higher percentage of a lower income.

Hypothecation can be a one-price entry ticket. It can, however, also be made a function of income. Proportional charging would be the more neutral way of making Penthouse and Yacht pay more than Bangers and Mash. Proportionality means that the ticket would cost a constant percentage of any income. The rate is the same but the absolute amounts are income-linked. A maximum income could be specified lest employers find the payroll component prohibitive. A maximum would also ensure that beneficiaries would not accumulate a wall of money that could feed through into care-cost inflation.

More discriminatory than proportional would be progressive hypothecation. Using income tax codes as the means-test that streams, such earmarking would not just redistribute from the healthy to the ill but from the prosperous to the deprived. Perhaps there will be a ceiling at which health-related contributions are capped. Perhaps there will be a floor below which the desperate will not have to contribute at all. Within those bounds, there is no technical reason why earmarked payments cannot also have the equalising, levelling bias that is one of the great selling-points of a State-run system. Solidarity is Good Samaritanship and social-ism is altruism scaled up to the whole. As Aneurin Bevan once said, looking back on the first decade of the British National Health Service: 'The redistributive aspect of the scheme was one which attracted me almost as much as the therapeutical.... What more pleasure can a millionaire have than to know that his taxes will help the sick?' (Bevan, 1958: Col. 1389).

(b) The tax-subsidised model

A second model of State insurance would rely, as before, on contributions. These, as before, could be either lump-sum or income-related. Crucially, however, the second model would dispense with the idea of a self-funding pool.

General taxation supplements the subscriptions. The earmarked component might end up merely as a token and a symbol.

Progressive income tax tracks the ability to pay. Assuming that rising personal income yields diminishing marginal utility, it makes perceived sacrifice more equal across the income brackets. Where the rates of personal tax rise steeply and the rich pay in graduated bands, the argument is that one citizen is assisting another and that the rich are assisting the rest of us most.

It is, however, a mistake to assume that all public finance is raised through the personal income tax. Value-added tax, the excise duty, the annual property tax, the road fund levy are all public burdens which fall proportionately more heavily on the lower-income groups. Estate duties, marginal rates, corporate tax, tax shelters, fiscal thresholds, capital gains taxes, mortgage interest relief, personal allowances, taxes on imputed income from owner-occupied dwellings will all have an impact on the *overall* and the *net*. So will tax rebates for the old, tax deductions for the ill and tax exemptions for basic necessities consumed disproportionately by lowest income-deciles. Taxation is a mish-mash and a mix. Adding up the various types of toll, Phelps Brown in the United Kingdom decided that the bias in each direction was likely to cancel the other out: 'Taxation, when the direct and indirect forms are taken together, does little to change relative incomes' (Phelps Brown, 1988: 331).

The same neutrality has been found in the United States, where Pechman and Okner felt that taxes as a whole were 'virtually proportional for the vast majority of families': 'Under the most progressive set of assumptions ... taxes reduce income inequality by less than 5 percent; under the least progressive assumptions ... income inequality is reduced by only about 0.25 per cent' (Pechman and Okner, 1974: 64). Pechman made the assumption that corporation tax and property tax are borne by the owners of capital while the incidence of the payroll tax is shifted on to the workforce. This led him to the conclusion that the redistribution was there but that it was slight: 'I believe that the US system has been progressive in recent years, but the degree of progression is very mild.... The tax system has relatively little effect on the distribution of income' (Pechman, 1986: 2, 39). The poor are not soaking the rich. The rich are not soaking the poor. No one in fact, is doing much soaking at all.

Any calculation is necessarily rough, and the net balance will alter year-on-year with each successive budget. Roach, who agrees with Pechman that there is currently a small element of redistribution, sees the bias as a leaf blown about in the wind: 'Overall, right now the U.S. tax system is slightly progressive. The progressiveness of the U.S. tax system in 2000 was at a similar level to that during the 1970s.... Even this small degree of progressiveness could be eliminated from the U.S. tax system in the future. Making state or federal social insurance taxes more regressive, or making the federal income tax less progressive, could be sufficient to make the entire U.S. tax system regressive' (Roach, 2003: 19).

The future is not likely to see a fiscal revolution. Even proportional taxation, however, will appeal more strongly to a collectivist than would lump-sum charges and premiums which by definition make private insurance regressive and skewed. It must also be remembered that the overall proportionality of a tax system as a whole refers only to the *rate* at which the tax is levied. The *amount* actually paid in tax will be greater the more the individual taxpayer ultimately earns and spends. To that extent it will still be the rich who put in the lion's share.

(c) Compulsion and freedom

The extent of the fiscal redistribution is a matter for debate. The medical redistribution, on the other hand, is clear enough. The healthy pay the cross-subsidy. The unhealthy take out more than they contribute. This is always the case in an insurance club. The difference in the case of State insurance is that the pool is the nation. The truth is the whole.

Yet there is a condition. For the insurance pool to be all-inclusive and all-embracing, there must be a Berlin Wall to lock in the citizens. The good risks cannot be allowed to opt out into a more attractive commercial alternative. Otherwise adverse selection would mean that only the medical catastrophes and the permanent loss-makers would remain behind. The multiple pool system stratifies the premiums and the packages. The national insurance system means that the assets and the liabilities are the same. Compulsion is freedom. Without the closed door national insurance would be only one insurance policy among many. It is the mandatory element in national health insurance that makes it unique.

Universal coverage, because no one is left out, is the embodiment at once of the caring externality and the self-regarding stake. The unemployed, the aged, the chronically ill all know that they do not have to rely on the safety-net of charity since as citizens they share in the common guarantee of *as much* and *as good*. The young and the robust are given the reassurance that they would not be shamed and stigmatised if disaster struck and they sank into the medically indigent. A State system does not exclude applicants on the basis of their current health status. It is more likely to credit in the genuinely deprived even when they have failed to pay their contributions or their taxes. It is a source of great reassurance. Mandated national insurance is always there. Our nation as a pool is our port in a storm.

National insurance allows professionals to concentrate on medicine without having to ask themselves if the destitute will ever pay. Contagious diseases are less likely to spread since patients who may have been exposed are less reluctant to see a doctor. Workers become occupationally more mobile since they are not held back from a productivity-enhancing change by job-lock, an occupational plan and non-portable cover. Social integration is promoted. Rich and poor, men and women, sneezing and non-sneezing all carry in their wallet or bag the same certificate promising the same entitlement. Even a Berlin Wall has its benefits as well as its costs.

Economically, big, it is often said, is more efficient than small. Large numbers and identical contributions mean economies of scale in respect of computer time, billing and administration. The marketing overheads of zero-sum competitiveness are eliminated. Investment portfolios become more balanced since the large pool makes it easier to predict claims. The sheer size of the fund gives it countervailing power in the negotiation of fees with doctors, hospitals and other providers.

Non-State entrants and innovators do not stand a chance against so popular, so economical a Berlin Wall. Nor should it be forgotten that, save where the fund is strictly hypothecated, the subsidy to the State monopoly is bound to be large and increasing. Impatient voters do not pay dividends to prudent leaders who say that the budget allows them no scope for supplementation.

The blankness of the cheque should not be exaggerated. Democracy does presuppose a certain amount of maturity and responsibility on the part of strong-willed politicians who want not just to win elections but to do a good job. It also assumes that there is an opposition party and a free press: they will alert the nation to the dangers of overspending by vote-buyers who promise more than the nation can afford. Yet the danger is there. A national insurance fund supported out of public revenues is a hostage to the political business cycle, the vote motive and the medical mystique. A national insurance fund that adopts the self-funding system will at least be insulated against the hidden expansionism of practical politics. The rule in hypothecated health care financing is that more must be put in if more is to be taken out. It is a safeguard against weak leaders. It might also leave the insurance fund too under-resourced to do its job.

A compulsory, comprehensive national insurance fund could be a cause of moral hazard. The feckless can take chances with their health since the entitlement, citizenship-based, can with difficulty be withdrawn. The lazy can go in for unemployment and malingering since national heath insurance is not bought through a consistent contributions record. A social consensus committed to a health care minimum is a target for abuse on the part of rational cost-minimisers who know that their fellow citizens will not allow them to die on the streets. Few threats are more challenging to the self-image of the social democrat than is that of the Atomic Bum when, wrapping himself in explosives, this blackmailing Bad Samaritan shouts 'Your money or *my* life'. National insurance is forever at risk from the feckless and the lazy who think that a decent commons can always support a few more sheep. Making the insurance mandatory will make it more difficult to travel free. When all is said and done, however, the Atomic Bum has got us dead to rights and there is not a lot that we can do.

4.3.2.   Payment *and* Provision

National insurance pays for medical attention. It contracts for health care services but it does not deliver them. A more ambitious national system is one that expands into delivery as well. In the private sector the prepaid plan undertakes the double function of budget-holding and purchasing. In the State sector too the same unified structure can be erected. The agency that pays can become the agency that provides.

It is a two-pronged attack. Demand and supply, finance and attention, become integrated in a single national bureaucracy. So huge will the monolith be that it is often divided up into regional health authorities. Even where the parts compete with each other for clients, still they are unmistakeably State. The State holds the property rights. The State determines the allocations. The State issues the guidelines. Top-down is *de rigeur*. It has to be. A National Health Service is a *national* health service. It is not cut off and separate like the private sector's HMOs.

In the case of pure national insurance the individual amasses claims which can be exchanged for medical services. Whether he has full freedom of choice or must select from a panel, there is no expectation that he will seek treatment in the public system. In the case of a National Health Service, he must. The reason is that treatment is free at the point of consumption. Purchase and delivery come already mixed. The entitlement is double. The two parts cannot be unstitched.

The service is provided in kind. It is, for economic and ethical reasons, a standardised one. The assumption is made that wants and needs are tolerably clustered around the mean. If the agreement is there, it might not be a violation of utility-maximisation for the service to be off-the-peg, subsidised and distributed without a user-charge. If there is dispersion, however, it might make more sense for discrete consumers to engage their own suppliers and for the national insurance fund passively to reimburse the cost. As David Collard writes: 'If consensus is pretty close (as was assumed at the time the NHS was set up) one might as well adopt the consensus allocation straight away on a "free" basis.... The less consensus or agreement there is, the more pressure there is to move from "free" provision to market prices' (Collard, 1978: 138).

Consensus is not easy to measure. Yet it is central to any discussion of the purchase-*and*-provision model. Economies of scale are all very well if they give the consumer what he wants. Long production runs are less attractive if the consumer values diversity and choice as ends in themselves, or wants a product other than the homogeneous service that the system provides. People are different. Yet there are limits to the diversity that a National Health Service can offer without sacrificing the very gains that are such a strong argument for conformity, uniformity and coordination. Henry Ford promised the motorist a Ford car of any colour he liked so long as it was black. Galbraith, referring to central planning and not to corporate capitalism, made the same observation: 'This may be the problem of socialism. Planners can provide for everything but color' (Galbraith, 1958: 28).

Much depends on what people expect. A national health system might meet the urgent needs of most people in a poorer society. It might find it more difficult to meet the discretionary wants of the multiple lifestyles that are the byproducts of individualism and development. Pluralism, devolution and autonomy are likely to have a high income elasticity. If they do, then the same pressures that led to market capitalism in the previously communist countries might lead to market capitalism in the national health service. Buchanan has predicted that the failure of national planning will also mean the victory of decentralisation and factoring-down: 'If socialism fails in the large it also fails in the small' (Buchanan, 1990: 23). Yet it might not be so. Different sectors might be subject to different laws of motion. What is true of Ford cars need not be true of health.

Especially is this true since the national health service has a social as well as an economic maximand. Socially, it is expected to provide a common experience that will give citizens from all backgrounds the feeling of national integration and an interlocking fate. Irrespective of colour, class or income group, citizens have adjacent beds and see the same surgeon. Togetherness and belonging triumph. Alienation and segregation are driven to the wall. The fact that some citizens will not want this kind of smothering togetherness is only a footnote in the work of social engineers and nation-builders who believe that viable collaboration presupposes a certain degree of cultural overlap. Such thinkers assign pride of place to social infrastructure like common language, common education and common health. These, they say, are the shared foundation upon which the Babel of business can later be built.

That is why the national health system must not be confused with the residual-supplier model. The National Health Service is not just a charity hospital to which only the hard cases will have recourse. The residual-supplier model is more Dickensian. It is payment-*and*-provision, but only for the absolutely deprived.

The State system in such a case will be a safety net and no more. The picture is easy enough to sketch. The destitute have no money. The abandoned need medical attention. The charitable State donates free-on-demand care. It opens up its soup kitchen because it wants all citizens and residents to reach a minimum level of decent life.

The outsiders might be the uninsurable: words like 'chronic' and 'catastrophic' cause markets to shut or premiums to shoot up. Affordability is a barrier: the unemployed, the retired, the part-time and the poor will often find it impossible to pay for such insurance as they can get. New immigrants will not have occupational plans. Single parents will no longer have the shelter of a former partner's policy. Even a national insurance system might fail those who cannot keep up the contributions. In such circumstances the State might have to correct the market failure because it is the last resort and no one else will.

Safety-net provision can be basic and no-frills. Where the society regards those unwilling to achieve and unable to save as indolent pariahs who have defaulted on the work ethic of personal responsibility and earned reward, it may take the opportunity to inflict stigma, to spoil identity, precisely because shame is part of the system. Where, however, the society is more tolerant towards those made medically indigent by a crippling disease or a long-term loss of employment, the concept of contributory negligence will not be invoked and the needy will not be dismissed as idle scroungers who ought to have planned ahead. A society that has made up its mind not to judge will offer something better than the basic minimum to all the celebrants in its community precisely because we as an articulated symbiosis have a common need to care. It is one of the advantages of the National Health Service that no one knows who has money and who came in off the streets. Clients share the same wards. They receive the same treatment. The sheep are not separated from the goats. Manager or worker, stockbroker or vagrant, no one is an outsider when the gloves go on and the needles come out.

4.4. PAYMENT BEYOND INSURANCE

Not all of health care is paid for out of a prearranged indemnity. There are other ways in which the patient can find the funds.

First and foremost, there is out-of-pocket. Here the patient remunerates the supplier out of current income, as he would do if he were buying any other market durable. Not every part of the medical encounter involves a CAT scan or a double bypass. Most people who are in work can afford to pay for a practitioner-consultation or to obtain a routine drug on prescription. In some countries user charges represent the major source of income for a doctor or clinic. Some of the charges are unofficial and illegal. Yet people do pay, and not from insurance.

Interpersonal transfers also contribute to the cost of care. Textbook economics maximises its utility on the basis of an isolated individual, absolutely on his own. The real world is more of a web. Many patients have friends and neighbours, workmates and fellow worshippers, parents and children to whom they can turn. Some people have a dense family network. Their extended degrees of kinship will reliably rally round.

Stranger gifts are a further source of support. Churches and charities provide money to cover medical bills. Doctors practise price discrimination when they learn that their patient is living in a shack. They often quote lower fees in Watts than at their branch in Beverly Hills. They often give a discount where the patient has no insurance. In extreme cases they will not charge at all. Doctors, like the rest of us, have a conscience. Their altruism is an inter-personal transfer which helps the patient to get well.

An employer will sometimes include care reimbursement as a fringe benefit. In such a case, typically in place of full health insurance, the employer will refund a certain amount of health-related expenditure each year. An alternative will be for the employer to offer a free-on-demand works clinic on the premises. This reduces travelling time and absence from work. It protects value-added and the throughput of the firm. It also ensures that the employee gets basic care without having to pay.

Savings are a further source of funds. For most people insurance is money paid for peace of mind. The same peace of mind might be purchased if the precautionary premium were invested in the stock market or placed in a high-interest account. Savings are a cushion upon which the individual can draw in time of adversity. Money held idle for a rainy day can be used to pay for health.

The Government, realising this, will sometimes opt not just for mandatory savings but for mandatory *medical* savings. Such medical savings accounts (called MSAs) could be voluntary. It is more effective for them to be compulsory. If they were opt-in, they would be chosen only by the healthy while the unhealthy would prefer generous insurance policies save where the premiums fully reflected their abnormal need. To avoid adverse selection, subscription to the MSAs will often be made citizenship-wide. In such a scenario the individual is obliged to set aside a percentage of his income every month. The funds are held by a commercial bank or a State-run agency. The interest they earn is often tax-free. Often a high-deductible catastrophic insurance policy can be purchased with the funds in the MSA. Once the deductible is met, the cost-sharing bias of an MSA-funded insurance policy is no different from any other third-party plan.

An MSA can only be withdrawn for approved, health-related expenditures. The individual and the family choose the provider for themselves. In that sense the model is the market. MSA holders have an incentive to shop cost-consciously to secure a competitive deal. The assumption is made that they have enough information to make a sensible choice. MSA holders also have an incentive to keep their health capital in good condition. Preventive care is economic. Account-holders do not want to deplete the savings which no one but the owner and later his legatees can touch.

MSA balances are savings and not insurance. There is no cross-subsidy within the pool. The rich will normally accumulate more than the poor. There is only a modest administrative overhead. There is no Exchequer top-up apart from any tax revenues foregone. No one can take out more than he has put in (Reisman, 2006). Within those parameters, the savings can build up quite rapidly. A healthy old person might be health-savings-rich but disposable-income-poor. But at least the money is there if there is a medical need.

5. The value of life

Medicine is about the quantity and quality of human life. Economics is about the dispassionate comparison of the costs and benefits. There is little love lost between the two disciplines. There was little love there in the first place.

In terms of ethics, there is an instinctive revulsion towards any policy that would reduce the sanctity of human life to pecuniary measurement and the rate of return. Life is the fulfilment of potential. Life is a human right. Policymakers, however, must live in the real world. Resources are finite and priorities must be assigned: 'Choices *must* be made and every choice necessarily reflects a set of values. These values underlie all implicit and explicit weighing of costs and benefits. Because resources are scarce relative to wants, we do not have the option of evaluating or not evaluating. The only option is whether to evaluate explicitly, systematically, and openly, as economics forces us to do, or whether to evaluate implicitly, haphazardly, and secretly, as has been done so often in the past' (Fuchs, 1983: 48). No decent person would say that economic trade-offs should be the only criteria. What most decent people would, however, say is that more information rather than less is essential if a democratic society is to get the policy-mix that best suits its tastes and preferences.

This chapter is concerned with the economic value of a human life. It follows the three groupings that were identified in chapter 3 to show that to satisfy Jack will often be to disappoint Jill. The bulk of Viscusi's estimates of the value of human life lie in the range from $3 million to $7 million but there is no obvious value that is 'right'. Aeroplane cabin fire protection costs $200 000 per statistical life saved; car side-door protection $1.3 million; asbestos regulations $104.2 million; gold-standard formaldehyde containment $72 billion (Viscusi, 1993: 1913). Choices *must* be made. That's the way it is in a fallen world where one kidney-transplant can cost the investment needed to sustain the jobs of 30 marginalised labourers and where expensive diagnostic scans can price deprived children out of free school milk.

5.1. THE PATIENT

Each consumer is an individual, a discrete subjectivity with a non-standard window on the world. Perception and self-perception mean that the unique client holds an opinion that cannot be reduced to objective medical parameters alone. The one-off bodyholder alone is in a position to know if extra life years accompanied by anxiety, pain and disability are genuinely preferable to premature death; or if unpleasant and risky treatments are really worth the putative outcomes; or if the fear of side-effects such as blindness, fatigue, nausea, incontinence or paralysis is greater than the attraction of a 65 per cent probability of full recovery. The doctor knows the statistical risks and the success-rates. The patient alone, however, can say what marginal life-years of varying quality will mean to the thinking subject of a life-or-death decision. That is why the morbidity and mortality tables must be complemented by information on the patient's own ranking of what he regards as right for himself alone.

5.1.1. Induction and Extrapolation

Market economics as a subject devotes considerable attention to marginal expenditure exchanged for incremental service. Revealed preference is taken to be the observable manifestation of consumer sovereignty and respect for persons. The same emphasis on devolution and decentralisation can be carried over from the market for fruit or meat into the market for gold fillings, weekend surgery, home deliveries and other health care services. The value of life is only one of many estimates that can be said to bubble up when people quantify the strength of their preference through the alternative benefits they are just willing to forego.

Life is not an economic tradeable. In that sense one may speak of a missing market that can only be tracked by its shadow. The demand schedule for health care is different. It is observed in a number of areas in the broad medical experience. A fixed fee for a drug leaves the patient free to determine the number of units he wants to consume. Stopping where he does, he is putting a value on the quantity of healthiness that he can afford. Negatively speaking, the refusal of expensive treatment or even the purchase of poison are ways in which the patient expresses the view that he has decided to reject what he believes to be a substandard existence. One reason might be that he ranks more highly than his life the bequest that he passes on to his heirs. In cases such as these the decision-maker is unwrapping the contents of his mind. He is signalling through his market responses what he thinks his own life is worth.

Induction and extrapolation are procedures that the economist can use to learn what private individuals really think. Even so, observation need not be a reliable tool. An obvious shortcoming will be the nature of the sample. One investigator studies the money–risk trade-off of young people living in a slum. Another investigator assesses the manifest preferences of old-age pensioners suffering from an incurable disease. A third investigator visits non-smoking, non-drinking clerks who repeatedly wash their hands, cut the fat off their meat and reduce

road-risks by walking to work. Which group, if any, throws up the more representative value? Which group, if any, expresses the median attitude that can be scaled up to pinpoint the proper cut-off for chemotherapy or to define the minimum safety standards needed to protect a toddler from a toy? Comparison and aggregation of utility are never very easy. Interpersonal valuation is that much more unreliable where the sample is divided into subgroups and not all people want the same thing.

Insurance complicates the interpretation of real-world choices. Willingness to pay will only approximate the intensity of desire where the individual himself is buying the extra satisfaction with his own extra sacrifice. Sacrifice prepaid through an insurance pool incorporates an incentive to overconsume since the consumer is not responding rationally to the economist's full price. The *quid pro quo* where payment is reimbursed does not constitute the same authentic metric that it would if the entire burden had to be supported out-of-pocket. Payment aside, there is also moral hazard. People with cover take risks that they would not have taken if they were uninsured. Their behaviour-patterns are altered by their insurance. The measured value of life is not the same.

Because insurance distorts the information, there is an argument for drawing policy-inferences exclusively from those who must pay the full cost themselves. Deductibles and thresholds are not enough. Deterrent and disincentive though they may be, they are less than 100 per cent. They are therefore not high enough to permit a direct estimation of how much the consumer actually values the intervention. Better information will be that collected where the consumer is uninsured. Such a sample is not, however, likely to be representative. The uninsured do not have insurance for a reason. Whether because of a high tolerance of risk, an uninsurable condition or a serious inability to pay, the danger is that they will be atypical exceptions who are not indicative of the mainstream. Policymakers would be making a mistake to estimate the value of life-saving interventions from the nature of care purchased only by the marginal and the fringe.

Extrapolation of the value of life from revealed preference is subject to a further difficulty. Faced with the choice of 'your money or your life', there is only one maximum that would logically be articulated by a life-lover who does not want to die. That one value would be all that he can pay. Assuming that he has no suicidal tendencies, assuming further that his decision-making horizon does not extend to a legacy for his heirs, there would be no reason for him to call a halt. Once the consumer has learned that he is under sentence of death, he will spend an infinite amount, up to the point where he exhausts his resources. A dead man cannot shop. In the words of E.J. Mishan: 'In ordinary circumstances, no sum of money is large enough to compensate a man for the loss of his life.... If, in ordinary circumstances, we face a person with the choice of continuing his life in the usual way or of ending it at noon the next day, a sum large enough to persuade him to choose the latter course of action may not exist' (Mishan, 1971: 693). This infinite valuation makes it impossible to put a price on a human life. An economic society, taking infinite to mean what it says, would have therefore to put all of its resources into the preservation of life. It would have to cut back altogether on the alternative claims to its national stock of wealth.

Certainty makes it impossible to assign a finite number to the value of life. Uncertainty, however, puts teeth into bottom-up consultation. Citizens who do not know what they will require must act on probabilities. Those probabilities allow the observer to calculate the maximum that the typical citizen would pay for life-enhancing intervention. Knowledge of the named life that must be saved forces policy down the road that leads to the infinite. Jim Jones, personalised through a photograph with his daughter and a puppy, is a castaway somewhere in the Pacific or an astronaut stranded in space. Probability, on the other hand, combines citizen consultation with the need to allocate finite resources in ways that do not stop short at life-saving intervention alone. We do not build the sea-wall despite the 10 per cent chance that 150 lives will be lost in a typhoon. We have decided to spend our money on chocolates instead.

Drawing aside the veil of unknowledge is not just to permit economising but also to encourage special pleading. Philosophy might suggest that life itself be given an absolute and lexicographic priority. Economics, however, would deny that any asset can be beyond price and next-best foregone. Overriding all is practical politics. What politicians know all too well is that agreement without the Rawlsian veil can be very difficult to secure. To assign an unchallengeable supremacy to the beating heart is to ring-fence the needs of the seriously ill but also to starve out the thriving and the glowing who want not just life but a good life as well. The healthy demand schools for their children. The frightened demand street lighting and police. The sickly demand cardiopulmonary resuscitation because lives must be saved. A pluralistic democracy must ensure that it does not scale up from the needs of only one of its groupings lest it produce a value of life that deviates significantly from the attitudes of the whole. Dissensus is a great obstacle to the derivation of the value of life from a single subsample alone.

That is the attraction of probability. While people might know their present wants and even their needs, the future is a *tabula rasa*. The willingness to pay cannot be infinite where people do not know what they will one day require. Thick Rawlsian ignorance may be a fiction but uncertainty about the course of history-to-come is a fact of life. Everyone dies of something. Will it be cancer or lead-poisoning or a heart attack not treated in time? Probability allows people to say what value they are willing to place not on a named, familiar human life but on a *statistical* life, a random and unknowable life that may or may not be their own. The focus shifts from the known to the possible. The value of life becomes an economic matter of extra payment in exchange for an expected diminution in risk. As Blomquist writes: 'Value of life is the marginal value of a change in risk of death. It can be interpreted as an individual's value of a small change in his own probability of survival or alternatively as an individual's value of saving the life of an unidentifiable person in a large group to which the individual belongs' (Blomquist, 1982: 37n).

Probability shifts the focus from the actual (the *ex post*) to the expected (the *ex ante*). Making the discussion a topic in the imagined rather than the factual, it is tempting to say that what is being measured is the value of the risk of dying and not the value of a human life at all. Life is Jim Jones's life when he knows with 100 per cent certainty that a blood transfusion has left him with HIV. Life is less convincingly a 5 per cent probability of being crushed by a cheaply-constructed building that collapses in an earthquake.

John Broome takes the view that it would be murder to act on the basis of the 5 per cent rather than the 100 per cent since life is life whichever way it is interpreted: 'It does not seem correct to distinguish in value between the death of a known person and of an unknown person' (Broome, 1978: 94). Hypothetically, one could downgrade the known life to the value of the anonymous statistic. Broome would prefer to upgrade the unnamed contingency to the value of the family friend. It cannot be morally right, he says, to value a human life differently before and after the same person is known to be suffering from a life-threatening disease. His recommendation is confidently utilitarian: the greatest number of survivals is the welcome result of the injunction to love one's neighbour as oneself. On the other hand, it is also expensive. The value of life is infinite again.

Broome's counsel of perfection does not leave room for actuarial economising in a second-best environment where resources are scarce. Nor does it adequately acknowledge the way in which real-world individuals actually conceptualise their life. Buchanan and Faith have this to say about Broome-type objective circumstances that make no allowance for the subjective perceptions of the individuals when they made their choice: 'To say that "costs" are infinite for the person who loses his life in the draw of a lottery in which he rationally chooses to participate is to say nothing at all about the *value* that such an individual placed on life in the moment at which the choice was made. These ex post "costs" can, in no way, influence the choice behavior that created the consequences' (Buchanan and Faith, 1979: 246). The gambler stakes his money on a horse and the speculator takes a view on the probable fluctuations in equities and bonds. A lifeholder is doing nothing different when he chooses a short-cut down a dark alley where dogs with rabies are known to lurk.

The choice made is the estimator of life as seen by the lifeholders who own the pulse. What happens then is only the unfolding of a historical skein that the individuals *when making the choice* knew that they could not precisely predict.

Broome ran together the *was* and the *is*. That was his mistake: 'The central flaw in his whole argument lies in a misunderstanding of *cost*. When does any attempt to *value* life arise for an individual or for a collectivity? Only when a *choice* is confronted does a valuation process become necessary. And only when choice is confronted is opportunity cost meaningful' (Buchanan and Faith, 1979: 245; original emphasis). *Ex post* is a game for historians. *Ex ante* is what real-world men and women actually do. The government would do well to follow the example of their constituents and not that of the philosophers who stand apart.

The *ex ante* approach is the approach that most ordinary people adopt. What this means is that the willingness to pay should be interpreted not so much as the payment for care as the payment for the *probability* of care that is the entry-ticket to the *probability* of survival. Jones-Lee and his colleagues sum up the position well: 'Briefly, the fundamental premises of the willingness-to-pay approach are (a) that social decisions should, so far as possible, reflect the interests, preferences and attitudes to risk of those who are likely to be affected by the decisions and (b) that in the case of safety, these interests, preferences and attitudes are most effectively summarised in terms of the amounts that individuals would be willing to pay or would require in compensation for (typically small) changes in the probability of death or injury during a forthcoming period. Consequently, the willingness-to-pay approach tends to be concerned principally with individual marginal rates of substitution of wealth for risk of death or for risk of injury' (Jones-Lee, Hammerton and Philips, 1985: 49).

It is all the willingness to pay. Yet there are different approaches and different proxies. The result is that there are different values. The next three sections examine the three principal options: questionnaires and surveys, safety and security and differential remuneration. It is not easy in the circumstances to recognise the *true* value of a statistical life. Melinek used a sample survey and found that it was £80000. Portney, working from the house price/air pollution trade-off, estimated that it was £150000. Olson, using compensating wage differentials, made it £5260000 (quoted in Jones-Lee, 1989: 91, 93). A government must do its best. Sometimes, however, it is not clear if the correct value for it to adopt is £50000, or £400000, or £11700000; or what discount rate is the appropriate one; or whether the valuation should reflect the mean of the distribution or its median; or whether American data should be employed in non-American policymaking; or how quickly the results are left behind by inflation, *ceteris paribus*, and fickle public opinion. One consequence is that policymakers are reluctant to put too much faith in a number that might be wrong.

The ideal of the democrat and the economic liberal is to build up an image of the value of life from the representative citizen's current preferences and practices. Translating the ideal into concrete social policy is more difficult. Is a human life worth £50000, or £400000 or £11700000? Which of the many alternatives is the right one? Philosophy is about principles and economics is about choice. Politics, however, is about action. It is very difficult for the State to act on the basis of a *true* value of life when in society there may not be a consensus on what it is.

5.1.2. Questionnaires and Surveys

The *ex ante* approach requires a good knowledge of what real-world people really think. The problem is that the contents of people's minds are not directly observable. There is no sophisticated polygraph that can measure the relevant brainwaves. People's willingness to pay must in the circumstances be estimated either from their words or from their deeds. The proxies are not the same as the substance. The alternative, however, is to dispense altogether with methodological individualism. So long as the observer insists that the individual alone has a right to put an economic value on a human life, so long as the assumption may be made that people are alert enough to articulate a valid preference, the top-down pronouncement will not be an acceptable choice. Ordinary people, if they are tolerably rational, must be listened to with respect.

Questionnaires and surveys are one way of getting at the contents of the invisible mind. To do this, a sample must be identified that will be representative of the surrounding population. The most relevant attributes are likely to be age, gender, education, occupation, income and wealth (the last-named often flagged up by the ownership of a car or house). The mix cancels out the dispersion. Young people think less about old age than old people do even if the same young people will think more about old age as they themselves progress further through their own life cycle.

Allowance must be made for health status. Those already suffering from a life-threatening condition will not be detached or impartial. Response rates can distort the finding. Where the candidates who reply do so because they are abnormally committed to good health, the result might be to bias upward the financial value of life. Sample size is relevant. The cross-section must be large enough to be free from selection bias. It cannot, however, be too large as then the study would be too costly and take too long. Different types of respondents will react differently to different kinds of risks. All of this makes the sampling of attitudes a minefield of ambiguities. Policymakers must keep their ear to the ground. They do not want, however, to copy the tail because they mistakenly assume that the tail is the dog.

The collection of information can be approached in a variety of ways. Sometimes the inquiry will be direct and transparent. Here the respondents will be asked to state the maximum sum they would be prepared to part with to reduce the chance of death by a specified percentage. Sometimes the respondents will be prompted by means of a story. They might be asked how much extra they would pay to upgrade to an airline with a better safety record, or to install air bags and a collapsible steering column in their car, or to dispense with cheap nuclear fuel from a reactor that might or might not melt down. Altering the focus from payment to remuneration, they might be asked how much money they would just expect to receive in order to agree to a small increase in the risk of death. They might be asked to name the bribe they would accept to allow toxic landfill producing radon gas to be situated near their home. There is a reference point and a final destination. The consumers put a value on the compensation that would make them feel neither better off nor worse off in their own estimation.

Some investigations give the subject a proposition and ask for reactions to be quantified on an interval-scale going from 0 to 10: while the rankings may be interpersonally comparable, it might be more difficult to determine the equivalence of the passions captured by a '3' or a '9'. Some investigations make a sophisticated distinction between the immediate and the deferred: a study produces different values if the damage is bang-bang (a car crash due to a substandard clutch) or drip-feed (leukaemia in later life caused by earlier exposure to benzene in fuel). No two investigations are precisely the same. What is constant is the object of the exercise. Questionnaires and surveys seek to tease out the marginal rate of substitution of resourcing for (the probability of) death that ordinary men and women hold in their minds in an imperfect world where some risk will always be there. The value once quantified, public policy will then be in a position to infer how much the people want to plunge into heart-transplants and well-patrolled underpasses, even at the expense of old-age pensions and subsidised research.

Consider the democratic benchmark of US\$28 000. This is the implicit value of a human life that was calculated by Acton (Acton, 1973: ix) based on a survey he conducted in Boston. Acton surveyed 93 Bostonians: the group, ranging from unionists to executives, broadly paralleled the income bands. He told his subjects that for the purposes of his study they should assume the probability of a heart attack to be 1/100 (0.01) and the probability of a heart attack proving fatal to be 2/5 (0.40). He then asked them how much they would be just willing to pay for a programme (such as an air-ambulance service or a mobile cardiac unit) that would reduce from 2/5 to 1/5 (0.20) the likelihood that the heart attack would be followed by death. The average sum quoted was \$56. Acton's focus was on a single, named reduction in risk. A different value might have been quoted had the base level of risk been different. As the chance of death without the intervention was (0.01)(0.40) and the chance of death following the improvement in policy was (0.01)(0.20), Acton was able to calculate the ratio of the extra cost (\$56) to the extra benefit (the reduction in the risk of death from 0.004 to 0.002, namely 0.002). He then solved for the economic value of an average human life. It turned out to be a rather low \$56/0.002 = \$28 000.

Questionnaires can pick up magnitudes such as $56. Interestingly, they can pick up supplementary details as well. An example would be the 37-question study conducted by Jones-Lee and his colleagues of 1103 people in Britain (Jones-Lee, Hammerton and Philips, 1985). The interviewers found, using the example of a safety feature costing £50 that halved the risk of loss of life to 5/100 000, that the implicit value of life was approximately £1 million. They also found, however, that the respondents were not indifferent to the mode of death. Financial implications held constant, when asked to say which of three forms of death they most wanted to see reduced, 11 per cent cited death in a car accident, 13 per cent said death from heart disease, and 76 per cent said death from cancer.

One death is evidently not the same as another. A study by Jones-Lee shows that the willingness to pay to avert a disaster in the London Underground is 50 per cent higher than the willingness to pay to reduce road fatalities by an equivalent number. A study by Tolley shows that citizens as a community are willing to pay $2 million to avoid an instant death but $4 million to avoid a death from lung cancer. A study by Pearce shows that people are willing to pay a high premium to reduce the risk of a Chernobyl-like nuclear disaster – and 25 per cent below the statistical odds to prevent fatalities from domestic fires which are held to be the responsibility of the household (quoted in Abelson, 2003: S6). All of this shows that dying itself can yield different amounts of disutility. A car crash is quick and can be painless. Cancer is slow death, leaving time for fear, anxiety and for simply feeling ill. It is morbidity as well as mortality. It is therefore that much more unpleasant.

Jones-Lee also discovered from his questionnaires that, for some people at least, death itself is not the worst thing that can happen. Fully 6.2 per cent of his sample said that the loss of a leg was as bad as death, 2.4 per cent slightly worse than death, 1.2 per cent much worse than death, 0.3 per cent very much worse than death. As for being permanently bedridden, the percentages, respectively, were 33.4 per cent, 11.9 per cent, 11.2 per cent and 6.9 per cent (Jones-Lee, Hammerton and Philips, 1985: 54). It is a sobering thought that 10.1 per cent of the respondents thought that losing a leg was at least as bad as death, 63.4 per cent that being bedridden meant that it was better to give up and die. Being alive is not the whole story. People clearly want a reasonable quality of life as well. That is why detailed psychometric studies of people's perceptions are so important if the value of life is truly to be built up from what ordinary people see and think.

Life is not an either/or but a spectrum. The willingness to pay makes more sense if the comparison is made with quality-adjusted life-years (QALY) in a state of average health. It is less realistic if the benchmark is arbitrarily taken to be statistical life-years in complete and perfect health. The crude number of life-years by itself overstates what it means to be alive but under-par. Thus

Johannesson and Meltzer (studying traffic accidents) found that the implicit willingness to pay for each *quality-adjusted* life-year gained in Sweden was $90 000. This was less than the willingness to pay per *statistical* life-year saved, which was $1.4 million (Johannesson and Meltzer, 1998: 5). Hirth and his associates used contingent valuation to calculate a willingness-to-pay value of $161 305 (in 1997 US dollars) per QALY saved: the comparable value implied in human capital studies was $24 777, in revealed preference safety studies $93 402 (Hirth, Chernew, Miller, Fendrick and Weissert, 2000: 338). The value of $161 305 was not the value of the earnings but the value of the satisfaction. Life is consumption. It is not production alone.

In Australia Abelson, following European precedents, took the estimated present value of life for a healthy prime-age individual to be about A$2.5 million. Using that stock, assuming a 40-year remaining lifespan, taking the interest-rate to be 3 per cent, he found a value per QALY obtained of A$108 000: 'A morbidity cost in excess of $108,000 implies that a health state is worse than death. Premature death may be better than quadriplegia (for some people). In this situation, the cost-benefit policy implication is euthanasia' (Abelson, 2003: S11). The economic value of a healthy day in Australia was A$108 000/365, or A$296 in 2002 values. That is the amount people were believed to be just willing to pay to avoid acute and chronic conditions. If total costs exceed total benefits, economics teaches that the human life is not paying its way. Economic logic is bad for your health. Pareto Optimality can kill.

Questionnaires and surveys build up the value of life from grassroots opinion. Contingent valuation allows the policymaker to induce policy options from real people's reactions, assumed representative, to hypothetical scenarios. Yet there is a problem. Ordinary respondents might not actually understand what it means to work outward from a risk-coefficient that is not a cast-iron guarantee. The questions can be opaque and the scenarios unfamiliar. As Jones-Lee states, there must always be 'cause for concern about the capacity of most subjects for *imagining* their response to this type of question in the first place' (Jones-Lee, 1976: 133).

In Acton's study (1973), the $28 000 is a response to the reduction in risk of death of 0.002 per cent. Confusion arises, however, where the respondents are not clear in their own mind about the thought-experiment they are being asked to perform. That is why it is useful for the interviewer to ask supplementary questions in order to force the respondent to think through the steps. Even a person who has been educated in trade-offs and statistical lives will not find it easy to say what 0.002 per cent means to him. A person unaccustomed to thinking in the language of probability will find it even more difficult to calculate the hypothetical value he is being asked to provide. One wonders how many respondents simply pluck a random value out of the air because the investigator is expecting something and basically they simply don't know.

The questions themselves may suggest their own answer. The survey must be designed in such a way as not to lead its respondents. It must attempt where possible to adjust for the expectational pitfalls and the psychological biases. Subjects might select values at the middle of the scale: compromise is reassuring while confrontation makes people nervous. Subjects might deliberately under-state their willingness to pay: calculative duplicity maximises their chances of enjoying something for nothing. Alarmists and ostriches, the indifferent and the manipulative all give answers that reflect their personalities because they are the people that they are. Policymakers trying to do the right thing will have to accept that there will probably be shortcomings in the answers they are given.

Subjects might in particular show a non-rational preference for outcomes that make them feel good. An illustration would be the experimental study done by Tversky and Kahneman on the private perception of language and its imagery: 'The prospect of certainly saving 200 lives is more attractive than a risky pros-pect of equal expected value, that is, a one-in-three chance of saving 600 lives.... The certain death of 400 people is less acceptable than the two-in-three chance that 600 will die' (Tversky and Kahneman, 1981: 453). From that pattern the authors, confirming Friedman and Savage, conclude that the majority opinion is less favourable to certain death than it is to probable recovery of an equal value: 'Choices involving gains are often risk averse and changes involving losses are often risk taking' (Tversky and Kahneman, 1981: 453). The implica-tions for survey design are striking in themselves: 'In a question dealing with the response to an epidemic, for example, most respondents found "a sure loss of 75 lives" more aversive than "80% chance to lose 100 lives" but preferred "10% chance to lose 75 lives" over "8% chance to lose 100 lives", contrary to utility theory' (Tversky and Kahneman, 1981: 455). The answers were not transitive in the strict sense of neoclassical economics. The framing bias altered the 'mental accounts' that flashed through the respondents' minds. The subjec-tive and the objective values were not the same.

5.1.3.   Safety and Security

Questionnaires and surveys are *what if*: they ask respondents how they would feel about for-instance contingencies. Observations of real-world experience are *what is*: they do not rely on words but merely shadow the deeds. Assuming that what people *do* gives some idea of what people *think*, such studies are in a position to deduce purpose from action and to take the realised as an indicator of the intended. Since, moreover, much of health care per se is unpriced, such manifestations of intent might be the only way to gain a purchase on what the lifeholder would prefer. Should the actual differ widely from the desired, should ordinary people not look before they leap, the outturns will not be a perfect in-dicator of the desiderata. Should people by nature be purposive, however, what they do might arguably give an insight into the wants that dwell nowhere but in their mind.

Observation shows that the drinker and the smoker trade short-term pleasure against the long-term damage to their liver and lungs. The worker dispenses with protective goggles and time-consuming safety ropes in order to increase his piecework return. The jaywalker crosses against the lights because time is money and a wait is disutility. People travel by motorbike and unlicensed taxis because the first-class alternative is sold at a higher price. People live in crime-ridden areas, or near firing ranges, or in flood plains, or on polluted main roads, or on fire-trap top floors, or without smoke-alarms, because rents there are cheap and the worst may never happen. People swim on secluded beaches because the beach with a lifeguard is crowded and noisy. People drink tap water although they know that bottled water will shield them from disease. People eat fatty foods rather than mackerel and reject organic vegetables because the pesticides and the insecticides cost them less. People turn down insurance upgrades because they think the likelihood of chemotherapy is low. People drive when drunk because public transport is not cost-effective. People fail to screw on childproof safetycaps because protecting the curious uses up scarce time. Evidence such as this gives an indication of just how much people value their lives. It allows the investigator to compute the maximum sum that people by inference would expect to spend on medical interventions that would save a life.

People who do not take their vitamins or wear their crash-helmets or install fire-alarms or dispense with fallout shelters, people who go in for gang warfare and climb sheer rock-faces and paraglide over crocodiles because it gives them an adrenelin rush, are all expressing a view. The preferences that they are revealing give little support to the hypothesis that they put an infinite price on the protection of a human life. What the evidence does suggest is that they are willing to exchange some probable survival for some present advantage in the manner described as follows by Rachel Dardis: 'Suppose 1,000 persons require a compensation of $100 due to a decrease in survival probability of 0.001, then the estimated value of a life is $100 thousand for individuals in the community.... This does not mean that any one individual will be willing to sacrifice his life for $100 thousand' (Dardis, 1980: 1078). Dardis studied the reduction in the probability of death and injury brought about by the purchase of residential smoke detectors. She calculated that a smoke detector produced an implicit value of life (taking the interest rate to be 5 per cent and assuming that death and injury were equally weighted) in the range from $189 049 to $256 652. The valuation is that of the households that opted in to this mode of risk avoidance.

The record is actual, not imagined. The evidence is the history of precisely what 1000 persons chose, the chronicle of how much that purchase was preferred to the next-best purchase foregone. It is in that sense the embodiment of the equilibrium price at which they were just willing to buy or sell their statistical life. Death, in other words, is not just a fact *out there* but an endogenous variable, self-selected at the margin. Life may be valued from the willingness to pay. It is the lifeholder's own value. The price that someone is just willing to pay is the measure of what the extra utility will mean to him.

It is methodological individualism. It is not necessarily selfishness. Consider a young child's car seat. The parent who voluntarily buys and correctly uses a safety seat is paying a cost but also buying a probability. The probability that the child will die in a road accident is reduced by 4.1/10000. Carlin and Sandy, using those values, calculated the imputed value of the child's life, taking into account the 'mother's surplus' (analogous to consumer surplus) and the discounted costs (in time and money) of raising the child up to the age of 18. The present value when added up was $526827 (in 1985 dollars) (Carlin and Sandy, 1991: 196). This is derived from the revealed preferences of the parent. It is close to Blomquist's (1979) capital value of $607200 (in 1985 dollars) which is based exclusively on the self's egocentric evaluation. It cannot be proven if the adult's implicit $526827 would be the under-four's own valuation of his or her life. Alter is not ego: Jones-Lee, Hammerton and Philips established that people believed the lives of friends and relatives to be worth little more than 40 per cent of their own (Jones-Lee, Hammerton and Philips, 1985: 69). Even close kin refuse to donate a kidney. Carlin and Sandy found that mother's love and self-denying altruism made the proportion a much higher 87 per cent. While 87 per cent is still less than 100 per cent, it is high enough to suggest that parents, as judged by safety seats, are reasonable guardians of their children's well-being.

Carlin and Sandy studied safety seats. Blomquist studied seat belts. The value he derived was $368000 (in 1975 dollars) (Blomquist, 1979: 556). A driver who voluntarily wears the belt is subject to three sets of costs: the financial cost of paying for and fitting the belt, the time-cost of earnings foregone while buckling and unbuckling the belt, and the disamenity cost of driving while restrained by the belt. On the plus side, however, there is the statistical benefit of lengthened life-expectancy. Blomquist compared the costs and the benefits. In that way he was able to calculate the implicit value of a human life.

Blomquist used a time-and-motion study: he established that the average American spent 3.3 hours per annum buckling and unbuckling the belt, and he made an arbitrary imputation of his own ($45, equivalent to 3.3 hours of average wages foregone) for the inconvenience of doing so. The marginal cost quantified, he consulted mortality tables to establish by how much the risk of death was reduced. He compared the costs with the benefits. In that way he derived the implied value of additional life-years purchased through prudence.

He established as well that his $368000 was double the value (using data on representative national earnings) that would have been thrown up by calculating human life as a piece of human capital. The willingness to pay for life is, evidently, not the same as the value of productive life. The man or woman in the street seems not to regard a human life as no more than the economic output that it delivers. Ordinary people would not support a policy of cost containment couched exclusively in the priorities of economic growth.

Blomquist was writing at a time when the seat belt was not compulsory in the United States. He found that 23 per cent of American drivers were voluntarily investing in this mode of reducing their risk. His study extrapolated values from the 23 per cent that did and not from the 77 per cent that did not. His low prevention-rate recalls that of Dardis, who established that only 13 per cent of American households had bought a smoke detector despite the negligible annualised cost (including the battery and a 5 per cent discount rate) of $4.34 (Dardis, 1980: 1082). His estimation of the value of life would have been different – it would have been lower – had he concentrated on the majority position and not on the safety-conscious exceptions.

Blomquist's case is a study only of the 23 per cent. It does not incorporate the subjective valuations of the 77 per cent, all of them probably aware of the benefits, who chose not to take preventive action. As always, it is not easy to identify the representative spokesperson for the social consensus. Some members of the community are so risk-averse that they drink caffeine-free coffee and refuse to talk to strangers. Others are so risk-loving that they go in for stock-car races and go out with promiscuous partners. Premature death is not an equal bad for all groups. Policymakers must understand that generalisation only makes sense where there is a conspicuous spike in support of a modal option. Otherwise all that Blomquist-type results will document is the attitude of the subgroup that belts and not of the nation that shares with them its social space.

Pluralism seriously undermines the notion that there is such a mode. Different people want a different balance between present enjoyment and possible extinction. Besides that, there is the intensity of desire. Frequency is simple head-counting. Utility, however, is cardinal as well as ordinal. What is at least as important as *how many* is *by how much*. Even a passionate minority can derive intense satisfaction from its choice. It is a well-known result in the theory of democracy that welfare in such circumstances can be maximised effectively by giving the minority and not the majority what it wants.

Studies that infer value of life from real-world consumables are useful. Yet there is a danger of double counting. Death and disability are the joint products of safety and security. Willingness to pay may refer to one, or the other, or both. The percentages are not clear. What is the meaning of the consumption foregone when the individual buys a seat belt? Does he think he is buying a lifetime endowment of years? Or does he think he is buying a lifetime stream of comfort? Willingness to pay keeps its own counsel on issues such as these.

Length of life may not be reduced by a car with ailing brakes or a job in the line of fire. Yet enjoyment of life, acute or chronic, almost certainly will be different when an accident or a shooting occurs. People do not want pain or disability. They do not want to lose all or part of their earning capacity. Their revealed preferences might refer to suffering, disfigurement or unemployment, not to the permanent and immediate absolute of being laid in the grave. Data collected by observing their choices relates, strictly speaking, to two kinds of utility and not just to one. It would therefore be a mistake to neglect the impact of quality of life while concentrating exclusively on the brute census of future life-days. It would make sense to do so only if the willingness to pay were seen by the lifeholders as a payment for physical existence alone. There will certainly be lifeholders like that. There are unlikely to be very many.

Even after regulation has been pyramided on the life values revealed, that is not by any means the end of the calculation. Enforcement itself imposes a cost. Food inspectors need only take one package off the shelf but factory inspectors must conduct expensive on-site evaluations. There will be evasion. A fine that is too low will be accepted as a legitimate business expense. Most important for a study that estimates life from the lifeholder's choice, there will be moral hazard. Policy based on safety and security can alter the probabilities which are encoded in the norms.

Thus do-it-yourselfers, aware that the drill is being protected by a perspex hood, no longer pay attention to the cable which gives them a shock. Childproof caps cause accidental poisonings where the compulsory safetycatch tempts parents to economise on the time-cost of hiding the bottle. A seat belt costs lives where it causes drivers to become overconfident about their speed. It can certainly be argued *a priori* that mandatory devices such as padded dashboards and shatterproof windscreens will lull consumers into a false sense of security. Regulation in cases like these will encourage them to let their guard down.

Whether the net feedback on the value of life is negative or positive is an empirical question. The results reported by Crandall and Graham are cautiously reassuring on the sum of the pluses and the minuses: 'The time-series evidence reported here reveals some offsetting behavior, but the intrinsic engineering effects of safety devices appear to swamp the behavioral responses' (Crandall and Graham, 1984: 330). The classic study by Sam Peltzman was not nearly so sanguine about the new fatalities that take the place of the old problem solved: 'The main conclusion is that safety regulation has had no effect on the highway death toll. There is some evidence that regulation may have increased the share of this toll borne by pedestrians and increased the total number of accidents' (Peltzman, 1975: 677). Peltzman does not say that the policy was actually *counter*productive. What he does say is that policies based on probabilities are the cause of new probabilities that will lead to new policies. Even in the field of health the Heisenberg Principle is all around.

5.1.4. Differential Remuneration

The labour market quantifies the danger differential. It may be taken as an indicator of the individual's personal valuation of his own human life. There are no markets in certain death. The labour market, however, does deal in the *risk* of death. Higher pay is offered for a higher probability of premature demise. The marginal payment measures the implicit bribe that the risk-averse will require to enter into the gamble. The premium is certain. The death is statistical. The value of life can then be worked out by an actuary who knows how to compute the flow into a stock.

Such a computation was made by Moore and Viscusi. Using statistics on the risk of death at work from the National Traumatic Occupational Fatality project in the United States, they discovered that there was 'a powerful and statistically significant positive relationship between job risks and worker wages' (Moore and Viscusi, 1988: 477). They found that the average employee required (in 1981 dollars) an extra \$43.4 per annum to accept a higher chance of death of 1/100 000. The implication is that the value of one human life lost as seen by the workers themselves is \$4.34 million. (Moore and Viscusi, 1988: 486).

Danger money measures the marginal hazard. It is a comparative measure. One form that the comparison can take is between high-risk and low-risk occupations: bodyguards, police informants and deep sea divers can earn more even than some graduate executives. Another way in which the difference can be seen is within a single trade: window cleaners willing to work on skyscraper floors will typically earn more than window cleaners who are afraid of heights. The latter is perhaps the better way of measuring the risk differential since it compares like with like. A test pilot going supersonic is being compared with the pilot of a cargo plane ferrying freight. Neither pilot is being compared with a doctor or a dustman. The job-functions are not similar enough to be able to spot the risk-element in the remuneration.

Education, skill, responsibility, gender, race, local amenities, unpleasant surroundings and alienating tasks all have an impact on the pay structure. So, interestingly, does union strength. Olson found that the value of a statistical life was about \$8.24 million for union members, \$1.5 million for non-members (Olson, 1981: 183). Risk of death is not the whole of life. Nor, however, is it an irrelevance. Increased risk of fatal accident is definitely part of Alfred Marshall's compensating variations (Marshall, 1949 [1890]: 463), part of Adam Smith's 'ease or hardship' (Smith, 1961 [1776]: I, 112) that is picked up by the offsets in the hierarchy of pay. Coalminers demand extra money if their job involves blasting underground. The extra money quantifies their subjective estimation of the extra disutility that is associated with the extra risk. It is their *willingness to accept* the small probability that something will go wrong. In that respect it is similar to the policyholder's eager *willingness to pay* for insurance lest uninsured damage lie where it falls. The two kinds of willingness will not, of course, be numerically the same. The willingness to pay is limited by the household budget. The willingness to accept is subject to no theoretical ceiling or constraint.

In conducting an empirical study, it is not easy to select a representative sample. Selection is a problem that extrapolation from differentials shares with questionnaires and surveys and with safety and security that were discussed in the previous two sections. Is a snake handler, a bomb-disposal expert or a quarryman dicing with explosives the 'typical' member of the community? Income-levels introduce a further complication. A sample must be class-sensitive since there are likely to be patterned differences in the marginal utility of money. If not all individuals are equally risk-averse, an important reason is that not all individuals can afford the luxury. Life and limb enjoy a high income elasticity of demand. Biddle and Zarkin, showing that 'job risk is an inferior good', situate the negative response in the range from −1.5 to −2.5 (Biddle and Zarkin, 1988: 667). That being the case, it is more likely to be the lower paid and the blue collar who self-select themselves on to the oil-rigs. It is less likely to be the senior executives and the leading accountants who mule the narcotics for the drug barons. Given the heterogeneity, it is not easy to know which part may be said to be speaking for the whole. The representative citizen, like the representative firm, may be a figment of the intellectual's imagination.

Lionel Needleman has nonetheless estimated the value of life from the danger-differentials of workers in the construction industry. Needleman seems to be suggesting that the pool in question is neither abnormally adventurous nor abnormally timid: otherwise he would be writing an anthropological case-study that would be lacking in broader applicability. He actually states that the group on which he is focusing is on average industrial earnings and is, objectively speaking, 'reasonably typical of male manual workers in general' (Needleman, 1980: 233). It is not clear how far the attitudes of the young, the manual and the male can be said to be representative of all construction workers; or whether their preferences can be made the basis for policies affecting the nation as a whole. The middle-aged, the professional and the female would probably be less willing to take risks with their lives. Young people, logically speaking, ought to be more risk-averse than the average since they have so many more life-years to lose. The stream of their expected future earnings, suitably discounted, is so much greater than that of an older worker nearing retirement. Logic only tells a part of the story. In terms of their attitudes, young people (especially young single people) are probably more willing than the rest to chance an injury; while older people are possibly less nimble on the roof.

Needleman collected data on the premium that British construction workers were demanding when they volunteered for higher-risk duties. He made the assumption that the workers had learned from experience and conversation what the hierarchy of falls was likely to be. His methodology is valuable even if his numbers have been left behind by inflation. Needleman found the following statistic, which measured the subjective valuation of working at heights: 'The hourly rate on one of [the] sites was two pence at heights between 30 and 75 feet, four pence at between 75 and 100 feet, six pence at between 100 and 150 feet, and thereafter six pence for each additional 50 feet' (Needleman, 1980: 235–6). Roofers, steel erectors and scaffolders got the most danger money. They were the most exposed to the risk of falls.

Their differential was their trade-off. It would be a representative value if the workers in the sample were a good cross-section of their trade. It would be a more representative value still if they were a good cross-section of their nation. It would be biased downward, however, if the workers who volunteered were idiosyncratically risk-tolerant. This nonlinearity explains why in some studies the wage differential associated with incremental fatalities is seen to be increasing at a decreasing rate (Olson, 1981: 173). Viscusi and his colleagues actually found a correlation between risk-providing jobs and risk-loving people: 'While smokers work, on average, in industries with higher injury risk than non-smokers, smokers also are more likely to have a work-related injury controlling for injury risk. Smokers also are prone to have had a recent non-work-related injury' (Viscusi and Aldy, 2003: 16). Even so, they were not so devil-may-care that they set their lives at nought. Their danger money was a measure of their anxiety. They were selling a small deterioration in the lottery of death for an agreed-upon payment which at the margin left them at least as contented as before.

Needleman found objective information on the actual magnitude of the incremental risk. His sources were the British *Annual Reports of the Chief Inspector of Factories*. Data on relative probability of deaths at work can also be obtained from the International Labour Organisation, the UK *Digest of Incapacity Statistics* and the actuarial bodies. Needleman learned, for example, that the average worker who volunteered to go up the scaffold was 0.52/1000 more likely to experience premature death as a result. Needleman also obtained data on extra remuneration ('condition money') for work involving extra risk and/or extra discomfort: the UK National Board for Prices and Incomes had collected this information, although a decade had passed. The statistics showed that the average labourer who became a scaffolder would be able to command an income 10 to 15 per cent more than that same person would have earned on the ground. Having been able to quantify the parameters, Needleman was then able to work out the implicit valuations for selected human lives: £7845 for a roofer, £16 565 for a steel erector and £45 980 for a scaffolder (Needleman, 1980: 240).

These estimates are low. Different studies using different samples will, of course, generate different values. Marin and Psacharopoulos derive very different values indeed: 'If the sample is split into groups, the value of life implied for manual workers is ... in the £600 000–£700 000 range, while the value of life implied for non-manual workers is over three times as high. This is expected given that safety is a superior good' (Marin and Psacharopoulos, 1982: 848). Other samples produce other results: US$7.2 million, $9.7 million, $10.3 million, $16.2 million, $2.8 million, $1.6 million and $700 000 are only some of the values that have been recorded (Viscusi, 1993: 1926–7). Most values lie in the range between $3.8 million and $9 million in 2000 dollars: the median is about $7 million (Viscusi and Aldy, 2003: 18). As always, it is by no means clear which group is the sensitive social indicator that makes the micro into the macro because it is absolutely in touch with the common mind.

A cook is not an electrician. A fireman is not a fisherman. Viscusi concedes that it might be difficult or impossible to find a single value in a thicket of heterogeneities: 'The value of life is not a universal constant, but reflects the wage-risk tradeoff pertinent to the preferences of the workers in a particular sample. The mix of workers in these samples is quite different' (Viscusi, 1993: 1930). It should also be mentioned that there is virtually no job-related risk differential for white-collar workers such as civil servants. A false inference, but also a logical one, would be that the life of a managing director has no economic value. The economic value of the supervisors and the administrators would have to be taken from that of the roofers and the scaffolders who fix their bayonets at the Front.

A sensitive social indicator is hard to find. Nor is it obvious that the labour market is the right place to look. Since work is a necessity and the children must be fed, it is possible that the scaffolder's premium does not lend itself to broader generalisations such as the number of traffic policemen that would reduce the kill-factor on the roads to an appropriate level. The differentials themselves, moreover, might not mean what the free-marketeers anticipate. If compensating variations are to be used to compute the value of life, then it must be assumed that the differences are indicative of supply and demand. Pay that is not market-driven cannot be taken to shadow the personal estimation of expected fatality. That is just the point. Wages, at least in the short-run, are not always flexible. Pay structures can be rigid, insensitive and sticky. Institutions and precedents can perpetuate outdated relativities. Economists assume rationality. Ordinary people just get on with their lives.

Differentials might not be proportionate to the risks because many workers will be isolated and provincial. Some workers are in the know. Miners repeatedly observe the decimation in their small occupational group that is caused by black-lung disease. Scaffolders see the blood on the ground each time that a roofer falls. Yet some workers will not be so sure. Laundry workers inhaling steam and solvent might not be able to put a figure on the healthy days they are *de facto* signing away. Nor is it easy for them to compare their pay with the next-best industry into which they might conceivably migrate. They do not know the mortality rate associated with working with lions in the zoo. They do not know if as laundry workers they are being offered enough to cover their opportunity cost.

Migration itself, moreover, is not a frictionless transition. Occupational and geographical barriers restrict mobility from one subtrade to another. Change of any kind involves transaction cost. Fear of the unknown is the greatest of all exit barriers. What this means is that windfalls and shortfalls can survive even into the long-run. Arbitrage cannot meaningfully be conducted where investors are stuck in a fixed habitat, in familiar territory which a combination of anxiety and myopia makes them reluctant to quit. Real-world danger money in the instant when the economist cross-sections his hierarchy is, one suspects, more likely to be indicative of a general direction than it is to be precisely calibrated, statistically fine-tuned: 'It is a bit like asking someone what the weather is like outside – they can give a reasonable idea, but not an exact temperature.... It would be a mistake to draw sharp conclusions based on an estimate' (Cutler, 2004: 16).

Adjustments take time. That, however, is precisely how markets work. People accept a job. They find out later about the particles, the acids and the rusty blades. They revise their expectations in the light of their flaking skin and the loss of hair. They move on as a consequence of what they have learned: 'Job risks raise worker quit rates.... Job risks account for as much as one-third of all manufacturing quit rates' (Viscusi, 1992: 109). Experience leads to switch. That is what is meant by an optimising process. Either the risks go down or the pay goes up or the worker goes out. Ignorance at the beginning does not mean ignorance at the end. It does, however, mean that an economist who wants to use differentials as a citizen's-eye perspective on the value of life must choose carefully the day on which he pops in to snap his still.

Time and space conceal the variations. A worker who ruins his health with phosphorus might only be seen to be terminally ill when, much later and far away, he is holding a job in a hamburger restaurant. The cause of his premature death will be even more obscure where he has held a succession of jobs: if the first involved lead-based defoliants, the second asbestos fibres, the third vinyl chloride, the precise carcinogen that finished the man off might never be known. Multiple causality and long gestation-periods make it difficult to determine the facts. Cognitive bias – a topic to be discussed in more detail in the next section – means that newsworthy disasters displace upwards the perceived risks of tanker piracy on the open seas while leaving neglected and unnoticed the higher-probability threat of heart attacks and diabetes among posh chefs who cater for Cordon Bleu. Mind and matter, in other words, might not move in step: 'Workers' demand for extra compensation is not necessarily based on the actual risks of each job but on what they think the risks are. Most of the occupational causes of death are not obvious' (Marin and Psacharopoulos, 1982: 831). New risks, meanwhile, are constantly coming on stream. Even if the old causes of death can be quantified or compared, the new ones are a black box. The new equipment might emit low-level radiation or put a strain upon the eyes. No one in the early stages might know.

Extra compensation is more than just pay. Non-pecuniary remuneration must be added to the wage differential. An illustration would be long periods of home leave for workers stationed in troubled war-zones abroad. Health insurance and/or workmen's compensation complicate the story. A worker who has free medical care will conceivably be more prepared to take risks than will a worker who must pay out-of-pocket. He might also be prepared to accept a smaller danger differential since *ex post* damages are his just-in-case right. Policymakers who want to use pay as their way in to the implicit value of life must in the circumstances make an estimate of the whole of the package and not just a part.

Compensating differentials are intuitively appealing where real-world actors make their own decisions. They are more open to debate where corporations and unions take over the haggling role. Monopsonies and countervailing monopolies complement productivity with power. They negotiate not for what each side deserves so much as for what each side can get. It is difficult enough to interpret the building workers' danger differentials in a world where smoking 20 cigarettes a day is twice as risky, riding a motorcycle three times as risky as working at heights. Yet it is even more difficult to read subjectivity into the resultant pay hierarchy when strong men hammer on the table and strong women refuse to deviate from their claim. Collective bargaining, in any case, is *collective* bargaining. It produces a standardised settlement for the group as a whole. Such a block booking does not leave much room for the non-standard labour-lump to shade his own remuneration in line with his own private perceptions.

Olson found that union members commanded a substantially higher fatal accident premium (9.1 per cent) than did non-union members (1.6 per cent). The difference as compared with riskless occupations translates into a value of life of $8 million and $1.5 million respectively: the weighted average might be about $3.2 million (Olson, 1981: 182, 184). The union wage can certainly be seen as a market-distorting disequilibrium pyramided upon imperfection and control. It can also be seen, however, as a higher-quality market signal that is more in tune with the relevant probabilities. Workers covered by collective agreements are likely to be better informed about chemical residues, toxic gases and other hidden risks. Their unions are there to obtain accurate information and to diffuse it widely. In that sense it might be the unionised and not the isolated who put the appropriate economic value on a human life. There is also a dynamic dimension. Agreements with management often guarantee the unions a seat on the firm's safety committee. Where the accident rate goes down as a result of local knowledge, the unions can pass the gains on to their members in the next pay round. The new marginal productivity curve *after* is not, Olson stresses, the same as the old marginal productivity curve *before*: 'Union firms are more efficient at producing safety' (Olson, 1981: 184).

Even if the objective frequencies are sensitively shadowed by market-determined differentials, still the relative wages will not be easy to interpret. Fires in oil-fields are put out by highly paid specialists whose remuneration reflects the real chance of death but also the need to be compensated for living apart from their home and family. Roofers might demand extra pay not just because of their exposure to fatalities but because of discomfort, inclement weather and the non-fatal fall which leaves them alive but nonetheless handicapped and unable to earn: 'Jobs that are risky tend to be unpleasant in other respects' (Viscusi, 1993: 1919). It would be misleading to extrapolate the value of life from a pay differential that emerged because of crashes and loose girders alone. Such a differential would be a measure of the implicit value of injury at work but not of a life-or-death decision that was never made. In order to put a value on a statistical *life*, it is necessary to separate the fatal from the non-fatal outcomes. Olson found that about 35 per cent of the wage premium was paid in recognition of possible death (Olson, 1981: 184). Danger differentials pick up more than death alone. They are therefore misleading when they are used to quantify the value of life.

5.1.5. Life Insurance

Dublin and Lotka in 1930 developed an economic approach to the money value of a man which effectively defined his value as his value to his dependants: 'Every individual who insures himself for the protection of the members of his family has in mind providing them, in the event of his death, with a sum of money that shall, as nearly as possible, take the place of his contribution to them while living. Human life in this sense may be equated to a sum of money' (Dublin and Lotka, 1930: v).

Human life in the sense of Dublin and Lotka is not the willingness to pay. It is taken to mean the expected stream of net future earnings lost, the discounted value of potential value-added foregone, the amount of human capital wasted. Allowance must be made for the individual's own future consumption destroyed to ensure that what is measured is the net value to others and not to oneself. Sentiment and the grief of loss are not a part of the calculation. Powerful as they may well be, the emotions, Dublin and Lotka caution, are lacking in 'practical, tangible quantities capable of numerical estimate in dollars and cents' (Dublin and Lotka, 1930: 3). Expected payments prematurely extinguished can be quantified: the age-specific mortality tables, the income tax records, the discounting rate all make it possible to grind out a single present value. Suffering and sadness, on the other hand, do not lend themselves to the precise pecuniary standard.

Life insurance empowers an individual to make financial provision. It allows him to put an economic value on the human life that he might be obliged rather early to quit. It is a mix of the subjective dimension (he chooses voluntarily to buy the policy) and the objective backup (he has data on earnings which allow him to project forward what he believes his human capital will be worth). Whether it is a measure of life or of death is more controversial. Life insurance is a way of compensating the survivors for the loss of their economic breadwinner. It is not a way of compensating the lifeholder for the loss of his blood and bones. Life insurance is the premium payer's valuation of his life as a capital sum to be handed on to his heirs. It is not a measure of the costs and benefits that the lifeholder would compare if he were working out what his human life is worth to himself.

Few lifeholders in any case hold insurance cover equal to the unexpired earnings-stream that they would command if they were still alive. They are more likely to select an insurance payout that will satisfy the future needs of their dependants. Alter's future needs are adequately met. Ego's own life is sadly wiped out. Jones-Lee is not impressed by the value of Ego's life that is registered as a result: 'All in all then, the sums for which people typically insure their lives or limbs would seem to give little if any guide to the appropriate level at which to set the gross output or willingness-to-pay based costs of risk or values of safety' (Jones-Lee, 1989: 24).

Ethically too, the insurance method is seriously flawed. It conveys the information that the life of a high-income earner is worth more than the life of the less well-paid. Many will feel uncomfortable with the idea that income distribution should be reflected in the economic value of a human life. Besides that, pay is an imperfect measure of productivity. The value to society will not be the same as the value to the beneficiaries if there are positive and negative externalities which have an influence on the value that should be put upon a deceased person's value-added foregone. No one compensates his workmates for the loss of a skilled manager who regularly secured them an above-average bonus.

The value of life extrapolated through the assurance method does not take moral hazard into account. Ideally it should do so. People who know that their family-members are protected might become less safety-conscious, less fearful of their own early death. Admittedly the amount reimbursed is the value of their life to their descendants. It is not the value of their life to themselves. Even so, the lifeholder can economise on precautions because he has a guarantee. This alters the nature of the game. The life-insurance method is obviously a source of misleading signals to the policymaker who is scaling up to the value of life.

Life insurance in any case is not able to quantify the life of the totally uninsured. An infant's life must have some value but the insurance method is not in a position to put an economic price on it. Nor is it clear what the appropriate value would be. Untapped potential, serendipitous luck, the work-ethic to come, have no known earnings-stream. Today's cross-section is not the same as a lifetime's time series. The future is unknown. Things will change.

Life insurance provides financial compensation to individuals who by definition have not borne the costs. The selfish premium-payer would to that extent be better off disabled. Insurance against what Dublin and Lotka call the 'acquired incapacity to fulfill the ordinary tasks of life', the 'depreciation of the economic value of the individual' (Dublin and Lotka, 1930: 68, 102), allows the party who has paid the contributions to claim back the benefits for himself. If he goes to court, the judge will set a comparable price on his economic value as damaged goods.

It is often suggested that judges are remote and out of touch. While it is difficult to generalise, court awards made for loss of function do seem to resemble the willingness-to-pay that is revealed through questionnaires and surveys. Kind, Rosser and Williams canvassed the opinions of 70 detached interviewees (both patients and professionals), approached in a calm and rational moment. They found a close correlation of 0.82 between the *ex ante* valuations of their subjects and some 202 court awards made for the purpose of *ex post* compensation: 'It appears that, compared with the psychometric evidence, legal awards tend to assign more moderate relative valuations to the most severe states, but otherwise there seems no identifiable source of systematic bias between the two' (Kind, Rosser and Williams, 1982: 165). If this finding is typical, then the willingness to pay for prevention may be said to approach the rectification that restores felt welfare to its original level.

Accident means damages for the injured party. Death means a payment made to the survivors of the deceased. In this latter case, once again, a parallel may be drawn with the payout that would be made from insurance. In making an award, in the British and similar legal systems, the judge does not take into account the disappointment of the deceased or the pain and suffering of his doting family. The judge fixes the sum exclusively with an eye to the economic well-being of those whose livelihood depends on the extinguished human asset. Such a valuation of life, as with insurance, concentrates on the value of earning capacity to others. There is no allowance for the loss of the bodyholder's *joie de vivre* in the estimate: the bodyholder, dead, is no longer there to claim. The valuation relates to a named individual: it does not have the detached impartiality of a statistical probability. It is private: it adds in no additional element to compensate the nation for the loss of its human capital.

Clearly, the award made by a judge will give incomplete guidance at best to a policymaker who is determined to find out the value that the discrete individual puts on his or her life. It is not a surprise that the value of life as an earnings-stream discounted is an approach which has largely been eclipsed by the willingness to pay. Yet the human capital approach continues to exist. Section

3 of chapter 6 describes it in detail. Anyone who wants to think of life wound up as productive potential ebbing into the sand is free to use discounted cash flow to calculate the economic value of a life.

5.2.   THE PRACTITIONER

The first constituency was the individual. The first section sought to show how the individual consumer proportions marginal payment to marginal benefit. He does so either to purchase additional life-years or to secure compensation for the life-years that he has had to sacrifice. This second section deals with a second kind of decision-maker. It is about the medical professional who can be asked to decide which life to save, and how much to spend.

This section is about authority. It is not about the best-judge client's authentic revealed preference. It begins with the shortcomings and the biases which undermine the validity of the bottom-up approach. It continues with a discussion of the skilled professional who has the knowledge and expertise to correct the market failure. In that way it looks forward to the third section of this chapter, which deals with the public interest. The third section suggests that the principal's best friend might be his parliament.

5.2.1.   A Fool's Valuation

In all studies of rational choice the assumption is made that the preference-revealers are in possession of the facts. The calculations discussed in the previous section lose their bite if the interviewees, the belt-bucklers and the roofers have no real idea of the risk of death. Unaware of the objective probabilities, uncertain as to the relative fatalities, people might be said to be expressing loose preferences but not informed magnitudes sufficiently well calibrated to serve as a basis for non-random public policy.

The individual as a consumer does not know if saccharine thins the amino acids or magnesium sulphate raises the glucose-level in the blood. He is not that much better off when he smokes a cigarette. He knows that high-tar is more carcinogenic than filter-tip but not that it starves him of precisely x years of expected life. Inference is profoundly ambiguous where people act on guesstimate or gut reaction because they have never troubled to search out the objective frequencies.

A general impression is at variance with the economist's logic. The marginalist is interested in 'a little bit more' or 'a little bit less'. His survey sample will, however, often be thinking in terms of yes/no. The economist is probing into small changes and shades of grey. Ordinary people will often stop short at the light-switch polarities of life versus non-life. The extremes are useful but they are not enough. Prompting and prodding will be required to ferret out the complexities. Otherwise the information will be no more than a busy respondent's unconsidered first approximation. The data will not be a reliable indicator of when ordinary people, if informed and thoughtful, would really want the life-support machine to be switched off.

Ignorance is the stuff of human life. It is a reason for thinking that the consumer does not know best. Yet there is another, more charitable way in which ignorance can be interpreted. People's perceptions might not correspond to the factual risks but they are people's perceptions nonetheless. A distinction should be made between a stable preference, well defined, and a fleeting whim, loose and evanescent. Even if neither is founded on the statistical distribution, at least in the former case people have a good idea of what they want. It is true that the perceived trade-offs are not those that would have obtained under perfect information. That by itself, however, is not a criticism but only a statement of the obvious. There is nothing in economics that says that a non-scientific choice is invalid: 'What *is* important', Jones-Lee writes, 'is that if people are, for whatever reasons, more averse to risk from nuclear power generation than to an "obviously" equivalent risk from, say, a natural disaster, then this comparative aversion should be reflected in decisions concerning the allocation of resources to reactor safety and disaster prevention and this is precisely what the economic approach seeks to do' (Jones-Lee, 1989: 224). So long as the rankings are consistent and transitive, felt satisfaction is being maximised when people get the cat that they want. It is not the job of the economist to complain that it cannot, will not catch mice.

Yet people do make mistakes. Psychological biases distort their perceptions. Information is falsely processed. Evaluations do not do justice to the facts that people have at their disposal. Systematic errors put all the clocks wrong.

Festinger uses the term 'cognitive dissonance' to describe the psychological discomfort that people experience when something deviates from the expected outcome: 'The presence of dissonance leads to action to reduce it just as, for example, the presence of hunger leads to action to reduce the hunger' (Festinger, 1962 [1957]: 18). Applied to the value of life, what this can mean is that people discount the facts when they undermine existing beliefs. People who see themselves as good drivers might dispense with their seat belts because 'it won't happen to me'. People who work with dangerous chemicals might not demand the appropriate danger-differential because they are convinced they won't fall ill. Most people find it distressing to think soberly about their own death. Wishful thinking rose-tints their risk-assessment: 'A majority of people view themselves as safer than average drivers, more likely to live longer than normal life expectancy, less likely than average to succumb to the dangers of smoking or excessive drinking' (Jones-Lee, 1989: 216). The result is that war correspondents badly overestimate the number of war correspondents who live to tell the tale.

Salience further biases the perceptions. People are disproportionately aware of the recent, the sensational and the well-publicised. They live in fear of a terrorist attack or a nuclear test. They underestimate the far greater risk from trans fats in a fast-food chain. They over-react to high-profile contingencies such as a farmer struck by lightning or a tidal-wave that washes away an island. They hardly notice the high-probability commonplace such as a chip-pan liable to catch fire or a Moaning Minnie who complains of pains in the chest. The ubiquity of the familiar lulls them into a false sense of security. It takes a disaster to shake up their short-term memory.

Conservatism too makes people non-rationally defensive of a status quo endowment. Surveys 'have consistently found that people say they would require a far larger sum to forgo their rights of use or access to a resource than they would pay to keep the same entitlement' (Knetsch and Sinden, 1984: 508). The mug once bought will only be resold for significantly higher compensation: the law of one price for a standard commodity is called into question not by ignorance but by a sentimental attachment to a bird in the hand. A study of gases and burns confirmed as much: 'Individuals were willing to pay moderate amounts for product risk reductions of fifteen injuries per 10,000 bottles of insecticide or toilet bowl cleaner used per year, but when faced with a product risk increase of 1/10,000 most consumers were unwilling to buy the product at all, and those who were demanded a considerable price discount. In this context, the risky choice focused on changes in the risk from the current risk reference point to which consumers had become accustomed' (Viscusi, 1992: 143). It is precisely the same reduction-in-wealth effect that lies behind the purchase of insurance.

The willingness to acquire is not the same as the willingness to give up. People quote a low maximum price in order to secure a desirable outcome. They insist upon high minimum compensation in the event of an uncertain change. Preference reversal drives a wedge between the bid and the offer. New drugs, new life-saving interventions, new cost-cutting procedures will be badly delayed if people are so protective of the health status that might be improved by the novelty – or might come under threat. Thalidomide did incalculable harm. Penicillin did inestimable good. Barbiturates were used in suicide attempts but benzodiazepines do not carry the risk of self-poisoning. The delay in the United States in licensing the benzodiazepines and delicensing the barbiturates meant the loss of 1200 American lives (Wardell, quoted in Peltzman, 1974: 89). The regulators were being cautious. Their minimax meant that 1200 unhappy Americans died.

Conventions and rules of thumb inhibit the open-minded absorption of new data. Decision processes, Simon writes, are characterised not by global rationality but by bounded rationality. They are dominated by a time-saving, intellect-saving reliance upon a tried-and-tested heuristic that the decision-maker has learned from experience to trust: 'One could postulate that the decision-maker had formed some *aspiration* as to how good an alternative he should find. As soon as he discovered an alternative for choice meeting his level of aspiration, he would terminate the search and choose that alternative. I [call] this mode of selection satisficing' (Simon, 1979: 503; original emphasis). Such history-dominated standards greatly simplify the filtering process. They also mean that the respondents and the sample-subjects might be acting on the basis of a systematic bias which leads them to give misleading responses on the value of life.

Emotion and intuition, finally, can affect the perception of risk-bearing activity. People are short-horizoned: they discount heavily the long-term probability of obesity and tooth decay. People are stubborn: they are too proud to admit to a mistake even if an admission of regret would lead them to error correction. People are simplifiers: because vegetarians are thought to have a longer life-expectancy, a vegetarian whose hobby is sky-diving will tend to be seen as long-lived. People are frightened: their obsession with catastrophes like tsunamis and plagues is a creature of their nightmares and not of their database. People are muddle-headed. They confuse a probability with a certainty. They do not grasp the distinction between a risk to their body and a risk to their wealth. In all of this people are demonstrating psychological complexities which are at variance with the positivist's dispassionate ideal of factual information in, impartial policy-recommendations out.

Cognitive mechanisms are not a camera but that is the way it is. Respect for persons is not something on which even the cost-conscious and the health-maximising will necessarily wish to compromise. That is why it might make better sense to estimate the value of life from *perceived* probabilities rather than from the true and objective probabilities of which ordinary men and women might not be aware.

Statistics on false consciousness are not easy to find. There is little information on the probable survival that real-world actors think they are selling or buying when they binge on carbohydrates or go for a swim. The University of Michigan's Survey of Working Conditions and its Quality Employment Survey are among the few investigations that have been conducted into grassroots evaluations of the attributes that ordinary people themselves associate with particular inputs and consumables. Such data must be collected. Perhaps it should even be made the basis for public policy. As Gavin Mooney writes: 'Although it may be accepted that where public funds are involved we ought not to use a fool's valuation in deciding upon their allocation, if ... society is comprised soley of fools, then the valuation of these fools is the correct one to use' (Mooney, 1977: 126–7). Revealed preference knows best. That is what tolerant liberalism came into being to protect.

5.2.2. The Doctor Knows Best

Patients are ignorant and misperception is rife. Ordinary men and women do not necessarily act on the basis of best-possible practice. Crucially, however, there is often a normative consensus that someone else should. The delegation of choice to an authority figure ensures that ordinary people will secure experienced guidance from a trained professional who knows best.

Often a rational choice is being made not to know. Even where information is a public good, time and effort are private costs which not all prudent shoppers will wish to incur. Often, moreover, the choice to hire an agent is a non-rational one. Not everyone wants the responsibility for a life-or-death decision. Many people would prefer not to know that a decision had to be made at all. Even if they did know that the life-support machine would have to be switched off, still many would prefer not to issue the order to terminate a spouse or a parent themselves. The doctor is believed to be wise, caring and impartial. He is believed to apply the same rules and procedures in an impersonal and a detached manner. The consolation to the constitutionalist is that at least each choice is based on intertemporal criteria and well-accepted conventions. It is not random, *ad hoc* or *ad hominem*.

The doctors are prepared to take on the role that they are assigned. They have been taught the precedents and have absorbed the traditions. They know what is tried-and-tested and what is a fool's valuation. They know in addition that decisions of this kind have long been made by doctors such as themselves. The decision as to whether to keep an old person alive at any cost is not new. Patients have confidence in conservatives who treat like as like and have done it all before.

From the perspective of public policy, however, the difficulty is that doctors might not be able to put a precise value on the lives that they *triage*, or even state in so many words what criteria they apply. Medical people rely on conditioned responses, knee-jerk reflexes, half-conscious rules of thumb and the autopilot of second-nature automaticity to deal quickly with any challenge that might arise. In an emergency they simply will not have the time to think through the background philosophy or to say what the correct values and standards should be. Philosophers verbalise. Doctors cut and paste. They do not get much satisfaction from thinking about the substandard life years that they pare away, the terminally ill that they do not resuscitate, the potential human beings that they abort at the mother's request, the mothers' lives that are lost because of the abortions that they refuse to perform, the feeding-tubes that they disconnect because the coma is expected to be permanent. The Hippocratic Oath precommits them to help the sick. It does not encourage them to say when a human life in their care is spoiled beyond the point of redemption.

Doctors do it but they like to think that they do not. What this suggests is that the doctors' valuation of a human life must be determined not through questions and interviews but by a careful inspection of their actual practice: 'The doctor who stays in theatre to finish a long and difficult operation and consequently misses an outpatient clinic is probably relying – implicitly or explicitly – on some sort of theory of justice whereby he can fairly decide to override his obligation to his outpatients in favour of his obligation to the patient on the table. So is the general practitioner who spends 30 minutes with the bereaved mother and only five with the lonely old lady who has a sore throat' (Gillon, 1985: 86). It is their deeds and not their words that allow the inductivist and the empiricist to get at the 'fair adjudication', the implicit price that is the maximum the practitioner is prepared to pay.

Thus the observer might find that the doctor will commit a particular amount to save a life but will refuse treatment where the cost is higher or the patient less likely to enjoy a cut-off quality of life. Inference from experience will suggest that food and water are withdrawn after x days in a persistent vegetative state or when a spina bifida baby is too handicapped for what the doctor, looking at the baby from the perspective of the parent, calls a reasonable life. Replicated and repeated, the observer will be able to infer *post festum* the criteria and the values that the doctors had at the back of their mind when, committing or omitting, they supplied the Herceptin or discontinued the antibiotics.

Buxton and West used data on long-term haemodialysis for chronic renal failure as the basis for a calculation on the undeclared value of life. They estimated that the cost to the UK National Health Service was £3500 per year of life extended through hospital dialysis (£2600 for home dialysis). They derived their numbers from the published statistic of £23m, the discounted cost in England and Wales of institutional dialysis provided to 1000 patients for a period of 20 years. Buxton and West said that the figures could be seen not merely as statistics but as revealed preferences, 'one estimate of the price society is prepared to pay to maintain life' (Buxton and West, 1975: 376). If society was prepared to pay £3500 for an incremental life-year, then, they infer, society must have believed that the life-year being saved was worth more than or the same as that sum. The doctor may have been operating without explicit reliance on an economics or a philosophy text. Yet the observer is able nonetheless to work out the contours of what the medical people thought a human life should cost.

It is possible to derive a value from the practice. Yet that does not mean that the value will be irreproachable. If economics is about maximisation, then the economist must also concede that the doctor's decision might not optimise the result.

The conservatism itself is a blunt instrument. Habituation and inculcation allow the doctor to make a quick decision. On the other hand, they also retard the adaptation of practices to new techniques and new ways of doing things.

Rationality is further discouraged where decisions are influenced by average cost rather than marginal cost, by medical considerations that are resistant to cost-effectiveness, by hospital committees that promote staff members based on rigid and traditional standards of performance. Where choices reflect past socialisation rather than cool reconsideration, there will inevitably be a risk that the corporatised valuation is something less than a careful balancing of the costs and the benefits.

Practice variation itself makes more difficult the task of generalisation. Doctors will always have some discretion and initiative. That means that different doctors will be suggesting different values. Doctors may disagree on whether an irreversible coma counts as an adequate standard of life; or whether quiet withdrawal of support is criminal *mens rea* on a par with a deliberate decision to kill. Doctors, again, may show different awareness of the extent to which neglected patients hidden away on a waiting-list should count as alternative claimants when a decision is being made on whether a hopeless incurable should be resuscitated into the long-stay ward. Different doctors will make different choices when they try to reconcile equal moral worth with finite economic resourcing. If the scholar wishes to reconstruct a value of life from the practitioners' practice, he must clearly select a representative sample that includes the outliers as well as the median. It is by no means easy to find such a sample. Each doctor is a one-off and each patient is different. Clinical freedom is a mixed blessing where it is also an invitation to inconsistency. One doctor will save the life. Another doctor will say that the game is not worth the candle. In choosing the doctor one chooses the life.

Accountability is, as always, a major consideration. The first constituency being the individual and the third constituency being the public, the question that must be raised about the second or intermediate constituency is the extent to which it is accountable to anyone at all.

As for the individual, the doctor might not be prepared to authorise a wonder-drug because it costs too much. He might not agree to bone marrow transplants because stem cell research is a moral affront. Here the patient might die because the supplier simply refuses the treatment. Reversing the sign, of course, the patient might live because the merchant is unwilling to sell euthanasia despite the fact that the lifeholder believes his asset to be qualitatively substandard. The doctor says that the patient's life has an intrinsic value. The patient says that his life, self-perceived, has outlived its sell-by date. There is a conflict of opinion between the two parties which the policymaker will do well not to ignore.

As for the public, once again there can be a disparity. The doctor might have no objection to selling a kidney to any patient who is willing to pay. The nation as a whole might, on the other hand, take the view that insurance and wealth must not be allowed to determine who lives and who dies. Studying organ transplantation, Neuberger's survey found that the general public believed 'priority should be given to younger children, those with a better outcome and those who had waited longest' but that the gastroenterologists (ranking medical need above popular want) 'gave highest priority to outcome alone' (Neuberger, Adams, MacMaster, Maidment and Speed, 1998: 174). The investigators also found that 40 per cent of family doctors put alcoholics with cirrhosis last but that only 17 per cent of the public were equally resistant to self-inflicted conditions. The public were more willing to save the life of an incurable alcoholic, a drug addict or a convicted criminal. The doctors, disagreeing, preferred that resources should go to patients who were responsible and upstanding. The values of life were not the same.

5.3.   THE PUBLIC

The social consensus might not be satisfied with the market-mediated exchange between patient and doctor. It might argue that neither sovereign consumers nor professional experts can speak for the whole; and that public opinion alone can say what is in the public interest. Democracy means that the groundswell gets what it likes, even if the national priorities are different from those of the seat belt wearer and the doctor who knows best. Observed risk trade-offs reveal the preferences of the discrete revealers. Tolerance, however, must extend to the bystanders and not just to the roofers and the scaffolders, out on a limb. The rest of us would like to go on record too.

The social consensus in certain cases will assign a high valuation to productivity and value-added. Such a consensus, judgmental and economystic, will not accept that an individual has an absolute right to health where that right is not secured by a contribution to the growing national product. It is this window on the world that confines kidney-transplants to the under-40s since it is they who are actuarially the more likely to pay back the investment. The value of life in such a perspective is not so much the value to the individual or even to his heirs but rather his value to his collectivity. The value of life is the value of the earnings the nation would have lost had the expensive piece of human capital prematurely met its knacker's yard. That is why a productivity-minded community will give higher priority to citizens on higher incomes. People who earn more must be worth more. They must be supplying more output and therefore be deserving of extra attention. No team sacks the footballer who is scoring all the goals.

Such a selective standard, concentrating on 'the economic impact of untimely death', treats the liquidation of the asset, in Schelling's words, 'more as a loss of livelihood than as a loss of life' (Schelling, 1973 [1968]: 295). Human capital is the key, discounted present performance the criterion that authorises the disbursements. Discrimination in health care is essential as otherwise the senile and the severely disabled would get what young high-flyers with socially-valued skills happen also to need. Such a nation can be criticised for putting material-ism before compassion. That, however, is beside the point. If the community as a whole wants to put its money into engineering graduates while condemning the down-and-out to the vestigialism of the back ward, then that is the kind of dog that the community wants to have. Philosophy is the last resort of the well-meaning when democracy lets them down. At the end of the day, however, no one is going to say that democracy should be scrapped because the *hoi polloi* don't know what is good.

Law tempers the autonomy of the free market choice. The law can be pater-nalistic – literally so, when the State forbids pregnant women from taking risky jobs that would endanger an unborn child, figuratively so where the leaders seek to create public opinion and do not follow it. It can be rights-based, as where even a single non-smoker insists that his neighbours may not invade his lungs with uncompensated addiction and an insurance company is not allowed to use race as a heuristic and a proxy for risk. Most commonly, however, it is demo-cratic. Public opinion guides the politicians in their determination of the value of life. It makes sure they understand what their constituents most want to see. Public opinion can even press for constraint by agreement on the model of the easily-tempted Ulysses who made a contract with his crew. Here the consensus is such that weak-willed citizens rationally expect the guardian State to put a constraining tax on their alcohol. They do so because their authentic self, favour-ing self-*control*, prefers them to stay sober instead.

Yet public opinion need not mean unanimity. Workers counting on their danger differential will not necessarily be pleased when public opinion pushes through safety regulations that protect them from themselves. As their risks go down, so does their money. A single-minded entrepreneur working himself into an early grave will deeply resent the discovery that his fellow citizens want to legislate for regular rest periods and an enjoyable game of whist. It is not rest or even whist that he has in mind when he builds overwork into his business plan. That, however, is beside the point. The will of all need not be the will of each.

One illustration of the *social* valuation imposed upon the individuals from the top would be a Pigovian tax levied to economise on expensive imported oil: 'The U.S. Department of Transportation estimates that 1,300 lives are lost per year because of the switch from larger cars to the smaller, more fuel-efficient vehicles. The principal drawback of the small cars is that they impose a higher probability of death on their passengers. The main advantage that they offer is a lower fuel bill' (Viscusi, 1992: 3–4). What then is the marginal social benefit that the market fails to deliver? Is it the conservation of scarce energy? Or is it the conservation of scarce lives? In correcting a market failure, the State has sometimes to accept that there is more than one non-market maximand and that it has to select.

A second illustration of State intervention would be legislation to impose a speed limit of 55 miles per hour. Brent has studied the implicit value of life. He found that the limit saved approximately 7466 lives per year when it was in force in the US. The average driver was 33.5 years old. Assuming a life-expectancy of 76 years, this means 42.5 years saved for 7466 persons. The outcome is a total of 316 558 life-years gained. Taking average earnings for the year of the study to be $15 496 and assuming the retirement age to be 65, the human capital value of a life at a net discount rate of 5 per cent would be $527 200 for one life, $4188 million for 7466 lives. On the other hand, the drivers and their passengers spent an additional 426 279 life-years on the road due to the lower maximum speed. Clearly, the 426 279 lost is more than the 316 558 gained. The market value of time lost, assuming the average wage to be $7.45 per hour, was $16 543 million. Brent sums up the meaning of the data in the following words: 'As $4188 million is less than $16,543 million ... the monetary net benefits of the speed limit decision were negative and this legislation would not be considered worthwhile' (Brent, 2003: 291). The results might have been different had they included the utility of the retired or the unemployed. Life-years in paid employment are not the whole of the story.

Data on consumption is needed to temper the investment-based case. The social consensus might argue strongly that even unproductive persons can have a claim to quiet enjoyment. It might argue further that some people can be other people's consumables. Even an aged grandparent can be a source of utility to a grandchild and the death of such an old person the source of unhappiness to their bereaved. A housewife is her husband's consumable. Apart from that, she can be an input in his production-function. Interrupting her career for children, when she resumes she will earn less money. It seems a bit unkind to say that a female life has a lower value than a male life simply because women have lower incomes than men and outlive them in retirement by expensive life-years that only the joy of being alive can make attractive and legitimate.

It is a shortcoming of the studies of safety and security and of wage differentials that they focus on self-interest. Surveys and observed transfers are better placed to put a value on altruism and benevolence. The information might be secured through a question about people's declared willingness (it is not known if they will actually pay up in a vote) to subsidise better brakes for local buses even though the respondents themselves might travel by car. It might also be obtained by a question on genetically-modified crops or the disposal of plutonium waste where it will be the health profile of generations as yet unborn that will suffer the consequences.

Surveys will help to put some information about attitudes towards other people into the public domain. It is unlikely that they will provide all the answers. Is it appropriate, for example, to project into the future using the interests and delicacies of the present? At the very least, later cohorts will probably be more demanding than current ones since their living standards will probably be higher. Also, it is not clear if public opinion would want human lives still to come to be given equal weighting with the human lives that are here right now. A discount rate would considerably lower the current commitment to unknown and distant descendants, even if an adjustment were made for the expected growth in income. The decision-makers simply do not have the information on public opinion that they require in order to produce the other-regarding policies that their constituents would prefer.

Yet there is another imponderable which is an even greater threat. If public opinion is indifferent to other people, if it sees no reason to incorporate Alter's needs into Ego's utility function, should the policymakers nonetheless act on the basis of non-consensual ethical absolutes? Or should the policymakers passively fit in with the expressed wish of the democracy that the freeloaders should die where they fall? Respect for constituents' opinions and respect for human needs may point the decision-maker in two entirely different directions. It may, fortunately, not be necessary to say what health care policy should be when public opinion is hard-hearted and cold. Public opinion probably does care. There is probably a certain amount of compassion in a society. That compassion, added to the seat belts and the scaffolders' differential, will raise upwards the economic value of a human life.

Dignity and belonging, solidarity and cohesion, introduce a humanitarian dimension that amplifies the more materialistic, more achievement-orientated discussion of investment and consumption. Where people think of their nation as a membership-based *Gemeinschaft* and not a gain-seeking *Gesellschaft*, they will not expect their brothers and sisters to justify their health care entitlement exclusively in terms of their expected contribution to national prosperity. We look after our own. The *quid pro quo* is not the primary standard that we use. One implication is that lives acquire a value which in a less altruistic society would have been written off as having no value at all. People become an end in themselves and not simply a means to the economic end. Public policy has got to take into account man's 'biological need to help' (Titmuss, 1970: 198). There is no point in making policy on the basis of selfishness if it is generosity that the citizens really want.

6. Efficiency

The primary condition is that the job must get done. A health care system cannot be judged by its good intentions or by the sheer numbers of its inputs. The only test can be that of success. The means must deliver the ends. They must do so with the minimum amount of slippage. Underachievement means that scarce resources fall through the cracks. It is not a luxury that any health care system in the world can afford.

The means–ends relationship has four dimensions. First, there is medical effectiveness: the treatment must be the best way of securing the desired outcome. Second, there is economic effectiveness: a given endstate must be secured with the lowest commitment of social resources. Third, there is cost-benefit: not only must the roads to a single destination be ranked by cost, the next-best targets must also be compared and assessed. Fourth, there is cost-utility: the members of the community must be able to secure the maximum amount of felt satisfaction from a given health care allocation. The first three dimensions will be examined in the three sections of the present chapter. Utility is the subject of chapter 7.

Different procedures entail different costs. Given the resources constraint, health care must be budgeted with a view to miles per gallon as well as the humanitarian objective of saving lives which a prudent use of the scarce endowment is itself likely to advance. No one would say that a parent should cost-benefit the resuscitation of a child who collapses in the street. Yet the trauma of a medical emergency does not mean that rational choice never has a role to play. Much of health care is elective. Very often there are alternative procedures. When all is said and done, the interests of competing claimants must also be taken into account. As Alan Williams writes: 'Economists, like doctors, are seeking to extend life and relieve misery. In the case of doctors, the premature mortality and the misery is due to disease. In the case of economics, it is due to scarcity. Health economics stands at the interface between these two important fields of human endeavour' (Williams, 1987: xi).

6.1. MEDICAL EFFECTIVENESS

This section is concerned with technical efficiency. Its topic is the marginal productivity of an intervention that is intended to bring about better health. It begins and ends with an unsettling revelation: the precise relationship between inputs and outputs is seldom certain. Even after allowing for the fact that no two patients are precisely the same, the problem remains that in many cases no real effort has been made to find out the little that can be established. As Henry Aaron writes: 'Most common medical procedures have never been subject to controlled evaluation to determine in which case the procedures produce expected benefits and whether alternative approaches might be superior. Some analysts hold that simply by eliminating care that produces little or no benefit, health care expenditures could be cut by as much as 30 per cent and that service could be extended and improved at no increase in cost' (Aaron, 1991: 49). If only the medical care production-function were better understood, if only preventive as well as curative care were costed at the planning stage, then unnecessary tests and spurious treatments could be eliminated and resources concentrated where they delivered the maximum return. Yet too little is known. The result is unnecessary uncertainty and an avoidable misdirection of effort.

6.1.1. Trials

It is clearly important for scientists to establish the medical difference made by a given intervention or drug. To do this, they must conduct trials comparing a treatment sample and a control. Each group should be selected at random so that non-trial characteristics are evenly distributed. The sample size in each case must be large enough for personal variations and asymptomatic latencies to cancel out. The two groups must have an equal probability of experiencing a given health status. Only the intervention or drug will make them different. The investigation that is conducted using a purified data set is called a randomised controlled (or clinical) trial (RCT). The objective is to eliminate selection bias. RCT weeds out irrelevant variables and puts teeth into the *ceteris paribus*.

RCT can be used to compare the effectiveness of diet versus insulin in managing the blood sugar level of a diabetic; of an old drug versus a new one in lowering the incidence of myocardial infarction; of action versus no action in areas such as a precautionary appendectomy or hysterectomy. It is specific to a group. What is effective for one country, community or ethnic group might not be effective for another. Mental health, for example, can have a cultural component. Sometimes members of the population with multiple health problems, or with known and relevant allergies, or with abnormally severe presenting symptoms are ruled out. While this does protect the integrity of the study into a single complaint, it also means that the trial tracks a lower-risk subgroup and is not a representative cross-section. Internal integrity may reduce the external validity. Generalisation might be more difficult.

The Papanicolaou smear illustrates the use that can be made of RCT. Without screening a 20-year-old average risk asymptomatic woman has about a 250 in

10 000 (2.5 per cent) chance of ever developing invasive cervical cancer in the course of her life. She has about a 118 in 10 000 (1.18 per cent) chance of dying from it. Historical evidence is available that demonstrates the fall in incidence and mortality associated with the introduction of large-scale screening programmes. There are also the trials. In Toronto a study was conducted of 1200 women, matched (by age, income, education, marital history, smoking habits, access to medical care) with comparable controls from the community. It showed that the relative risk of cancer for screened women was 0.37/1 as compared with those who had not had a smear. In Milan (191 women) the relative risk was 0.44/1. In Denmark (428 women) it was 0.33/1. In Scotland (115 women) it was 0.11/1 for the two years after a smear, 0.28/1 for the year after that, 1/1 after six years (Eddy, 1990: 216). These studies confirmed that screening with Papanicolaou smears is highly effective in detecting cancer in its preinvasive stage.

Mather and his colleagues conducted a very interesting trial on home versus hospital treatment for acute myocardial infarction. The investigators studied 1203 patients, divided into the outpatient group and the inpatient group. The subjects (all males under 70) were similar in non-trial characteristics such as age and gender. The investigators ensured that there was no selection bias in relevant areas such as a past history of angina, hypertension, hypotension or coronary heart disease. The study established that the mortality rate was not the same. It was 4.4 per cent lower for men cared for by relatives and their family doctor than it was for men treated by hospital specialists in well-equipped institutions (Mather, Pearson, Read, Shaw, Steed, Thorne, Jones, Guerrier, Erault, McHugh, Chowdhury, Jafary and Wallace, 1971: 336). Women, usually the family carers, were better off in hospital, as were men taken ill at work or on the street. For others, however, the clinically effective option was also the cheaper one. This finding has obvious implications for the investment a nation makes in costly hospitals and beds.

RCT is intended to eliminate any systematic bias in cause and effect. Yet it is not without its shortcomings. Clearly, unless the trial is double-blind the practitioners might not devote equal attention to both groups while the patients might not show the same interest in the old therapy that they would in the new one: 'Knowing that one is involved in a trial may induce strategic behaviour on the part of the participants, and consequently distort the results' (Kristiansen and Mooney, 2004: 9). Differences in practice culture can make a trial institution-specific. This is the argument for conducting the trial in a number of centres and even in different countries. Payment patterns are a further consideration. Doctors on fee for service may supply more tests or drugs than doctors on salary. They will in that way tilt the thrust of the trial.

Industry sponsorship may introduce a publication bias. While downright mendacity would rightly be counterproductive, discreet manipulation is believed to be a fact of life. Trials funded by the pharmaceutical or device industry do not always reach the technical journals if they find that a comparator product delivers more favourable results. A medical system may itself select the statistics that keep down its costs. It would be embarrassing for a Ministry to be supplying treatments that are less effective. Problems arise where the scales are not uniform and the statistical tests not consistent.

There is also an ethical objection. Patients given the placebo are being denied the benefits of the breakthrough experiment that could stop their tremors. The sample testing the mould-breaking innovation might later find out, perhaps after a considerable time lag, that it had serious and irreversible effects on their heart or kidneys. Participants are asked for their consent. No one, however, can know precisely what they are foregoing or consuming. Guinea pigs and mice might have been exposed to the procedure first. What works for a dog might not work for a human. There is only one way to find out.

Follow-up is costly of scarce resources. Not only must the doctors put time into the study that could have been devoted to treating patients, they and other professionals must monitor the patients over time to determine the delayed consequences. A study of screening versus no-screening is a case in point: it might be many years before the false negatives and the unscreened controls are actually diagnosed as ill. The administration of longitudinal studies is costly and can be tricky. The investigators might never learn if the patients were later admitted to a different treatment centre suffering from the same complaint. They might never hear of unexplained complications that might be the downstream side-effects of the trial. Patients are not always helpful in reporting a change in address or circumstance, in telling the investigators about unusual symptoms, or even in adhering to the course of drugs that is being monitored. Economists building on such trials will find it difficult to calculate a long-term variable such as life-years saved on the basis of a short-term study that does not track the recurrences and the survivals far enough through social space. One year or even five years might not be enough.

Nor will the clinicians normally be able to obtain subjective data from the trial. Patients may experience vomiting in the short-run, intermittent spasms on a permanent basis. Irrespective of the differences, patients who remain alive are recorded as one added to one on the mortality scale. Comfort is not included in the data on crude deaths. The omission introduces a bias. Undifferentiated life-years are not the same as the patient's felt quality adjustment. If the scientists want to know by how much the felt life-utility falls short of 100 per cent, they will have to broaden their investigation beyond medicine and conduct a supporting trial.

Morally charged research areas raise problems of their own. Not all doctors will want to be associated with a study of abortion or contraception: the absence of Muslims, Catholics and others with ethical reservations complicates the process of randomisation. Also, in some cases the disease is so rare that a statistically-representative sample is difficult to find. Self-selection might influence the drop-out rate from the trial or the extent to which remaining patients comply with the regimen. Not all doctors are in any case equally adept at concealing from the patient whether they are getting the new development or a sugar-based makeweight. Tests would have to be double-blind if the doctor without a poker face were not to give the game away. Tests would have to be triple-blind if the researcher analysing the data were to be as much in the dark as the patient and the doctor.

The treatment administered to the RCT sample must be of best possible standard, and so must the alternative treatment delivered to the patients in the control group. A test of best-possible *efficacy* is valuable since it studies the new departure in pure, ideal and optimal conditions. Yet real-world *effectiveness* is not likely to match up to the rarefied circumstances of the trial. Doctors might spend more time with the patient in a trial. Patients might be better motivated to conform and more closely monitored to ensure their compliance. Motivation aside, a researcher conducting a gold-standard trial might have access to above-average equipment. Clinical conditions in the non-trial day-to-day are going to be different. The question is whether they will be *different enough* to reverse the trial rankings. A trial more representative of the real-world treatment setting would give a better picture of what will happen once the protocol is actually adopted.

6.1.2. Practice Variation

The doctor knows best. Yet different doctors do different things. Each practitioner believes that his is the 'right', the 'optimal' treatment. Yet the procedures are alternatives, different routes to the end. Andersen and Mooney are concerned at the range of disagreement and ambiguity that obtains even in a science-based, evidence-based area like medicine: 'Substantial variations in utilisation of modern medical care seem to be more of an overwhelming rule than an exceptional phenomenon. Practice variation has revealed to a greater extent than ever before, and in a way which denies the essentialism of modern medicine, that medical practice floats on a sea of uncertainty' (Andersen and Mooney, 1990: 7). It is not much comfort to a patient down for an amputation and not a drug.

(a) Cross-country variations
Much seems to depend on the doctor one consults. Vayda's examples illustrate the disparity that can result. Vayda, comparing Canada with England and Wales, found major differences in the (age-adjusted, sex-specific) rates of surgical intervention. The likelihood of (non-obstetric) surgery in Canada was 1.6 times greater for women and 1.8 times greater for men than it was in England and

Wales. For specific procedures the differences were greater still. The hysterectomy rate in Canada was 2.3 times that in England and Wales. The rate for partial or radical mastectomy was 3.2 times greater (Vayda, 1973: 1225). A representative woman was more than twice as likely to lose her womb through surgery in Canada, more than three times as likely to lose a breast.

England and Wales were different. So was New York State. The overall age-adjusted rate of coronary artery bypass graft surgery was 1.79 times greater in New York than in Ontario. It was 8.97 times greater in New York for patients with only moderate heart dysfunction. Tu and his colleagues try to say which rate is right. They conclude that it all depends: 'We suggest that there is probably neither one "right" rate nor a simple relation between service rates and appropriateness of case selection. Instead, policy makers must work within a paradigm of trade-offs' (Tu, Naylor, Kumar, DeBuono, McNeil and Hannan, 1997: 18). What that means in non-medical language is that a patient who is not very ill is almost ten times more likely to get heart surgery in New York. In Ontario the money is being used for something else.

California, like New York, supplied more surgery than Ontario. The Canadian government imposes global limits on the number of intensive surgical procedures that can be provided. In Ontario, for example, no more than ten open-heart surgery units can be in operation. California has no such limits: 'California, by contrast, has three times the population of Ontario but ten times the number of bypass surgery facilities.... As a result, a typical heart attack patient is many times more likely to get bypass surgery or angioplasty in the United States' (Cutler, 2004: 58). Canadian doctors prioritise their patients and Californian doctors do not – 'and yet, survival after a heart attack is virtually identical in the two countries' (Cutler, 2004: 58). Not everyone in the United States needs intensive care. A cheaper form of therapy might have done just as well.

Pearson and his colleagues conducted a similar investigation. Their comparison was based on three areas (Liverpool, UK, New England, USA and Uppsala, Sweden). These, they believed, were sufficiently similar in terms of background health indicators such as mortality rates, socio-economic composition and standard of living. Their finding was that the recourse to specific interventions was by no means the same. Inguinal herniorrhaphy was performed twice as often in New England as in Liverpool; the reason could not be variance in bed availability since the waiting time in Liverpool was then a mere two months. Cholecystectomy was performed seven times as often in Uppsala as in Liverpool; the fact that it was also performed three times as often as in New England suggests that insured fee for service cannot explain the whole of the variance in gall bladder corrections. Tonsillectomy and adenoidectomy were performed more than twice as often in New England as in Liverpool, more than four times as often as in Uppsala. Disaggregating, the differences were greater still: 'When T. & A. [tonsillectomy and adenoidectomy] operations are considered by age-groups, about ten times as many operations are performed in New England as in Uppsala in preschool children, and six times as many in school children; Liverpool is intermediate' (Pearson, Smedby, Berfenstam, Logan, Burgess and Peterson, 1968: 563). Were preschool children in New England really ten times more sickly than their counterparts in Uppsala?

The ratio of coronary artery bypass graft to population was, according to Brook, five times higher in the United States than it was in the United Kingdom (Brook, Kosecoff, Park, Chassin, Winslow and Hampton, 1988: 750). Hysterectomy too seemed to follow no medical law. The rate in New England was twice that of Liverpool, four times that of Uppsala. It is likely that some hospitals were irresponsibly performing too many hysterectomies – or that other hospitals were regrettably performing too few. Medical considerations apart, the economic implications are clear enough: 'If the British rate was to rise to U.S. levels, at an estimated cost of £1000 per hysterectomy, it could cost an additional £60 million per year' (Coulter, McPherson and Vesey, 1988: 992). Coulter's calculation is based on the finding that the hysterectomy rate was 67 per 10000 women in the United States but only 28 per 10000 women in England and Wales. The figure was 11 per 10000 women in Norway. If the Norwegians got it right and the Americans got it wrong, a very large sum of money could be freed up.

(b) Intra-national variations

Doctors disagree from one country to another. They also disagree within the borders of a single nation. Overuse and underutilisation are not problems that foreigners alone will have to address. Wennberg is sharply critical of the randomness and the lack of a guiding light: 'The "system" of care in the United States is not a system at all, but a largely unplanned and irrational sprawl' (Wennberg and Cooper, 1999: 4).

Thus Wennberg found that cardiac bypass surgery rates have a coefficient of variation of approximately 4: adjusted for age, sex and race, they are three per thousand in Albuquerque, New Mexico, but eleven per thousand in Redding, California. There is a six-fold variance in recourse to surgery for lower back pain. The average number of hospital days per Medicare decedent in the last six months of life ranged from 4.6 in Ogden, Utah to 21.4 in Newark, New Jersey. The average number of specialist visits per Medicare decedent in the last six months of life ranged from two in Mason City, Iowa to twenty-five in Miami, Florida (Wennberg, Fisher and Skinner, 2002: W100–101). Radical prostatectomy was 0.5 per 1000 Medicare enrollees in Binghampton, New York but 4.7 per 1000 enrollees in Baton Rouge, Louisiana (Wennberg and Cooper, 1999: 141). Tonsillectomy rates varied from 13 per 10000 to 151 per 10000 persons between the 13 hospital districts of the small state of Vermont. The appendectomy rate varied from 10 to 32, the total surgery rate from 360 to 689:

'Hospitalization rates for specific admitting diagnoses and for surgical procedures are almost ten times greater in some hospital service areas as in others' (Wennberg and Gittelsohn, 1973: 1104, 1105). The studies of small area heterogeneities such as these suggest that the treatment a patient receives depends in no small measure on who happens to be on duty. Medical opinion is not unanimous. Best practice is not a single value. Medical 'need' is not set in stone.

Wennberg conducted a study of two top-grade medical centres in the United States. He found that the residents of New Haven are about twice as likely as the residents of Boston to undergo a coronary bypass. Bostonians, on the other hand, are more than twice as likely to have a carotid endarterectomy. They also experience a higher rate of hip and knee replacement. Admission to hospital for discretionary treatments (asthma, bronchitis, gastroenteritis, to take three examples) is, weighted by population, higher in Boston than in New Haven. There are 55 per cent more hospital beds in Boston than in New Haven. Whether the beds lead the professional conventions or passively follow them, the differences are clear enough: 'For adult and paediatric medical cases, the admission rates are 1.49 and 1.47 times greater, and the length of stay 1.09 and 1.16 times longer for residents of Boston than for residents of New Haven' (Wennberg, Freeman and Culp, 1987: 1186–7).

It all costs money. The equivalent of 16 per cent of local value-added is invested in health care in Boston. In New Haven it is only 9 per cent: 'Their expenditures per head for inpatient care were $451 and $889, respectively. The 685,400 residents of Boston incurred about $300 million more in hospital expenditures and used 739 more beds than they would have if the use rates for New Haven residents had applied' (Wennberg, Freeman and Culp, 1987: 1185). It is a surprising result. Both Boston and New Haven are university towns with teaching hospitals fully up to date with current international thinking. Demographically, the populations are comparable. Medically, however, the neighbours disagree. What is standard procedure in the one is dubious science in the other.

Roos, Roos and Henteleff studied practice variations not simply within Canada but within the single province of Manitoba. They found that the number of tonsillectomies and adenoidectomies performed on children 14 years of age and younger varied, in nine areas of the same province, from 80.8 per 100 000 to 163.6 per 100 000 (Roos, Roos and Henteleff, 1977: 362). The dispersion seemed not to be correlated with the differential incidence of respiratory ailments or the unequal availability of surgeons and beds. Even more striking, however, is the amplitude of practice variation within the British National Health Service. The nationalised, collectivised, coordinated system is explicitly committed to universalising the best. In spite of that, different regions do things in different ways. Selecting the single year of 1988 for purposes of comparison, there were 679 operations per gynaecological consultant in the Yorkshire

Regional Authority but 1320 in Trent; 740 per Ear, Nose and Throat surgeon in Wessex but 1211 in Mersey. In the case of prostatectomy, there was a three-fold variance between the region with the highest rate of surgery and the region with the lowest (Ham, 1988: 13, 19). Manitoba is Manitoba and Boston can look after itself. A single, unified national organisation is a different matter again.

As with the likelihood of intervention, so with the length of stay. Inpatient convalescence can be two days or it can be 16 days: one hospital's 'excessive' is another hospital's 'inadequate'. In the British National Health Service, the mean length of stay in the Wessex Regional Health Authority was 3.9 per cent below what would have been predicted based on the health-related characteristics of the catchment population. In the North East Thames Regional Health Authority, however, the figure was 4 per cent above the level that age, gender and health profile would have suggested. For the over-65s the mean length of stay was 18 per cent longer in Oxford than it was in Wessex (Martin and Smith, 1996: 285). Heasman and Carstairs discovered that recommended stay for peptic ulcer in Scotland varied from 8 to 23 days; for myocardial infarction 10 to 36 days; for a hysterectomy 3 to 18 days; for an appendectomy 3 to 10 days (Heasman and Carstairs, 1971: 497). Hospitals in Holland were no more likely to do the same thing. A sample of five treatment centres, casemix adjusted, revealed that the average length of inpatient stay for an appendectomy varied between hospitals from 6.8 to 8.9 days, between doctors from 6.5 to 9.5 days. For inguinal herniorrhaphy it varied between 5.9 to 6.7 days for the hospitals, 3.9 to 7.1 days for the doctors (Westert, Nieboer and Groenewegen, 1993: 835). There is nothing so unstandard as the standard practice.

It is a cause for concern since it can be indication of waste. Wennberg found that surgery for benign prostate removal in the United States varied in the ratio of 10:1 but that the outcome indicators were more or less the same: 'For most men, surgery does not increase the length of life and, in fact, might shorten life expectancy slightly, because of the risk of operative mortality' (Wennberg and Cooper, 1999: 225). The intervention might for that matter reduce and not enhance the quality of life. Comparing the opinions of patients made aware of the impotence and the incontinence with surveys of patients who did not know about the side-effects, it is likely that more surgery was being performed than fully-informed patients themselves would have preferred. In 1992–3 the Medicare reimbursements for benign prostatic hyperplasmia exceeded \$1.8 billion. About 1.6 billion hospital days were involved. It is a lot of money to pay if there is to be no improvement in well-being. Nor is it always the case that the outcomes are not much affected by the treatments. The best hospitals in New York State have mortality rates that are one-fifth those of the worst. The variance between the individual doctors is greater still (Cutler, 2004: 104). Some of the patients who are walking in are not walking out again.

Greenspan found that 20 per cent of a sample of 382 permanent pacemakers implanted in Philadelphia County in 1983 were medically unnecessary. Each implant costs $12000 (Greenspan, Kay, Berger, Greenberg, Greenspon and Spuhler, 1988: 161). Chassin said that 17 per cent of the coronary angiographies, 17 per cent of the upper gastrointestinal tract endoscopies and 32 per cent of the carotid endarterectomies performed on elderly beneficiaries studied in 5 sites in the United States were not medically justified. The clinical slippage was not a function of the willingness to spend. In the high-use area (where angiographies were performed fully 2.3 times as frequently), the appropriateness of angiographies was 72 per cent. In the low-use site it was, at 81 per cent, not very different (Chassin, Kosecoff, Winslow, Kahn, Merrick, Keesey, Fink, Solomon and Brook, 1987: 2533, 2535). Winslow, conducting a further study of endarterectomies delivered to 1302 Medicare patients in three geographic areas, estimated that 32 per cent were inappropriate, 32 per cent were equivocal and only 35 per cent were supplied for appropriate reasons. Since the rate of major complications was 9.8 per cent, it was also found that the risks outweighed the benefits and that the procedure was overexpanded (Winslow, Solomon, Chassin, Kosecoff, Merrick and Brook, 1988: 724). The methodology in all of these studies was Delphi: medical records (all obtained from Medicare and relating therefore to the over-65s) were shown to a panel of expert cardiologists. The professionals then peer-reviewed treatment on a scale of appropriateness going from 1 to 9. Physical examinations were not conducted. As the appropriateness was exclusively medical, relative cost was not considered.

Even if the figures are too high, the consensus seems to be that someone is doing too much. Someone is pushing up the total cost. In the US, haemorrhoid injection varies regionally from 17 cases for 10000 residents to only 0.7. The variance in skin biopsy is 190 to 41, in knee replacement 20 to 3. Even in relatively consensual appendectomy the range is 5 to 2 (Chassin, Brook, Park, Keesey, Fink, Kosecoff, Kahn, Merrick and Solomon, 1986: 287). About 49 per cent of people in Newark, New Jersey, die in hospital but only 19.7 per cent of the residents of Tucson, Arizona, do so. It did not make any difference to the outcomes. More attention or less attention, the flat-of-the-curve came to them all: 'The intensity of care, while raising spending, does not appear to have had an impact on the overall mortality level of the community. Regions providing more intensive levels of medical intervention to the elderly sick yielded no discernible improvement in life expectancy' (Wennberg and Cooper, 1999: 178, 190, 196).

Outcomes were not much affected by throwing more money at the patient: 'Residents of the highest-spending quintile received about 60% more care than residents of the lowest-spending quintile.... We found no evidence to suggest that the pattern of practice observed in higher-spending regions led to improved survival, slower decline in functional status, or improved satisfaction with care'

(Fisher, Wennberg, Stukel, Gottlieb, Lucas and Pinder, 2003b: 284, 293). Life-expectancy or even felt quality of life were not much affected by prolonged hospitalisation or aggressive therapy in the flat-of-the-curve. Yet the difference in lifetime Medicare spending between a typical 65-year-old in Miami and one in Minneapolis was more than US$50000 (Wennberg, Fisher and Skinner, 2002: W97). Clearly, a high proportion of Medicare spending could be saved – perhaps as much as 20 per cent of its budget – if Miami were to convert to Minneapolis's cost-effective practice style: 'Debates over the need for further growth in medical spending and expansion of the medical workforce are largely based on the assumption that additional services will provide important health benefits to the population served. Our study suggests that this assumption is unwarranted' (Fisher, Wennberg, Stukel, Gottlieb, Lucas and Pinder, 2003b: 298). If the waste in the medical system as a whole is equal to Wennberg's 20 per cent waste in Medicare, the potential savings would be about $1000 per person. It is, as Cutler says, 'a very large amount' (Cutler, 2004: 67).

6.1.3. The Reasons for the Variance

Mooney and Andersen admit that they are not certain what is happening: 'Doctors do different things. Is this because their bests are different? Or are some of them not achieving their bests?' (Mooney and Andersen, 1990: 193). It is nonetheless useful to hazard a guess. The rate of coronary artery bypass graft to population was five times higher in the United States than it was in the United Kingdom (Brook, Kosecoff, Park, Chassin, Winslow and Hampton, 1988: 750). It is important at least to understand why this is so.

One reason might be patients' preferences. The patients might simply be asking for the interventions and the hospital stays. The difference is not in their medical needs but their tastes, preferences and values; it is a valid difference nonetheless. Where there are at least two potential alternatives, each with its own costs and benefits, voiced wants can play a role. These in turn may reflect previous experience in the same or a different treatment setting: 'The observation that native Vermonters of similar age and income use physician services approximately one-half as often as nonnatives suggests the importance of consumer behavior' (Wennberg and Gittelsohn, 1973: 1105). Different people want different things. One person wants to die at home. Another person wants to die in hospital. It is hard to say that the lost causes do not really belong in an intensive care unit merely because a friendly face and a word of comfort will have no impact at all on their quantifiable days on earth. Perhaps the customer is at least sometimes right. Can, however, regional preferences really account for more than a small fraction of the variance? Admission to intensive care in the last six months of life is, in America, 49 per cent of the cohort in Sun City,

California but only 14 per cent in Sun City, Arizona (Wennberg and Cooper, 1999). In the last six months of life most people are ill wherever they live. Demand, age-adjusted, is not likely to vary by a factor of 3.5:1.

Demand, needless to say, must be effective demand. That is a possible link to practice variation. Regional variations might mirror regional differences in incomes, insurance coverage, family support, savings accounts. Patients with fewer resources will turn to bed rest and informal carers. Patients with first-dollar policies will be less eager to discharge themselves from hospital. The doctors might even prescribe different programmes depending on what the patients are able to afford. Ability to pay probably explains a part of the variance in treatment patterns. Whether economic clout explains geographical variance as well is an empirical matter. Its influence will depend on the definition of the regions and the balance of their population. International comparisons will probably be more sensitive to spendable resources. America can pay for things that Bangladesh cannot.

Heterogeneities in lifestyle provide a further explanation for practice variation. Studies normally make an adjustment for age, gender and (ideally) household income. Other variables have explanatory power as well. Appropriate allowance must be made for illness levels (higher in Louisiana than in Colorado) and price per service (higher in New York than in Iowa). Diet influences how quickly the body will bounce back to health. Cultural attitudes impact upon the seriousness of one and the same complaint. A society dominated by aggressive competitiveness, risk-taking and status insecurity might arguably report a greater intensity of stress-related complaints than would one that is more tranquil and more accepting.

Folland and Stano, conducting an empirical study in Michigan, felt that social underpinning was the principal reason for variance: 'Standard economic and demographic factors account for both differences in market area per capita utilization rates and the average intensity with which patients are treated' (Folland and Stano, 1989: 87). Standard socio-economic factors account for the small-area differences in what the doctors do. This means that the scope for reduction in total cost through the diffusion of best-practice information is less than it would have been had doctors been involved in excessive interventions because of radical uncertainty as to what to do.

Yet the uncertainty is there. It is another reason for variance. Given the subjectivity and the doubt, doctors often conclude that there is safety in numbers. They conform to the expectations of their peers. Hospital boards perpetuate tried-and-tested drills because the old ways have worked well in the past. Doctors who join an institution snowball the done thing because they do not want to be criticised or asked to go. One curious result is that the same surgeon operating in different hospitals will differentiate his post-operative practices in line with the respective institutions. Confidence is self-reinforcing. Doctors have no reason to make a careful study of what other cliques and coteries are doing. They may never know.

Medical schools teach different things. Education too is a cause of variance. Where the doctor trained will have an impact on the tests, benchmarks, referrals and disclosures that he regards as appropriate. Vintage is relevant: different cohorts will have been exposed to different techniques at different times. Professional bodies in different regions replicate distinctive fashions, norms and conventions in an honest attempt to keep the local standards up. The result in Maine is that 70 per cent of women in one city will have had their uterus removed before age 75 but only 25 per cent will have had the same procedure in a neighbouring city only twenty miles away. The highest rate of tonsillectomy is six times the lowest, of prostatectomy four times. The populations are similar in economic status, number of doctors, health insurance and – crucially – general health. There is no significant difference in the pattern of illness. What makes them different is 'the style of medical practice of the physicians in the two cities': 'In one city surgeons appear to be enthusiastic about hysterectomy; in the other they appear to be skeptical of its value' (Wennberg and Gittelsohn, 1982: 100). They follow the herd. Learned reactions and local traditions are good enough to get them through the day.

The herd explains part of practice style, but so does the doctor himself. The doctor's own personality will count for something. Doctors differ in their ability to think in terms of probability, in their aversion to risk, in their willingness to exercise discretion, in their readiness to trade excellence against cost. They differ in the extent to which they will forego reimbursable interventions in order to supply sympathy and counselling that pays them less. They differ in their ability to spot the early symptoms of diabetes or a heart attack. They differ in their responsiveness to patients' preferences even when the expressed wish seems to them to be trivial or marginal. Depression can be a sadness that is a part of life or an intolerable abnormality that cries out for tablets and electroconvulsive therapy. A limp can be a minor inconvenience with which the patient has to live or an unacceptable gap between the actual and the ideal that must be corrected through surgery. Your want is not a need in this office: we take the view that you should not let things get you down. Your want *is* a need in the office next door: they say that even the hypochondriac has a condition that must be addressed. The wants that are validated as needs depend on the buzzer that the patient presses.

Doctors, where they are both agent and provider, face potential conflicts of interest. These will impact upon what Wennberg calls their 'surgical signature'. At its mildest, professionals might resist day case surgery because it increases the throughput and therefore the workload. The same is true of doctors when they fail to seek out information about new treatments simply because their existing stock of know-how has always performed well in the past. Variations can exist because the doctor is out of touch with the latest research. Just as the consumer can suffer from ignorance and tunnel vision, so can the supplier when he settles into a rut: 'One reason that physicians do not write prescriptions for beta-blockers is that they are not up on the latest literature; specialists in cardiovascular medicine prescribe beta-blockers more than generalists' (Cutler, 2004: 69). Cutler says that the doctors should stay on top of the medical literature. Since there are more than 10 000 clinical trials conducted annually, he recognises that processing all the information would be an impossible task.

Mode of payment can influence variance. Capitation and salary can keep the interventions down. Fee for service can turn loose the demon of supplier-induced demand: 'Practice style is an *exogenous* set of beliefs about the efficacy of various treatments. SID [supplier-induced demand] in contrast is an endogenously chosen level of influence on patient demand' (Folland and Stano, 1989: 89–90). Information, persuasion, vicarious choice, voluntary delegation, advertising, insurance status and even exaggeration can sway the patient's demand in line with the profit maximiser's wish to induce. Suppliers of equipment such as pacemakers and pharmaceuticals have a profit-motive of their own. The patient who goes in for an aspirin might come out with an implant. Economics brings out the worst in people.

As, however, was pointed out in Chapter 3, the power to over-treat is not without its limits. Monopolistic competition means that choices are made from a menu of perceived substitutes. Also, many patients are referred by their general practitioners rather than selecting their own specialist when they are at their most exposed. It is possible that variations in the rate of self-referrals will have an impact on the rate of practice variations. It is unlikely that the effect will be very great. Perhaps it is this gatekeeper relationship that explains why Folland and Stano in their study of SID found little evidence of prior-income protection, target-income inducement and supply-sensitive utilisation: 'Increases in the availability of physicians, including general surgeons, do not affect the intensity with which general surgeons treat their patients' (Folland and Stano, 1989: 103).

Escarce calculated that 57 per cent of the dispersion in cataract surgery rates in the United States Medicare programme could be explained by differences in practice style. The remaining 43 per cent was due to demand-side variables such as patients' preferences (the decision to seek an ophthalmologist's care), demography (the percentage of enrollees aged over 75 in the area) and economics (per capita income and supplementary insurance) (Escarce, 1993: 1114). His 57 per cent, high enough in itself, would be regarded as low by an author such as Wennberg. In Maine, one hospital service area does 56 per cent more hysterectomies than the state's (age-adjusted) average. Another is 89 per cent above the average in the surgical treatment of varicose veins. The availability per capita of surgeons or hospital beds does not differ to such an extent as to explain the variance. That, Wennberg says, is best put down to the momentum of the done thing: 'Physician and resource supply are a less likely explanation than differences in opinions of physicians about the proper indications for surgery' (Wennberg, Barnes and Zubkoff, 1982: 815).

Yet that is not to say that doctors and resources contribute nothing to the explanation. If the beds and the doctors are there, then Roemer's Law comes into play. Medicare spending in 1996, adjusted for the demographics of age, race and gender, was $8414 per enrollee in Miami. It was only $3341 per enrollee in Minneapolis. Fisher and his associates say that the explanation must be sought on the side of supply: 'The greater-than-twofold differences observed across U.S. regions are not due to differences in the prices of medical services or to apparent differences in average levels of illness or socioeconomic status. Rather, they are due to the overall quantity of medical services provided and the relative predominance of internists and medical subspecialists in high-cost regions' (Fisher, Wennberg, Stukel, Gottlieb, Lucas and Pinder, 2003a: 273, 284–5).

Vayda confirmed that inputs influence treatments. Less use was made of elective surgery in England and Wales at least in part because of supply. The number of acute care beds was 30 per cent lower in England and Wales than in Canada and the ratio of surgeons to patients was only 19 per 100 000 of population. The ratio in Canada was 27 per 100 000, 1.4 times greater (Vayda, 1973: 1227, 1228). The differences probably reflect the higher prestige of the specialist relative to the general practitioner in North America. One consequence was that discretionary procedures in North America were relatively more common.

Wennberg, Fisher and Skinner examined the impact of equipment and availability on cardiac bypass surgery rates (age-adjusted). They found that the explanatory power was high: 'The rates are strongly correlated with the numbers of per capita cardiac catheterization labs in the regions but not with illness rates as measured by the incidence of heart attacks in the region' (Wennberg, Fisher and Skinner, 2002: W101). The authors established that a good predictor of death in hospital rather than at home was not the patient's expressed preference so much as the local supply of resources.

Wennberg and Gittelsohn studied 193 small areas in 6 New England states. Their finding once again was that the omelettes and the eggs tended to go together: 'The overall rate of surgery ... in a given area is correlated strongly with the number of surgeons there and with the number of hospital beds per capita' (Wennberg and Gittelsohn, 1982: 100). Roemer's Law makes the treatment possible: 'Variations in the rates of hospitalization for most conditions are driven by supply, rather than need.... Capacity, not medical science, drives the rates of hospitalization, even in regions served by distinguished teaching hospitals' (Wennberg and Cooper, 1999: 69, 88). A built bed is a filled bed. Yet there are surprises. The same area that was below-average in tonsillectomies was above-average in the removal of the prostate gland. The wide variations in the rates of individual procedures are not caused by differential resourcing alone.

6.1.4. Trimming the Fat

The routine and the reflex is yet another of the issues in the social sciences that are explained with the conversation-stopping affirmation 'because that's the way we do things around here'. It is not clear what recommendations can be made. Perhaps one ought to say that medicine is not an exact science and that different opinions will always get in the way of a single standard procedure. Lack of knowledge is inevitable. What one can say is that opinion should be as informed as possible. Evidence-based medicine will not mean that consensus converges on a single option. It might, however, make it easier to rank the success rates of the alternatives on offer.

An example of the research that is needed is the tracking of inputs and outcomes. Hysterectomy and mastectomy were more common in Canada than in England and Wales. Death rates from cervical, uterine and breast cancer were, however, approximately the same. Vayda found that the gallbladder was even more discouraging: 'For diseases of the gallbladder, the mortality rate in elderly women and men was twice as high in Canada although the cholecystectomy rate was five times higher. Some of the excess mortality may conceivably be attributed to the increased surgery' (Vayda, 1973: 1227). More surgery was correlated with more spending. More spending was correlated with more deaths. A knowledge of medical care productivities and treatment production-functions will help to identify an appropriate procedure. It is the precondition for cost-effective budgeting.

Thus hospital league tables, utilisation reviews, Internet websites and performance-related supplements will motivate administrators to concentrate on high-quality procedures that have a good track record. A liberalisation of professional licensing and restrictive accreditation might loosen the dead hand of the traditional response. Consensus conferences, giving doctors in the same speciality the opportunity to exchange information, can coordinate, adjust and focus. Peer review, medical audit and second opinions, Wennberg suggests, might be able to bring about convergence on an accepted mean: 'A national trend toward decreased use of tonsillectomy appears to have accelerated following feedback, suggesting that information comparing performances among neighboring areas may per se enhance diffusion of state-of-the-art opinion and promote greater uniformity in clinical decision-making' (Wennberg, Blowers, Parker and Gittelsohn, 1977: 825). Utilisation rates can alter in response to comparative data that countervails the physicians' uncertainty.

Feedback and monitoring, both by scientists and by the insuring agencies, can provide valuable guidance in bringing about convergence on a single standard of clinical excellence. Evidence is the antidote to ambiguity, uncertainty and inconsistency. Data collection would document variables such as diagnostic tests, patients' preferences, day case surgery, hospital admission rates, casemix adjusted length of stay, casemix adjusted cost per case, targeted outcomes, complications in surgery, avoidable deaths. It would reduce both under-provision and over-provision of service where both extremes can be detrimental to health and where the latter is wasteful and costly as well. It would make delivery systems more accountable to the administrative leadership and reduce professional uncertainty at the doctor–patient level. Politically, and allowing for the valid preferences of the local democracy, it would level up the disparities and equalise the success-rates. So rational an approach would, however, require a detailed database on which to draw. It would also necessitate a willingness on the supply-side to convert to the best-possible techniques.

Apparently both the necessary and the sufficient conditions were fulfilled in Vermont. The result, according to Wennberg, was a dramatic fall in the tonsillectomy rate: 'Providing information on tonsillectomy rates to the Vermont State Medical Society led to a decline in the pre-adulthood risk for children of tonsillectomy in the highest rate Vermont area from 65% to 8%' (Wennberg, Barnes and Zubkoff, 1982: 816). In 1969 there was a 13-fold difference between the lowest and the highest age-adjusted per capita rates of tonsillectomy as between the hospital service areas in the state. In the area with the highest rate, fully 63 per cent of the resident population had had a tonsillectomy before the age of 25. In 1971 the Utilization Review Committee of the Vermont State Medical Society tried to establish justifiable criteria for a spread. By 1973 the average rate was 46 per cent lower than in 1969, the range of variation was only 4.5, and only one of the 13 hospital service areas (in contrast to seven in 1969) was still above the national average (Wennberg, Blowers, Parker and Gittelsohn, 1977: 821).

It is not always so, however, as the *Dartmouth Atlas of Health Care* (Wennberg and Cooper, 1999) has shown. Among patients with heart attacks who were 'ideal' candidates for beta-blockers, medically speaking, those who actually got the needed drug ranged from 5 per cent to 92 per cent. The proportion of female beneficiaries aged 65–69 who received a mammogram at least once over the recommended two-year period ranged from 21 per cent to 77 per cent. Only a quarter of hypertensive patients had reduced their blood pressure to the recommended levels. Fewer than half of diabetics had controlled their blood sugar (Cutler, 2004: 59). Most of the 306 regions included in the *Atlas* exhibited substantial underuse: 'Compliance with evidence-based practice guidelines exceeds 80 percent of patients in only eight regions; in ten regions, compliance was less than 20 percent.... The most important explanation for such variation in effective care appears to be the lack of infrastructure to ensure compliance with well-accepted (evidence-based) standards of practice' (Wennberg,

Fisher and Skinner, 2002: W99). Knowledge is power. By itself, however, knowledge is not enough. At the very least computers could be used to identify at-risk patients and monitor the follow-up. Existing knowledge would then be put to best advantage. There would be an electronic signal if the prescription did not seem to be appropriate or the patient did not return for a check-up.

Institutions such as the Professional Standards Review Organizations (PSROs) in the United States, the European Agency for the Evaluation of Medical Products (EMEA) in the European Union, the Danish Centre for Evaluation and Health Technology Assessment (DCEHTA) in Denmark, the Canadian Coordinating Office for Health Technology Assessment (CCOHTA) in Canada, the National Institute for Health and Clinical Excellence (NICE) in the UK encourage controlled clinical trials and make evidence-based recommendations on alternative interventions. In some cases they will combine scientific testing with Delphi group judgment. Once approved by the Department of Health, NICE recommendations on best practice in the National Health Service become mandatory. This makes allocation more efficient and performance more accountable. New drugs, although more costly, might be no better than the old ones in ensuring stated probable outcomes. Integrated health systems such as HMOs and the NHS are more likely to be made aware of new research and to comply with it. The elimination of excess capacity will reduce the temptation to exceed the target.

Insurers could refuse to pay where the service is deemed medically inappropriate. They could rely upon preoperative screening to bring about greater uniformity of procedures. They could proportion premiums for medical insurance to the amount of treatment per capita in the member's area of residence. Surcharges in higher-cost areas and rebates in more economical ones would focus the mind on value for money. The insurers could also reimburse using a standard schedule. The same for all would mean that they would no longer be cross-subsidising areas with a high rate of care at the expense of areas which look askance at more marginal treatments.

Yet the patient too has a role to play: 'A better informed and sophisticated role for the consumer as a purchaser of health care is essential to any strategy for improving market performance' (Wennberg, Barnes and Zubkoff, 1982: 821). People need to be made aware of utilisation rates and comparative treatments. They should know the limits and the risks of each. They should not hesitate to ask for a second medical opinion. Obviously insurance with low or no coinsurance provisions does dampen down the incentive to shop around. The price incentive would otherwise reinforce the provision of information in reducing practice variation.

Not all treatments are subject to variation, however. In some cases discretion is low. Also, deductibles and cost-sharing can 'have only an indirect and attenuated influence on those who make far-reaching decisions on the distribution of resources' (Wennberg, Barnes and Zubkoff, 1982: 822). The members of hospital boards will only tangentially take patients' utilities as encoded in their co-payment schedules into account in reaching a decision on additional beds and physicians. Politicians will find it difficult to reduce disproportionate funding for high-cost procedures even if the success rate is no better than that of the lower-cost alternative. The result is that inequitable transfers from low use to high use communities within a single pool are likely to continue.

6.2. COST-EFFECTIVENESS ANALYSIS

The cost-effectiveness approach does not evaluate the anticipated benefits. It provides no justification for the pursuit of any particular end or goal. It does not say why *x* life-years gained or *y* children screened is in itself a desirable thing. Nor does it place a financial value on the stream of benefits expected: the costs are monetary but the health effect is expressed in pulse rates, subjective satisfaction or survival days alone. The maximand is treated unambiguously as an exogenous constant. Since it is a prespecified objective, all that the investigator has to do is to rank the alternative routes to the agreed-upon destination in order of their respective costliness. In that way the approach puts the spotlight on the mix of (incremental) input means that is the least expensive in terms of securing a change in a targeted and valued clinical end: 'For any level of expenditure, the greatest benefit can presumably be achieved by adopting those interventions which offer the greatest benefit per unit of cost and abandoning those interventions which offer the least' (Meltzer, 1997: 33).

A business selects the production-function that will most economically deliver the output that it plans to sell. It minimises the cost of reaching a specified target or maximises the benefit it reaps from a fixed budget used up. A Ministry is no different when it seeks ways to reduce deaths from cancer of the colon by 10 per cent or works out how most cheaply to reduce blood pressure in men aged 50 and above. It will often insist that reimbursement for an innovatory drug should not be approved until cost-effectiveness evidence is available. It will want to be sure that the new departure will be better value for money than the existing alternatives of tried-and-tested medication, diet therapy and lifestyle counselling.

Scarce resources focus the mind. The availability of interventions exceeds society's ability to pay for them. Economic criteria and businesslike priorities are the normative response. They are not the only response. Medical best practice is also a yardstick that can be used to decide on the proper, the necessary course of action. So is the authorisation of the insurer who might say that the intervention, if still deemed experimental, lies beyond the remit of the contract. Distributional considerations and public opinion can discredit a valuation which most people find unethical. Not everyone likes to put a money value on health. The cost-effectiveness approach is not the only game in town.

The approach begins with clinical effectiveness. Quality of service and practice variation must be smoothed into representative generalisations. Randomised controlled trials (RCT) must be conducted to determine which procedure (if any at all) is the most likely to clear up a standardised complaint. The alternatives selected must be the most suitable comparisons: 'The control therapy used in a clinical trial may not be an alternative therapy that is appropriate for cost-effectiveness analysis' (Detsky, 1995: 25). One test will compare a new drug with placebo. Another test will compare the new drug with the established procedures already in use. The RCT incorporated must be the RCT that targets the alternatives that the policymaker has defined to be the most relevant.

The precise outcome of an intervention can never be known in advance. The important thing is that full use should be made of such medical evidence as can be collected. Probability does what certainty cannot: it makes the unforeseen into the expected while still not denying that the surprise of the random can shock. It is at that stage that social *science* becomes possible. The economists put a cost on each benefit in the set. They are only able to do so, however, because they have gained access to trustworthy clinical results: 'We are not interested in the efficient provision of ineffective services, i.e. those services which have been shown to do no more good than harm.... *If something is not worth doing, it is not worth doing well!*' (Drummond, O'Brien, Stoddart and Torrance, 1997: 31; original emphasis).

6.2.1. Selected Illustrations

Piachaud and Weddell studied varicose veins. They showed that the medical effectiveness of surgery and scelerotherapy three years after the intervention was about the same but that scelerotherapy cost less money per cure. Scelerotherapy was clearly the more cost-effective buy: 'The method of choice should be one that leads to as good clinical results as any other and should be the method most economical of man-power, money and resources' (Piachaud and Weddell, 1972: 287). The British National Health Service, the authors reported, would save over £1 million if it were to substitute that which was relatively cheap for that which was relatively pricey.

Gavin Mooney (1982) employed a similar methodology when he studied the alternative modes of breast cancer screening (other than self-examination) for women in their 40s and 50s. He identified three treatment packages. The first was mammography, thermography and clinical examination. The second was mammography with clinical examination. The third was thermography with clinical examination. Each of mammography, thermography and clinical examination could be performed either once or twice. He could have added still more options, each of them an increment or a decrement to the one before. Five of these are no screening at all, screening conducted at different frequencies, screening conducted in a local as opposed to a central facility, screening conducted by medical practitioners or by nurse auxiliaries and screening that targets abnormal risk profiles within a single age cohort. There are still more. Just as it would be meaningless to conduct too narrow a trawl, so an over-long spectrum of neighbouring comparators makes the study unwieldy, expensive and even open-ended.

Mooney collected his data at a single clinic in Edinburgh. In terms of capacity, it was capable of screening approximately 4000 women a year. The reservation must be entered that a different clinic (and/or a different volume of throughput feeding through into different economies or diseconomies of size) could possibly have produced a different profile of relative costs. There is no *a priori* reason to think that the variance would be very large, however; or that the rankings (as opposed to the *absolute* values) would be significantly affected. It should also be stated that research too imposes a cost. A larger sample might not itself be cost-effective.

Yet context-specific investigations undeniably limit the wider applicability of the findings. Eddy, studying the United States, found not only that the hospitals charged the patients but that the charges varied widely: for breast physical examination from \$3.50 to \$60, for mammography from \$25 to \$200 (Eddy, 1989: 390). Mooney's single institution might not be speaking for anyone but itself. Eddy's conclusion is that breast physical examination costs \$10000–\$15000 per year of life-expectancy for women over 50 while mammography would mean a marginal cost of \$20000–\$90000: 'Thus, breast physical examination is fairly easy to justify. Adding mammography is more difficult to justify' (Eddy, 1989: 395). Eddy's focus was on life years while Mooney's maximand was successful detections. They made different assumptions and they selected different targets. It is no surprise that their rankings were not the same.

Mooney found that the cheapest package cost £11.30 and the most expensive £16.50. These costings led him to the following conclusion: 'Mammography with single reporting and 1 clinical examination emerges as the "best buy" in that it is at least equally as effective and results in as few false negatives as any other screening package considered and is less costly in terms of (a) screening costs *in toto* (with the exception of single reported thermography and 1 clinical examination); (b) health service costs (both screening and biopsy costs) per cancer detected; and (c) the costs falling on women screened per cancer detected' (Mooney, 1982: 1282). Mammography with single reporting therefore emerges as the best value that money can buy.

Screening for asymptomatic bacteriuria provides a further illustration of ordinal quantification. Bacteriuria is not life-threatening. It is, however, unpleasant for the individual, and can be costly for the system if it is not caught in time.

Early diagnosis is desirable to protect the kidneys. Since the condition is asymptomatic, this can only mean screening.

Rich and his collaborators conducted a study of 1329 schoolgirls in seven Newcastle schools in order to discover the least-cost mode of detection. Medical opinion was that there were two treatment alternatives that would be appropriate. The first involved supervised collection of urine samples at the school: here the average cost per child screened was 77 pence for the high response rate of 96.3 per cent (the figure would have been 55 pence for the lower response rate of 85 per cent) and the average cost per successful detection ranged from £22 (for junior girls) through £34.37 (for senior girls) to £39.29 (for infants). The second related to dipslides self-administered in the home: the average cost per test went down to 26 pence (the response rate also fell, to 70 per cent) and the average cost of detection became £10.40, £17.50 and £20 respectively (Rich, Glass and Selkon, 1976: 59). Dipslides are clearly the more cost-effective choice. They are medically as effective as supervision and, economically, have a far lower cost.

Tosteson and her associates studied the economics of perimenopausal, asymptomatic white women at risk from osteoporosis. They found that there were three treatment strategies: no intervention, unselective, universal hormone replacement therapy, and bone mineral density measurement followed by selective oestrogen-progestin therapy for 15 years for women with low bone mass. Each strategy was estimated at the societal level (regardless of the source of payment) and expressed as a present value (discounted at 5 per cent). Account was taken of the low rate of compliance with the HRT programme (only about 30 per cent). No intervention would cost nothing at the preventive stage but far more in terms of disability after hip fracture, long-term hospital stay and even death: it was ruled out because of its poor impact on the quality of life. Universal treatment without screening would protect more women from fatal fractures but would expose more women to the adverse side-effects of HRT: it would have an incremental cost of $349 000 per life-year gained. Screening at the menopause combined with selective treatment would cost $11 700 per additional life-year gained. The figure is net of treatment costs saved because of fractures that never occurred. This third strategy was identified as the most cost-effective choice (Tosteson, Rosenthal, Melton and Weinstein, 1990: 601).

A final illustration of cost-effectiveness is Acton's study in Boston of policy options to reduce deaths from heart attacks. Four of the choices involved hospitalisation: the list included an improved ambulance service (so many of the victims dying in the first hour after an attack, especially where they cannot reach a treatment centre) and the average cost per expected life saved lay between $8400 and $10 300. The fifth of the schemes was outpatient only: the method was selective screening (the target group might be candidates with a history of heart disease) accompanied by preventive treatment (by statins, say, where an

ECG picks up an abnormality). The average cost per expected life saved in that case was only $6800 (Acton, 1973: 109). The fifth or preventive option was the most economical choice. It was also the most congenial. It was the only one of the five to reduce mortality without waiting for the patient first to have a heart attack. Most of health care spending is currently directed to the acute, the curative, the therapeutic and the individual. Acton's finding is a salutary reminder that prevention and public health might, economically as well as medically, be the more rational choice.

6.2.2. The Evidence Appraised

The results on varicose veins, breast cancer, asymptomatic bacteriuria, osteoporosis, heart attacks all suggest that the cost-effectiveness approach can usefully rank the scenarios. A ratio is produced in which the numerator is the net cost of bringing about a change in health status and the denominator is the net improvement in health status that results from the intervention. In each case there is a relevant comparator. The next-best can be no intervention at all, or the status quo protocol, or a different treatment for the same complaint. It can even be attention transferred to a different medical condition which produces the same number of life-years more cheaply. The assumption must be made that the treatments can be administered to any of the patients (otherwise they would not be alternatives) and that no other variables have an impact on the outcomes (that age, gender, diet and co-morbidity can all be controlled away).

The outcome measures vary. Timely detections or reduction in serum cholesterol (proximate outcomes), life-years, quality-adjusted life-years, sight years, illness-free days, improved functioning, reduction in pain (final outcomes) are only some of the success indicators that have been employed. All are physical. The heterogeneities like excess mortality are not standardised by a common measure such as price. What is standard is the estimation of best-attainable value for a budgeted amount of money (the lowest cost-effectiveness or C/E ratio). The calculations are, however, only as good as the data that is used. Reliable numbers are not always easy to find.

One problem is the bundling of data. Information on a treatment centre such as a hospital will frequently be presented as a total. It will not be disaggregated by department, let alone by service. Economists have no choice but to work out the *pro rata* shares, assigning due weight to the hotel and catering and to the medical components. They will do so on the basis of arbitrary assumptions about the allocation of kitchens, laundry, heating, lighting, record-keeping, administration and other institutional overheads. They must in addition work out the marginal cost of the operating theatre, the laboratory tests, the X-rays, the depreciation of the capital equipment (at historical or replacement cost), the time spent by the nurses and the surgeons (as approximated by the share of their wages). The information will have to be separated out from the aggregates (often with the aid of an expensive time and motion study) in order to isolate the costs exclusively imposed by a specific condition. Published sources will not provide the decomposition that is required.

The data, following economic theory, should be marginal. Public policy, since it is about the change in outcomes, should conceive of costs as incremental too. The choice is not whether to treat the complaint at all but by how much the supply of treatment should change. In practice the statistics are often uncritical summations. Economists must work with averages precisely because the marginal values they require are not known. Fixed and variable costs are a further complication. Costs are dependent on whether a change is possible using existing plant combined with labour on contract (excess supply) or whether constant as well as working capital must vary in order to accommodate further clients. Putting one more patient into a vacant bed costs little. Building a new ward or hospital costs much more. Conducting the research and development that will make the new technology a reality can cost even more. Rankings can be reversed depending on the new fixed costs that will have to be sunk. The short-run and the long-run results will not be the same.

Marginal and average costs themselves vary with the level of utilisation. Spreading the overheads can make the treatment rankings alter places: 'Due to economies of scale, a smoking cessation program for pregnant women conducted in an urban setting might be less costly per person than the same program in a rural setting where there were fewer pregnant women' (Torrance, Siegel and Luce, 1996: 63). The choice of the target population is also the choice of the costs. It would be more convenient for the investigators if the costs of production were constant. Typically, however, they vary with throughput – and with experience. Average cost is likely to fall as use of the new equipment becomes second nature. Doctors travel down their learning curve as they become more adept at prescribing the optimal dosages and at the early identification of side-effects which will become expensive if not corrected in time.

Generalisation is always a problem. Practice varies: one doctor's necessity is another doctor's luxury. Quantities are influenced by insurance: the cover is not the same. Input prices depend on factor endowments. An imported drug will cost more than a labour-intensive procedure in a poor country. In a developed country the bottleneck is more likely to be high wages. Presumably a different cost-effectiveness test should be carried out in developing and developed countries rather than carrying over results which might not tropicalise well. Comparative advantage is in any case not what it appears once the whole of the treatment sequence has been taken into account. Cost-effectiveness should audit not just the wonder-drug itself but also the extra nursing and the extra counselling that are its complementary inputs. Expensive pharmaceuticals in this scenario are supported by cheap labour. Cheap labour may be so cheap that it makes the capital-intensive scenario the most cost-effective buy.

Not all treatment centres, regions or countries will spend the same amount on the same protocol. Nor should cost be confused with price. Competitive markets will set their fees close to the economist's minimum or opportunity cost. Imperfect markets will be less accommodating. The monopoly price can be so far above the normal profit that a procedure found to be cost-effective in competitive conditions might have to be rejected once the supplier gains the power to pad out the surplus.

Hull and others, comparing the USA and Canada, found that the cost of two tests for deep-vein thrombosis (outpatient venography and impedance plethys-mography plus leg scanning, respectively) differed between the two countries so markedly that it reversed the ranking. Scenario one imposed an incremental cost of $1224 per successful detection in Canada, $11 159 in the US. Scenario two cost $1621 in Canada, $8650 in the US (Hull, Hirsh, Sackett and Stoddart, 1981: 1567). Relative prices in one country made one protocol the more cost-effective buy. In the other country different costs suggested the alternative method.

The cost even of a well-defined procedure is likely, all things considered, to be a range and not a singleton, an interval and not a point. The cost of time off work is different for women and men: women, like the non-white and the semi-retired, have lower average earnings. Externalities and spillovers extend the catchment of cost: advice to pregnant women to give up smoking will reduce the number of low birth weight babies but will also protect the woman herself from lung cancer and her other children from passive smoking. Being ill means a sacrifice of the nation's potential value-added: a full cost-effectiveness ratio would have to reflect the growth that is lost. The selection of the target popula-tion, the inclusion of the value-added variable and the redefinition of the neighbourhood that shares the social costs clearly shape the results that are ob-tained. It is cost-effective for at-risk fishermen and for local property speculators if mercury that leads to high medical bills is not discharged into the river. It is cost-ineffective for the consumers of batteries and tanned leather if the burden of chemical scrubbers and waste disposal is passed on to the public in the form of higher prices. What is cost-effective for the microcosm might not be cost-effective for the whole.

It is not easy to know which costs should be included and which should be suppressed. The choice will depend on the client-group whose needs are the focus. Some costs will fall narrowly on the clinic or the hospital budget. Others will be borne by the patient. Others will be shifted to the insurers. Still others will be a charge on the Ministry, the taxpaying public or society as a whole. The various cost centres need not have the same C/E rankings. Nor will full data be available for any.

Consider the hidden costs that are borne by the patient. Sometimes these will be as subjective as the anxiety costs of a woman biopsied for a false positive, the fear of pain of a child waiting to see a dentist, the inconvenience experienced when a cheaper drug leads to an inpatient stay, the disappointment suffered when the denial of a procedure means career advancement blocked off. Sometimes they will be as objective as the opportunity cost of waiting time, the earnings foregone at work (including the imputed earnings of a non-working spouse), the monetary cost of travel, the out-of-pocket payments net of the insurance reimbursement. Either way, the private costs should not be ignored simply because they are not normally included in the narrow definition of the cost of supply.

One example is fixed versus mobile dental clinics: 'The fixed facility was found to be cheaper whenever there were 75 persons to be treated, or more than 300 treatments a year to be provided. But no account was taken of travel costs for patients. These would be likely to be considerably lower in the case of mobile practices. Consequently the results would be biased' (Yule, van Amerongen and van Schaik, 1986: 1133). A second example is mammographic screening in ten small Australian towns: 'The *break even point* across the 10 towns is calculated to be at 29.04 km. The economic benefits of mobile screening outweigh the economic costs when a rural town is located at a distance greater than this break even point from a fixed screening unit' (Clarke, 1998: 783; original emphasis). Another example is varicose veins in the British National Health Service.

Piachaud and Weddell in their study included days off work when the patient was being treated in hospital or was convalescing postoperative at home. They found that the patient who had undergone surgical intervention for varicose veins lost on average 31.3 working days. This was a median sacrifice (using national data on average remuneration and making an allowance for sickness pay) of £118 in earnings foregone. The corresponding figures for sclerotherapy being 6.4 days and £29 respectively, the authors were able to report that the ranking based on private cost was the same as the ranking that was based exclusively on the cost to the institution (Piachaud and Weddell, 1972: 292). What is worrying is what would have been the implication if the rankings had pointed to different treatments.

This is especially relevant where more than one cost centre is involved in an intervention. Thus the patient's family might pay for a wheelchair, or might lose money when a room rented out must be converted for home dialysis, or might pay across-the-counter for medication that would have been supplied free of charge in a hospital, or might have to have time off work to ensure that a patient suffering a relapse receives appropriate follow-up care. The local community, again, might bear the burden of transportation for the disabled, the provision of day centres, the home visits conducted by social workers or charitable volunteers, the demands upon the police when mental patients are discharged without a network of support. The choice of the cost centre will influence the choice of the most economical procedure. Early discharge is an economy for the provider but is a new expense for the patient. In each case the appropriate centre will be a matter for debate. The decision will be a crucial one. Cost-effective analysis typically proceeds on the assumption of a fixed budget constraint. Different centres will budget in the light of different constraints. What is expensive for one cost centre in the community will be cheap for another. In choosing his viewpoint the observer chooses his view.

Time always complicates the issue. Brand names and patents at first inflate the price with a monopoly rent. Generics, embedding and the public domain subsequently make the new departures cheaper and more accessible. A transitory observation is not a permanent result. The C/E ratio at the start is not the C/E ratio once things settle down. It is always the way with a medical investigation. At the beginning of the innovation's life cycle the doctors will follow detailed instructions carefully. Later on there may be some slippage from best possible standards as reflex action takes over. Marginal patients initially turned down may later reduce the success rate. Marginal doctors not in the first tier of consultants may have a similar effect on the performance indicators. Still later the innovation will become obsolete and will be superseded by something new. A study, clearly, must be conducted when the new development is neither too experimental nor too routine. It is not easy to recognise the ideal moment when the evaluation should be conducted. If, however, an unrepresentative moment is selected, the costs of the study may exceed the knowledge that is gained.

Time makes it difficult to name the best possible moment. Time also dictates that sometimes cost must be recorded as a flow. A stream of costs such as lifetime hospital dialysis will often have to be included – and discounted – to allow for the fact that, in contrast to surgery, the expenditure was not once-for-all. For symmetry, some would say, the benefits should be discounted as well to the extent that they are reaped with a lag (the deferred effect of not smoking on the lungs) and/or can be cumulative (the long-term impact of a keep-fit class on health capital). Treatment for a headache or the common cold has an immediate payoff. Most major medical decisions, however, have an intertemporal dimension: 'The entire notion of investment in human health implies some concern with future well-being' (Viscusi, 1995: 125). To track every procedure through the whole of the relevant life-years is not feasible. Follow-up being difficult, investigators therefore draw a line after an arbitrary period of perhaps one to five years. A line drawn for convenience might not be a proper measure of the long-term effects of a new drug or procedure.

Also, there are the knock-ons, the waves, the sequences for which the initial intervention will serve as a foundation. The market fails to internalise the long-term multipliers. Vaccinations and screenings today mean fewer treatments tomorrow: a cost incurred becomes a greater cost saved. It is not, however, always so. Cancer diagnosed through a screen will trigger expensive chemotherapy as a result. Angioplasty initially is 50 per cent cheaper than coronary artery bypass but the saving falls to 20 per cent after only two years because of the greater need for continuing procedures. Malaria prevented when the child is young can mean the additional medical burden of unrelated hip replacements (unknowable and impossible to quantify) when the pensioner is old. Initial intervention can, for that matter, mean non-health-related costs (net of production) that could be avoided if the life earlier on had been evaluated out using economics: 'Cost-effectiveness criteria for the allocation of medical expenditures are strictly consistent with a model of lifetime utility maximization only if they account for effects on future related and unrelated medical expenditures.... It does seem rather counterintuitive that a hamburger eaten or cholesterol level checked 20 years after someone's life is saved by a given medical intervention should be counted as a cost of that intervention, but that is the implication. The intuition behind the result is that the benefits of extending life include the utility generated by those future expenditures and the analysis must also include the costs necessary to obtain that utility. If the intervention had never taken place, those resources would have been available for other uses' (Meltzer, 1997: 41, 59).

The lesson is therefore this, that in each case the study can concentrate on the cost-effectiveness narrowly defined or it can incorporate the full sequence of nodes and debits that a given programme can unleash. Letting the patient die at the outset (allowance made for extinguished productivity and the taxes foregone) would save a great deal of money that is not usually included in the data on the detections and the prophylactics. Perhaps it would not make sense to stray too far from the present or to include the whole of the decision tree. It would not be cost-effective to research too much, or to impute a value to a variable which cannot realistically be known: 'Any study can become a career in itself if the investigator chases down every ripple and linkage. In circumscribing the study, the analyst must attempt to balance the need to capture all significant effects of the intervention that will be relevant to the decision maker with the need to contain the study to the form of a manageable and feasible project' (Torrance, Siegel and Luce, 1996: 67–8). The study focuses *ceteris paribus* on a single issue or treatment. It cannot normally be expected to identify the whole of the patient's medical history to come. Nor can it incorporate every side-effect, intended or unexpected, that has an impact upon the calculus.

Abnormal cases must, however, be given their due. Some interventions are so closely connected that to select one is automatically to select the other. The abortion of a foetus with Down's syndrome is often followed by a second pregnancy to make up for the tragedy of the first. The side-effect of a drug to correct tachycardia can be a malfunction in the prostate. Treatment for high levels of cholesterol can lead to premature cataracts. Sequential interventions like these illustrate the need to cost the whole of the package and not just a part. The steps are inseparable. Abortion is birth. Heart is waterworks. Cholesterol is eyes. The treatments are as if one.

Ends are treated as exogenous. The cost-effectiveness approach ranks the techniques but not the benefits. The problem is that it is sometimes very difficult to separate them in practice. A study by Neuhauser and Lewicki demonstrates clearly that outcomes need not be insensitive to the treatment options that are chosen. The authors did not study differentiated treatments but rather the different number of times that a single test was performed. The aim was to detect cancer of the colon. Initially asymptomatic in nature, the task was to discover how the cost per detection altered as the number of sequential stool examinations per patient rose from one to six.

Neuhauser and Lewicki found that the average cost per case detected did not first rise and then fall as the series was extended. Rather, it rose continuously, from $1175 for the first test to $2451 for the sixth. Marginal cost expanded exponentially from $1175 to $47 million: the reason for the high figure was that the sixth test (costing in absolute terms an extra $13 190) would produce an improvement in the detection-rate amounting to only 0.0003 cases out of each 10 000 persons tested. This is much less than the success rate of 91.67 per cent produced after only a single stool (Neuhauser and Lewicki, 1975: 226). Unhappy about the $47 million, Brown and Burrows found that the marginal cost was more likely to be in the range from $1931 to only $4883 (Brown and Burrows, 1990: 441). Even $4883 can be a substantial drain. It is hard to say since the approach precludes the assessment or comparison of ends.

As interesting as the numbers are the implications. In the sample of 278 patients screened, Neuhauser and Lewicki found there were an unknown number of false negatives, 22 false positives and two patients actually suffering from cancer. These results were dependent on the number of times the tests were performed. Marginal tests saved more lives. Doing less saved more money. The end was not independent of the alternative selected. Like was not being compared with like. The effect was not a constant throughout the sequence of comparisons.

Eddy's results on the optimal frequency of Pap smears for cervical cancer were equally open-ended. The clinical effectiveness is not in question but the cost rises with the number of tests. The decrease in lifetime probability of death from cervical cancer is 92.7/10 000 where the screening takes place every three years. The marginal cost per year of life expectancy is $15 501. The comparable figures where the screen is made annual are 101/10 000 and $503 700 respectively. Cutting the charge per smear by 50 per cent cuts the marginal cost per year of life-expectancy by the same proportion. The 8.3/10 000 need not give up hope (Eddy, 1990: 222). Assuming constant charges, however, the philosophical question is whether the further decrease of 8.3/10 000 is worth the further increase of \$488 199. Eddy calculates that the move will increase the life-expectancy of the average woman by about three days. After discounting the cost at 5 per cent, the difference in life-expectancy is about nine hours (Eddy, 1990: 219). The study cannot say if the move to annual screening should be made. Common sense suggests that a frequency of once every three years is a reasonable compromise: it captures 92 per cent of the benefit of annual examinations and saves on the costs and the inconvenience. Common sense, however, is not enough. Once again, the maximand is not a constant but is determined simultaneously with the means.

The cost-effectiveness approach ranks the treatment alternatives by their respective costs. It does not say how much should be budgeted in order to secure a given benefit. It does not say why that benefit is worth having at all. It does not say whether the treatments should be ranked in terms of a broad objective (*x* more life-years in the nation as a whole) or a narrow objective (*y* fewer traffic accidents at the intersection of two rush-hour thoroughfares). All that it does is to identify the best buy, the cheapest means to secure a specified amount of health-related success. It ranks the programmes by the ratio of costs to outturns. In that way it enables the decision-makers to work downwards from the highest C/E ratio until the budget is exhausted.

The units in the C/E table are mixed. The cost is monetary. The benefit is medical. The result is that comparisons cannot be made between one investment project and all the other means/ends relationships that are in competition with it for the nation's scarce resources: 'Suppose we are attempting to compare a hypertension screening programme, aimed at preventing premature death, with an influenza immunization programme, aimed at preventing disability days. Here the outcome of interest differs between alternatives. Consequently, a meaningful cost-effectiveness comparison is impossible' (Drummond, O'Brien, Stoddard and Torrance, 1997: 14). A more ambitious reckoning is necessary if a general equilibrium is to emerge.

6.3. THE COST-BENEFIT APPROACH

Efficiency in economics is not a single turning selected once. It is a global matrix, an overall balance. Efficiency in economics is an exercise in thinking big. The maximisation of efficiency is the search for a point, optimal in the sense of Pareto, where it is impossible to make any person feel better off without making any other person feel worse off in his own estimation. Redistribution is possible on ethical grounds: it is the job of the social welfare function to say which optimum is the optimum *optimorum*. What is not possible is to move further outwards towards the production possibilities frontier. All the slack has been taken in. Every bed is continuously booked. Every doctor is fully employed.

Opportunity cost makes every gain a loss. The cost of a new paediatric ward opened is an old geriatric ward in decay. The cost of cervical cancer treated is prostate cancer left undetected. The cost of an angiogram in the capital is kwashiorkor in the villages. Health care is expensive. Priorities must be set. Means must be matched to agreed-upon ends. The *ought-to-be* is a normative judgment. The economics, however, is value-free. The margin is the modern missionary. Cost-benefit analysis is a body of techniques which, going beyond cost-effectiveness, makes efficiency global. It ensures that maximum juice is being squeezed from limited resources which will never be enough.

The cost-benefit approach enables the rational collectivity to ensure that it is maximising its return per unit of input. It uses discounted cash flow to decide if a new benefit will be worth the extra outlay that it entails. It uses the common denominator of money to make possible the comparison of heterogeneous outcomes for which simple cost-effectiveness provides no metric. Comparisons of costs and benefits can even be made with other programmes such as education or road building. A monetary total and a rate of return allow the option to be selected which maximises the net social payoff. In that way an economic value is placed on the good or service just as it would have been in a competitive economic market. Four case-studies will show the use that can be made of the cost-benefit approach. The stages in conducting an empirical investigation will then be explained and evaluated.

6.3.1.   Selected Illustrations

Acton quantified preventable deaths from heart attacks in the Boston area. He put a price not just on the means but on the benefit as well. He then worked out the present value of a life-saving intervention such as an air ambulance system. Assuming a discount rate of 8 per cent, he said, it would make economic sense to invest in the intervention so long as the cost did not exceed an average of $21 000 for each of the statistical lives that would be saved. If the outside rate of return were assumed to be only 4 per cent, the economic value of each statistical life would rise to $26 700 (Acton, 1973: 67).

Jackson sought to establish if university students should be vaccinated against meningococcal disease. Treatment of the sufferers is expensive: it could cost as much as $8145 per case for the doctors, the medicines and seven days in a hospital ward (two of them in intensive care). The fatality rate is 15 per cent: where premature death occurs, lifetime earnings of $1 million (the calculation is done for a male aged 20–24) could be lost. On the other hand, there is the cost of universal student vaccination: at $15 per dose (plus another $15 for administering the vaccine and treating occasional side-effects), the annual social outlay would be $56.2 million. Estimating the on-campus disease rate at twice the baseline for the age cohort and making the assumption that the vaccine is efficacious in 85 per cent of the cases (and that 80 per cent of the students actually receive their jabs), the investigators calculated that, at a discount rate of 4 per cent, the maximum present value the society could rationally afford would be $46.9 million. Only if the incidence were 13 times the baseline would the stream of benefits begin to exceed the costs. Otherwise it would be preferable, economically speaking, to leave the students (except for a small high-risk minority) unvaccinated and exposed (Jackson, Schuchat, Gorsky and Wenger, 1995: 844). The study uses the human capital approach. Willingness to pay would generate different values since it would make an allowance for the probable pain and grief of those afflicted with a condition which, objectively speaking, is relatively rare.

Boyle and his associates studied the costs and benefits of neonatal intensive care being provided automatically for all infants weighing less than 1500g at birth. Their investigation was conducted in a single county (Hamilton-Wentworth) in Ontario. What they found was that it would be an inefficient use of scarce resources to keep the number of infant deaths at its medical minimum: 'For example, neonatal intensive care of infants weighing 750 to 999g at birth resulted in the largest gain in survival rate for any subgroup (from 19 per cent to 43 per cent). However, neonatal intensive care of this same subgroup also produced a net economic loss that was the largest for any subgroup ($25 500 per live birth). Thus, the introduction of the economic perspective leads to a quite different conclusion about the effects of neonatal intensive care than does consideration from a purely clinical perspective' (Boyle, Torrance, Sinclair and Horwood, 1983: 1335).

Neonatal intensive care means that more money will have to be spent on capital and staffing. On the other hand, more survivals mean more working years. Comparing the costs with the benefits, Boyle and his associates concluded that the programme would consume more resources than it saved were the discounting rate to be 5 per cent. At a lower discounting rate of, say, 3.5 per cent, the position would, however, be different. Robust infants with a birthweight of at least 1000g would then become an economic proposition. Low interest rates mean surviving babies. High interest rates mean a rise in the price of black cloth.

Geiser and Menz used the same methodology to assess the economic efficiency of public sector dental programmes in two American cities: Richmond, Indiana, and Woonsocket, Rhode Island. The initiatives were intended to detect and treat caries in a target population of schoolchildren aged between 5 and 15. The authors collected information both on the costs of the programmes (including the fillings and bridges that would not have been demanded had the new-style screening not picked up unnoticed decay) and on the expected benefits (approximating the value of a tooth saved by the replacement cost of an artificial tooth, and making a largely arbitrary allowance for appearance and comfort).

Unlike Acton and Boyle, Geiser and Menz did not need to take the long time-period of the life span as a whole. The choice of the number of years as well as the selection of the discounting rate are a strong reminder that even accurate calculations are no more convincing than the assumptions upon which they depend. That said, their conclusions are as follows: 'With our "best estimates" – $350 benefit for each tooth saved, $10 cost per each surface restored, and an 8 per cent rate of discount – it would be six years in the Richmond program, and seven years in Woonsocket, before positive annual net benefits accrued. It would take 11 years for the Richmond program and 14 years for the Woonsocket program to generate sufficient total benefits for each program to cover total costs.... The results of this investigation may explain the reluctance of communities to institute publicly financed dental care programs for children' (Geiser and Menz, 1976: 197–8). There will be a gnashing of the teeth in Richmond and a gnawing of the gums in Woonsocket. Dentistry is about healthy teeth. Economics, however, is about value for money. The two are not the same.

6.3.2.   Cost-Benefit: The Four Stages

The cost-benefit approach compares the extra cost incurred to support a marginal treatment with the differential benefit resulting from the incremental care. It seeks to provide decision-making criteria comparable to those used by any cost-conscious investor, manager or accountant when deciding whether it is worthwhile to sacrifice today's pleasures in order to secure greater gains later on. The approach is a flexible one. It can be employed for virtually any marginal treatment, quantity, specialism or institution. It can be employed at the microscopic level of the individual, the family, the hospital or at the aggregative level of the society (through its legislators) as a whole. Whatever the level of aggregation, however, the approach expresses both inputs and outputs in comparable (monetary) terms. It proceeds by means of four steps.

(a)   Cost
The first step is to calculate the marginal cost of a small change in the treatment provided. To society as a whole this will involve a direct cost (the capital cost of equipping ambulances for specialist coronary care, the current cost of paying the doctors and nurses who run a vaccination programme) plus an opportunity cost (notably the amount of output the patient was unable to contribute to the national pool, as approximated by gross earnings foregone). To the individual and the family the cost will once again be the direct cost (fees, charges, medicines, home helps, fares and other out-of-pocket expenses, calculated net of eventual reimbursement by an insuring agency) plus the opportunity cost (usually income not earned while receiving treatment, calculated not gross but net: society retains the income tax but the individual taxpayer does not privately

pocket a share). Theory teaches that the relevant cost is the marginal cost. Most studies use the average cost. Total cost divided by total patient days is often the nearest the investigator can get to the facts that are required.

Some costs are concealed: this would be the case where a relative refuses paid overtime in order to look after a housebound invalid. Some costs are shiftable: consider the shorter inpatient stay, where the counterpart of less food, heating and lighting consumed in the hospital is a greater burden on the general practitioner, the voluntary organisations, the local authority backup services and the family support system. Some costs are sunk: the overheads of construction and capital are irrevocable bygones. Some costs, however, are sequential. Cost can be a river and not a lake. Thus an operation might be once-for-all but the immunosuppressants needed to prevent a recurrence might be a financial drain for life. HIV/AIDS requires permanent medication bunched by the phases of the disease. The total cost is clearly a function of early detection versus late. The discounting process must allow for the fact that the cost was incurred in instalments, not plunged in a single investment.

Some costs are background: basic research is not expected to innovate a named and specific breakthrough. Some costs are non-quantifiable: an example would be pain which has no market price save the willingness to pay for painkillers which may or may not be a reasonable proxy. Some costs are policy levers: tax relief for patients' travel, cash grants to family carers, an appointments system to reduce waits, are all examples of ways in which the decision-makers can alter private costs in line with social objectives. Some costs are joint: common goods like the recovery room, food service, heating, cleaning and accounts are difficult to apportion to the level of the representative patient, division or marginal episode. Crucially, however, all costs are calculated in an institutional setting. Different places do things in different ways. The rate of return in Woonsocket need not be the rate of return in Sheffield, or in Taipei, or in Dar-es-Salaam.

The capital commitment is always a Pandora's box. The investment decision can be delayed (where an existing hospital has empty beds that have become a fixed cost) or it can be immediate (where the hospital has no excess or slack and must build from the ground up). Nor need the cost per case be linear. Economies and diseconomies of scale (including the ability of large purchasers to negotiate discounts) mean that average and marginal cost are a function of the output level that is chosen. Quantity is a function of cost. Cost, however, is a function of quantity. Economic analysts are clearly taking a risk when they generalise on the basis of a single ward or a single hospital at a single moment in time.

The appropriate time period is not easy to identify. As Alfred Marshall says, 'time is absolutely continuous' (Marshall, 1949 [1890]: vii). Labour on tenure is retiring and job functions are being redesigned. Rent and insurance are coming up for renewal. Capital is wearing out every day that it is used. New wings are going up and old wings are being converted. Economies of scope mean that new departments are being added and old ways of doing things rethought. Technology itself *semper facit saltum*. Marshall's short-run and Marshall's long-run are artificial distinctions in a world where everything is variable and all is on the move. It is no simple task to generate useful results if the numbers will change radically before the policy-proposals have even been implemented.

(b) Benefit

The next step is to estimate the extra benefits which are the direct and unambiguous consequence of the extra cost committed. These benefits would not have come into being had it not been for the intervention. The benefits can be estimated using the willingness to pay approach or the human capital approach. As willingness to pay was considered in chapter 5, the present discussion will concentrate on human capital.

The approaches need not be mutually exclusive. Future wages rescued can be interpreted as the reason for the willingness to pay. It is, after all, the medical intervention that makes possible the stream. Many individuals and nations do regard health care as a way of getting on and moving up. They see their lives as an investment good.

Future leisure too can be seen as a part of the product that human capital is expected to deliver. People buy the machine for its utility and not just its bottom line. In such a case the investigator would cost leisure at the average wage rate and then make a human capital calculation, suitably augmented to allow for consumption. Thus Keeler, using the broader canvas, found the value of all future hours for a 20-year-old male to be $2 771 000 in 1990 dollars. This was five the times the discounted value of all future *working* hours, $532 000 (Keeler, 2001: 142). Only one-fifth of the individual's future hours would be devoted to work. The present value of $2 771 000 is likely to have been closer to the willingness to pay. It is logical that it should lie above the sum of expected lifetime earnings. People believe that health status is a benefit even where it cannot be said to be adding to the national product.

To society as a whole the marginal social benefits will principally take the form of the higher gross differential earnings-stream (taken as a proxy for productivity and adjusted upward to allow for growth). This will be the extra income accruing, say, to a schizophrenic placed on a community care programme rather than confined in a hospital. It will be the extra output produced by a worker whose active life would have been terminated by a heart attack had his hypertension not been detected early by a precautionary ECG. Manpower is highly valued. Most of all is this so in a fully-employed economy where labour is scarce.

Social benefits are the value-added secured. Contagious diseases are arrested where all children are given compulsory medical checks. Scientific research is advanced where doctors set aside time to participate in trials. Consumption is boosted since premature death destroys a producer who is a spender as well. Crime is reduced where drug addicts have easy access to rehabilitation. Medical costs are less where prevention eliminates the need for future treatment. Externalities such as these must be added on in order to obtain a full picture of the gains that are made possible through care. In doing so, the public-good spillovers enjoyed by future generations must also be taken into account. Weisbrod calculated that the most likely rate of return on the Salk and Sabin vaccines was between 11 and 12 per cent. Yet he also commented that infinity is a very long time: 'The more distant the horizon, the larger the rate of return on polio research' (Weisbrod, 1971: 538).

To the individual and the family, the marginal private benefits will naturally include the higher (net) lifetime earnings that result from timely detection and cure. No one wants days off work, blocked promotion or a shortened life span. Yet the benefits must also extend to the subjective welfare that is the improved quality of life of the person whose pain is less and mobility more. Good health is an end in its own right as well as a means for rendering oneself a more valuable piece of human capital at work. In Klarman's words: 'Man is not a machine, and consumption is the ultimate goal of economic activity' (Klarman, 1965: 379). What this means is that cost-benefit analysis, where it is done, should not omit the felt satisfaction of the patient when he discovers that there will be a few more good-quality life-years on the clock. Willingness to pay measures that subjective satisfaction.

It is all too easy to assume that a benefit is an objective magnitude. It is not. The controversial nature of a benefit is well illustrated by Brent when he writes: 'A reduction in the number of persons born stemming from a population control program may be considered an advantage if one is trying to ensure that existing food supplies enable the most people to survive; but it would constitute a disadvantage if one were trying to build a large (human) army for defense purposes' (Brent, 2003: 13). In such a case the births controlled would be not a benefit but a cost. Should the citizens fail to agree on what they want, there is no way to decide on what kind of welfare is being maximised, and by whom.

(c)   The internal rate of return

Once the costs and the benefits have been enumerated, it is necessary to combine them into a single statistic. Comparisons are made using the discounted cash flow formula that is employed by the investment analysts when they are assessing any other multiperiod project. This formula identifies the rate of return which makes a marginal benefits stream extending over at least two years just equal to the marginal cost of acquiring that stream. Put in other words, it identifies the maximum price – the present or capitalised value – that a rational, profit-motivated entrepreneur would pay for an asset if it were his intention consciously and exclusively to equate the rate of return on that asset with the compound rate of return (explicit in the case of multiperiod investment, imputed in the case of multiperiod consumption) on his next-best alternative under review. Total benefits increase at a decreasing rate since additional satisfaction accruing to additional medical services becomes less and less. Total costs increase at an increasing rate since diminishing returns make each extra unit cost more. At some point the value of the two increments will be the same.

The formula may be written as follows:

$$PV = \sum_{i=1}^{n} (B_i - C_i)/(1+r)^i.$$

In the formula, PV is the present value of the incremental benefits that are expected to accrue over time. It is the most a rational investor would pay to acquire the discounted stream. The total of $\Sigma(B_i - C_i)$ is a measure of the net gain. B_i is the greater income and/or utility made possible by the treatment. C_i is the marginal (not the total or the average) cost of the intervention. The summation sign Σ indicates that the differential (expressed in monetary terms) is to be aggregated for each year (each i) that falls within the domain extending from the treatment to the end (the n). The end will be the end of the working life in the earned income perspective. It will be the end of the period in which utility continues to be enjoyed where the study takes felt satisfaction into account.

PV is the highest economic price. $\Sigma (B_i - C_i)$ is the flow that is being bought. The r in the formula is the internal rate of return. Different levels of aggregation will give different values for r. The return to the society is not the same as the return to the individual since the costs and the benefits are not the same. If the incentives are incompatible the government might decide upon taxes and subsidies in order to bring the private incentive structure into harmony with the social.

(d) The rate of discount

The internal rate of return only acquires a meaning in investment analysis when it is compared to the next-best rate of return foregone. The discount rate is used to incorporate opportunity cost into the discussion of time preference. What it pinpoints is this: even if the differential benefits stream and the marginal cost of the treatment produce an internal rate of return that is greater than zero, still it might be uneconomic to proceed with the project so long as the return on a close-substitute project is higher still. Our hospital compares hernia repair at 5 per cent with drugs for Parkinson's Disease at 7 per cent. Our politicians compare investment in a new scanner at 4 per cent with investment in a new motorway at 10 per cent. Even a positive internal return pales into insignificance when an opportunity, easily missed, is seen to pay better dividends to an investor who is constrained by a fixed budget and does not want to miss his chance.

The outside rate is called a rate of *discount*. The name picks up the intrinsic uncertainty which surrounds any multiperiod investment project. Higher earnings might not accrue because of the obsolescence of the patient's skill. Even if the operation is successful the patient might be killed while crossing the road. A drug that costs millions for research and development might in the end fail to meet safety standards. It is never easy to be as confident about the unforeseeable future as it is about the been-and-gone past. An intertemporal discount is applied because risk-ridden predictions are always imprecise and might simply be wrong.

A discount is also applied for the related reason that people are deficient in telescopic vision. They are attracted by what the money can give them now and are repelled by an invitation to defer their gratifications. A bird in the hand is worth more than a bird in the bush. A given sum ten years in the future is believed to deliver less satisfaction than the identical sum today. To make the lagged and the current equal in attractiveness to short-horizoned decision-makers who want to live for today, an extra inducement must be added on to allow for the fact that people are impatient as well as anxious. Future satisfactions must therefore be discounted in order to capture the full value of felt time preference.

The discount rate is in addition a way in which the next-best foregone may be incorporated. Money plunged into a medical intervention is not by definition money put into a profitable enterprise or saved in an interest-bearing account. The purchase of the transplant means not just the loss of the purchase price but the loss of the project in which the purchase price could otherwise have been invested. Opportunity cost at compound interest is a real incentive not to have a hip replaced. The higher the opportunity cost, the lower the present value. The use of the trade-off rate makes the medical intervention equal to the competing investment into which the initial capital would have grown over time. In the case of a childhood vaccination, the time period in which the benefits are secured could be as long as three score years and ten.

It is, of course, possible to imagine a society in which the future enjoyed equal weighting with the present. A highly conservative community will regard any breach with perpetuated convention as revolutionary iconoclasm: it will say that the future is a joint product bundled together with today's status quo and that mould-breaking changes destroy the harmony of the eternal chain. It is, for that matter, possible to imagine a society in which the discount rate actually reversed its sign: 'Near-term consumption delivers only consumption utility whereas future consumption delivers both consumption utility and anticipatory utility.... Utility from anticipation creates a downward bias on estimated discount rates, and this downward bias is larger for goods that create more anticipatory utility' (Frederick, Loewenstein and O'Donoghue, 2002: 371).

The future will be valued above the present by dedicated parents who desperately want their children to succeed. It will also be valued above the present by growth economists who anticipate based on past performance that incomes, life span and productivity in the future will be much higher than they are in the present. Most people, however, will probably say that impatience is a stronger force than anticipation, parenting or even productivity. Today's aspirin cures today's headache. Today's operation, however, drip-feeds its benefits so slowly that a discount rate is needed in order to countervail the taste for immediacy.

More problematic is, however, the precise rate that ought to be selected. The same rate will clearly not be appropriate at all levels of aggregation. A good knowledge is required of what actual investors themselves regard as the nearest substitute when they are deciding whether to invest in surgery to correct their myopia or in a costly resort complex which has a 50 per cent probability of making them as rich as Croesus.

In calculations relating to society as a whole (and particularly if a significant part of the burden is borne by the State), an obvious choice for the health care discounting rate would be some other rate of return in the public sector. The comparison might be with a proposed rail link to open up the interior; or a marginal investment in an engineering school; or a nuclear reactor to break the dependence on imported oil. Sometimes the government will propose a specific discount rate for studies that it sponsors: in the UK a recommended rate has been 5 per cent. Taking a rate from the borrowing rather than the spending side, the social opportunity cost or social rate of time preference might be said to be the bill or bond rate that the government has to pay when it incurs new debt in order to fund new public goods publicly provided by the State. A long-term rate of this kind reflects the public's awareness that the interests of future generations must be protected. Their resources cannot be unduly depleted nor their genetic drift poisoned with disease merely because they do not have a vote.

In calculations relating to the individual and the family, the rejected alternative might be the bank interest offered by a financial intermediary on a similar balance over the equivalent period of time. It might even be the appreciation in a portfolio of stocks and shares or a new home not purchased because of a need for an expensive course of drugs. Where the patient borrows to finance the intervention, the borrowing rate could be taken to be the appropriate one. The evidence cited in chapter 5 on the implicit rate at which people discount expected life-years saved through seat belts and low-risk jobs can provide still further benchmarks. As there are no real-world markets where health status is explicitly traded across time periods, the reconstruction of a reasonable substitute is not straightforward. Not least is it problematic because a medical

intervention will seldom be delivered to a population of patients with an identical attitude to personal finance. A range of estimates would be more democratic
than the single right answer that does not exist.

Whatever the rate that is selected, the calculation is then a simple one. The
discount rate can be plugged in to the discounted cash flow equation. Solving,
this will reveal the present value, the maximum price (the V) that a rational investor should pay for a medical intervention in the light of the next-best return.
Alternatively, the equation can be solved for its own internal rate and that rate
can be compared with the outside option. If the inside rate is higher, it is the
better buy. If it is lower, the government on economic grounds alone ought to
buy a new stealth bomber paying 11 per cent and not a new dialysis unit that
pays back only 3.

Arbitrage in general equilibrium makes all the rates equal. Comparing like
with like, netting out unrepresentative projects, the final result is a situation in
which it is impossible to increase one's rewards by shifting resources to a better-
paying investment. This may be called a position of maximal (allocative)
efficiency. No one is saying that such a state *ought to* be chosen. All that can be
claimed is that cost-benefit information amplifies and enriches the assessment
made by the medical practitioners when they put their Hippocratic Oath above
the gains from trade.

6.3.3. The Interpretation of the Results

The cost-effectiveness approach opts for medical success indicators. Such indices have a stronger appeal than do percentage rates of return to doctors and
anti-economists who say that health and not money ought to be the dependent
variable. Cost-benefit studies are more ambitious. They have the advantage that
they measure benefits, like costs, in money terms. Cost-benefit selected, however, there are a number of problems that must be addressed before full
confidence can be placed in its investment-based analytic.

An obvious problem is the relationship between earnings and productivity.
In the human capital equation, differential incomes are used as a proxy for differential value-added. Such an assumption would make sense in a highly
competitive market economy where pay responds sensitively to fluctuations in
supply and demand. It is more of a problem in a settled labour market where
monetary hierarchies are ossified by conventions, unions and pay policies stand
in the way of cuts and rises, and the bureaucratic career structure proportions
rewards to seniority rather than to contribution. Entry barriers ensure that pay
does not fall to the lowest acceptable level. Professional bodies restrict occupational mobility. Housing tenures contain movement between geographical areas.
Race, age and gender are often the glass ceiling to merit. Pay is clearly a rough-
and-ready measure of the economic significance of days lost through illness.

The question is whether remuneration is *close enough* to marginal productivity to be the credible basis for an investigation.

Costs as well as benefits are, of course, subject to the same *caveat* about imperfect competition. Hospitals run by charities do not price their services by the textbook $MC=MR$. Taxes and regulations drive a wedge between reality and homeostasis. The prices of inputs like beds and drugs are not necessarily *free* market prices. Maybe monopoloid prices following output restriction are close enough to the invisible hand to serve as a tolerable proxy for something that does not exist. Maybe they are not.

A further problem is the reliance on today's cross-section when what is required is a time-series into the future. Today's pay structure provides information about today's differentials and gaps. It does not reveal how much a young barrister will earn over the next 25 years if his or her life is saved through an organ-transplant. Today's data can, of course, stand in as a basis for extrapolation. Yet today's pecking order is an imperfect measure in view of the economic and technological changes that are likely to take place in the microeconomics of pay. An aggregative measure is at once safer but less finely tuned. National average annual earnings could be used in a study. The figure would have to be adjusted upward in line with probable growth in productivity.

Higher incomes generate higher returns. The implication is that an elderly black woman will be worth less than a white male professional in his prime. It is an economistic value judgment. Where benefits are legitimated by production, the poor, the retired and the unemployable will go to the end of the queue. A different value judgment would be that it is the less intelligent and the less well-paid who on the grounds of the humanitarian spillover are the most deserving of the compensating distribution. The income structure in the future could be radically altered as a result of an egalitarian investment decision made in the present. Most of all would this be so if cost-effectiveness and cost-benefit analysis were able to identify projects that could be scrapped in order to free up resources for a more equal society.

Studying tests for cervical cancer, prostate cancer and high blood cholesterol, and allowing for the high incidence of false positives necessitating expensive treatment that the patient does not need, Louise Russell has used the economic line of reasoning to suggest that the community would have been better off if the screening had never taken place: 'The billions of dollars involved in these three screening tests alone are enough to finance a system of basic care for the poor and uninsured' (Russell, 1994: 92). Overinvestment is a great concern, but so is the medical gain if even one true positive turns out to have saved a life. That is the problem of interdisciplinary communication. Economists say that the treatment costs too much. Louise Russell says that the poor deserve their turn. The doctors say that they did not go to medical school in order to default on their duty to the sick.

The theory of diminishing utility reinforces the welfarist ideal: the marginal utility of income is likely to be higher among the lower income-groups. Subjectively if not objectively, the poor earn more than the statistics reveal. Cost-benefit analysis should therefore massage the figures and make the numbers say what they should. Not everyone will agree. One among many, Pauly is unconvinced that it would make economic sense to tinker with the market-measured evidence in this way: 'If a dollar's worth of benefits to poor people were worth more to society than a dollar's worth of benefits to rich people, it follows that society should be redistributing more income from rich people to poor people. If we observe, however, that society, whichever decision it makes, does not seem disposed to make further transfers from rich to poor, then we are not justified in asserting that the same society would value health benefits of a given money value more if they go to poor people than to rich people.... It is not legitimate to doctor the books in cost-benefit analysis in order to bring about by subterfuge what would not be tolerated in the standard political process' (Pauly, 1995: 118).

It is not always easy at the best of times to say who are the 'low paid'. Teachers and nurses are not highly paid in money terms but they do receive an above-average stream of psychic income which leaves them no worse off in their own estimation. Housewives are not paid in cash but they do supply value-added nonetheless. A possible solution would be to record housewives' implicit incomes either as their own opportunity cost in the outside labour market or in the currency of the average female wage in the appropriate locality and pool. Another solution would be to proxy their value as the paid-out cost saved had they had to hire a housekeeper to take over their domestic chores. Each solution is better than nothing. None, however, is entirely satisfactory.

An important difficulty is the need to put a value on consumption. Even a retired person who has left remunerated labour behind can still derive final utility from the quantity and quality of life. Retired people who do not want to die say that their life still has value in their own eyes despite the fact that their economic contribution has fallen to zero. Parents who want to learn the gender of an unborn child approach a doctor despite the fact that their knowledge of pink and blue adds nothing to the nation's wealth. Material improvement, in other words, is not the whole of individual preference. Consumption and investment are properly treated as joint products in a cost-benefit study of health. There is much overlap. There would be double counting if patients were asked to compartmentalise into work and play the improved well-being they gained from medical intervention. The expenditure incurred to get back one's earning capacity is difficult to separate in one's mind from the ability to walk again.

Investment is less difficult to quantify. Studies, partly for that reason, concentrate on the differential earnings component. It is easy enough to write off felt utility as an unmeasurable unknown. Yet not everyone would abandon the chase. Chapter 7 explains some of the techniques that can be used to incorporate personal satisfaction where the stream of benefits is all in the mind.

The benefits are difficult to measure. So, however, are the costs. Inputs purchased in the outside market may be subject to price-fixing by oligopolies and public sector regulators. Further distortion of market-clearing values occurs where inputs are not bought in the outside market but exchanged at a notional value in-house. Some costs have subjective content (as where a prescription charge is proportional to marginal utility) but other costs are accounting values that are not true opportunity costs, tested through supply and demand. Externalities and third-party effects are not easy to recognise or to quantify. Many of the indirect effects are very indirect indeed. It is not always obvious where to draw the line.

The rate of discount can itself be a problem. The higher it is, the lower the present value, the lower the price that the rational investor will be prepared to pay. Hospitals in that way will be put on hold and new equipment rejected at 10 per cent that would have been installed at 5. Intertemporal quickly becomes intergenerational. Future generations will not thank us for leaving farmers-to-come without water for irrigation because we decided that a low discounting rate was unsuitable for a dam. Individuals' time preference is short-term: it reflects the fact that they will die. Nations, however, go on and on: the social optimum must include the future's preferences. Equity means being fair to our descendants as well as to our neighbours despite the fact that it is the here-and-now that is making the choice.

What that suggests might have to be a low discounting rate even if the observed opportunity cost is high. Even the unborn are utility-seeking consumers. *Their* sovereignty too must be a part of today's intertemporal collective choice. Our consensus might incorporate ethical as well as economic arguments. Our politicians will disregard these preferences at their cost. Our *collective* trade-off is in any case extremely difficult to measure. If we do not all discount future consumption at the same rate, our politicians will have to cut the Gordian Knot on our behalf. They will have to invent a consensus where no consensus is to be found.

They will be on firmer ground in the imposition of a solution if they can argue that the financial markets have a tendency to fail. Public policy is less obviously a market distortion if the capital market is incompletely informed and imperfectly competitive. Individuals might reveal preferences which are irrational and inconsistent in the light of their life cycle options. The banking sector might be administered, imperfectly competitive and insensitive. In such circumstances the market rate might not have the same normative primacy that it would if the pricing of savings and investment had been frictionless, powerless and index-linked against inflation. In the public sector the appropriate *social* discount rate might not be the market rate of interest after all. The State rather than the people might be the best judge of the structural needs of an interdependent whole. The State might be within its rights to proclaim a discount rate of its own.

7.   Utility

Ends are problematic where the success indicators are as objective as illnesses cured, life-expectancy extended, five-year survival met, blood pressure reduced, asymptomatic bacteriuria detected. They are even more problematic where the clinical outcomes are equal but the subjective meanings are not. Individuals have preferences. It would be a mistake to concentrate on the sick days never taken, the throats swabbed, the splints stuck on, the human capital accumulated, the internal rates made equal while neglecting the passionate stakeholder's personal satisfaction from life.

There are three constituencies that expect to be consulted. These are the patient, the practitioner and the public. This chapter, in three successive sections, analyses the contribution of each to the identification of the health-related quality of life. The chapter is about cost-effectiveness and value for money. More like the psychologist than the engineer, however, it quantifies its desiderata through the perceptions of thinking human beings who think they have a need to be heard. The mind speaks and the accountant listens. The product of the health care production-function must be – or must also be – the psychic well-being that all three constituencies experience when medical intervention solves a problem that to them had been a blight.

7.1.   THE PATIENT

Liberal democracy is imbued with individualism. Welfare is in the eye of the beholder. Rational choice, revealed preference and consumer sovereignty can be trusted to produce an optimum that no doctor and no dictator can ever know or impose. The greatest felt happiness to the liberal democrat is the direct result of the weights that are applied by discrete one-offs when they reveal their preferences and quantify their desires. Only the bodyholder can say if, and by how much, he believes kidney dialysis to be inferior to an organ transplant; or if he fears a surgical scar so much that he would prefer a herbal remedy that just might do the trick. Only the patient offered hormone replacement therapy can say if she is willing to exchange a lower risk of osteoporosis for a higher risk of cancer or whether a lower probability of heart disease has the same value to her as a higher probability of postmenopausal surgery. Only the one-off can know if he discounts the future at a high rate or a low one; or if he is risk-averse enough to refuse a gamble that might save his life. The World Health Organization comes down in favour of 'complete well-being'. Since the discrete atom alone knows what is 'complete' for him, since every mind is a stranger to every other, the liberal democrat will say that self-rating is the bedrock measure of health.

One year of life spent in one health state does not yield the same satisfaction as one year of life spent in a different state. Crude life-years and calendar time do not tell the whole story: 'The difficulty is that everyone who remains alive is given the same score. A person confined to bed with an irreversible coma is alive and is counted the same as someone who is actively playing volleyball at a picnic' (Kaplan, 1995: 31). It can be misleading to code death as No, life as Yes, without inquiring into the multiple stages along the continuum that track out how it feels not to be on form. Some of those stages might actually be the side-effects of a treatment designed to extend calendar life. High blood pressure is controlled but exhaustion is the price.

The pluses come with minuses attached. The quality-adjusted life-year (QALY), health-related, is a mixed statistic that marries up the length and the enjoyment that are the joint products of medical care. The QALY has the attraction that it combines information on both morbidity (quality) and mortality (quantity). In that way it serves as a single benchmark, a single standard of excellence and indicator of success: 'The basic assumption is that two years scored as 0.5 add up to the equivalent of one year of complete wellness. Similarly, four years scored as 0.25 are equivalent to one completely well year of life…. The disagreement is not over the QALY concept but rather over how the weights for cases between 0 and 1 are obtained' (Kaplan, 1995: 35).

The validity of the statistic stands or falls with the sensitivity of the weights. Liberal democracy is a noble ideal. It is, however, no better than the quality of the information that is passed upwards from the people. This section explores the extent to which the statisticians can reconstruct the direction and intensity of the preferences on which the citizens would like their leadership to act.

7.1.1. Rating Scales

Daly and her colleagues studied 63 British women (with a mean age of 52.1) in the menopausal years. Using a questionnaire and a rating scale, they found that, in the women's own judgment, if full health was 1 and death was 0, severe menopausal symptoms made the utility 0.29, mild symptoms 0.61. Things improved (to scores of 0.85 and 0.79 respectively) when the women were given hormone replacement therapy (Daly, Gray, Barlow, McPherson, Roche and Vessey, 1993: 838). Only the women themselves were in possession of this information. Psychometrics here only reconstructed their felt quality of life, self-perceived. It is important to understand what the discovery means. If the woman with the score of 0.29 suddenly dies, what is being extinguished is not 100 per cent of her expected joy from life but only 29 per cent. In a cost-effectiveness ratio, her life will count as less than a third if the data she revealed to the investigators gives an accurate picture of her state of mind.

An important illustration of the experimental procedure is the influential (and much replicated) study done by Rosser and Kind. The authors constructed a double scale of negative outcomes. The first proceeded in eight steps: 'no disability', 'slight social disability', 'severe social disability', 'choice of work or performance at work very severely limited', 'unable to undertake any paid employment', 'confined to chair or to wheelchair', 'confined to bed', 'unconscious'. The second had four grades: 'no distress', 'mild distress', 'moderate distress' and 'severe distress' (Rosser and Kind, 1978: 349). Respondents were asked to correlate felt distress with the medically-measurable outcome-anchors, each carefully described by the interviewer. Permanent unconsciousness counted as 0, perfect health (a 'well year') as 1, everything else as intermediate. This is not the traditional bipolarity of life versus death but an interval scale.

Respondents were first asked to rank the states of illness in order of perceived severity. Thereafter, in order to establish *how many times* less satisfactory one health status was when compared with another, they were asked to arrange the states of illness on a scale. They were asked to put the state of death on the scale and to assign a value to it. Prognosis was introduced twice: once as treatment leading to cure, once as a permanent state of illness. Respondents were invited to say which condition was half as severe, one quarter as severe, and so forth. This is fractionation. As a cross-check they were asked ('split-test reliability') which condition was twice as severe, four tines as severe and so on. This is multiplication. The questions were repeated ('test-retest reliability') after a short lapse of a week. A week was long enough for subjects to have forgotten their earlier answers but not long enough for their preferences to have altered significantly.

Rosser, with others, expanded the index of health-related quality of life (IHQL) by adding an extra scale. The eight levels of disability were to be evaluated in terms of five levels of distress and five levels of pain (Rosser, Cottee, Rabin and Salai, 1992). Kind and his colleagues developed the EuroQol EQ-5D questionnaire. It defines health in terms of five dimensions: mobility, self-care, usual activities (work, study, housework, family, leisure), pain or discomfort, anxiety or depression. Each dimension is subdivided into three categories of disutility: no problem, moderate problem, extreme problem. Combinations of these categories produce a range of discrete health states. At the end of the study the respondents are asked to rank their health status on a visual analogue scale. It extends by single percentage points from 'worst imaginable' to 'best imaginable'.

Conducting a study of 3395 representative British residents, Kind found that one in three respondents reported some pain or discomfort. The mean state of health on the visual analogue scale was, on the other hand, quite high: 82.5 per cent. The questionnaire was able to pinpoint the respondents' perceptions in terms of age, gender, social class (as approximated by occupational group), education, housing tenure, economic position and propensity to smoke. Smokers, women, the unmarried and the unemployed, for example, were twice as likely to report problems such as pain or discomfort (Kind, Dolan, Gudex and Williams, 1998: 738). Such quantification makes it possible for policymakers to practise positive discrimination towards the beneficiaries who were the most distressed with their quality of life.

All studies are crucially dependent on the rationality of the respondents. Rosser and Kind found that 97.2 per cent of the sample produced test-retest responses that were internally consistent with their earlier answers (Rosser and Kind, 1978: 350, 351). Torrance in his own studies found correlations in the range from 0.86 to 0.94 (for rating scales), 0.77 to 0.92 (for the standard gamble), 0.77 to 0.88 (for the time trade-off) (Torrance, 1986: 26). High values such as these suggest that self-aware respondents were not making up their answers or blurting out their integers at random.

Other studies have, however, turned up inconsistencies even within a single method of measurement. Tversky, Slovic and Kahneman found that 46 per cent of their subjects in a study of monetary bets, 52 per cent in a study of delayed payment, displayed irrational preference reversal due to inappropriate heuristics and framing biases (Tversky, Slovic and Kahneman, 1990: 209, 213). New information is processed sequentially through the biases of the older endowments. A gain is weighted more highly than an equivalent loss. Scale intervals are so small that respondents cannot see the differences. Probabilities are harder to work with than are certainties. The conclusion is in the form of a word of caution. It is hard to infer the preferences from the payoffs if the payoffs have the same expected value but the matching and the weighting are observed to alter between the plays.

Rosser and Kind, like Torrance, regard inconsistencies like these as the exception and not as the rule. The scale used by Rosser and Kind is analogous to the points on a thermometer between the temperature at which water freezes and the temperature at which it boils. Combining morbidity with mortality, it takes into account people's own perceptions of the different combinations and of the distance between them. Minus values can be assigned: if people prefer death to being arthritic or bedridden or unable to wash without help or unable to climb the stairs, they have the chance to express the opinion that the disabled life-year carries a minus sign. It is no small problem, however, that different people might assign different meanings to an anchor benchmark like 'good health'. Evaluations articulated might also vary by role function, by age and gender, and over the life cycle.

A bottom-up study of especial interest is that conducted by Kind, Rosser and Williams into the intermediate values that lie between 100 per cent enjoyment of faculties on the one hand, irrevocable extinction on the other. The investigators said that it had been their wish not explicitly to quantify the earnings potential saved or lost but to construct 'what might be called "warmblooded" or joy-of-living valuations' (Kind, Rosser and Williams, 1982: 159). They investigated the subjective meaning of satisfaction from life using a questionnaire incorporating the eight states and the four grades of the earlier study. Subjects were asked to grade each state of disability. Each subject had to rank the eight states (ordinal utility) and also to say *by how much* the states differed in their psychic payoff (cardinal utility). The results allowed the investigators to quantify the relative values that individuals attached to different standards of health or illness.

The interviews found a distress rating of 0 (equal to death) for the immobile state where the patient is confined to a chair or wheelchair. The rating for the severely disabled state (where the patient cannot leave his bed) was −1.486. Unconscious but with no distress was, at −1.028, once again worse than death. At the opposite end of the scale, an intermediate impairment of physical ability (able to do light housework only) was scored as 0.87, being housebound (unable to continue education or employment) as 0.70 (Kind, Rosser and Williams, 1982: 160). Other studies have found distress-discounts for a range of other conditions: 0.89 for sore throat, 0.80 for headache, 0.76 for mild food poisoning, 0.58 for emphysema, 0.30 for lung cancer, 0.16 for severe brain damage (quoted in Abelson, 2003: S10). Such values can complement precedent in setting damages in court.

Individuals in a psychometric study have the chance to say that the side-effects of the treatment are worse than their expected life-years. They can state that they prefer to live with the depression, the seizures, the faints, the angina or the intermittent ulceration. Not every intervention promises a complete and one-time cure without any further symptoms or medication. The respondent (who may be a patient or may be an outsider prompted with a pictorial or a verbal scenario) has to decide if the less-than-perfect quality of the long-term outcome is worth the discomfort of the therapy. Each scenario has a variety of dimensions, attributes and implications. Some are relevant to a respondent who lives alone on a high floor without a lift but will be of less concern to a respondent in a bungalow with a supportive network. Not every programme does more good than harm. Some can cause the patient's marriage to break up. Some can drive the beneficiary to suicide.

7.1.2. The Standard Gamble

Rosser and Kind abstract from unknowledge and uncertainty. The hidden assumption is that individuals, risk-neutral, make the non-rational assumption that the status quo is an equilibrium that will not be disturbed. The 'standard gamble' is a different window on the world. Its concern, incorporated into the rating scale, is expected utility, not actual utility. Its decision-making calculus is in the tradition of Neumann and Morgenstern.

In the original game as outlined in 1944 by the two pioneers, the player is presented with a choice between a certain outcome (a one-way bet) and a gamble with two payoffs. One of those payoffs is worse than the certain outcome but one is better (Neumann and Morgenstern, 1972 [1944]: 18). In the case of health this crossroads would be the fate of a patient considering an operation for cancer of the larynx where one option is total recovery and the other is the inability to speak. Surgery for lower back pain has a high probability of a successful outcome, free from pain. It also has a small probability that the patient will never walk again.

The standard gamble, Torrance says, is a tree with two branches. Alternative 1 is the certainty of the chronic state (permanent dialysis, quadraplegic paralysis) for an expected life span of t years more. Alternative 2 is the crossroads: 'Either the patient is returned to normal health and lives for an additional t years (probability p), or the patient dies immediately (probability $1-p$)' (Torrance, 1986: 20). Even if the probability is slim that function will be satisfactorily recovered, the patient might still say that he is willing to take the risk. Siamese twins might say that the possibility of an irreversible vegetative state would be preferable to them to survival in a quality of life which they regard as worse than death.

It is the task of the investigator to find the probability p at which the respondent is indifferent between the current health status and the treatment which is being offered. In the interview the probability is varied until the equilibrium balance is found. Where the alternative is death, the likelihood of a successful outcome would have to be very high. Where no cure exists (as with arthritis), the choice would be no more than relief of symptoms; and then only if there is a slight but non-negligible risk that the drug might do permanent damage to the joints.

7.1.3. Time Trade-Off

Many people are uncomfortable with hypothetical scenarios and imaginary *what ifs*. The time trade-off approach has the attraction that it treats both alternatives at the crossroads as certain. In each case the number of life-years is specified. What the respondent is being asked is not about probabilities but about preferences. He is being asked how many life-years he would just be willing to give up in exchange for a move from the less healthy to the more healthy state. The number of compensating years is varied until the subject declares himself indifferent between the quality and the length that he is being promised. A cardinal value is then constructed from the ratio of the relative desirabilities that the individual himself has packaged into his mix.

Thus a subject might say that one year in a wheelchair delivers the same satisfaction as six months in perfect health; or that home dialysis for 8 years means a debased existence equal to only 0.65 of a full-quality life (Sackett and Torrance, 1978: 701). In one study women were asked how many years in normal good health they would regard as equivalent in utility to five years with menopausal symptoms. The median reply was 3.2 for severe symptoms, 4.25 where the symptoms were mild: this may be rewritten as utility values of 0.64 and 0.85 respectively (Daly, Gray, Barlow, McPherson, Roche and Vessey, 1993: 837). Interestingly, not all of the women interviewed had opted for hormone replacement therapy. The QALY ratings for the users and the non-users were in fact almost the same.

As death is not one of the anchors, the time trade-off is useful where the disability is chronic but not life-threatening. At the same time, one would have thought that the respondents would have felt uncomfortable with a question which invited them to purchase present comfort at the cost of future years (and, commonly, at the cost of the opportunity to care for their dependants). The shortening of life inevitably introduces a psychological bias. No one (the 'endowment effect') is other than reluctant to give up something he already has. Life-years are more salient than mugs.

A modification of the time trade-off would involve equivalence. Here the subject is not asked directly about himself but is required to make a choice between groups A and B. The numbers in each group are stated, as is the fact that each health state is a suitable case for treatment. Limited resources mean that a choice must be made. The population in each group is varied until the subject is indifferent between them. The ratio between the groups may then be taken to be a bottom-up valuation of the utility of care.

7.1.4. Willingness to Pay

Chapter 5 showed that the downward-sloping demand curve for life can (on the assumption of calculative rationality) be estimated from the preferences that economic men and women reveal when they respond to a survey, fit a seat belt or work at heights. The same may be said about the outcomes and profiles that informed people *de facto* select when they spend scarce resources in ways that impact upon their health. One life is not the equivalent of one life. The lifeholders themselves reveal reservation prices implying that it is not.

A thing is worth what the market says it is worth. The willingness to pay or to be paid is the sole measure in market economics of how much better off people think they will be as a result of their choice. It is the fundamental value judgment of market economics that the individual actor, proportioning marginal loss to marginal benefit in the light of the next-best foregone, knows best how to maximise felt welfare from a limited resource endowment. Shadow-data on utility, it must follow, can only be derived from what heterogeneous people do or say when they spend their time or money and get back more pleasurable life-years in return: 'The benefit from a program is then defined as *the sum of the willingnesses to pay of all persons whose welfare is affected by the program*. Note that this definition does not limit benefits to persons directly, or physically, affected by a program. If my welfare is affected by a program that affects my parents' health, my willingness to pay should be included (along with theirs) in defining the benefits from a program for elderly people' (Pauly, 1995: 102; original emphasis).

People spend money to buy hazards or to avoid risk. Revealed preference sheds light on the median attitudes of the population as a whole. It also serves to separate out the microscopic groupings most willing to splurge on cigarettes and alcohol from those most willing to give up the overeating and the laziness in order to make an investment in their future health: 'The distributional issue is then: should the health service value health benefits more highly if they accrue to people who, by their behaviour, clearly value their own health more highly? Put more bluntly, should we discriminate against heavy smokers, heavy drinkers, obese people, freefall parachutists, unclean people, etc? ... Should we value that (most costly) benefit differently if people appear *from their own behaviour* not themselves to care much about their own health?' (Williams, 1997b: 289; original emphasis). Such people are the most costly to the health service since they are the ones who take the risks. Willingness to pay adds fuel to the fire. Not only do they cost us more, they seem to value themselves less.

Questionnaires as well as induction can be used to measure the quality of life-years. Old people (or their relatives) can, for example, be asked just how much more they would be willing to pay for the greater comfort of a nursing home rather than a hospital ward. They can also be asked how much less, should they be planning to downgrade their care to the inferior option. Donaldson in a UK-based study invited a panel of 83 relatives to quantify the appropriate difference in value to them of the publicly-provided, tax-financed facility. The immediate payment would be from the State: the core National Health Service is effectively free at the point of consumption. That meant that money-minded respondents might be demanding too much because of their strategic self-interest. It also meant that the interviewees might be underestimating the fiscal burden since they would have had no occasion to find out what it is. Donaldson plugged both leaks at a stroke by spelling out to his sample precisely how much the respondent's own taxes would have to go up. The evidence enabled the investigators to calculate the marginal net benefit of an NHS nursing home place over hospital care as seen by respondents with a preference for the nursing home option: £11 837.50 (Donaldson, 1990: 108, 114).

The tax is a price. Olsen and Donaldson used that willingness to pay (WTP) in their study of popular preferences towards alternative public sector health programmes in Norway. Their 150 interviewees were told that extra helicopter ambulance services would impose the same cost as 80 extra elective heart operations and 250 extra elective hip operations. The respondents were asked what would be the maximum amount they would be willing to contribute in earmarked additional taxation for each of the competing options. The values per annum were NKr316, Nkr306 and Nkr232, respectively. The cost per QALY ratios could then be calculated. The ordering of the priorities was the same. The actual sums, however, were not proportional: NKr67000, Nkr50000 and NKr8900 (Olsen and Donaldson, 1998: 8).

The order in which the options were presented may have influenced the amount people said they were (still) willing to spend. Stewart and others confirmed that 'fading glow' is behind a systematic tendency for utility values to fall: 'Asking people to put a monetary WTP value on a sequence of health care programmes will likely yield different results depending on the order of the programmes because answers to earlier questions will affect responses to later questions' (Stewart, O'Shea, Donaldson and Shackley, 2002: 594). A further bias may result from the academic nature of the exercise. Whatever they told the interviewers, people knew that their taxes would neither go up nor go down.

A bias does not necessarily invalidate the results of a study. It means, however, that the policymakers must make an appropriate adjustment before they take the evidence to be a perfect measure of the democratic mind. Stewart's 'fading glow' will weaken the pull of the tail-end preference. The tendency towards satiety is likely to be especially strong among respondents without personal experience of the conditions. All they know is that they are being asked to pay more and more for additional programmes. This sequence makes them more sensitive to their diminishing utility. The growing strain, conceivably, can even reverse their rankings.

Thompson, also interested in willingness to pay, asked 247 subjects with rheumatoid arthritis what percentage of their household income they would be willing to pay for a complete cure. They were told to assume that such a cure existed and that their health insurance would not cover it. The mean response from the sample as a whole was 22 per cent (Thompson, 1986: 396). People unable to climb stairs at all were willing to pay on average 35 per cent. The percentage of income rather than a pecuniary amount was selected in order to eliminate differences in the utility of money and the level of wealth. The rich and the poor in Thompson's study were seen to sacrifice the same proportion of their purchasing potential.

Froberg and Kane comment that the logic can be carried even further. Investigators could conduct a progressive canvass of opinion that 'takes into account the likely possibility that 10% of a very low income constitutes a larger burden than 10% of a very high income' (Froberg and Kane, 1989: 681). They are opening the door to the debate on the legitimacy of unequal incomes. Since purchasing power is unevenly distributed, all market preferences encode data which track not demand so much as *effective* demand. Assuming that pay mirrors productivity, this is no more than the acknowledgement that people who put more into society have the right to take more out for themselves.

Doing so, since the commodity is health, the high-flyers will be investing more heavily in high-powered human capital that is of growth-producing value to all. As the prosperous will also have invested in better housing and food, it is possible that they will be cheaper to treat than will less cost-effective members of the community whose lifestyle itself will often have contributed much to their relative deprivation. Yet the envy and even the malice will, rightly or wrongly, still mean that the net utility will be less than the gross. Where some people can afford to pay for high-utility life years while others must come to terms with the dyspepsia and the toothlessness, QALYs will not pick up the hidden frustration that exists when the willingness to pay is not matched by the ability to do so.

Some people will have neglected both their earning capacity and their health capital. One could say that they are the authors of their own low willingness to pay. Egalitarian philosophy might not be very interested in the historical by-gones which can no longer be changed. Vertical equity dictates that the most help should go to those who are the most in need even if the most deprived find it the most difficult to scrape together the effective demand. The criterion is at odds with the willingness – and the ability – to pay.

There are compromise methodologies. One solution is to quantify the QALY using a non-monetary price such as the waiting time, travelling time or duration of illness. Another is to use a negative price such as willingness to accept compensation. In both cases there is a market-like response to a non-market problem. Costs and benefits are compared at the margin.

Questionnaires at least are not income constrained. Talk is free. Yet talk is not action. Induction from experience has the advantage over unreliable verbalisation that people are observed to put their money where their mouth is. Policy based on stated rather than market-revealed preference has, on the other hand, the feature (which may be an advantage or a shortcoming) that it gives lower-income people benefits that higher-income people must finance. That is the policy implication when the truth comes to light that lower-income people have articulated a want for a good or service that they cannot afford to buy. It is, of course, possible to stratify a sample in order to isolate the differences in attitudes between the income groups. In such a case it would be possible to tell in which social group the preference actually originates. It would also be possible to weight the answers.

Utility-adjusted years are not cost-adjusted years. Cost-effectiveness analysis can incorporate the QALYs into its benefits stream. It will not expect, however, that the gains have already been prudently juxtaposed to the losses. Cost-effectiveness fills in the blanks in the balance sheet. Intuition and common practice suggest that it concentrates the attention when the subject is being asked to estimate the benefit not in isolation but in the light of the next-best foregone. Unanimity of consensus occurs when the buyer and the seller trade. Most people are familiar with the choices that double-entry exchanges entail. Most people understand the notion of opportunity cost.

7.1.5. The Choice of the Sample

Sampling is fraught with problems of size and representativeness. The desire to generalise must be balanced against the cost of data collection. Where trained interviewers conduct extended interviews, where doctors are required to explain carefully the risks, symptoms and treatment alternatives, time and money necessarily limit the scope of the investigation. The task can be a mammoth one: while kidney disease has only four possible outcomes (transplant, hospital dialysis, home dialysis, death), neonatal intensive care has 960 (Torrance, 1986: 11). So much detail can lead to overload. A certain amount of background information is needed to understand the issues. Some people only really grasp the meaning of scarcity if scarce resources are presented in terms of physical units like finite kidneys available for transplants. It is no surprise that the respondents are often of above-average education.

Information is a real constraint. The uninformed are a part of the general public to which public policy must respond. Yet, in contrast to patients already afflicted and doctors who are in touch, the citizen in the street might simply not know what Crohn's Disease involves or how long it is likely to last. Torrance expresses the 'sticking point' in the following words: 'How do you describe, in a complete and yet unbiased manner, a particular dysfunctional health state (for example, kidney dialysis) to a healthy individual who has no experience with the condition? And how do you know when you have done it right?' (Torrance, 1986: 15). Descriptions are provided. Visual aids are employed. Dreaded labels such as cancer or leprosy are replaced by neutral terminology. At the end of the day, however, if the respondent does not understand the intricacies, it must be questioned whether he should be asked what he thinks about Crohn's Disease when the fact is that he does not think about it at all.

Information asymmetry introduces the further complication that even the afflicted might not know exactly where the goalposts stand. Needs are not wants, and consumer's awareness might only be the result of the practitioner's sensible recommendation. As Murray and Acharya write: 'Individuals' perception of their own health may not coincide with their actual health status.... Hence, allocation that maximizes consumer satisfaction may not actually yield the best possible health outcomes' (Murray and Acharya, 1997: 708). Subjective perceptions might not mirror the objective frequencies. Subjects might not understand that all predictions in the health care field are no more than probabilities. Respondents might not grasp that all decisions in the health care field are gambles involving trees where all they are buying is a known chance of moving to the next decision-making node. People think they are being asked about life-years. The truth is that they are being asked about path, iteration and risk.

Speculation appeals more strongly to the risk-loving than it does to the risk-averse. In that way it resembles danger money at work, where the valuation of life is generalised not from the average or the median but from the marginal person taking the marginal chance. A representative sample would have to parallel the attitude to time preference of the population as a whole and not just of the fringe. The willingness to pay is a measure of those who are willing. It is not a measure of the intramarginal who are indifferent, unwilling or even strongly opposed. Perhaps a study should include evidence on the *number* of persons known to share the willingness in order to establish if the utility value is autobiography or social science.

Dispersion in discontentment and exhilaration make it difficult to identify the median or typical citizen. Rawls draws attention to the possibility of hijacking and crowding in on the part of utility monsters who have an abnormal capacity to be over the moon: 'Imagine two persons, one satisfied with a diet of milk, bread and beans, while the other is distraught without expensive wines and exotic dishes' (Rawls, 1982: 168). In such a case it is the complainer who is given the most exclusively because deprivation to him would cause the greater unhappiness. Utility is maximised because the subjectively underattended get extra resourcing while the stoics feel grateful when they are given an aspirin and a cup of tea. A representative sample is hard to find.

In choosing the sample, it must be decided what weight to put upon a 'fool's valuation'. Trapped in a traditional rule of thumb, blinkered by yesterday's reference point, twisted by fear and emotion, much that is said is not fully rational, cool-headed and actuarial. It must be decided whether to interview the sufferer alone or to include the spouse and children: their QALYs too will be affected if their breadwinner cannot work or must go into expensive long-stay care. It must be decided how to incorporate the patient with co-disability (diabetes and loss of sight) or with multiple disability (the heart patient who is also HIV). It must be decided if the raters are being asked to assess the utility of a hypothetical patient; to imagine their own utility if they themselves were in need of the intervention; or to express their own feelings in the knowledge that they were selected for the survey because they were known to have cancer. It makes a difference if the exercise is imagined or real. There are also important ethical considerations when hypothetical scenarios become the basis for public policy decisions.

This is especially so if subjects are being asked about the quality of life of other people. It is difficult to know what is going through the mind of a sufferer from dementia, a drug addict, a schizophrenic or an alcoholic. Even so, it is always on the fringes of the immoral for an outsider to make his own interpersonal comparisons or to fall back on empathy to plug in plausible impressions that his sample has never confirmed. Infants and the as-yet-unborn cannot be included in a representative cross-section. Yet they too have a right to a quality life.

Even where the respondent is informed and alert, the same problem of imputation arises where a sample is mixed. In the Rosser and Kind study (1978), there were six groups of subjects: medical patients, psychiatric patients, general nurses, psychiatric nurses, experienced doctors, healthy volunteers. That in itself suggests the possibility of disagreement and bunching within the sample. More weight should arguably be given to the opinions of those who have experienced or are experiencing the condition or treatment. An older man facing a choice between surgery and embarrassing trips to the toilet has local knowledge which a younger person cannot share. Different ethnic groups can be susceptible to different complaints which they refract through the different value systems of different cultures. The preferences of outsiders should in the circumstances be treated as secondary and supporting rather than as cutting edge. Outsiders find it difficult to imagine life in a wheelchair. The wheelchair-bound, living with their condition every day, are better placed to discount the happiness they get from life.

Yet, as Loomes and McKenzie say, there is a problem of bias: 'Current sufferers ... may tend to overstate their own cases relative to other groups, thus undermining the notion of some general basis of comparison' (Loomes and McKenzie, 1989: 305). Sackett and Torrance found that home dialysis patients assigned a higher utility to kidney dialysis than did the general public (Sackett and Torrance, 1978: 702). Dolan too established that those in poor health tended to value the appropriate interventions more highly: 'Current poor health results in higher health state valuations. This might be termed *valuation shift*' (Dolan, 1996b: 558). In the interests of transparency it might be better not to mix the pool.

Where individuals express preferences that are the reflection of bias and self-seeking, the logical expedient would be for social policy to opt for the anonymity, the impartiality of the Rawlsian veil. Priority setting in such a case would not be distorted by personal interest since no one would be in a position to be the judge in his own cause. The problem is that in the real world people do know who they are. They know that they are already receiving treatment. They know that they are old. The temptation is undeniably there to exaggerate their disutility in order to ensure that their health state will not be neglected. Only the allocation of medical procedures by means of a lottery would meet

this objection. It is unlikely that the community would ever vote for the allocation of organs on the throw of the dice.

The future is, of course, an unwritten book. Looking to the future, there is
radical uncertainty. A person healthy today does not know how he will feel if
and when he falls into bad health. Nor does he know what treatment he will
need. Nor does he know if *ex ante* expectations will be borne out by *ex post*
outturns. That is an argument, statistically speaking, for going for low-cost
treatments that can be supplied in large quantities. Instead of the organ transplants there is across-the-board testing to pick up the asymptomatic and the rare.
More people will be drawn into the net. Indeed, such diversification might even
prove the most popular option: 'It is quite conceivable that the majority of a
healthy population might prefer the allocation which offers each of them as individuals a larger probability of a smaller benefit. In other words, they might be
willing to pay a kind of "risk premium" by choosing the allocation which, in
QALY terms, offers a lower expected value' (Loomes and McKenzie, 1989:
305). Something for everyone means that the symptoms you treat might be your
own.

7.1.6. Adaptation

Valuation shift, Dolan suggests, occurs not just when the patient is ill but when
the patient is well again: 'Past experience of serious illness is found to have a
less powerful effect, leading to the conclusion that as experience of illness becomes more remote, its effect on health state valuations becomes less' (Dolan,
1996b: 558). Even within a single pool of sufferers, the inexperienced freshers
and the knowing old lags might not think as one. The reason is the rebasing of
the reference points. Patients with long-term disabilities adapt to their handicaps
once they have become accustomed to the loss of a leg or the need for insulin
injections. In this respect they are similar to lottery winners whose happiness
level is documented to rise at first and then to return to a long-established pla-
teau. It is therefore not clear at which point to conduct the investigation: is the
'correct' QALY the QALY just after the accident or the QALY several years
down the road? The fox writes off the grapes it cannot reach. The general public
might express a degree of compassion that exceeds the disutility of the sufferers
themselves. It would save money, if the prediction is accurate, to base public
policy on the patients themselves and not on healthy respondents trying desperately to imagine how the victims must feel. They might be wasting their pity on
business-as-usual human beings who have learned to live with their disability.

Cognitive dissonance was discussed in chapter 5. Coping strategies in chronic
illness mean that well-being might not be significantly affected in the long-run
by the loss of the initial endowment: 'Patients with a particular condition often
assign it higher utility than do persons without the condition. It appears that

people with a disability manage to compensate in a manner which causes them to deny its disutility' (Froberg and Kane, 1989: 681). Preferences, given time, might even return to 1. Proper weighting, clearly, is essential, as is the ability to recognise when the disutility has levelled off and expectations have been adjusted. The *when* of the survey can be as important as the *who*.

An illustration of duration and coping strategies is provided by Meyerowitz's study of 113 postmastectomy women: 'Level of cancer-specific denial emerged as the variable most strongly associated with postmastectomy distress. This coping strategy was more important in explaining distress than were availability of social support, treatment group, time since operation, or age' (Meyerowitz, 1983: 117). Emotions had to be kept under control. Meyerowitz found that, following a low in the aftermath of treatment, the overall outlook tended to bounce back to something approaching its normal state. Cognitive avoidance or minimisation made the women over time better able to write off the effects of their surgery. Patients unable to control their bygones at least learn to control their reactions.

Not every woman is cheerful in adverse circumstances. Richardson and his colleagues, interviewing 63 women about three breast cancer treatment states, observed that one discrete stage is often seen first and foremost as an anteroom to something else: 'Patients typically face multiphase scenarios, and a knowledge of later stages of a health state may well affect the utility of earlier phases.... A poor health state may be more tolerable if it is perceived as a temporary hardship' (Richardson, Hall and Salkeld, 1996: 152). The converse is also true. The respondents in the Richardson study told the investigators that a negative prognosis alone would alter their viewpoint for the worse: 'The knowledge of future suffering and death casts a shadow over, or devalues, the enjoyment of earlier life years' (Richardson, Hall and Salkeld, 1996: 157). Importantly, not one of the women in the Richardson study had actually had breast cancer. It is impossible to say how they would have adapted, Meyerowitz-like, if they had actually had to make the best of their holistic sequence.

7.1.7. Duration

It is easy to fall into the trap of assuming a stable, proportional, monotonic relationship between expected utility per year and the number of years in which that utility will be enjoyed. It is easy to reason that an individual who regards 15 years in impaired health as equivalent to 12 years in perfect health will regard 30 years as equivalent to 24 and five years as equivalent to four. The previous section on coping strategies called into doubt the facile assumption of invariant utility. It said that some people tend to come to terms with their disabilities. The present section on duration says the opposite, that sooner or later some people become profoundly disheartened.

The inference from the classic investigation by Rosser and Kind is that each additional life-year tends to be valued equally. Changing the prognosis from 'treatable' to 'permanent' had little impact on the results in their scale (Rosser and Kind, 1978: 351). Not all studies, however, suggest a link that is a linear function of time. Sackett and Torrance, randomly sampling the general public in Hamilton, Ontario, through 246 home interviews, found that satisfaction was negatively correlated with time: 'For each health state the mean daily utility fell as the duration of time in the health state lengthened' (Sackett and Torrance, 1978: 701). Home dialysis for 8 years delivered only 0.65 of the mean daily satisfaction attached to perfect health. Home dialysis for life was 0.40, hospital dialysis for life 0.32. Hospital confinement for life for an unnamed contagious disease scored 0.16. The fall was dramatic (although the high standard deviation is a reminder that there was variability and disagreement even within the groups). Length of time was relevant, they found, as well as the intensity of the suboptimality.

If the complaint is life-threatening, one would expect studies to show that more life-years are preferable to less. Sutherland discovered, however, that the proportion of her sample (made up opportunistically from 20 health care-professional colleagues) who preferred immediate death to guaranteed survival in all but one ('able to work ... sleeping poorly') of five substandard health states went up as the duration of the complaints increased. There was a 'maximum endurable time in a given state of dysfunction' (Sutherland, Llewellyn-Thomas, Boyd and Till, 1982: 300) beyond which people responded to the scenario *what ifs* ('a nurse bathes, dresses, and feeds me', 'confined to my home' and so on) by stating that they did not wish to live. Previous periods were affecting choices in subsequent periods. The preferences were not independent.

Sutherland's result is in line with Grossman's theory of human capital. Machines as they depreciate towards scrap satisfy their capitalists less and less. Dolan in his own study found additional evidence that there was a diminishing marginal utility of extra years where the extra years were seen as ever more inferior: 'The results suggest that the valuation given to a health state is a decreasing function of both its severity and its duration: the (estimated) score for a state lasting 10 years is lower than when the same state lasts for 1 year which in turn is lower than when that state lasts for only 1 month' (Dolan, 1996a: 200). He also found that states were more likely to be rated 'worse than death' if they lasted 10 years than only 1 month. People might reject a longer life if it is accompanied by pain.

7.1.8. The Life Cycle

The QALY need not be a constant. It can mutate due to adaptation or duration. It can also vary as a consequence of where it is situated in the stream. Impatient people might opt for jam today: they might apply a high discounting rate to future utilities that (perhaps because their life expectancy is short) they might not live to enjoy. Caring people might prefer that scarce QALYs be redirected to their children and beyond: they might apply a negative rate of discount in order to transfer worthwhile resources to the sunrise cohort. Anxious people might abnormally defer their current gratification since their time preference is such that future stages have to be given the lion's share: 'For example, it is conceivable that a young single adult may place a lower weight on good health *now* than on good health a few years ahead when he/she may be raising a young family; the weight placed on good health in years beyond that, when the children have grown up, may then fall; but may rise again for the years immediately following retirement' (Loomes and McKenzie, 1989: 301). This saw-tooth up-and-down casts doubt once again on the assumption of a constant proportional trade-off. Calendar time and felt utility need not move in step.

Choices must be consistent and transitive. The question is *for what period* since stability over a lifetime is unusual, even pathological. Some observers say that it is impossible to conduct the required evaluation in practice: 'It may be conceptually appealing to ask individuals to convert into a utility index a whole-of-life scenario in which health and social states change with age and disease progression. However, in the absence of a reliable and valid technique for converting such scenarios into a numerical score the approach cannot be operationalised' (Richardson, 1994: 15). Other observers feel it is possible at least to see the shadow on the wall. Alan Williams belongs to the optimists who believe that adequate information can be found.

Alan Williams and his colleagues asked 377 individuals randomly selected from the electoral register to consider ten life-stages, from 'as infants' to 'getting very old'. Respondents were asked to pick out and rank the three sets of circumstances in which they thought good health in general was most important. The most frequently selected first-choices were 'when bringing up children' (32.9 per cent), 'as infants' (27.3 per cent) and 'when getting very old' (7.2 per cent) (Williams, 1997b: 285). There was a high degree of consensus across the genders and the age groups both on the rankings and on the proposition that one life-year cannot be treated as the equivalent of any other. A responsible carer (more frequently a woman) looking after children or elderly dependants must be given extra points. A single-person household affording no one else either a healthy start or a dignified finish loses out since he or she will not be missed. Age does matter. Role does matter. Gender does matter. Relative values drive a cart and horses through the non-judgmental rubber stamping of equal treatment for equal need.

Williams found that his sample subjects wanted their fellow citizens to be sensitively prioritised. What his study did not elicit was the actual difference (the *by how much*) that lies between the life-steps. Make-believe values like

2.75 or 0.26 can be selected at random to illustrate graphically the discrimination by consensus that is missing. Hypothetical values might say that, 'in order to give one extra year of healthy life expectancy to an infant (valued at 2.75), it would be worth sacrificing about 10.5 years of healthy life expectancy (each valued at 0.26), which might have been given to someone setting up home for the first time' (Williams, 1997b: 286). What is needed, however, is not hypothetical values but the concrete calibration of grassroots discriminators.

To quantify the preference intensities Williams conducted a trial study. He used a small cross-section (nurses, secretaries, managers, psychologists, academics, doctors) as his initial (convenience) sample of ordinary citizens. The infants and the carers once again scored well, but there were some surprises. The doctors were disproportionately in favour of those who had looked after their health. Older respondents were disproportionately in favour of the young.

7.2.   THE PRACTITIONER

Sometimes the QALYs will be built up from questionnaires and interviews, revealed preferences and money committed. In other cases it will be deemed more appropriate to turn to the medical professionals for an expert's-eye opinion. The doctor knows the objective parameters and can compare the probabilities. The doctor has some idea of what standard practice in the public domain takes to be normal or average. The doctor knows his patients. He knows what they regard as minimal or acceptable. He is in a position to give his opinion of *their* opinion. The doctor, in short, has access both to utility-related information and to the clinical intelligence which is essential if the self-rated symptom is to be matched up to the cure that can put things right. That is why the investigators will often turn to the medical practitioner when they want to put a concrete value on what a year of life with insomnia, tinnitus or palsy means to the median sufferer who might not be well-placed to translate disabled life-years into an acceptable common *numéraire*.

The doctor might express a need that is not a want. The doctor might try to guess what the great majority of the patients would say if they could. Either way, there is always a chance that a gulf will emerge between the counselled and their advisers. Rosser, Kind and Williams identified just such a disparity: 'Doctors place relatively less emphasis on the importance of death in comparison with other states; i.e. regard *more* states as worse than death. Doctors also place more emphasis on the importance of subjective suffering' (Kind, Rosser and Williams, 1982: 163). Doctors, the investigators found, had a greater aversion to disability and distress than did the population as a whole. Medical people would overvalue interventions to reduce the suffering. The investigators also identified major differences between medical patients and psychiatric patients. Psychiatric patients were less willing for virtually any kind of disability to put up with severe distress.

Doctors can come up with utilities which are idiosyncratically their own. To minimise bias, it is common to approach a panel of advisers rather than to rely on a single clinician who says he knows best. An example would be the consensus meetings on disability weights convened by the World Health Organization. Experts at these sharing sessions were asked to assign disability weights to 22 health states (including deafness, below-the-knee amputation, dementia, quadriplegia) (Murray, 1996: 37). Insider judgment was in that way the source of the value. The problem is what to do when there is a conflict: 'In general, health-care providers and families of persons in a specific health state rate health states as worse than the general public does, and the general public in turn rates the same health states worse than those living in the health state do. As responses vary, considerable debate has emerged on whose values should be used' (Murray, 1996: 29).

Coronary artery bypass grafting is one competitor for scarce resources. Some alternatives are heart-related (pace makers, transplants) and some lie in other fields (renal dialysis, hip replacement). The question must be if more, less or the same number would maximise felt happiness. Data is obtained on life-expectancy and on perceived quality of each year of life. The results can be unexpected. Williams, quantifying his QALYs in the light of the advice he received from three cardiologists, finds that the present value of extra service costs per QALY is £14000 for hospital haemodialysis, £11000 for home haemodialysis and only £750 for a hip replacement. The respective values for the QALYs themselves were not as different: 5, 6 and 4. The deciding factor was the cost: £70000, £66000 and £3000. The data suggest that happiness would be increased if resources were to be redirected from coronary artery bypass grafting and put into hip replacements (Williams, 1997a [1985]: 247). Others have found that dressings were placed above appendectomies. Economics is about comparisons and opportunity costs. The question must be the extent to which the three cardiologists really had their finger on the popular pulse.

Information obtained from the experts can be used by policymakers to maximise felt satisfaction. An example would be Williams's study done at Guy's Hospital, London. He asked five general surgeons to quantify both life-expectancy and improved quality of life associated with a series of interventions. They were to use Rosser and Kind's eight-times-four scale of normal function and relative comfort. On that basis he was able to build up a ranking scheme per hour of operating time for the top 22 conditions, accounting for 90 per cent of patients' waits. The list was based upon relative benefit of treatment to the patient. It went from male bilateral inguinal hernia (no. 1) to epigastric hernia (no. 22) by way of piles (no. 8) and skin lesions (no. 13) (Williams, 1997b: 259).

This makes more rational the shifting of resources from one treatment to another in the National Health Service.

Doctors help the policymakers to quantify the QALYs. The QALYs introduce calculated weighting of subjective utilities into the waiting lists. While the quantification of distribution and redistribution goes against the individual doctor's clinical freedom to do his best for his unique patient, so does the constraint of scarcity itself. More will not necessarily be better where it comes from someone else. The real bind is not the ethical but the economic one. Paternalism and elitism have the great disadvantage that the doctors might get the utilities wrong. If they do, then they are biasing the community's cost-effectiveness away from what the community itself would have preferred.

7.3. THE PUBLIC

Neither the patient nor the doctor can speak for the wider community that surrounds the consulting room. The community has attitudes and opinions. These, as Murray observes, cannot responsibly be excluded from an index of quality-adjusted life-years: 'If many individuals after deliberation hold a preference or value then this value should be considered seriously. We should investigate, and if need be, speculate on, the likely reasons why many individuals hold such a view. If these reasons appear to be persuasive and do not contravene important "ideal-regarding principles", these preferences should be incorporated' (Murray, 1996: 5). Externalities such as contagions and fellow-feeling are common in the field of health. Norms and institutions are everywhere because people are socialised into groups. The democrat is in the circumstances obligated to consult a representative cross-section of the citizens who hold a stake.

It is not enough to delegate the public interest to consumer sovereignty in collaboration with clinical freedom. Spillovers and values aside, it is the taxpayers who must pay all or part of the bill: 'It could be argued that it is appropriate to weight more heavily the preferences of those most directly affected by a particular policy or intervention. However, there are also grounds for supporting the notion that, since the general public pay for health care, their preferences should be given the greatest weight in the resource allocation process' (Dolan, 1996b: 559).

Inference from the general public could lead to overestimation of a chronic dysfunctional health state to which the healthholders have already adapted well. Inference from the general public could also lead to the denial of a heart transplant to a chain smoker who is a poor steward of his – of our – value-adding health capital. Discrimination based on compassion or on economic contribution can in that way become a democratic distortion of the patient's own preferences. Whether too much or too little, it would be unpopular and insensitive for the politician and the bureaucrat to spend the public's money without knowing what the voter believes his public health service ought to be doing.

7.3.1. Utility and Public Policy

An individual can act on the basis of his own private utility. The policymakers have to reconcile the differences and arrive at a single figure. Drummond and his colleagues summarise results which show that the adjusted cost per British QALY gained in 1990 was £270 if the money went on GP advice to stop smoking, £7840 on heart transplantation, £21970 on hospital haemodialysis, £107780 on brain surgery for cancerous tumours (Drummond, Torrance and Mason, 1993: 34). The same measure is applied across the programmes. The common standard allows them to be ranked by their QALY-benefit per unit cost. A health budget of £21970 produces one quality-adjusted life-year if spent on kidney dialysis in hospital. It produces 81 quality-adjusted life-years if spent on practitioners' advice to give up smoking.

Health care costs money. Weinstein points out that the US GDP per capita when he was writing was about $20000 (Weinstein, 1995: 95). By that standard, using Torrance's price list, it would cost what the average American would earn in almost three years to buy one extra QALY through hospital haemodialysis ($54000) but only 6 months to pay for a QALY rescued from severe hypertension ($9400). It would cost a mere 1.6 months to restore a QALY under threat from postpartum depression ($1220) (Torrance, 1986: 6). Exercise, Hatziandreu and his co-authors calculate, costs $11313 per QALY saved. Of that, only $1395 is the direct outlay on the shorts, the shoes and the doctoring for minor injuries sustained.

Interestingly, the purchase of utility-adjusted life-expectancy jumps to the cost-ineffective present value (discounted at 5 per cent) of $48775 for the sub-sample of 'exercise haters'. All exercise-time for them is costed at average hourly wage foregone since athletophobes derive no positive satisfaction from cardiovascular aerobics such as jogging. Doctors should encourage their patients to start (despite the high subjective cost) in the hope that they will develop a taste for physical activity. If they do, then their new-found sportiness will reduce or, conceivably, eliminate the subjective cost of preventing coronary heart disease. It will make exercise more rather than less cost-effective than the curative alternative of hospital care later on (Hatziandreu, Koplan, Weinstein, Caspersen and Warner, 1988: 1419, 1420). The Hatziandreu study was of necessity limited. It concentrated on one cohort (35-year-old males) and on a single threat to health (coronary heart disease). What it makes clear is nonetheless the economic value of finding out the facts. Knowledge makes informed public policy possible. Should it wish to do so, the society using the common QALY can then target the maximum utility it can secure from its health care allocation.

Budgets are limited. The ethical standard of greatest happiness might be interpreted as the greatest number of persons treated or as the feasible maximum of QALYs squeezed from a given health budget. The latter tends to be the more popular standard of efficiency: 'Procedures should be ranked so that activities which generate more gains to health for every pound of resources take priority over those which generate less; thus the general standard of health in the community would be correspondingly higher' (Williams, 1997a [1985]: 239). The task of the policymaker is to maximise the community's well-being. The community's well-being is measured not in statistical years but in the sum of the QALYs enjoyed by the individual citizens.

Garber and Phelps accept the intuition behind all forms of cost-effectiveness analysis, that 'in order to maximize expected utility, one should adjust the intensity of all medical interventions so that they have a common CE ratio' (Garber and Phelps, 1997: 9). Wagstaff too is persuaded by the microeconomic rule that marginal benefits, for maximum welfare, ought to be in proportion to marginal costs. He says that, for equal costs, one person's higher QALY relative to another's clearly suggests that the former person has the greater potential to benefit: 'Health maximization leads to the conclusion that resources ought to be redeployed away from people (or groups of people) who have a low capacity to benefit from treatment' (Wagstaff, 1991: 26).

The policy inference is that treatment should be funded based on relative cost per QALY or on the rank order of procedures as determined by the QALYs. More satisfying years count more than second-rate ones. Resources should be channelled to treatments which produce more QALYs for a given cost and away from under-performing treatments for which the QALY payoff is less. Different diseases and different persons may be the winners and the losers. In Boyle's study of very low birth weight babies, a random sample of parents of school-age children told the investigators that disabled lives were worth less than healthy lives: the cost per life year gained through intensive care was US$9300 but the cost per QALY until death was US$22 400 (Boyle, Torrance, Sinclair and Horwood, 1983: 1333). In Klarman's investigation into the perceived quality of life-years, a life on dialysis was taken to be less enjoyable than a life following a kidney transplant. The differential was 25 per cent (Klarman, Francis and Rosenthal, 1973 [1968]: 232).

Physical survival is a part but is not the whole. Utility-adjusted life-years help the policymakers to put scarce public finance where it buys the most satisfaction. There can be a problem of implementation, however, where one-person-one-vote points in one direction while the maximisation of social felicity points in another. In such a case the politicians would have to channel scarce resources towards the nearly-indifferent and to abandon the high-intensity outliers to the tyranny of the majority.

Health status is not the only reason to be alive. A discussion of QALYs must recognise that there is more to utility per year than disabilities and operations alone. Broome writes as follows in defence of the broader vision: 'Good health is plainly not equally good for everyone. Good health is only a state of good *health*, and nothing else in one healthy person's life may be good, whereas everything else in another's may be. Qalys to one person will represent more good than qalys to another. Prolonging the life of, say, a happy person will do more good than prolonging the life of an unhappy one' (Broome, 1993: 161). Good health can be the passport to the other attributes of happiness: income, employment, friendships outside the home. Broome nonetheless sees that the implications of narrow *ceteris paribus* can be disturbing. Even if every individual's health is treated equally, even if medical *like* is treated as medical *like*, the fuller picture is unlikely to be as idyllic: 'The assumption that healthy life is equally good for everybody is just false' (Broome, 1993: 161).

7.3.2. Old Age: An Illustration

Society wants QALYs. Yet it wants affluence and equity too. Affluence could suggest discrimination by age, productivity and scarce skills in order to maximise the nation's flow of future value-added. Equity could imply that the community should be even-handed towards the young who have their whole life to live even as it should behave justly towards the old who have had their seven ages of man, their three score years and ten: 'The fair innings argument takes the view that there is some span of years that we consider a reasonable life.... The fair innings argument requires that everyone be given an equal chance to have a fair innings, to reach the appropriate threshold but, having reached it, they have received their entitlement. The rest of their life is the sort of bonus which may be cancelled when this is necessary to help others reach the threshold' (Harris, 1985: 91). Few decent people would go on record in support of racism, sexism, caste-ism or religion-ism. Ageism is, however, the new taboo that dare not speak its name: 'While it is always a *misfortune* to die when one wants to go on living, it is not a *tragedy* to die in old age: but it is, on the other hand, both a tragedy and a misfortune to be cut off prematurely' (Harris, 1985: 93; original emphasis).

In a study of 721 adults in Cardiff, 94 per cent preferred saving a 5-year-old over a 70-year-old; 80 per cent preferred saving a 35-year-old over a 60-year-old (Murray, 1996: 55). Busschbach and his associates, sampling 30 students and 35 old people in Holland, found a similar pattern: 'Being healthy during childhood is about twice as important as being healthy during the last period of life. The utility of health at age 35 is likely to be located somewhere halfway between these two extremes' (Busschbach, Hessing and de Charro, 1993: 157). The utilities expressed by the two groups of respondents were very close: 'This is a strong indication that the utilities for health found in the investigation belong to a value system that exists throughout the whole population.... Without an age correction, the QALY analysis is, according to our findings, more egalitarian than judgments of the general public imply' (Busschbach, Hessing and de Charro, 1993: 157). Ordinary people are apparently not willing to treat an old person's life-year as having equivalent value: 'The results are quite consistent ... that individuals prefer, after appropriate deliberation, to extend the life of healthy individuals rather than those in a health state worse than perfect health' (Murray and Acharya, 1997: 726). Dementia and maybe even hearing loss should be given a low priority. A new paediatrics ward or prepubescent anti-bipolars to extend a young and promising life have a greater appeal.

Public policy must be *as if* an implicit referendum on defining characteristics such as age and gender. Equity must be seen and felt. It must also be gauged. Busschbach in Holland discovered that health in childhood was believed to be twice as satisfying as health in old age. Johannesson and Johansson in Sweden found that one QALY gained by a 30-year-old was believed by their community sample to be equal at the point of indifference to 7.7 50-year-olds securing one QALY each (Johannesson and Johansson, 1997: 595). One QALY consumed by a person aged 50-plus was worth 0.13 of a QALY if that QALY were consumed by a 30-year-old in his prime.

Johannesson and Johansson interviewed 1000 subjects on the telephone. All were 15 years of age and older. Their answers to the question about policy were rather unexpected. The respondents said that, compensating for the lower quality of life and ignoring the lower number of innings still left to play, a programme which saves 100 lives among 50-year-olds had to be regarded as preferable to a programme which saves 50 lives among 30-year-olds. Policy had to be social-needs-based. Education and earnings were not all there was to what society needs to be able to look itself confidently in the mirror.

Johannesson and Gerdtham conducted a related study on the perceived value of age. They asked a cross-section of the community (in this case, a small and even unrepresentative subset made up of 80 university students in Stockholm) for their views on the number and distribution of QALYs in their society. The authors found that people once again were generous. The responses indicated that individuals in a group with more QALYs were willing to give up one QALY (discounted at 5 per cent) in order to secure an increase of 0.58 (discounted) QALYs in the group with fewer QALYs. The trade-off was not affected by the size of the difference in QALYs between the two groups: 'It was thus as if the respondents focused on inequality as such rather than the size of the inequality' (Johannesson and Gerdtham, 1996: 366).

The implicit weight given to the lower group was $1/0.58 = 1.724$. So self-sacrificing, so redistributive a general will lends support to the Rawlsian 'Difference Principle'. Rawls anticipated that rational people would want to see an allocation of basic claims that worked 'to the greatest benefit of the least advantaged' (Rawls, 1972 [1971]: 302). The Swedish students confirmed that even without a veil of ignorance they still wanted to share. Every blood donor is like a Swedish student in that respect. Titmuss (1970) on social interaction as a brotherhood of gifts should evidently not be written off too soon.

7.3.3. Procedure as Utility

Rawls, who is not an Aristotelian, says that justice as fairness accepts the liberal presupposition that 'there are many rational conceptions of the good': 'The consequence is that the unity of society and the allegiance of its citizens to their common institutions rest not only on their espousing one rational conception of the good, but on an agreement as to what is just for free and equal moral persons with different and opposing conceptions of the good' (Rawls, 1982: 160). The claims it is appropriate for citizens to make must be filtered through these procedures: 'Justice is prior to the good' (Rawls, 1982: 184).

Different people might want different things. Manual labourers might have different attitudes from managerial-professionals or the seriously rich. The old might need different services from the young. The doctors might articulate different preferences from either their patients or their community. The different groups, subgroups and unique one-offs might not see eye to eye: 'Although home dialysis may be more cost-effective than hospital dialysis from the societal point of view, the reverse may be true from the viewpoint of some patients and their families' (Torrance, 1986: 7). Aggregation and generalisation are less difficult where there is a bunched distribution with minimal deviation in the tails.

Kaplan reports a remarkable convergence in QALY weights between rheumatoid arthritics and the general population, between Arizona Navahos and a random selection in San Diego, between Oregon and the United Kingdom: 'The evidence for differential preference is weak at best.... Overall preferences for health states appear to be quite similar.... Preference differences across groups appear to be small and are not sufficiently large to justify their use in influencing policy decisions' (Kaplan, 1995: 51, 52, 60). Where there is not universal concord, however, the democratic option is different strokes for different folks. The alternative would be to force a single choice on a plurality of heterogeneities. One man's meat is another man's poison: 'A more sophisticated approach would be to plan different styles of care to satisfy the preferences of people who, for example, place different emphasis on the relief of disability relative to the relief of distress' (Rosser and Kind, 1978: 357). Each of us is unique. Each of us has valid QALYs to report. Not all of us feel the same about our condition.

Different studies spotlight different utilities as seen by different people in response to different questions relating to different functions put right through different procedures. The difference of focus can cause the respondents to articulate different values. Thompson found this when he juxtaposed the standard gamble (when the trade-off was life in pain versus either diminished pain or immediate death) to the willingness to pay (when people were looking at functional improvement and putting a price on their recovery). The latter answer was 22 per cent of household income. The former answer was a mortal risk of 27 per cent (Thompson, 1986: 395). The focus was different. The results cannot be compared.

Cook, Richardson and Street, studying treatment options for gallstone disease, confirmed Thompson's finding, that the view is different depending on the perspective that is adopted. When the questions were asked *ex ante* (allowance made for uncertainty and medical risk) the respondents selected extracorporeal shockwave lithotripsy. When the questions were asked *ex post* the respondents (having experienced the unpleasant vomiting and the diarrhoea that accompany the non-invasive shocks) said that they would derive a better quality of life (despite the 1/1000 chance of death in the operating theatre) from laparoscopic cholecystectomy instead (Cook, Richardson and Street, 1994: 167). Democratic accountability means that responsive decision-makers will eschew discretion in favour of the random cross-section that voices the opinions of the mass. That, however, is just the problem. The citizen in the street says lithrotripsy when he is interviewed *ex ante*: like any economic subject he must buy his ticket before he attends the show. The citizen in the street says cholecystectomy when he is interviewed *ex post*: like every tourist who has gone there and come back, he wants his vomiting and his diarrhoea to be fed through to future travellers. On the one hand there is anticipation. On the other hand there is experience. It is not very easy to be a responsive decision-maker these days.

One study is of Parkinson's and another is of Tourette's: the Rosser scale may not be sensitive enough to allow for QALY comparisons between the conditions. Heterogeneity in intervals and weights makes it a guesstimate to juxtapose the QALYs from the investigations: psychometrics is not comparing like with like where the measuring rod is itself a rubber standard. Interpersonal comparisons are fraught with difficulties: Jack's ordinal scale cannot be aggregated with Jill's unless there is a warning that the cardinal utilities might actually be very far apart. The patient, the practitioner and the public might express preferences in a scatter: implying that pain, technique and tax can legitimate the reliance upon different informants, Torrance writes disarmingly of the three constituencies that 'the appropriate viewpoint depends upon the question to be answered' (Torrance, 1986: 7). Overriding all is the problem that few of us are able to evaluate our present or our future in the language of 'how many times worse is A than B': 'It may be conceptually appealing to ask individuals to convert into a utility index a whole-of-life scenario in which health and social states change with age and disease progression. However, in the absence of a reliable and valid technique for converting such scenarios into a numerical score the approach cannot be operationalised' (Richardson, 1994: 15).

The costs are at least as confusing as the benefits. Costs are a moveable feast: some studies concentrate on the direct costs of treatment while others include opportunity costs, private transport, personal expenses, psychic costs, social spillovers. Costs are a judgment call: some studies include a 'do nothing' option while others include only treatments for which receipts can be obtained. Costs are context-specific: different institutions, different cultures, different clinical practices, different lifestyles, different age structures can all throw up different rankings. Costs are time-dominated: where utility is an intertemporal flow accruing to an initial stock, it makes sense to use a discount rate. Not all studies will select the same one.

The benefits and the costs are hard to measure. Cost-utility rankings must evidently be accompanied by a health warning and a word of caution: 'QALY league tables: handle with care' (Gerrard and Mooney, 1993: 59). Drummond, Torrance and Mason agree that it would be sensible to proceed with care: 'Although cost per QALY league tables can potentially assist decision makers in the allocation of resources, they can also potentially mislead. In this way they are analogous to many medical interventions which do good but carry risks' (Drummond, Torrance and Mason, 1993: 39). It is always sensible to proceed with care. That does not mean that one should not proceed at all.

8. Equity and equality

Equity means fairness. It means that the entitlements are as they ought to be. It means that each member of society is getting his just deserts.

Fairness can refer to the starting point. Here each entrant is known to enjoy the appropriate opportunities when the starting gun goes off. Fairness can refer to the race. In this case each runner is seen to be treated properly within the accepted guidelines of the rules. Fairness, finally, can refer to the finish. Fairness at the end of the game means that each player receives the prize that he deserves and that no one is getting less nor more.

Fairness is a moral absolute. It is a correct procedure or a just outcome. In that sense it is different from equality, which is a statement of fact. Jill is precisely as tall as Jack. Tom is precisely as fat as Dick. There is no normative suggestion that they ought to be the standard size. Equality is measuring up. And that is all.

This chapter is concerned with equity. Yet it is concerned with equality as well. The reason is that, rightly or wrongly, equity is often the moral principle that is invoked to make equality a desired objective and not just a dispassionate yardstick. Many people attach normative significance to a levelling of interpersonal distance. Many people say that in core areas of social life it is proper for the disparities to be kept within manageable limits. Many people are at one with Tawney when he says that it is *right* for fellow citizens to have uninhibited access to the social minimum: 'Whatever their position on the economic scale may be, it shall be such as is fit to be occupied by men' (Tawney, 1964 [1931]: 108).

Political democracy is one area where equality is believed to be a desideratum: the norm there is one citizen, one vote. Health status and health care is another such area. The first section of this chapter says what is equal about equality. The following four sections, headed 'A Human Right', 'Maximin', 'Generosity and Compassion', 'The Structural Imperative', suggest reasons why consensus might converge on the perception that it is equitable to be more nearly alike.

8.1. EQUALITY AND HEALTH

There is a *what* and there is a *why*. This section says what, precisely, is equal about equality in health. One reason why policymakers approach equality with caution is that there is no real agreement as to what the term actually entails. On a good day it is unclear. On a bad day it is divisive. It is curious that something so widely welcomed and desired should also be so elusive, so difficult to pin down.

There are four equalities in equality. Not all are equally useful in the formulation of health policy that, normatively speaking, is fair and just. The four conceptions of equality are equality of per capita expenditure, equal treatment for equal need, equality of contribution and equality of outcome.

8.1.1. Equality of Per Capita Expenditure

Each child at a school picnic is given an identical piece of cake. 'One size feeds each' is the moral principle that the teachers invoke. Equality of health care spending is a horse from the same venerable stable. Whether the equality targets public spending or the whole of the health care encounter (private and public alike), the lump-sum principle is the same. Equal-share consumption is the expectation that each citizen will be putting an identical strain upon the fund.

Tawney did not think that the expectation made much sense: 'Equality of provision is not identity of provision. It is to be achieved, not by treating different needs in the same way, but by devoting equal care to ensuring that they are met in the different ways most appropriate to them' (Tawney, 1964 [1931]: 49). Different people need different treatments. Some people do not need doctoring at all. Every system of risk pooling, capitalist and socialist alike, is the same in this respect. Illness is to a large extent random. Unlike most other commodities, the demand for the product is not within the control of the individual. It cannot be equalised since it is not fully a function of choice and behaviour. Uncertainty makes it a thing apart.

The demand for care is erratic and peaked. Even if the option (supply) is the same, the take-up (demand) will not be. The sick use up more care inputs than do the well. The health-conscious claim more of their entitlement than do the short-horizoned. Clients who take the blue tablet cost more than do patients who take the white one. The over-75s absorb several times more health care resources than do the mid-20s. No one would say that their drugs should be discontinued once they reach the national entitlement of £500. Nor would many people say that healthy people should be given a free television licence to make up the commitment to the £500 that is their equal share.

8.1.2. Equal Treatment for Equal Need

The famous professor needs radiotherapy and the unemployed labourer needs radiotherapy. When Titmuss was dying in a National Health Service hospital, he was gratified to find that both he and a young West Indian from Trinidad, aged 25, had the same access to the same expensive equipment: 'Sometimes he went into the Theratron Room first; sometimes I did. What determined waiting was quite simply the vagaries of London traffic – not race, religion, colour or class' (Titmuss, 1974: 151). 'To each according to his need' means that each should have an equal opportunity (whether or not he actually exercises his option) of receiving the attention that his condition dictates. This need should be met irrespective of age, income, gender, caste, place of residence, ethnic background, difficulty of access or any other non-medical irrelevancy. Horizontal equity means that no one should be able to secure fast-track treatment merely because of non-need selection criteria such as influential friends or ability to pay. It might even suggest positive discrimination in order to overcome history-dominated inequities that have imposed an unjustifiable handicap.

The debate centres round the general case versus the specific exception. In the general case of pins, cars, clothes, oranges, apples and yachts many people would argue for allocation by supply and effective demand: 'No exchange will take place unless both parties do benefit from it. Co-operation is thereby achieved without coercion' (Friedman, 1962: 13). In the specific case of PhD degrees and professional certificates many people would argue the opposite: the consensus would probably be that academic merit and not willingness to pay should be the deciding factor in allocating an examination pass. Then there are bedrock commodities like basic nutrition, basic shelter, legal assistance and medical services. Like the PhDs and the certificates, these too are exceptions even in an economy where most people are broadly satisfied with exchange. Tobin has used the phrase 'specific egalitarianism' to encapsulate the notion that the distribution of 'basic necessities' such as these cannot be left to the economist's haggling and bargaining. Bought and sold degrees distort the information they are expected to convey. Bought and sold basics are at variance with the common value core. They make us feel bad about ourselves.

The 'social conscience', Tobin stresses, is offended by 'severe inequality in … commodities essential to life and citizenship' (Tobin, 1970: 264, 265, 276). Moral obligation in respect of pins is not the same as moral obligation in respect of life-or-death resuscitation. Equity, as Walzer writes, is specific to a sphere: 'The principles of justice are themselves pluralistic in form.… Different social goods ought to be distributed for different reasons, in accordance with different procedures, by different agents' (Walzer, 1983: 6). Health care is different from pins. It must be distributed in accordance with a standard that is in keeping with the nature of the beast. Social conscience provides that standard. Haggling and bargaining can price and sell the luxuries. In the case of health care, however, *ought-ness* comes from *need-ness* and *need-ness* comes from *us-ness*. *Want-ness*, good in its place, somehow leaves us hungry for another meal.

Bernard Williams says: 'Leaving aside preventive medicine, the proper ground of distribution of medical care is ill health: this is a necessary truth' (Williams, 1973 [1962]: 240). Williams, in 'The idea of equality', raises the objection that in many societies ill health works as a necessary but not a sufficient condition for receiving medical attention: 'Such treatment costs money, and not all who are ill have the money; hence the possession of sufficient money becomes in fact an additional necessary condition of actually receiving treatment' (Williams, 1973 [1962]: 240). Inequality is inseparable from health care in the obvious sense that the ailing consume more than the hale. Yet there is a second inequality that is marbled into the first: the rich sick take out more than the poor sick. This is likely to happen even where the *medical* needs of the top and the bottom income deciles happen to be the same. Williams finds this second inequality objectionable and illogical. It is, he says, 'an irrational state of affairs': 'It is a situation in which reasons are insufficiently *operative*; it is a situation insufficiently controlled by reasons – and hence by reason itself' (Williams, 1973 [1962]: 241; original emphasis). Williams states that the right to a fair trial cannot be regarded as safe where the litigant cannot afford to pay the counsel. Williams concludes that to believe in liberty it is necessary to believe in some supported equality, a moderately supported equality, as well.

The model is 'one person, one vote' in the political democracy. It is as familiar as equal access to the police services and the law courts in the protective State. As health care is a mixed bag, the equality of entitlement would have to be confined to the fundamental services, to the core of need. The need is for greater equality. It is not for straight-line access that knows no mountains or troughs. Above the basic minimum, equal access might not even be equitable access in any sense. Infinite elasticity might, on the contrary, be a bloated over-commitment that over-satisfies the need. The basic minimum is different. Up to the basic floor, equality of access would be singled out as a distributional imperative by Tobin's 'social conscience', by Williams's 'proper ground'. There at least, threshold access cannot be refused. There at least, needs take precedence over wants and ethical absolutes marginalise the effective demand.

Basic access is just, noble, humane and impartial. Translating allocation by need into normative policy is more difficult. A list must be drawn up; and a number of health care systems have had to do this. The list would have to include access to a primary care doctor, a hospital inpatient bed, an ambulance in an emergency, a tried-and-tested generic (but not an experimental drug or a luxury brand), palliative alleviation of intolerable pain, necessary X-rays, necessary dental care, necessary laboratory tests. Perhaps the list would include preventive care such as a tetanus injection and health education in areas like family planning. Perhaps it would include mental health services such as counselling and psychotherapy.

Some services will be core necessities. Emergency antivenom when the snakebite victim would otherwise have only hours to live is probably 'basic'. Other services will be top-up amenities. Chemical injection to look young and attractive is probably not 'basic'. The problem lies with the ambiguities in between. Suppose that one diagnostic test is called 'basic' but that it false-negatives one cancer in ten thousand. Is a battery of sequential tests 'basic' where the outcome might be to save the ten-thousandth human life that, snuffed out, will leave three small children penniless, orphaned and alone? Dictionaries and encyclopaedias to their discredit have no set-in-stone table revealing the essence of 'basic' care. It is easier to be in favour of equal access than to say what is being covered by the guarantee. What is clear is that the guarantee extends only to the satisfaction of needs. Preferences and wants, however defined, will have to look after themselves.

Levelling up could mean benchmarking the services and/or the financial entitlement by the bundle that the median citizen is already enjoying. A cohort somewhat above the median could be selected in order to build generosity into the standard of decency. The social wage of services would in that way be of greatest proportionate value to those citizens whose earned incomes are low. In a sense, however, this replication of the status quo may be said to negate the message of earlier chapters in this book. Night visits and home visits may or may not deliver health. A full annual check-up might not make any difference. Medical efficacy is not cut-and-dried. Some treatments are not cost-effective. For some complaints like Ebola and herpes there is no cure. The side-effects and the cross-infection are sometimes worse than the disease. The total cost of care is subject to escalation. Patients' ignorance and information asymmetry make it unclear what the bodyholder wants or needs. Supplier-induced demand and defensive medicine build in an upward bias. There is at least a chance that what the median is demanding is already too high. Or perhaps it is too low. Or perhaps it is just right. Defining basic needs in terms of current practice is a theory held up by its own bootstraps.

A less relativistic, more medically-informed specification of irreducible care would be less controversial. An objective measure would in particular minimise the divisive polarisation where the community is being asked to back equal access with its own pooled subsidy. It is, however, not easy to come by so invariant a definition of need. To say that the doctor knows best is to say that the individual and the public should mind their own business. Not everyone who sees medicine as a topic in social rights and duties will be prepared to sign over his opinions. An alternative is to say that the kaleidoscope knows best and that objective need laid up in Heaven simply cannot exist. Adequate health, the relativist will say, is what is regarded as an equitable minimum in a given society at a specific time in its continuing evolution. The definition of 'basic' changes with time and place. *How much* inclusion is a variable and not a constant.

Equal access to basic care is an end in itself. It is the passport to a more enjoyable use of leisure, a wider range of consumables, a longer and more productive retirement. What should not be forgotten is that basic care is a means as well as a utility. The gateway to tolerable health, basic care is twice blessed in that tolerable health itself is also access. As Daniels writes: 'Health care is "special" because of its connection to the special social good, opportunity. Health-care needs are things we need to maintain, restore, or compensate for the loss of normal species functioning. Impairment of normal functioning means that an individual might not enjoy his fair share of the range of opportunities normal for his society' (Daniels, 1985: 86). Health care is about economic success. It is not just about getting rid of a stubborn cold.

That is why there is a strong temptation to say that the definition of 'basic' should be shaded to incorporate the equalisation of life chances as well. Tuberculosis gets in the way of promotion. Anxiety affects concentration. Basic health is basic not least because it empowers the left-behind to obtain and retain a decent job. Public subsidisation of medical care has in this sense the same social mission as skill formation through schooling. It levels up the low paid through public finance raised by means of progressive taxation. Basic care is liberalism and it is socialism. It opens doors. It gives everyone a chance.

Yet basic care might not be the only commodity to which the principle of allocation by need might have to be applied. Many diseases are the result not so much of inadequate doctoring as of bad housing, poor diet and a polluted neighbourhood. It is a blank cheque. As strong as the case for basic health will be, the danger is that the argument is also open-ended. Williams and Cookson describe the porous boundaries well: 'One difficulty with needs-based theories lies in drawing the line between goods which should be distributed according to need and those which should be distributed according to market forces. Should goods other than health care also be distributed according to need (e.g. nutrition, shelter, transport, employment)? For that matter, should some forms of health care be distributed according to market forces (e.g. cosmetic surgery)?' (Williams and Cookson, 2000: 1888). The concept of 'basic' means that someone must draw the line. When asked to do this, even Williams and Cookson wisely fall back on rhetorical questions and pass the poisoned buck.

Basic care is access defined by validated need. Validated need, however, conceals as much as it explains. Cost-effectiveness is a high-profile absentee. If person A has only a 20 per cent chance of survival and person B has an 80 per cent potential to benefit, should their needs be adjusted to incorporate the probability of success and the maximal utilitarian endstock of welfare? If need C costs ten times as much as need D, should equal treatment for equal *needs* mean that Big C can never be discontinued? If technique E delivers the same endstate as technique F, can the patient hold out for a gold-standard new hand or is his basic need satisfied by an adequate-enough metal hook? Once the questions are answered, the conclusion is then inevitable: 'There is nothing egalitarian about distribution according to need' (Culyer and Wagstaff, 1993: 448). Nor would equality by itself be enough. If all are given one grain of rice and all desperately need two grains instead, equality by itself cannot satisfy the need. Resources will be required to ensure that minimum standards are met.

8.1.3. Equality of Contribution

Equality of contribution can mean that each citizen pays an equal sum into the fund. This means that each not only has the same entitlement to receive care, but that each puts in the same amount of money each month. Rich or poor, sick or healthy, each citizen each month sticks on his two-shilling health care stamp.

Equality of contribution can also mean that each citizen sacrifices the same psychic satisfaction. The objective magnitudes are made unequal in order that the subjective sensations should be the same. Proponents of this interpretation would say that progressive income tax is better than the equal lump-sum since the poor value their marginal income more highly than the rich. It need not be so: the rich might have more sensitive tastes while the poor might be more accepting, more used to a hard life. Since utility cannot be measured, since interpersonal comparisons are therefore speculative, Braybrooke prefers to defend progressive tax with the documented empiricism that 'the poor find it difficult to cover their basic needs, while the rich can indulge in the most frivolous preferences' (Braybrooke, 1987: 173). Other thinkers, uncomfortable with unbending needs, will nevertheless return to the celebrated *a priori* of falling incremental happiness. Unequal payments, they will say, make the diminishing marginal disutility the same. They make the redistribution double. The healthy cross-subsidise the ill. Simultaneously, the successful cross-subsidise the less advantaged.

Equality of contribution, finally, can mean equal payment for equal utilisation. At the stage of provision, the sick would subscribe more each month towards their care since it is the sick who are blocking up the beds. At the stage of finance, the higher risks would pay higher premiums upfront since it is they who are likely to spend more days on a drip. Where payments are standard, moral hazard would empower the risk-prone and the careless to take advantage of other people's assiduity. It is hard to call it equitable when people who have worked hard all their lives have to pay for people who have put drunkenness and crime before their social duty.

Le Grand has argued for a two-part approach to equal charging. Discrimination, he says, is not acceptable at the stage of provision. In respect of finance, however, it is not inequitable to shade the user-fee. One way of doing this would be by income: 'The extension of means-tested charges would raise the cost to the high income groups, hence perhaps reducing their use relative to that of low income groups, while at the same time perhaps promoting equality of cost' (Le Grand, 1982: 50). Another form of shading could be based on risk. Thus all smokers might be asked to pay a hypothecated supplement to cover the additional costs of medical treatment. The result would be actuarial social insurance that recalls the microscopic bias of the sin-excising excise duties. Yet there is a conflict of ethics. On the one hand, sin fills up the beds. On the other hand tolerance, even of sin, is the mark of a liberal society. Is high-risk sexuality not as valid a choice as motoring to work or eating red meat in a society that does not want to judge? Does society really want the poorest of the poor to pay a risk premium merely because they have to dive for pearls in shark-infested waters while the plutocrat sips his tea at home? Should the married really pay more than the single because they are more likely to have children and impose a burden?

Equal contribution need not be in money. It can also be in the equal execution of the duties that validate the rights. T.H. Marshall writes as follows about the social compact: 'Social rights imply an absolute right to a certain standard of civilisation which is conditional only on the discharge of the general duties of citizenship' (Marshall, 1992 [1950]: 26). Equal access to the service seems in his view to be dependent on equal recognition of other citizens' claims.

Breaking the social contract can cost the offender more than his friends. It can also have major implications for the medical care he can expect. Compare a criminal injured while robbing a bank with his innocent victim who got in the way. Compare the murderer who fired first with the member of the public who was shot while rescuing a policeman. Would most people really find it fair that the aggressor and the defender should be able to claim the same entitlement? Equal rights might have to be tempered by equal duties in order to ensure that equality is equity and not just a flat, level line. It would be the thesis of judgmental contractors that the characteristics and history of the patient, and not just his current and present need, ought to be taken into account when he is being assigned his priority for care. Equal treatment for equal need might not always be equally fair.

8.1.4. Equality of Outcome

Health will never be dead-level. There will always be differences in quality-adjusted life-years. Inherited genes are a fact of life. The biological endowment marks out the playing field. Women live longer than men. Women hold a monopoly in the reproductive function. The old man does not have the same life-expectancy as the beardless youth. We may be equal but still we are not all the same.

Some inequality, indeed, is self-selected. It is a topic in equality of respect. Freedom includes the freedom to take a chance. A society cannot stop boys from playing football merely because they might break a leg. It cannot force girls to become active in armed robbery merely because they are statistically under-represented in premeditated homicide. It cannot force mercenary soldiers to convert to whist merely because mercenary soldiers have rates of attrition that make the Minister of Hospitals look bad. A society cannot prohibit hang-gliding, skate-boarding, tiger-shooting merely because it has made a decision to bring the mortalities and the morbidities closer together. A society cannot force reli-gious minorities to have blood transfusions merely because death ranked above a violation of the moral code introduces a spike into the equality of status. Equal liberty in cases such as these is actually incompatible with equal outcomes, equal incomes or equal levels of satisfaction. Different people opt for different risks. They regard different amounts of care as right for them.

A smoker is revealing that he is less risk-averse than a non-smoker. He may be said to have made a considered purchase of the ill health that he experiences. A misanthropist choosing freely to live in an offshore lighthouse has some control over the medical facilities he can enjoy. He may be said to have waived his equal access to a world-class local hospital. Such inequalities might not be unacceptable inequalities: 'If one individual receives less than another owing to her own choice, then the disparity is not considered inequitable' (Le Grand, 1991: 87). Students who put in different amounts of effort must not expect to score equally well in a test. If some people have gone for a trade-off that dam-ages their health, it might not be in the spirit of T.H. Marshall or even of common usage to say that they have an equal right to restorative care that makes their health outcomes equal again.

The rule of equal outcomes tends to lose its appeal where the effort is not the same and the deserts and sweets are well within the individual's control. The student who works hard should not have to share his grades with the student who is lazy. The saver who defers his gratification should not have to share his dividends with the spender who squanders his wealth. Two individuals cutting a cake might not intuitively find the rule of 'half for you, half for me' equally fair to both: 'Suppose that one of the two individuals concerned had baked the cake; might not she have a claim, on equity grounds, to a larger share? ... Equal-ity of outcome will sometimes be equitable and sometimes not' (Le Grand, 1991: 66, 71). In comparing the outcomes, a decision must be made on whether or not to include the accomplishments, the aspirations and the values that made the more healthy and the less healthy the unequal persons that they are.

So must a decision on whether to incorporate the capacity to benefit. Musi-cians who can play the piano are given first refusal when only a few pianos are around. Linguists who can read Bulgarian are offered books in Bulgarian that Romanians could only use to make a fire. Patients who are more likely to get well are pushed up the list for surgery when not all operations can be performed. People left out and left behind will complain that their outcomes are disregarded. They will insist that they are plants and not weeds that can legitimately be culled. Scarcity, however, is not on their side. Limited resources rule out an egalitarian solution: 'People with greater aptitude for legal studies justly gain admission to law school, while other people, however worthy in other respects, must accept rejection' (Braybrooke, 1987: 141).

Equality of outcome, if it is to be an objective, cannot be defined as uniformity, constancy or a strict convergence on the mean. Yet it does have a meaning. It can usefully be defined as an equalisation of differences that are at once avoidable, unwanted and properly understood: 'What is important is not that everyone achieves the same level of health but rather that everyone has the *opportunity* to achieve the same level' (Wagstaff and van Doorslaer, 2000: 1817). An equal chance, not an equal finish, is the objective that must be pursued. Levelling of access to care is not a guarantee that across-the-board health status will converge on the mean. Income, education, occupation and lifestyle have a role to play as well. Conspicuous and flagrant differences are nonetheless an indicator that something has gone wrong. Unequal rates of morbidity or child mortality suggest that some groups might be suffering from neglect.

Named individuals have freedom within the law. Equitably equal outcomes can only mean that non-random patterned pathologies should not force broad categories or recognisable groups into a position on the health status map which they would not have selected had the material constraints and the unequal information not shoehorned them into a dystopia that was not of their own choosing. While accidents of birth have to be accepted, preventable handicaps should be made less arbitrary, less of a lottery that rides roughshod over the meritocrat's justification of reward.

That said, pluralism and volition are a part of democracy. Different people want different standards of health, just as they target different levels of effort, of income, of expensive consumables, of job satisfaction. It is *their* cardinal utility and *their* quality-adjusted life-years that make the inequality an equitable one. They do not want dead-level equality in the health biographies that describe their lives.

8.2.   A HUMAN RIGHT

The charters and the manifestos state that health care is an absolute right: 'The enjoyment of the highest attainable standard of health is one of the fundamental rights of every human being without distinction of race, religion, political belief, economic or social condition.... Governments have a responsibility for the health of their peoples' (World Health Organization, 1962 [1946]: 1). The 'highest attainable standard' is a counsel of perfection. Even a threshold minimum can, however, be enough to ensure that human dignity does not fall victim to discrimination or even to economics.

8.2.1. The Threshold Minimum

It can never be just to violate a fundamental right. Health is not a market tradeable that is no more than wants and interests, utility and profit, competition and efficiency. That is why the desired equality cannot be achieved by selectively refusing treatment to applicants with above-average health status or by deliberately cross-infecting patients with above-average access to hospitals. Envy and malice can easily shunt the car of equalisation on to the siding that leads to *Schadenfreude* and even *Birkenau*. The focus on the human essence keeps the car on the path of reason. To level down rather than to level up would be an immoral violation of the human essence that the healthy as much as the ill must be deemed to possess. To be equally healthy means to be equal *and* to be healthy. It does not mean that Peter can be robbed of life-years in order to reduce the distance that separates him from Paul.

The healthy have a fundamental right to retain the health status that they possess. What the World Health Organization would say is that the unhealthy too have a fundamental right to move up. Without a reasonable access to health, other personal objectives cannot be achieved. The unhealthy human being is unfree. Held back, he iş unable fully to become himself. In that sense a target level of health care is a primary good and a strategic input. Ideologically, it is a part of the career open to the talents. It puts a stamp of legitimacy on to unequal finishes proportioned to innate talent, focused assiduity, demonstrated accomplishment and entrepreneurial alertness. These and other achievement-related characteristics make it possible for a liberated human being to turn to best advantage the historical accidents of good genes and good luck. Health care is not the same as shopping-mall consumables such as television sets and designer labels which deliver final satisfaction alone. It is closer in function to other primary entitlements like decent shelter, sufficient exercise, adequate companionship, recuperative leisure, physical security, reproductive gratification and nutritious food. Without primary entitlements such as these stunted people would never escape the vicious circle of under-fulfilment.

The 'highest attainable standard' is an ideal that no society can meet. Nor is it necessary to do so. The human right is the right to satisfy a basic need. It is the right to 'flourish as a human being'. The basic need met, the concept of right can then safely drop away. Birth control through abortion is not a human right. It is on the luxury side of the 'decent adequate minimum' (Daniels, 1985: 56) since family planning is possible without expensive medicalisation. Frills like a private room with a cable TV are not a human right. Such services contribute something to comfort and marginally to self-respect but do not realistically deliver the core faculties that make a man a man. Society can reasonably turn off the tap where the fringe is not the right. Preferences do not carry an *ought-to-be*. Basic needs are different.

Having a pulse is necessary but not sufficient to fit the dictionary definition of being human. The full flowering of the human essence means more than the simple beating of the heart. Wagstaff and van Doorslaer write as follows about the implications of the freedom to grow into oneself: 'The extent to which medical care is needed is to be judged not so much in terms of its impact on health, as reflected in, say, freedom from pain and mobility, but rather more generally in terms of its ability to enable individuals to flourish. A hip replacement, for example, aids mobility and enables a person to flourish. But some items of care, such as IVF, might do little to improve a person's health narrowly defined and yet might make a big impact on their ability to flourish as a human being' (Wagstaff and van Doorslaer, 2000: 1815–6). Health care is about full and unfettered functioning. Mortality and morbidity are a part of the story of growth. The biological minimum does not, however, exhaust the syllabus.

8.2.2. Natural Rights

The commitment to levelling up may be derived from what it means to be human. A human being is not *human* in the full sense of the word if he does not have a reasonable set of faculties. It is in the nature of a human being that he should be able to move about. It is in the nature of a human being that he should be able to propagate and reproduce. It is in the nature of a human being that he should be able to forage for food which in the market economy means holding a job.

The term *homo sapiens* picks up the idea that it is in man's nature to be wise and alert. Adequate function within the 'normal opportunity range' (Daniels, 1985: 35), a philosopher like Daniels would say, is a characteristic of the species. It is typical, normal and suitable. Even the old, the frail, the disabled and the incurable are human. Their humanness is their passport to their right. The mentally and the terminally ill cannot reasonably be shot merely because their economic value has gone into the red.

Locke started from the premise that 'one omnipotent and infinitely wise maker' had imposed a law of nature upon the state of nature which was a source of absolute obligation: 'And reason, which is that law, teaches all mankind who will but consult it that, being all equal and independent, no one ought to harm another in his life, health, liberty, or possessions' (Locke, 1993 [1689]: 263–4). The right to life or liberty might be cancelled out by a crime and the right to property become inoperative where the estate has been secured through force or fraud. In the normal course of things, however, the claim to retain that which is my own is an irrevocable imperative, a clause in the social compact, a universal *nolo tangere* that even an overwhelming majority cannot override.

Locke's criterion is the negative injunction that 'thou shalt not harm'. It can, however, be amplified into the doctor's Hippocratic duty 'to help the sick'. To make this extension it is only necessary to say that the right to a body is the right to a *functional* body. Possibly the extension is actually implied by Locke when he says that men are 'all the servants of one sovereign master, sent into the world by his order and about his business' (Locke, 1993 [1689]: 264). No one can serve God's purpose if his bodily capital is not up to the task. In such a case 'to each according to his need' would have to be translated as 'to each that which is the distinguishing mark of the species'. *Salus populi* would quite literally be the *suprema lex*. The right to *good* health would mean more than merely the protection from harm.

Nozick does not include the National Health Service alongside the night watchman on his list of the polity's fundamental prerequisites. His manifesto is as follows: 'Individuals have rights, and there are things no person or group may do to them (without violating their rights).... A minimal state, limited to the narrow functions of protection against force, theft, fraud, enforcement of contracts, and so on, is justified. ... Any more extensive state will violate persons' rights' (Nozick, 1974: ix).

Nozick is clear on the conflict that can arise when the government does too much: 'No one has a right to something whose realization requires certain uses of things and activities that other people have rights and entitlements over' (Nozick, 1974: 238). Nozick is referring to a conflict of commission: my estate is invaded when the government billets the homeless in my barn. The problem is that there can also be an error of omission: my net worth is under threat yet again because well-baby clinics have been abandoned in order to keep down the deficit. Nozick is prepared to include the protection of property. Good health, however, is not regarded as a part of the capital.

Gillon questions this choice. If the right to *good* health is included on Locke's list, then even an advocate of the minimal State such as Nozick would have to accept the legitimacy of taxes to provide doctoring for the sick and the poor (Gillon, 1985: 88). Even the sick and the poor were sent into the world by 'one sovereign master'. They too are expected to do their duty. The acknowledgement that they too have human rights imposes a duty on the community to ensure that even *their* philosophical essence is made *de facto*. Altruism is a choice. Natural rights, however, are an obligation that is as absolute as the laws of the tides. Even if justice is refracted through mutual agreement, still the underlying principles upon which we agree are not up for grabs. It cannot be called just for a democracy to murder Bill merely because 99 per cent of his fellow citizens do not like his face. Health and health care have some of the properties of the vote to murder Bill. Equity cannot be allowed to be as contingent as the willingness and the ability to pay.

Locke himself sows the seeds of doubt when he introduces a *caveat* into his theory of property. What is acquired by my labour is mine alone, he writes, so long as there is 'still enough – and as good – left': 'Nobody could think himself injured by the drinking of another man, though he took a good draught, who had a whole river of the same water left him to quench his thirst' (Locke, 1993 [1689]: 277). Locke's natural rights become problematic where there is not *as much* and *as good* left behind. Nozick sees what such engrossment of the means of life implies: 'A person may not appropriate the only water hole in a desert and charge what he will…. An owner's property right in the only island in an area does not allow him to order a castaway from a shipwreck off his island…. The rights are overridden to avoid some catastrophe' (Nozick, 1974: 180). Scarcity of resources throws the natural rights back into the melting pot. It is not obvious what will come out.

Medical care might be said to fall in Locke's no-man's-land between the doctor's natural right not to treat and the patient's natural right to be restored to tolerable health. Nozick's island that is necessary for survival somehow undermines the reader's confidence in Locke's river that is a free gift to all. Nozick is not convinced that *as much* and *as good*, at least in the long-run, call into question the legitimacy of libertarian *laissez-faire*: 'I believe that the free operation of a market system will not actually run afoul of the Lockean proviso' (Nozick, 1974: 182). Others will be less certain that the free market genuinely makes the threshold minimum as well-protected a property as Nozick's island in a storm.

The guarantee of medical care can mean an unavoidable conflict of rights. On the one hand it might be said that people have a right to possess good health. This is the logic of care delivered in proportion to medical need. On the other hand, it might be said that people have a right to spend their money as they see fit. This is the argument that high taxes (especially high progressive taxes) put ability to be squeezed above the entitlement to hold on to one's own.

It is difficult to be both an egalitarian and a libertarian at once. If society's reward system legitimates unequal wealth, and if the freedom to choose extends to health care as well as hamburgers, then the inference must be that more or better care is something, at least at the margin, that the autonomous citizen must be allowed to select. Natural rights cannot be invoked to impose a standard bid. That is not a concern. As long as natural rights are given the support of a floor, that should be enough to satisfy the conflicting objectives at once.

8.2.3.   Citizenship Rights

Nature is one way of explaining the existence of a human right. Affiliation is another. Citizenship is 'a status bestowed on those who are full members of a community' (Marshall, 1992 [1950]: 18). All citizens are full members of the club. As such, they are all entitled to make full use of the facilities.

Citizenship rights are different from natural rights. They are more in tune with sociology, less in awe of nature. In the case of citizenship rights, the entitlements are derived from belonging and membership, consensus and community. They are not therefore absolute but strictly relative. They are rights which a given group of people has come to attribute to one another. The citizens do this because to be a participant in a nation's activities is voluntarily to accept the mutual responsibilities that knit together the separate individualities. T.H. Green was in no doubt that the life in common was the sole source of reciprocal obligation. Negatively speaking, he wrote, nature has no imperative: 'If the common interest requires it, no right can be alleged against it.... There is no such natural right to do as one likes irrespectively of society' (Green, 1941 [1879]: 109–10). Positively speaking, he emphasised, rights are other people: 'A right is a power of which the exercise by the individual or by some body of men is recognised by a society, either as itself directly essential to a common good, or as conferred by an authority of which the maintenance is recognised as so essential' (Green, 1941 [1879]: 113).

T.H. Marshall, like Green, made much of citizenship as 'a claim to be admitted to a share in the social heritage' (Marshall, 1992 [1950]: 6). Citizenship to Marshall meant not simply a cold passport legality but 'a direct sense of community membership based on loyalty to a civilisation which is a common possession' (Marshall, 1992 [1950]: 24). He made perceived integration in an evolving organism with a link to past and future the basis for civil rights like valid contracting and political rights like full adult suffrage. He also made it the basis of social rights such as the right to health: 'By the social element I mean the whole range from the right to a modicum of economic welfare and security to the right to share to the full in the social heritage and to live the life of a civilised being according to the standards prevailing in the society' (Marshall, 1992 [1950]: 8). The rights of assembly or speech are negative freedoms that do not cost any money. Social rights are more expensive. Where the consumer cannot pay for medical care, the social whole must tax and spend to make his equal right into a social fact.

Equality is equity because our fellow citizens want it that way. Sometimes through market processes, sometimes through consultation and democracy, they name the rights that they think we ought to have. As in economic exchange, however, each of us must do his part to make the social contract two-way: 'If citizenship is invoked in the defence of rights, the corresponding duties of citizenship cannot be ignored' (Marshall, 1992 [1950]: 41). The right to education implies the duty to study hard. The right to health implies the duty to look after oneself. The right not to be infected implies the willingness of a citizen with a contagious disease to surrender his liberty to an isolation ward.

It all sounds suspiciously like what Nozick calls a 'utilitarianism of rights' (Nozick, 1974: 28). Absolutes give way to functions. Social good is superordinated to personal good. Nature cedes its primacy to thee and me. It is a far cry from the Categorical Imperative, which in Kant's sense is intended to universalise the Golden Rule: 'Act in such a way that you always treat humanity, whether in your own person or in the person of any other, never simply as a means, but always at the same time as an end' (Kant, 1961 [1785]: 86). Welfare rights are a city of glass. They make it difficult to be left alone. At least they are not philanthropy or charity. He who puts in what is required has an incontrovertible expectation that he will be allowed to take out what he needs.

8.3. MAXIMIN

Equality can be regarded as equity because the national family looks after its own. It can also be called fair because it is even-handed and impartial. Situated in the here-and-now, the ill person knows that he is ill and the well person knows that he is not. Each has a vested interest in his own known stake. Neither will in the circumstances approach here-and-now levelling with an unbiased eye. Looking to the future, however, the prospect is less certain. No one can know what his future requirements will be. Human beings are situated behind a thick veil of unknowledge. Anything might be out there. It is precisely that ignorance that led John Rawls to his prediction of redistribution down (Rawls, 1972 [1971]: 302).

People are afraid of what might happen when the truth is revealed. As things stand, the 'objective probabilities' are unknown and unknowable: such is the power of the 'principle of insufficient reason' (Rawls, 1972 [1971]: 168). In the great emptiness a careful calculation is not an option. Rawls suggests that, uncertain whether the future is the lady or the tiger, the most rational choice is to 'rank alternatives by their worst possible outcomes' (Rawls, 1972 [1971]: 152–3). The most rational choice is maximin. People buy insurance. They do so because the darkness turns the nightmare loose. It is the tiger and not the lady that most occupies their imaginings when as frightened Hobbesians they think themselves through the closed door.

People behind the 'veil of ignorance' do not know their social class, their intelligence or strength, their ideological principles. Torn between the ambitious big win and the pensionable nine-to-five, they decide to minimise the damage that might be caused by the worst possible outcome. In making their choice, they are also electing not to maximise the gain that they would reap if they later found themselves to be on the winning side. The hypothesis is rather stark. The Rawlsian damage-averter is assumed to have 'a conception of the good such that he cares very little, if anything, for what he might gain above the minimum stipend that he can, in fact, be sure of by following the maximin rule' (Rawls, 1972 [1971]: 154). He is not a self-denying moralist who wishes to assist the less advantaged because their inequality is unjust. He is certainly not a fearless entrepreneur who throws caution to the winds because he values his winnings above his losses. Instead he is a self-seeking, risk-averting cost-counter who out of calculative self-interest pays his progressive income tax, makes distributive justice *re*distributive and insists upon a generous National Health Service.

Interestingly, Rawls does not include health care as one of the primary goods which equity dictates must come under the umbrella of the social guarantee. The list of primary goods extends to income and wealth, occupational opportunity, liberty under the law, access to positions of authority and 'the social bases of self-respect' without which people would not have the confidence to act in their interests: 'The primary goods are necessary conditions for realising the powers of moral personality and are all-purpose means for a sufficiently wide range of final ends' (Rawls, 1982: 166). Doctoring is not on the list. If it were, there would be an argument for intervention with the legitimation that the service satisfies a need that is more than a desire alone: 'Society, the citizens as a collective body, accepts the responsibility for maintaining the equal basic liberties and fair equality of opportunity.... If these requirements are not met, persons cannot maintain their role or status, or achieve their essential aims' (Rawls, 1982: 170, 172–3). Health, he seems to reason, is distributed by nature, not just by society. It is not easy in any case to convince the medical professionals that the Rawlsian priorities are the right ones for their patients. A doctor would probably accept that the health of the worst off should be improved. The problem is that the doctor would regard it as a success indicator if a wealthy executive were to get well too.

Buchanan, like Rawls, believes that equity is defined in a state of unknowledge. All of economic action is such a state since, while no one is so ignorant that he does not know his Rawlsian age or gender, all are radically uncertain when they plan for a future that is yet to come. Justice to Buchanan is procedural rather than endstate-based. It is intimately connected to the rules of the game that were settled through consent: 'A "fair rule" is one that is agreed to by the players in advance of play itself, before the particularized positions of the players come to be identified. A rule is fair if players agree to it. Note carefully what this definition says: a rule is fair if players agree to it. It does not say that players agree because a rule is fair' (Buchanan, 1986: 126).

Taking agreed-upon rules to be the arbiter of equity, it would be difficult to say that any particular outcome is in itself unjust. Whether the final allocation is the result of skill or luck, the fact is that the players agreed to the social contract. The endstate of a spontaneous process that they themselves voluntarily initiated is a dispassionate verdict that cannot fairly be renegotiated. Yet there is more. Like Rawls, Buchanan is a frightened conservative. Walking backwards into the future, he predicts that the rules that emerge will be such that 'citizens will act as if they were risk-averse' (Brennan and Buchanan, 1985: 55). Buchanan writes that it is rational to take precautions: 'We need not predict that each child will fall off the cliff to justify the installation of railings. Minimax is descriptive of deeply felt human precepts of rationality' (Brennan and Buchanan, 1980: 207).

Buchanan's world-view is explicitly politico-economic. Protecting the best by guarding against the worst usually means a constitution to prevent the policymakers from abusing their power, printing money and running a budget deficit. His minimax can, however, be of broader applicability. Even a self-reliant captain of industry can become brain-damaged, crippled, impoverished and unemployable after a single catastrophic accident. That is why it is absolutely in the spirit of Buchanan's minimax for a sympathetic constitutionalist to come down decisively on the side of the safety net and the welfare State. The chronically ill and the irrevocably old are susceptible to denial of cover in the profit-seeking commercial sector. That does not mean that they want to be levelled out because effective demand takes no hostages. Minimax is another way of saying that right wing can vote left wing because the alternative is being left with no wing at all.

Intuition confirms that there is no smoke without fire. Even so, uncompromising risk aversion would be an unusual orientation for a health economist to adopt. While the market may be able to survive without intended endstates, the neglect of cost-effectiveness is a more serious problem. Many of the least advantaged, medically speaking, are the ones least likely to survive for long. There seems to be no ceiling limit to the money that can disappear into their care. Economic growth is bound to be held back by a policy that explicitly funnels scarce resources into a never-filled black hole. There is no suggestion that justice is bound up with merit and achievement. The healthier and the more productive go to the end of the queue.

Maximin in addition cannot explain why so many citizens demonstrably fail to insure. Equality out of self-interest, narrowly defined, may exaggerate the impact of fear on social institutions. One reason is that history-to-come is not in truth radically and completely unpredictable. People do know the age at which their parents died and from what. They do infer from their peer group what is likely to happen to whom and how soon. Probabilities are not the future; and the unforeseen does happen all the time. It all comes down to psychology. It is very difficult to know what goes on in people's minds when they imagine the lady or the tiger that is waiting just behind the closed door.

Maximin assigns no role to altruism, ethical commitment or *pro bono publico*. It is ego and not other that steers them through the day. Yet people do care. Famine relief and subsidised doctoring suggest that the approach cannot be a full account of why other people's health status becomes a selfish stakeholder's valued concern.

8.4. GENEROSITY AND COMPASSION

Whereas Rawls would derive the sharing imperative from self-love, Titmuss would explain it in terms of attachment, responsibility, cohesion and community. He believed that the gift made to unknown strangers had become embodied and embedded in the British National Health Service: 'The most unsordid act of British social policy in the twentieth century has allowed and encouraged senti-ments of altruism, reciprocity and social duty to express themselves; to be made explicit and identifiable in measurable patterns of behaviour by all social groups and classes' (Titmuss, 1970: 225). The National Health Service had its origin in other-regarding self-determination. It also had the function of reinforcing the attachments that made State provision and public payment into a consensually desired crusade. Private charity would not be enough. Nor would it ever be seen as a synonym for the All.

Nor would it satisfy the need for belonging that is the cause and effect of the National Health Service. Michael Walzer writes as follows about the ritual need that the species-being satisfies when he worships in the same waiting room with an unbiased and representative cross-section of his fellow communicants: 'Membership is important because of what the members of a political commu-nity owe to one another and to no one else.... This claim might be reversed: communal provision is important because it teaches us the value of member-ship' (Walzer, 1983: 64). Matter is in motion. History is shaping our mind: 'Goods in the world have shared meanings because conception and creation are social processes' (Walzer, 1983: 7). What we *regard* as just is a function of what we *regarded* as just. Institutions once created acquire a momentum of their own.

Health policy to Titmuss and Walzer was more than the doctoring and the nursing alone. It was also a topic in nation-building and the transcendence of isolation. Giving the citizens a shared experience, the common health made them see themselves as fellow participants in a going concern. The externalities spilled over into all areas of social life. People donate blood, tell the truth, bag their litter, pay their taxes. They would no longer be so eager to volunteer if the children's chores were to be secularised into the for-hire maid's bought-in ob-ligations. The privatisation of free-on-demand services, Titmuss writes, can cause far-ranging damage indeed: 'It is likely that a decline in the spirit of altruism in one sphere of human activities will be accompanied by similar changes in attitudes, motives and relationships in other spheres.... Economists may fragment systems and values; other people do not' (Titmuss, 1970: 198). Hobbesians are made and not born. The same is true of Good Samaritans. In the one case as in the other, what matters most is getting the institutions right.

Privatisation would be a certain way of setting people free from the biological imperative that protects the herd through the self-immolation of the lookout deer that sounds the alarm. The repression of fraternity is in that sense an economically-inefficient choice. Nor is it necessarily the one that will make people feel good about themselves. The free rider does not pay for his ride. Yet it is not really the most satisfying ride that he could have experienced. As Hirschman writes: 'There is much fulfilment associated with the citizen's exertions for the public happiness.... To elect a free ride under the circumstances would be equivalent to declining a delicious meal and to swallow instead a satiation-producing pill that is not even particularly effective!' (Hirschman, 1982: 90, 91). It is fair to do one's part. It is satisfying to get involved.

Relatives and friends are the model. Thinkers like Titmuss would extend the commitment to the national family as a whole. There is a spillover effect where good neighbours join community watch schemes and water a holidaymaker's plants. People suffer from spoiled identity and the pinch of conscience when they cross the road and pretend not to see. People, unless they are pathologically insensitive, manage to empathise with what they believe to be the suffering and anxiety of the needy sick. They therefore sacrifice a part of their self-centred hedonism in order to make sure that there will be good quality health standards for all. It is emotion and involvement rather than rationality and interest that motivate them to incur a cost. Citizens take pride in a continuing whole. Mutual aid is in their blood. They want to do their share.

The caring externality is the cause and effect of a preference. Such a 'sacrifice' is not a duty but a pleasure. It is a benefit that exceeds its cost. Yet it is not for all that the same as sharply-defined equity. Justice is an absolute. Justice, unlike sentiment, cannot be traded at the margin when wealth falls or the cost of production goes up. Equity may be said to be the source of a beneficiary's unequivocal right. A personal and private desire to do good is, however, no more substantial than a donor's fleeting whim.

Compassion is productive of a non-market distribution that is built on sand and not on rock. Yet built it is, and that is what counts. Charity satisfies the residual need once the recipient's rights have been exhausted. Consensus validates the rights. A broad groundswell determines what is tolerable and what is unfair. Agreed-upon processes legitimate the prizes. The winners beat the house. The losers end up hungry and alone. Benevolence fills the gap when equity does not provide a strong enough reason to relieve the uncorrected distress of the widow, the orphan and the dental patient who cannot pay.

Individual benevolence is inclination. Collective representations, however, can be a true source of constraint. Social standards are external to the individual. They are a social fact that does not lend itself to opportunistic redefinition. In that sense collective altruism can be a 'categorical imperative' even if private altruism is only a private taste.

8.5.   THE STRUCTURAL IMPERATIVE

Commitment is subjective and motivational. It is refracted through individual choice. Structure is the logic of the system. It is collective and it is functional. Agreement is demand. Structure is supply. If both pillars are not there, the entire edifice will collapse.

The microscopic approach proceeds piecemeal, bottom-up. The structural imperative begins and ends with the whole of the social edifice. It derives the case for equity as equality from the perceived need for intervention in order to ensure that the social machine functions well. It therefore declares the equalisation to have gone far enough where the worst-off have been sufficiently upgraded for the collectivity to be able to get on with its life. Equalisation is not the same as equality. If *our* minimum is adequate, *your* maximum is a waste. At least there is some improvement in status and access on the part of the health-deprived who would otherwise have had more sick days and swallowed fewer pills.

One illustration of the structural imperative is economic growth. The economic system requires not only a stock of educated skills but also a reliable supply of labour. Its success is put in jeopardy by interruptions caused by disease, debility or death. Townsend and Davidson, making a calculation for 1970–2, found that if the mortality rates for the lowest two occupational groups had been the same as that for the upper two occupational groups, then '74,000 lives of people aged under seventy-five would not have been lost. This estimate includes nearly 10,000 children and 32,000 men aged fifteen to sixty-four' (Townsend and Davidson, 1982a: 15). Over and above the loss to the lifeholders and their relatives, the loss to the nation in terms of production, consumption and skill was great.

It is *our* growth that is dependent on *his* health. We therefore invest our money in bringing his health capital up to the standard that is needed for our nation's advance. Even in a market economy, the most efficient distribution of entitlements need not be the allocation that is brought about by the invisible hand. Economics suggests that no one should be suffering from jaundice when he ought to be making microchips or delivering the milk. Equity, seen from that perspective, can be welcomed as a cause of *dynamic* efficiency. Moral philosophy can sometimes shift the production possibilities out.

For the philosophy to be *moral*, however, the utilitarian outcome must be unintended and unexpected. Consequentialism is not the same as deontology. Otherwise the nation would be in the amoral position of sentencing people to death merely because they had grown too old for economics. Equality can be justified on the grounds of productivity and growth. Equity is a harder nut to crack. Fairness is still fairness, even if the patient will never supply any goods or services in return.

A second illustration of the structural imperative was touched on in chapters 3 and 4. It relates to felt integration. Race, gender, occupation, income group, social class, place of residence, insurance qualification, the age profile all draw the fellow citizens apart. Perceived distance can be incompatible with the over-lap in life experiences that is necessary to make one nation out of a multiplicity of separate tribes. Universalistic provision of health care services might be seen as a way of smoothing out the disparities that could otherwise lead to riots, strikes and alienation: 'Civil rights legislation in Britain ... would be a poor and ineffective substitute for the National Health Service' (Titmuss, 1968: 142). New perceptions and conventions take the place of the old castes and ghettoes. Universalism means adjacent beds in a standard ward. It also means that no so-cial group feels that a disproportionate number of its members are dying young because they lack a threshold ability to pay.

Integration as well as affluence would seem to suggest that equality has a payoff. Equality protects the social structure against the under-performance and the divisiveness that could throw sand into the gears. As before, however, the structural legitimation is derived from the *ex post* consequences. The moral code is an ethic. It can teach that the narrowing of the health gap is somehow right and just. As far as structure is concerned, it is beside the point. Even without the ethic, we might still opt for the levelling up since otherwise the alienated will stone our cars in the street.

The end justifies the means. The decoupling of endstate from popular valida-tion gives paternalistic leaders considerable discretion to take action in line with the national interest. The whole is different from the sum of its parts. The public interest is an entity *sui generis*. The structural imperative cannot be ignored. The most optimistic verdict on the action that must be brought about from the top would be that Plato's philosopher-rulers are wise enough to recognise the needs of the collectivity irrespective of the wants that its citizens express – or fail to express. The shepherd knows better than the sheep. Equality can be the result of the social engineer's omniscient and beneficent response.

The solution is simple. Social engineers who know everything they need to know and are able to sacrifice their private interest to the public good must take command. God is equal to the task. God will not let us down. Social engineers who are as good as God will never be out of a job.

9.   Equality and health

The White Paper of 1944 that led to the creation of the British National Health Service on 5 July 1948 took equality in health to mean equal access for equal need. It built on the historic Beveridge Report of 1942 which had declared war on the 'five giant evils of Want, Disease, Ignorance, Squalor and Idleness' (His Majesty's Stationery Office, 1942: para. 456). The White Paper said precisely what it understood by the commitment to levelling up: 'The Government … want to ensure that in the future every man and woman and child can rely on getting … the best medical and other facilities available; that their getting these shall not depend on whether they can pay for them, or on any other factor irrelevant to the real need' (Ministry of Health, 1944: 5).

The aim was the generalisation of a common standard. It was to be the universalisation of the best possible entitlement. Like was to be treated as like. Resource allocation was not to be driven by profit maximisation and the ability to pay. All citizens were to be given what their doctors defined to be medically appropriate. The inference was that the equality of inputs would feed through into an equality of outcomes. In the end a national health status, like a national language, would emerge as the badge of a citizenship shared. The common culture would extend to the common health culture. Professional or manual, rich or poor, the children of Shakespeare, England and St George would have recognisably the same life-expectancy and the same incidence of scabies. They would have attained this standard irrespective of their achieved purchasing power in the judgmental economics of supply and demand.

The aim was ambitious. The realisation was elusive. In countries as market-centred, as payment-oriented as the free enterprise United States one would expect the disparities to survive. What is surprising is the extent to which they survive even in the solidaristic United Kingdom which is committed to high-quality care that is free or nearly free of user-charge at the point of consumption. This chapter examines the two principal kinds of disparity in morbidity and mortality indices: those based on social distance and those based on geographical location. It then suggests social and health care policies that can be relied upon to narrow the gap.

9.1.   SOCIAL DISTANCE

Aneurin Bevan was the Minister of Health who was responsible for the introduction of the National Health Service. Negatively speaking, he regarded it as the welcome antithesis of competitive individualism: 'A free health service is pure Socialism and as such it is opposed to the hedonism of capitalist society' (Bevan, 1961 [1952]: 106). Positively speaking, he saw it as *primus inter pares* in a bundle of social services that all conferred disproportionate benefits on the have-nots, the excluded and the left-behind: 'The Socialist Party ... rushes to the defence of state spending: their supporters are the poor and the defenceless who most need it' (Bevan, 1961 [1952]: 136). It is likely that he would have been bitterly disappointed by the failure of the British Health Service to live up to his high aspirations.

Half a century after the establishment of the National Health Service the Independent Inquiry into Inequalities in Health (chaired by Sir Donald Acheson) revealed that rising living standards backed up by the generous welfare State had not put paid to persisting inequalities in health outcomes: 'Although the last 20 years have brought a marked increase in prosperity and substantial reductions in mortality to the people of this country as a whole, the gap in health between those at the top and bottom of the social scale has widened' (Stationery Office, 1998: v).

Acheson proxied social stratification through the occupational hierarchy. The focus was on the occupation practised by the head of each household. Since people tend to marry within their own social class, the fact that the head of the household is normally a man does not unacceptably prejudice the statistics on women's socio-economic location. Acheson used the five-category schema (adopted by the Registrar General) in which group I is made up of high-end professionals like doctors, lawyers and accountants, group II is intermediate-grade professionals like managers, teachers and journalists, group IIIN is skilled non-manual (clerks, cashiers, retail staff), group IIIM is skilled manual (plumbers, electricians, bus drivers), group IV is partially skilled manual (security guards, care assistants) and group V is unskilled manual (labourers, cleaners, messengers) (National Institute for Health and Clinical Excellence, 2006: 6). In 2001 the National Statistics Socio-economic Classification (NS-SEC) superseded the five-occupation scale. The revised rubric has eight classes. These range from higher managerial and professional occupations through semi-routine occupations to the long-term unemployed. Five classes or eight classes, it is the job function, as in the Acheson Report (Stationery Office, 1998), that determines the social location.

In the early 1970s, Acheson found, the mortality rate among unskilled men of working age was twice that of equivalent men in the administrative, managerial and professional grades. By the early 1990s it was three times higher. For men in classes I and II life expectancy increased by 2 years. For those in classes IV and V it increased by only 1.4 years. Infant mortality in the mid-1990s was 5 out of every 1000 births for the higher groups, 7 out of every 1000 for the lower ones. About 17 per cent of professional men reported long-standing illness: the figure for unskilled men was 48 per cent. Babies with fathers in classes IV and V had a birth weight which was on average 130 grams lower than that of babies with fathers in social classes I and II. Mortality from suicide for men was four times greater in the Vs than it was in the Is. As for hypertension, 'average blood pressure increases as social class decreases'. And, Acheson discovered, there is more: 'At any level of blood pressure people from lower socioeconomic groups appear to be more vulnerable to the associated diseases, as evidenced by their higher rates of coronary heart disease and stroke' (Stationery Office, 1998: 11, 13, 14, 66, 69). Disparities like these are what we expect from foreigners living abroad. In England, however, we have the National Health Service.

Almost a decade before Acheson the Association of Community Health Councils had been reporting that equal care for equal need had not delivered the equalisation in outcomes that had been intended: 'In 1987, babies whose fathers had unskilled jobs had infant mortality rates over 70 per cent higher than those for babies whose fathers had a professional occupation.... In the major killer diseases lung cancer, coronary heart disease and cerebrovascular disease, manual classes have a considerably higher risk of death than non-manual classes (comparing all non-manual classes against all manual classes). For example in the 20–54 age band, men in manual work are more than twice as likely to die from lung cancer as non-manual workers.... Nearly all the major and minor killers now affect the poor more than the rich' (Association of Community Health Councils, 1990: 3–4). Working class women remained 'three times more likely to suffer mental illness than professional women'. Babies born to women of Pakistani origin continued to experience a death rate 'almost 50 per cent above that for the white population' (Association of Community Health Councils, 1990: 6). Only in a very small number of areas (notably breast and prostate cancer, leukaemia, malignancies of the lymph glands, skin melanomas) did the social gradient work to the disadvantage of the affluent and the privileged.

A decade earlier the Working Group on Inequalities in Health had reported a similar, and an equally disturbing, lack of progress towards the eradication of socially-proportioned gaps. Sir Douglas Black and his colleagues had found that differential mortality rates as between the broad occupational groups had not narrowed at all since 1921 for the 15–64 age cohort despite the introduction of the National Health Service. The mortality gap between groups I and II (professional and managerial) and groups IV and V (semi-skilled and unskilled) had actually widened. In absolute terms the mortality rates for all occupational groups had declined. In relative terms the spread had become more marked.

Inequality had increased and not decreased: 'Mortality tends to rise inversely with falling occupational rank or status, for both sexes and at all ages' (Townsend and Davidson, 1982b: 63). An individual born into group I who remains in group I is likely to have a life-expectancy five years in excess of his counterpart in group V. Five years is a lot of life to lose merely because one never managed to make the climb from blue collar to white.

The inequalities related to inputs as well as to outcomes. Very early on in the history of the classless National Health Service Richard Titmuss had found that the higher occupational groups had managed to secure a disproportionate share of the screening, radiography, referrals, antenatal care, infant care, dental care that were supposed to be allocated on the basis of clinical need alone: 'We have learnt from fifteen years' experience of the Health Service that the higher income groups know how to make better use of the Service; they tend to receive more specialist attention; occupy more of the beds in better equipped and staffed hospitals; receive more elective surgery; have better maternity care, and are more likely to get psychiatric help and psychotherapy than low income groups – particularly the unskilled' (Titmuss, 1968: 196).

Stigler (the proposition is sometimes called 'Director's Law') used libertarian public choice to predict that the squeaking wheel gets the oil: 'Public expenditures are made for the primary benefit of the middle classes' (Stigler, 1970: 1). Brian Abel-Smith was sad to report that the expectation of manipulation, assertiveness and special pleading was borne out even in Britain's welfare State. He concluded that the upshot of the good intentions had been perverse, 'that the major beneficiaries of these changes have been the middle classes, that the middling income groups get more from the State than the lower income groups, that taxation often hits the poor harder than the well-to-do, and that in general the middle classes receive good standards of welfare while working people receive a Spartan minimum' (Abel-Smith, 1959: 55–6). Le Grand's finding on the distribution of the citizen's social wage documented the extent of the upward bias. Drawing his data from the General Household Survey (an annual sample of 14 000 households totalling 40 000 individuals), he found that the members of socio-economic groups I and II in Britain were receiving 'at least 40 per cent more expenditure per person' than were the members of socio-economic groups IV and V (Le Grand, 1978: 132). The actual inequality was even greater. The figure of 40 per cent relates to National Health expenditure alone. Many of the affluent had private cover as well.

The same invisible hand appears to be in business in the United States. The Medicare system was created in 1965 expressly to enable the elderly to seek medical treatment without regard to the rationing constraint of finance. Well-intentioned, the unexpected outcome has nonetheless been to favour the better off. Medicare payments per enrolled beneficiary are greater for the higher-income elderly than they are for their low-income counterparts. Davis and

Reynolds calculate that, 'when adjustment is made for health status, physician visits increase with income' (Davis and Reynolds, 1975: 369). The rich elderly in the United States were consuming as much as 70 per cent more of Medicare-funded doctor consultations than were the poor elderly. The class-gradient for other Medicare-sponsored interventions was steeper still. The perverse correlation in publicly funded care might not be Le Grand's 40 per cent more. It might be as much as 100 per cent more.

At least there has been progress. In 1964 those with incomes less than $15000 were 79.6 per cent as likely as those with incomes of over $50000 to have seen a doctor in the previous year and 92.5 per cent as likely to have been in hospital. By 1995 the figures had become 94.6 per cent and 128.4 per cent. For the over-65s as compared with the total population the figures were 69.7 per cent rising to 90 per cent, 190 per cent rising to 266.9 per cent respectively (Folland, Goodman and Stano, 2007: 479, 480). Outcomes are another matter: a study done in the 1980s showed that, across all age groups, those self-reporting their health as excellent had 74 per cent more wealth than those who said their health was fair or poor. White men with family incomes below $10000 could expect to live 6.6 fewer years (for black men it was 7.4 fewer years) than white men in families with more than $25000 (Smith, 1999: 146, 147). Examining the geographical distribution nationwide, in 1996 in 56 of the 306 hospital referral areas Medicare spending was at least 25 per cent *below* the national average; in 19 regions it was 30 per cent *above*. The average reimbursement was $9033 in McAllen, Texas. It was $3074 in Lynchburg, Virginia (Wennberg and Cooper, 1999: 12). It is unlikely that differential rates of illness can explain the whole of the marked inequality. Be that as it may, government schemes like Medicare and Medicaid have clearly improved access and promoted social justice.

They may even have equalised outcomes. Black women enrolled in New Jersey's HeadStart Medicaid programme experienced increased birth weights, reduced incidence of abnormal birth weights and lower newborn hospitalisation costs, although there was no evidence of such a change among whites (Reichman and Florio, 1996: 471). Currie and Gruber found that a 30 percentage-point increase in Medicaid eligibility among pregnant women aged 15–44 nationwide (from 12.4 to 43.3 per cent of the total) was associated with a decrease in infant mortality rates of 8.5 per cent. Increased insurance led to increased utilisation. Increased take-up led to improvement in health status. The improvement is long overdue: at 7 per 1000 births, the infant mortality rate in the United States is among the highest in the industrialised world. On the other hand, each infant life saved cost the Medicaid programme $840000 (Currie and Gruber, 1996: 1276, 1287). This is a great deal of money, equivalent to 206 child years in full-time education. It may not be cost-effective to level up the birth outcomes or to buy incremental health status where the economic outlay is so high. Chapter 5 has submitted the quotes. Olson's (1981) $3.2 million suggests that $840000 is cheap at the price. Blomquist's (1979) $368 000, on the other hand, is a reminder that children can be a ruinous luxury.

Public schemes may have slanted the patterns of utilisation. The poor may have overused (subsidised) inpatient care when (unsubsidised) outpatient care would have been more appropriate and also less resource-intensive. It is, however, hard to generalise in the United States as Medicaid operates on a state-by-state basis. There are 51 separate programmes, with significant differences in eligibility, coverage, payments and benefits. In some states the eligibility cut-off is generous but in others it has been below the poverty line. Also, top-ups in the private sector, as they do in Britain, make the class-correlated inequality even greater than data on the public sector would suggest. The age-adjusted number of doctor visits per 100 bed disability days was 80 per cent higher among higher-income whites than among whites below the poverty level. In the South insured whites made two-and-a-half times as many physician visits as uninsured blacks. Among those who rated their health as poor, the insured saw a doctor 70 per cent more often than the uninsured. Yet the uninsured in surveys disproportionately self-report themselves as being in poor health (Starr, 1986: 117–8).

It is the inverse care law, the law 'that the availability of good medical care tends to vary inversely with the need of the population served' (Tudor Hart, 1971: 412). The Black Report in Britain, using mortality as its principal indicator of relative need, found that the children of social group V were at least four times as likely to die in the first year of life as were the children of social group I; while boys aged 1–14 in social group V were twice as likely to die while in that age-range as were boys in social group I (Townsend and Davidson, 1982b: 53, 64). Blaxter found that the differences in deaths were paralleled by the differences in sickness: 'Even if examination is confined to the more stringent and objective conditions of handicapping chronic illness, prevalence rates in social class V, at over 200 per 1,000 people, are well over twice the rate of 75 reported in class I' (Blaxter, 1976: 117). The lower-income groups report more illness and take more sick days per annum. Their medical need is proportionately more. Yet they consume proportionately less of the health care budget. This is not the warm-hearted generosity of the Good Samaritan who wanted to alleviate conspicuous distress. It is not even the even-handedness of the Hippocratic Oath that commits the doctor 'to help the sick'. It is a *prima facie* violation of the social engineer's commitment to equity and equal access.

Patterned inequalities have survived. They have survived in the social distance that separates the genders and the age groups. They have survived in the inequality that draws apart the British ethnicities: 'For example, since mortality from coronary heart disease in South Asians is 40 per cent higher than the general population, intervention rates for large Asian communities might be expected to be higher than average. The evidence shows the opposite after adjusting for socioeconomic and geographical factors' (Stationery Office, 1998: 113). They have survived not least as a hierarchy of layers that goes from top to bottom. They are vividly demonstrated by the differences in QALYs that cannot be reduced to crude life-years which take no account of pain, immobility, depression or an inability unassisted to wash or dress: 'Surviving members of social classes 4 and 5 have noticeably worse health than their contemporaries in social classes 1 and 2, especially when they are past 40.... We find that the quality-adjusted life expectancy at birth of someone in social classes 1 and 2 is about 66 QALYs but for someone in social classes 4 and 5 it is only about 57 QALYs. To achieve the mean value of about 61.5 QALYs (a 'fair innings') they would need to live to be 65 and 71 years old respectively, a feat achieved by about 76 per cent of social classes 1 and 2 but by only 46 per cent of social classes 4 and 5' (Williams, 1997b: 336–7). Social stratification counts. Yet there are a number of conceptual and statistical problems that must be addressed before the evidence on the vertical inequity can be taken to mean what it says.

First, the empirical studies tend to approximate the social strata using broad occupational categories. The categories document the work function. They do not document what lies beneath it. There is no explicit reference to Marx's distinction between capital ownership juxtaposed to pure labour power; or to net household income as the passport to healthy diet, consumer durables and good living conditions; or to education (general, vocational, higher) as an indicator of lifestyle culture and a school for disciplined assiduity. It may be that occupational group is no more than an umbrella category, and that the active ingredients ought to be unpacked one by one. Black-boxing has the disadvantage that it vacuums up the variables despite the likelihood that they are doing unequal amounts of work. It makes a difference if both partners are earning money, or if one or both has health insurance through work. It makes a difference if the family has adequate house room, or if there is good access to a hygienic hot and cold water supply, or if there is an inside toilet not shared with another family. It also makes a difference if the will to win is there: an individual determined to rise up the occupational ladder will probably take better care of his health than will a self-perceived dead-ender who is passive, live-for-today and undisciplined. It would be useful if the specific micro-linkages could be investigated. It explains too little to aggregate the hidden hypotheses into a mixed bag of causes. Too many explanatory variables make the analysis unwieldy. Too few explanatory variables, however, leave the breakdown incomplete. Besides that, different countries use different categories and different variables. The heterogeneity makes cross-national comparisons very difficult unless the data is recalculated using a standard grid.

Second, the numbers in each of the government statisticians' broad categories tend to alter in relative significance over time. Upward mobility, dynamic *embourgeoisement*, the improvement in skills, tend to mean that fewer people will be left in the lower groups at the end of a period than were there at the beginning. Thus, in Britain, groups IV and V contracted from 38 per cent of the population in 1931 to 26 per cent in 1981 while groups I and II expanded in size from 14 per cent to 23 per cent in the same period. Le Grand and Rabin have recalculated the crude death rates per group using a weighting scheme that picks up the total numbers of which each group is comprised. Their finding for 1931 to 1981 is different from that in the Black Report: 'Over that time the death rates in adult males in classes I and II fell faster than those for classes IV and V, creating an impression of widening inequality. However, because of the changes in the composition of the classes, the numbers of deaths in classes I and II actually increased (in fact, nearly doubled) over the period while the numbers in classes IV and V fell (by about a quarter). Hence if inequalities in health are measured by differences in numbers rather than in rates (a not indefensible procedure), the same data show a decrease rather than an increase in inequality' (Le Grand and Rabin, 1986: 118).

Third, there are practical problems in establishing the correct occupational group. The information that the survivors provide might be exaggerated or simply ambiguous. The occupation given on the death certificate might not be the group in which the individual spent the bulk of his working life. Data on deaths pick up the historical experience of an elderly cohort that was young in a different environment. Changes in the definition and classification of occupation complicate comparisons over long periods of time. The out-of-work are difficult to situate: the link with health will be insurance retained as well as the earnings-stream cut off. The stage in the life cycle has a feedback effect both on health (as the body's systems atrophy) and on wealth (since savings are drawn down and medical bills mount up once the retired stop work). Married women raise issues about the nature of the household: they tend frequently to be placed in their husband's occupational group irrespective of their own level of earnings, education and employment status. Children are often subject to the same proxy classification. Stocks and flows invite an analysis of fluidity and mobility in an open society where occupational group might not be a lifetime constant but a temporary stopping place. A few years spent in V is not a lifetime spent in V. Information is needed on how long the typical transient has to wait before the dynamic of progress moves him on. Information is also needed on the baggage of neglected health that he brings with him when the V ceases to be a coalminer and becomes a Cabinet Minister who is thereafter recorded as a I.

Fourth, there is the problem that the differences *within* the groups can be at least as great as the differences *between* the groups. Thus British university teachers (in occupational group I) have a standardised mortality ratio of 49 but engineering foremen (in group III) have a ratio of 47 and pharmacists (in group I) have a ratio of 116. British fishermen (in class IV) have a ratio of 171 but office cleaners (in class V) only 88 and innkeepers (in class II) as high as 155 (Jones and Cameron, 1984: 43). The averages indicate a smooth gradient. It rises from 77 for the Is to 137 for the Vs. Yet the averages only serve to conceal the heterogeneities. The differences within each pigeonhole are large enough to call into question the generalisations that the broad socio-economic groupings make possible.

Fifth, there is the possibility of reverse causality, that health influences occupation ('health selection') rather than bearing the imprint of present day economic distance ('social causation'). *Post hoc* need not be *propter hoc*. Both health and occupation could for that matter have been shaped by an antecedent third variable ('indirect selection') such as parental education, a problem gene, inadequate self-control, blind-alley time preference or simply the drive to get on which makes upwardly mobile people invest in every kind of capital (including education, which is correlated with health as well as marketable skills). Health at any rate can lead and not lag. A person who is chronically ill will not have access to a full range of jobs. He might have to take early retirement on a considerably reduced pension. He might become exhausted before he has earned a full day's pay. The employment that he finds may be the best he can secure given his handicap. Health status can be a cause of downward social mobility (or, less dramatically, an impediment to rising up). It need not be the effect. Clearly, the policy inferences are different where health influences occupation than where life chances are frustrated because of the dead hand of inherited class.

9.2.   GEOGRAPHICAL LOCATION

Both health status and access to health care resourcing are different in different parts of the world. Male life-expectancy is 52 years in Cambodia, 78 years in Japan, 65 for the world as a whole. Infant mortality per 1000 live births is 87 in Laos, 3 in Singapore, 56 for the world. There are 283 doctors per 100 000 population in the United States but only 10 in Ghana and 25 in the Congo. Different countries report different outcomes and different inputs. The level of economic development seems to account for much if not most of the dispersion.

More surprisingly, there is dispersion even within a single nation. In the United States infant mortality is 10.3 per 1000 live births in rural Mississippi but 3.7 on the Upper East Side of Manhattan. Black males have a life-expectancy at birth that is 6.8 years less, black females 5.2 years less, than do their white counterparts. The slums are a law unto themselves: 'A boy born and brought up in Harlem has less chance of living to 65 years old than a baby in Bangladesh' (Wilkinson, 1996: 158). In the Philippines the infant mortality rate in Metro Manila is 35 per 1000; in Central Mindanao it is 103. In Metro Manila the dentist–population ratio is 1:2533; in the Eastern Visayas it is 1:33 433. Comparing Sweden with Bangladesh is bound to produce marked geographical variations. Comparing America with America, the Philippines with the Philippines, is less obviously a reason to expect dispersion within the matrix of a single economic, political and social system.

Many countries have opted for health care allocated by means of the ability and the willingness to pay. Britain, however, has chosen a National Health Service. That is why disparities in Britain are in a real sense the most worrying of all. British citizens are given an explicit undertaking that each naked Adam has equal worth in the sight both of God and of Westminster. Yet the endstates and the inputs seem nonetheless to vary depending on the area in which they live.

Peter Townsend, 30 years after the institution of the National Health Service, compared the least healthy with the healthiest areas in the North of England. He found a dispersion of approximately 4:1 for lung cancer in both sexes and for female deaths from circulatory complaints (Townsend, 1987: 52). In Bristol, likewise comparing the worst with the best, he found a dispersion of over 2:1 in the ratio of still births, of infant deaths, of deaths of adults in the economically productive age-band from 15 to 65 (Townsend, 1987: 52–3). Looking at national disparities in mortality rates (and taking 100 as the base for the calculation), Townsend and his colleagues were able to identify a sizeable gap between the performance of the bad areas and that of the good: 'If Middlesbrough's age-specific death-rates occurred nationally 125 deaths, not 100, would be experienced, with the greatest percentage increase over the national rate being in the 45–64 range; whereas if Guildford's death-rates applied nationally, only 83 deaths would occur, with the largest decrease being in the 45–64 range' (Townsend, Phillimore and Beattie, 1988: 27). At every age children living in the north have more dental decay than children living in the south: 'For example, at 5 years children living in the North West NHS Region show a 59 per cent excess compared with those in the South Thames NHS Region. At 12 years there is a 75 per cent excess' (Stationery Office, 1998: 72). Differences such as these, combined with similar disparities in permanent sickness, chronic disability, low birth weight, all underline the fundamental proposition that British health had not become *national* health despite the high ideals of Bevan's common service.

Ham writes as follows about the differences between the English regions: 'In 2002, the infant mortality rate in England stood at 5.3, and within England the rate varied from 4.4 in the South West to 6.5 in the West Midlands. In the same year the perinatal mortality rate for England was 8.4, and within England the rate varied from 7.5 in the East to 10.1 in the West Midlands' (Ham, 2005: 206). Life expectancy at birth in Kensington and Chelsea is 86.2 years for females, 82.2 years for males. In Manchester it is 78.3 and 72.5. In Glasgow City it is

76.7 and 69.9 (National Statistics, 2006). Moving from Glasgow City to Kensington and Chelsea could add more than 12 years to an average man's lifespan. Life expectancy in central Glasgow is less than in Vietnam or Egypt. Small areas show up even greater variations. Those born in Middlehaven, the dockland area of Middlesbrough, have an average life-expectancy of only 67.8 years. Those born in Moreton Hall, just outside Bury St. Edmunds, can expect to live to 93.4. The North–South divide has not gone away despite the fact that average life expectancy in the whole of UK is the highest in its history.

Health status is not the same in all areas. Yet the whole of the variance cannot be put down to regional differences in formal health care. As with social patterning, so spatial disparities reflect a multiplicity of variables, including occupation, income and wealth, education, culture. Working conditions are more hazardous in a factory than in an office: areas with a high concentration of manufacturing industry are likely to report a higher incidence of mortality and morbidity. Environmental pollution is more likely where slash and burn is the standard way of clearing forests for crops: even white collar workers in such areas will experience illness and a shorter life.

Incomes are lower in areas where productivity is poor and joblessness high. Affluence has a direct impact on health. Townsend and his colleagues studied the 678 electoral wards (other investigators have used the postal code) that make up the Northern Regional Health Authority in the United Kingdom. They found that the closest correlation was between economic prosperity and the state of health: 'The link between measures of health and socio-economic measures reflecting deprivation could scarcely be more firmly demonstrated. Unemployment is almost four times worse, overcrowding four-and-a-half times as likely, and car ownership and owner-occupation levels nearly three times lower, in the 10 per cent of wards with the worst overall health, as compared with the best 10 per cent' (Townsend, Phillimore and Beattie, 1988: 75). Low income and low wealth were closely correlated with above-average rates of mortality and morbidity. Material deprivation was the cause. The economic system had left the excluded in the lurch.

The disparities were more than the doctors and the nurses alone. Yet access to medical facilities was unequal as well. It is a problem in every country save a small city-State like Singapore where public transport is good and distances matter less. Urban areas will normally be better served than the countryside. Doctors in pockets of crime and material deprivation will tend to have longer lists. They will often be older and less well qualified. They will usually have less access to a medical library, less opportunity for in-service updating, less contact with a well-situated medical school. Waiting times in local hospitals can be longer. The ratio of beds to catchment can be less adequate. The stock of diagnostic equipment can be less up to date. The number of complementary professionals such as psychiatrists, pharmacists and physiotherapists can be lower. It is never easy to prove that the availability of formal care is directly and unambiguously linked to the outcome indicators that separate the social classes. What can be said, however, is that misdiagnosis, ignorance and the absence of a much-needed scanner are likely to have some impact, however small, on the quality and quantity of the patient's life.

9.3. NARROWING THE GAP: SOCIAL POLICY

The inequalities in the health status outcomes pick up more than the doctors and the nurses alone. Narrowing the gap must therefore mean a bundle of policies if citizens are to have equal access to the precise standard of health that they regard as right for themselves. Such a bundle must target the principal risk factors that draw the fellow citizens apart.

9.3.1. Occupation

Different people do different things. Different jobs carry different risks. It cannot in the circumstances be expected that all citizens will have the same number of injuries or will die at the same age. Office workers suffer from carpal tunnel syndrome, dry eyes and glare. Deep-seam miners are exposed to cave-ins and coal dust. Drum makers working with untreated hides can inhale anthrax spores. Block printers dipping fabric in dye are open to cancer of the bladder. Street prostitutes are vulnerable to HIV. Policemen have access to guns when they are feeling low. Pharmacists can kill themselves with poisons. Cooks face a temptation to overeat. Barmen have a tendency to over-drink. Not all members of the labour force are equally at risk from lead and mercury, radiation and radioactive wastes, insecticides and sulphur dioxide, asbestos fibres and falls from heights. That is what the division of labour means. We are not all average. It is a fact of life.

As was argued in chapter 5, a free society must give people the freedom to select some risk. Just as some people will want a safe life with an index-linked pension, so others will become test pilots, Everest explorers and stunt doubles because the thrill of excitement combined with the lure of the danger differential will make them feel better off in their own estimation. So long as the transaction is 'bilaterally voluntary and informed' (Friedman, 1962: 13), so long as no prohibitive externalities are imposed on innocent third-parties who are not signatories to the contract, there is a sense in which differences in health status are an indicator of a healthy society and not the scarlet letter of intolerable inequity.

The problem arises where the choice is not free. A conscript or a convict cannot be said to have selected his own preferred level of health when he parachutes into an inhospitable jungle or works on a railway in subzero cold. An indentured coolie does not have the libertarian's highly valued personal autonomy when he hauls excessive loads or gathers cockles in the face of the incoming tide. Yet the same restricted freedom may be observed as well where the unbonded and the undrafted have to drive buses with exhausted brakes or work in a badly-lit sweat shop because they lack the skills that would give them meaningful options, or because unemployment is rife and there are not enough good jobs to go round. Policy in such a case must at the very least ensure that citizens have an equal opportunity to become educationally unequal. It must also create the conditions for an adequate level of demand for labour. If then people continue to choose the less healthful occupations, at least society can be confident that it was their tastes and preferences, not forced and resented exchange, that made them opt for the challenge and excitement that cost them the frostbite and gangrene in the end.

Forced exchange can make the poor die young. Yet even prestigious and well-paid jobs can be a threat to good health. Medical doctors in Britain are a case in point. They experience as many deaths in road accidents as the wider population; they have a cirrhosis problem three times the national average; and their drug addiction (including regular reliance on sleeping tablets and tranquillisers) is many times that of the wider community. More than a third see themselves as overweight (but only one in ten is on a diet). One general practitioner in eight continues to smoke. Women doctors (but not men) have above-average leanings towards suicide (Richards, 1989). In the United States the position is very similar. One in five American doctors takes no exercise. At least 11 per cent drink alcohol every day. Only 50 per cent consult another doctor about their health. Less than half (despite the ever-present threat of needle-stick injury) are immunised against hepatitis. Peer pressures, stress at work, burn-out, exceptional responsibility, irregular hours, continuous exposure to illness and death must all play their part. Even so, it is remarkable that such well-informed and health-conscious professionals were knowingly taking chances with their health. Weakness of will is evidently not just the shortcoming of the *hoi polloi* but of their wise paternalists and their role models as well.

Another white collar group that seems to be at risk is the middle ranking civil servant. Marmot and his collaborators conducted two studies in the United Kingdom: the first in 1967 (17 000 subjects, all males over 40), the second in 1985–1988 (a further 12 000 middle-aged subjects, both male and female). Both studies documented 'a steep *inverse* association' (Marmot and Theorell, 1988: 661) between coronary heart disease, cancers and level of employment. The lower grades (even after controlling for age and lifestyle factors like smoking and obesity) were several times more susceptible to heart attacks and premature death than were their bosses. The higher grades, pressured and stressed as they were, had more discretion, more security, more variety in their job-functions.

They had more flexibility, more autonomy, more power, more self-esteem. The higher grades had freedom to choose. The lower grades knew that they were merely cogs in the wheel.

Marmot and his collaborators also found that 28 per cent of the administrative staff but as many as 53 per cent of the clerical officers indulged in smoking; while 43 per cent of the lower grades (as opposed to 26 per cent of the higher ones) preferred an inactive to an active use of leisure time. They chain-smoked because they were frustrated and bored: 'Giving up smoking is easier when your self-esteem is high, you feel optimistic about life and you feel in control' (Wilkinson, 1996: 185). They watched television soaps. They self-medicated through comfort anti-depressants like cakes. They put sugar in their caffeine. They took more sick leave. They were more likely to self-report that they 'see little meaning in life'. Their American counterparts are just as down: 'Increasing levels of occupational prestige are associated with decreasing levels of depressive symptoms and decreasing rates of major depressive disorder.... The lowest stress levels [are] found in the highest occupational category' (Turner, Wheaton and Lloyd, 1995: 109–10, 114).

Financially speaking, the lower Whitehall grades were not absolutely deprived. They could afford decent food. They had job security. They were not normally labouring to exhaustion. They were not ordinarily at physical risk. The mind, however, is refractory to such Polyannaing. The fact is that relativities and alienation at the place of work seem to have turned them against themselves. Cardiovascular disease was the self-destroying consequence of the monotonous, uncongenial and unwelcoming situation that they faced every day when they clocked in their bodies and switched off their souls.

Rank rankles. More bottom-up consultation and more self-controlled teamwork might be a preferable alternative to the emergency clinic where the insecure, the insulted and the unfulfilled might otherwise have to go for a cure. The medical palliatives in any case are unlikely to narrow the gap: 'If the experience in Britain is a guide, even the achievement of universal access to medical care would not substantially reduce socio-economic differences in health and disease.... The determinants of inequalities in health lay elsewhere.... Attention must be paid to the circumstances in which people live and work' (Marmot, Ryff, Bumpass, Shipley and Marks, 1997: 901, 908).

Public policy is not in a position to reverse the division of labour. Private enterprise has found that job rotation, consultation, team responsibility have raised the productivity of the cog in the wheel; so perhaps capitalism itself will produce its own turning points. Yet there is much that the State can do to equalise health and safety at work. Minimum standards of hygiene, protective equipment, compensation schemes, environmental controls, are all ways in which legislation policed by inspection can force all competitors without bias to internalise the costs of an accident or an illness that might otherwise have been a burden on the unfortunate worker alone. In that way the costs do not lie where they fall and some people are not made 'the social pathologies of other people's progress' (Titmuss, 1968: 157). The tort-feasors then cease and desist. The polluter pays.

Such privatisation is an overhead that many would regard as a tax on jobs. Even those who have argued for what has been termed 'microeconomic welfare' (Reisman, 2001: 60–64) would accept that a policy to eliminate regressive bads can create some involuntary unemployment among grades of workers who might well have preferred the deadly fumes, the lidless acids and the visorless lathes to life without a regular income. The upward equalisation of the blue collar health status is not something that every self-respecting member of the IVs and the Vs will regard with real warmth.

9.3.2. Income and Wealth

Different classes have different amounts of purchasing power. The Gini Coefficient is the standard measure of relative income equality. In Britain as everywhere else in the skill-based society, it is moving against the relatively deprived: 'The median real household disposable income, before housing costs, rose over the period 1961 to 1994 from £136 per week to £234 per week.... The top decile point more than doubled, from £233 per week to £473 per week. The bottom decile point rose by 62 per cent from £74 per week to £119 per week' (Stationery Office, 1998: 16). The proportion of British people whose income was less than half the national average (the European Union definition of poverty) went up from 10 per cent in 1961 to 17 per cent in 1995. Many of the left behind were from minority ethnic backgrounds (black men, women of Pakistani origin) or were in difficult age groups (new school-leavers seeking a first job, older workers passed over for employment).

Unemployment rates are four times higher among the unskilled than among the professionals, three times higher for the disabled than for the non-disabled. Disability is an illustration of reverse causality where the joblessness is the result and not the cause of the perceived shortcoming. Unemployment is generally believed to be correlated with poor physical and mental health: coronary heart disease, stroke, anxiety, spoiled self-image, depression, suicide are some of the manifestations. Gardner and Oswald report that, at least for men, unemployment increases the risk of premature death: each additional year out of work raises the probability by 1.4 per cent (Gardner and Oswald, 2004: 1191). Unemployment can mean hardship and poverty. A leaky roof and an inadequate diet do little for health.

Ruhm's result is a surprising outlier which challenges the mainstream opinion. Ruhm showed that a little unemployment actually had a good effect on people's health. A one percentage point *rise* in cyclical unemployment was associated with a 0.5 per cent *fall* in the total death rate in the United States over the period from 1972 to 1991. It was associated with a 1.6 per cent reduction in bed days, a 3.9 per cent decline in acute morbidities and a 4.3 per cent decrease in ischaemic heart disease. While fewer accidents at work must have played a part, and while the exhausted and the over-stressed are more prone to injuries in traffic, changes in lifestyle are likely to have been the main reason for the improvement in physical health: 'Risky behaviours become less common when the economy deteriorates' (Ruhm, 2005: 351). Smoking, heavy drinking and excess body weight went down when discretionary income collapsed. Exercise filled some of the involuntary leisure created by a downturn. Home-cooked meals took the place of fatty food consumed outside. The lower time-price of health maintenance was conducive to increasing investment in a good health status which unemployment had made less costly (Ruhm, 2005: 341, 342, 360). While a transitory fall may have been mistaken for a permanent one, the evidence does suggest that people were quick to scrap old conventions and to break with an equilibrium way of life. Bad habits were evidently not irresistible addictions after all. In the upswing the reemployed once again rethought their behaviour patterns and returned to the previous status quo. The long-term unemployed, it must be presumed, sank into the low income/poor health trap which most observers believe to be the most common consequence of being out of work.

Money, it is often said, allows the better off to buy better health. A balanced diet, restful accommodation, vitamin pills, health club memberships, a smoke alarm in every room all presuppose that the consumer will be in a position to pay. Not every consumer, relatively speaking, is equally well-placed to do this. In 1996 as many as 14 per cent of all British households were living in 'poor conditions', 7 per cent in 'unfit dwellings' (Stationery Office, 1998: 20). Yet it is important not to confuse adequate resources with unequal resources. Below some basic social minimum the very poor will not be able to afford more costly consumables like the fish, green vegetables and fresh fruit that would inject much needed nutrients into their diet, raise their efficiency at work and shield their future offspring from birth-born debility. Above the floor, however, the absolute malnutrition of the poverty trap ceases to be a problem; while the damp walls of squalid slum hovels give way to accommodation less likely to be a breeding ground for cholera, respiratory ailments and gang warfare.

For those countries at the lowest income levels a little more purchasing power can mean a great deal more health. The Preston Curve (the curve which plots life expectancy against GDP per capita as a time series for a single country or as a cross-section for a selection of countries) rises to the right as the national wealth advances from Nigeria through Korea to the USA (Preston, 1975: 235). It rises, however, at a decreasing rate. For those countries which have reached the cut-off minimum at which the basic necessities become easily affordable the causal relationship is tenuous to say the least: 'Within developed countries, the relationship between mortality and income is ... tending to disappear, except for those at the lowest income levels' (Fuchs, 1974b: 181). Even the poorest quintile in the richer countries tend to have central heating, a refrigerator and often a freezer. A rise in absolute income no longer makes the difference between health and sickness. Preston in 1975 had found that only about 12.2 per cent of the improvement in life-expectancy in a world-wide scatter was actually associated with the rising standard of living (Preston, 1975: 237). Wilkinson in 1996 found that the piggy-backing was no more than 10 per cent (Wilkinson, 1996: 36).

It could even be argued that, beyond some trigger threshold of income, the association becomes perverse. Overeating, unhealthy eating, driving too fast, a sedentary lifestyle, constant worry all cause even affluent people to make their way to the doctor's office. If malaria goes out, then hypertension, coronary heart disease, skin cancer and duodenal ulcers come in.

The policy inferences for the poor are clear enough. Food vouchers, means testing, income supplementation, unemployment benefits, medical insurance, vaccination campaigns, child benefits, concessionary eye tests, earnings-linked pensions, heating allowances, subsidised school meals, council housing, rent rebates, halfway hostels, home helps for the elderly or disabled, selective discrimination in favour of geographical black spots, well equipped local clinics with high-quality staff, fluoridation of drinking water, tax zero-rating for food staples and public transport, concerned social workers who counsel the hard-to-reach on the take-up of their stigma-free citizenship rights – these and other instruments are all ways in which a welfare society can bring the less-healthy up to the threshold entitlement and neutralise the poverty trap. In terms of macroeconomics, full employment and economic growth are crucial if the needy are to earn enough for nutritious food. In terms of microeconomics, policy could be deployed to assist the relatively neglected to catch up. Apart from minimum wage laws, security of employment, training and retraining schemes, support for geographical mobility, the prohibition of racial discrimination, quotas for the economically under-represented, nursery and child-minding facilities such that low-income (often single) parents can return to work, flexible working hours where there is a sick child at home, there might be an argument for concessionary interest rates and tax holidays for firms selecting labour-intensive technologies in areas where long-term unemployment is high.

The policy inferences for the rich are more of a problem. Apart from health education and the appeal to role-models, there is a limit to the laws a free society can introduce to stop an obese executive from grabbing a hamburger in his car when he should have been going to his meditation class, eating nutritious lentils or doing keep-fit in the gym. A high income will not protect him from gout. It will if anything make it easier for him to afford extreme sports, luxury absinthe and a yacht which might sink. A health-conscious democracy can at least impose punitive taxes on the plutocrat's cigarettes and gin. It can even prohibit altogether the health-threatening opiates that a good income is bringing within his affordable choice set. The outcome of the guidance can be unexpected. Making the rich healthier against their will, such policies may be pro-health but also contra-egalitarian. It is easier to redistribute income than it is to reapportion health status.

Abject destitution ceases to be a major cause of unequal health outcomes once most members of the community have passed beyond the cut-off level of prosperity (the 'epidemiological transition') where infectious diseases give way to degenerative and chronic complaints. Relative deprivation is a harder nut to crack. Even after the problem of low incomes has been solved, the problem of *unequal* incomes (and with it *unequal* power, *unequal* security, *unequal* respect) is likely to remain.

One dimension of the problem is the non-linearity of need: 'People with incomes below the average lose more years of life than are gained by people at the equivalent distance above the average. The greater the spread, the larger the net loss' (Preston, 1975: 242). It is the distribution of the national income and not just the average GDP per capita that must apparently be used to predict the life-expectancy link. Preston cites the index computed by Kuznets in support of his contention: 'Mexico and Colombia have the most uneven distributions of income on this index of any countries considered here, ranking 14th and 15th. These countries have life expectancies which are 6.7 and 2.1 years respectively below the levels predicted on the basis of average incomes' (Preston, 1975: 242). Relative material conditions are correlated with health status. Even if the effects of raising living standards for all are minimal for the well-off, the implications for the most deprived – the Vs and not the Is – can be more tangible. Poorer countries where relative deprivation is also absolute will want to take the lesson to heart. Resources transferred from the richest to the poorest can prevent the poorest from dying on the streets.

Objective shortfall is one dimension of relative deprivation. Subjective perception is another. It is especially relevant in richer countries where people finally have enough to eat. If contaminated drinking water, infectious diseases, overcrowded hovels, smoking chimneys and open sewers can make people ill, the possibility is no less real that conspicuous consumption, flagrant ostentation, self-advertised distance and zero-sum promotion can lead to insomnia, anxiety, cirrhosis and even a stroke. Frustration can lead to homicide. Unhappiness can lead to suicide. Alcoholism is a form of Russian roulette that some Russians might appreciate because the cold winter nights and the aggravating waits to see a bureaucrat make them want to drink themselves to death. Everyone knows that laughter is the best medicine and that mothers can't spare the time to be ill. Is it possible that other health-related states too have psychosomatic and psychosocial roots? Is it possible that those roots go back to relative deprivation?

Is it possible that the privatisation of the commons is making people physically and mentally ill?

Tawney's common culture is not the same as the common *health* culture. No one should assume that Tawney's good society is only about health. Yet social connectedness for all that was to him a topic in the health status production function. It was Tönnies's (2001 [1887]) *Gemeinschaft* and Putnam's (1995) social networks as well as free school milk and Keynesian full employment that protected mental health in Britain once the bombings in the Blitz began. It was, Titmuss writes, the sensation of belonging, cohesion, camaraderie, unity and nationhood that kept health-sapping individualism and the rationally marketeering mindset at bay: 'The civilian war of 1939–45, with its many opportunities for service in civil defence and other schemes, also helped to satisfy an often inarticulate need; the need to be a wanted member of society.... The absence of an increase in neurotic illness among the civilian population during the war was connected with the fact that to many people the war brought useful work and an opportunity to play an active part within the community' (Titmuss, 1950: 347). An integrated community in wartime remained an integrated community at peace. Public health was one consequence of the new togetherness and the new culture of material support. History could, as Szreter and Woolcock report, easily have taken a different course: 'Where urban neighbourhoods and rural communities (and particular sub-populations) are demonstrably low in social capital, residents report higher levels of stress and isolation, children's welfare decreases, and there is a reduced capacity to respond to environmental health risks and to receive effective public health service interventions' (Szreter and Woolcock, 2004: 651).

Social support is status rather than contract. There is no reason why it should not stop short at voluntary service in an old people's home, personal contacts in business negotiations or joining a sports club in preference to bowling alone. Wilkinson, however, thinks that something less decentralised and more directive than *laissez-faire* politics will be the *sine qua non* if shared and cooperative norms are to be properly embedded. Wilkinson identifies a reasonable level of egalitarianism at the expense of achievement as the precondition for good national health. Going beyond the need for felt community and mutual respect to focus specifically on the narrowing of economic distance, he says that income inequality is unnatural to the human condition, out of keeping with biological evolution and a threat to people's health.

Dominance, conflict and submission are shaming. Low-ranking baboons suffer from high blood pressure. The pecking order breeds chronic anxiety. Radical loss of confidence weakens the immune system. It is not just toxic waste and arctic hypothermia that make people ill. No one wants to feel excluded or neglected, stigmatised as an also-ran who could not make the grade: 'To feel depressed, cheated, bitter, desperate, vulnerable, frightened, angry, worried about debts or job and housing insecurity; to feel devalued, useless, helpless, uncared for, hopeless, isolated, anxious and a failure: these feelings can dominate people's whole experience of life, colouring their experience of everything else. It is the chronic stress arising from feelings like these which does the damage.... Psychosocial stress can kill' (Wilkinson, 1996: 175, 215). It is clearly the whole population and not just the least well-off who stand to gain from a reduction in perceived and resented stratification.

Besides that, the consensus required for health-promoting public goods like education, slum clearance and the British National Health Service presupposes robust social capital and a sense of interdependence which is likely to be lacking in an unequal society where the rich go private for what they need while the poor lie awake worrying about redundancy and eviction. That in turn highlights the need for political democracy. Political deprivation denies the poor their voice and stifles their input. One-person-one-vote is an input in the production of good health. Tawney was neither the first nor the last to have concluded, in Deaton's encapsulation of the integrationist's credo, that 'equal societies have more social cohesion, more solidarity, and less stress; they offer their citizens more public goods, more social support, and more social capital; and they satisfy humans' evolved preference for fairness' (Deaton, 2003: 113). To frustrate the basic human need for dignity, sharing and mutual support is to stunt the individual's health. If the theorists of the common *health* culture are correct, then not all health-related needs are the exclusive preserve of the doctor who knows best.

Lynch and his co-authors (using US Census data) write that the (age-adjusted) excess mortality in urban areas with high as compared to low income inequality was 139.8 deaths per 100000 in 1990: 'An appropriate comparison would be that this mortality difference exceeds the combined loss of life from lung cancer, diabetes, motor vehicle crashes, HIV infection, suicide, and homicide in 1995.... Initiatives to reduce income inequalities should be a high priority' (Lynch, Kaplan, Pamuk, Cohen, Heck, Balfour and Yen, 1998: 1079). Deaton summarises his own reading of the raw correlations on health by concluding that there is insufficient proof.

Deaton is aware of Waldmann's evidence, for 57 developed and developing countries, that the rising share of income going to the top 5 per cent of the population (holding constant other variables such as female literacy, urbanisation and the number of doctors per capita) was associated with an increase in the infant mortality rates among the poor. This was true even when the absolute incomes of the bottom 20 per cent did not actually go down: 'When incomes are unequally distributed, the true welfare of the poor may be lower than measured real income suggests' (Waldmann, 1992: 1298, 1299). Deaton acknowledges Wilkinson's conclusion, that life-expectancy went up more rapidly in countries like Greece and France which reduced income inequality than it did in countries like Britain and Ireland where social distance increased (Wilkinson, 1996: 7).

He is aware of Wilkinson's assertion that Japan has the highest life-expectancy in the world in no small measure because it has 'the narrowest income differentials of any country reporting to the World Bank' (Wilkinson, 1996: 130). He recognises the value of studies such as those of Marmot which seem to document the medical relevance of hierarchical relationships, not just in Whitehall but in the former Soviet Union. There life-expectancy at age 15 declined by about five years in the period from 1989 to 1997 – a period in which inequality as measured by the Gini coefficient also made a significant advance (Marmot and Bobak, 2000: 1125). Violent crime claims more lives in countries where living standards are flagrantly unequal. Suicides are more common in countries where each is determined to overtake all. Yet there is just as much evidence on the opposite side. That evidence shows that *absolute* income is correlated with mortality and morbidity but that *relative* income is no more than the politics of envy and spite. Overall, Deaton says, the evidence on invidious comparison is not strong enough to permit robust generalisations.

The proof is the bind. It is never easy to find reliable data on disparities in income and wealth. Episodes are not trends. Resented inequality is *perceived* inequality rather than statistical inequality which will often be out of sight and salience. A distinction must be made between inequality with social mobility and inequality where the road up is blocked. Studies do not use comparable indices. Improvements in medical techniques distort the time series. Cross-cutting distinctions such as race make it difficult to interpret the results. Income inequality might be a proxy for power-disparities that might be the real cause of disease. National statistics conceal regional disparities. Single indicators like child mortality or heart failure are no substitute for a weighted index of health outcomes that does not exist.

Above all, groupings themselves are hard to define. The Whitehall ranks were as clear as the organisational chart. Most reference groups are, however, amorphous, multiple and unobservable. Other reasons must be found to justify the levelling of incomes, Deaton says, besides the desire to make the health indicators less far apart: 'My conclusion is that there is no direct link to ill health from income inequality per se; all else equal, individuals are no more likely to be sick or to die if they live in places or in periods where income inequality is higher' (Deaton, 2003: 115).

9.3.3. Education

Work and resources are matter. Education and culture are mind. Work and resources are external constraints. Education and culture are attitudes and motives. If money is the way, then mind is the will. The necessary and the sufficient condition are both required if morbidity and mortality indices are to be made acceptably equal.

Education, Grossman says, is the *sine qua non*: 'Among socioeconomic variables years of schooling completed is probably the most important correlate of good health in adult populations' (Grossman, 1982: 191). It is impossible to be certain: since incremental education is cross-correlated with higher income, attitudinal capital and a non-manual job function, since brighter people get more education *and* go further at work, since better health empowers children to learn more and perform better at school, it is hard to say if education is the cause or simply a fellow traveller along the road.

Genes and upbringing will sometimes contribute as much or more to life chances as do qualifications and chalk. Intuitively, however, there are grounds for thinking that formal education plays an active role. Evidence on correlation seems to bear out the conjecture: 'Those with no qualifications are significantly less likely to eat breakfast and those with a degree are significantly more likely to do so. The more educated are less likely to smoke, while those with no qualifications are significantly less likely to exercise than other groups. Those who have a university degree are less likely to be obese' (Contoyiannis and Jones, 2004: 979). The outcomes bear out the breakfasts. Guralnik and his colleagues, studying American adults aged over 65, found that those with at least 12 years of education had an active (non-disabled) life expectancy 2.4 to 3.9 years longer than those with less than 12 years of education. There were no large differences between blacks and whites when education was taken into account. Since only 14.6 per cent of black men but fully 31.9 per cent of white men have 12 years of schooling, the differences when education was *not* taken into account were, on the other hand, very large. Not immutable, they can be altered by policy (Guralnik, Land, Blazer, Fillenbaum and Branch, 1993: 113). Adriana Lleras-Muney, using US census data for American whites, discovered that there was 'a large causal effect of education on mortality.... An additional year of education lowers the probability of dying in the next 10 years by approximately 1.3 percentage points or even more. This could represent as much as 1.7 years of life' (Lleras-Muney, 2002: 23).

Elo and Preston showed that the adult mortality rate per 1000 working-age males was 7.41 for those with 0–8 years of schooling but only 3.33 for those with at least 16 years. They characterised educational attainment as 'the primary marker of socioeconomic status': writing of the US, they regarded as less indicative the grouping by occupation or income that investigators in the UK have tended to prefer. Elo and Preston calculated that each additional year of education in the US reduces deaths by 7.7 per cent. The causality runs partly through the cognitive effect of education and partly through the indirect effect, in the form of higher earnings. Their figure is comparable to equivalent results for Denmark (8.1 per cent), Finland (9.2 per cent), Sweden (8.0 per cent), England and Wales (7.4 per cent). The similarity is surprising in the light of the debate on health policy: 'It suggests that educational differentials may not be very responsive to the organization of health care services' (Elo and Preston, 1996: 47, 48, 49, 56). The returns to education clearly go beyond book learning. On grounds of health status alone, it would appear, the educational budget should be increased most rapidly in disadvantaged areas where less healthy children need the greatest help.

At its most basic level the school teaches human biology. It imparts factual information on body maintenance. Preventive care and early detection are more likely if the patient knows what causes tooth decay, why cigarettes are bad or how to avoid venereal disease. Besides that, there will often be lessons in home economics which give pupils background knowledge on household budgeting, the washing of vegetables, how to store meat, when water is safe, the nature of a balanced diet, the threat from cholesterol, alcohol, tobacco, salt, sugary drinks, saturated fats, chemical additives, aluminium saucepans. Possibly children from more privileged backgrounds will have acquired much of this knowledge informally in the home. They will have been given more fruit, vegetables, iron, calcium, vitamin C, wholemeal bread and dietary fibre. In such a case it is the less advantaged children who gain the most from the academic increment that facilitates the catch-up.

All of education, moreover, has an invisible curriculum which can instil health fostering habits and goal orientated predilections. Formal education demands regular and punctual attendance: the intellectual stance is identical to that which favours the disciplined swallowing of the contraceptive pill, careful tooth brushing at least twice a day and the conscientious completion of a course of antibiotics. Formal education rewards candidates who are willing to exchange time and effort for technique and enlightenment: the *quid pro quo* is the same as that which Grossman has in mind when, postulating a 'production function of healthy days', he makes use of an eggs-produce-omelettes, jugs-fill-mugs approach to derive the result that 'the level of health of an individual is *not* exogenous but depends, at least in part, on the resources allocated to its production' (Grossman, 1972: 225, 233). Formal education requires present sacrifice in order that a future dividend might one day accrue to human capital laboriously built up through lessons: it is the valuation of disciplined sowing in order to reap, the notion of gratification deferred later rewarded by a productivity differential that leads Fuchs to conclude that 'the most likely explanation for the high correlation between health and schooling is that both reflect differences in time preference' (Fuchs, 1996: 6). The link between incremental education and marginal healthiness continues up to the PhD level. The only reason Fuchs can find is that people willing to invest in human capital also have the future-facing attitudes that will make them invest in health capital as well. In both cases, it was the values that preceded the responses. Yesterday's conversion to deferred gratification is today's improvement in education and in health status both.

Fuchs's interpretation of the correlation that bears the stamp of a third variable – mind – reinforces the conclusion reached through Grossman's model of healthy time. Grossman's theory, incorporating the long-term utility from a better health status and the long-term differential earnings-stream that is the payoff for more and healthier days, states that consumption and production presuppose an economist's sensitivity to the machinery that makes it all possible: 'An increase in the stock of health reduces the time lost from these activities, and the monetary value of this reduction is an index of the return to an investment in health' (Grossman, 1972: 225). Investment, abstention and exchange – these core features of the hidden curriculum demonstrate that more is learnt at school than academic content alone that is of direct relevance to the production of good health. Early patterning and the conditioning of reflexes are an acquisition for life.

The foundations for good health are laid in childhood: 'The concept that individuals somehow choose their socioeconomic pathway through life is too simplistic.... The health-related behaviours and psychosocial characteristics of adult men are associated with the social class of those men's parents.... Efforts to reduce socioeconomic inequalities in health must recognize that economic policy is public health policy' (Lynch, Kaplan and Salonen, 1997: 815, 816, 818). Poor people behave poorly because their parents were poor. Smith summarises the evidence on a British study into the long hand of childhood by saying that adult diabetes can be a consequence of malnutrition before a child was even born: 'Poor conditions at home during early life predict high systolic blood pressure at age 43.... Development of schizophrenia by age 43 was related to difficulties in infancy in walking and talking.... More than half of those physically disabled by age 43 had a serious childhood illness.... Those whose parents had divorced by age 15 reported higher levels of male alcohol consumption and female smoking' (Smith, 1999: 161). The risk of bronchitis for children at age two was greatest for those whose parents had had a respiratory illness in their own early childhood. Blaming the victims is to rob the atom of its history and its memory.

A study of 2674 middle-aged Finnish men has demonstrated vividly the continuity of the inheritance: 'Men born into the poorest childhood circumstances had 28% lower intake of fruit, 15% lower non-root vegetables, 12% lower carotene, 8% lower vitamin C, 6% higher levels of salt' (Lynch, Kaplan and Salonen, 1997: 814). Lifecourse for such middle-aged men was not solely a function of their own free will and their personal preference. Marmot in his study of British civil servants found a much weaker link: 'Taking into account the social background of parents does not change the relationship between grade of employment and health' (Marmot, Ryff, Bumpass, Shipley and Marks, 1997: 905). Should the Finns be the rule and Whitehall the exception, however, then the conclusion would be that today's alcoholism, estrangement or 'cynical hostility' are a function of yesterday's socialisation. In the light of such inter-generational moulding, there is then a strong argument in favour of educated parents. Most of all is there an argument in favour of an educated mother.

A childbearer's nutritious diet in pregnancy is an investment in her child's cardiovascular system: 'Birthweight is determined by the weight and height of the mother, which in turn reflects her own growth in childhood' (Stationery Office, 1998: 69). Currie and Moretti found that an additional year of maternal education reduces the probability of low birth weight by 10 per cent (Currie and Moretti, 2003: 1516). Since educated women are less likely to smoke, they are presumably less likely as well to be on narcotics while pregnant. It is just as well. Joyce found that between 1482 and 3359 low birth weight babies in New York City (3.2–7.3 per cent of all low birth weight babies in that city) were born to women on cocaine. The cost to the system for excess neonatal health care was between $18 million and $41 million (Joyce, Racine and Mocan, 1992: 312).

It is women who are the most directly involved in antenatal care, breastfeed-ing, vaccinations, shopping, menu planning. It is more often the woman than the man who takes the child to the doctor and sees to it that fatty crisps and low-fibre starches are consumed only in moderation. Women's education is in that sense high-powered education. The woman is being equipped with family-related as well as economically-relevant skills. These skills have the character of an intergenerational transfer: 'Children and teenagers of more-educated mothers have better oral health, are less likely to be obese, and less likely to have anaemia than children of less-educated mothers' (Grossman, 1982: 192).

Better educated women will have higher-than-average incomes. They are more likely to marry educated men who will themselves be able to command above-average pay. As the living standards go up, moreover, so the size of the family goes down. Better educated mothers tend to have fewer children because of the higher opportunity cost of their earning time foregone. The result is more resources concentrated on fewer beneficiaries, with a consequent improvement in the mother's own and her dependants' health. The education of women is the most reliable form of family planning.

Thus Colle and Grossman, looking specifically at the take-up of medical services (office visits, preventive medication, diagnostic tests, specialist consul-tations) on the part of a national sample of American children aged 1–5, reached the conclusion on the demand for care that 'the two basic forces are mother's schooling and the number of children in a family' (Colle and Grossman, 1978: 150). A black woman is less likely than a white woman to have completed high school. American blacks have larger families than American whites. The policy inference is then the following: 'Black-white differences in use of services would be dramatically altered by eliminating black-white differences in mother's schooling and in family size' (Colle and Grossman, 1978: 149).

Colle and Grossman say that education will help to narrow the gap. Morris, Sutton and Gravelle were less convinced that education was the key to equal use for equal need. Studying the English experience in 1998–2000, they discovered that, with respect to GP consultations, the correlation actually was pro-unschooled: those with less education were more likely to see their primary care doctor. The correlation was also pro-poor: consultations became more frequent as the level of income fell. It was, for good measure, pro-non-white as well: non-white patients saw their GP more often than did whites. Improving the education of the lower groups would, it would seem, only lead to more of the same.

Yet the statistic is misleading. For one thing, the non-whites in question are disproportionately ethnic Indians, not Pakistanis or Afro-Caribbeans. Selective discrimination in education could help to upgrade a health-neglected group. Also, there is horizontal inequity in the more expensive hospital referrals and inpatient services: 'Low-income individuals and ethnic minorities are ... less likely to receive secondary care' (Morris, Sutton and Gravelle, 2005: 1264). Seeing the gatekeeper *more* is not enough if the primary practitioner has a systematic bias towards opening the gate to the later stages *less*.

9.3.4. Culture

People are socialised into a peer group. They internalise the norms that other people expect. Values and attitudes are the consequence of informal learning. They are closely related to recorded inequalities in mortality and morbidity.

Some peer groups make it a convention that members will smoke and drink. They would ostracise a deviant who rejected the done thing and refused to share an unsterilised needle. Some peer groups gamble on fate and trust in luck. They say 'it can't happen to me', think 'devil-may-care' and live for today. They resist the calculative rationality that would have led them to don crash helmets or move out of flood plains. It is not simply a matter of disposable income. Smoking costs more than not smoking: advocates of nicotine replacement patches on National Health prescription are the first to recognise this fact. Yet it is the unskilled and the manual rather than the prosperous and the professional who spend the most on cigarettes that actually widen the health divide.

Other peer groups have long horizons. They plan for the future and invest in success. They are more likely to settle disputes through consensus and cooperation rather than through punch-ups and reckless abuse. They reject the red meat and chips in favour of a low-salt diet and an occasional glass of wine. Entrepreneurial, competitive and individualistic, however, the focused and the calculative might also be more susceptible to stress-related complaints like acid stomach and sleep disruption. A cooperative, consensual, communitarian culture is less fragmented. The glums and a barbiturate overdose may there be the result of nannying over-regulation but they are less likely to be the escape route from radical *anomie* for which the Juggernaut life in common will have little room.

Different peers want different things. In America in 1995 40 per cent of men who had not completed high school smoked; the comparable figure for male graduates was 14 per cent (Smith, 1999: 148). In Britain in the lower occupational groups 10 per cent of men are dependent on alcohol, 41 per cent of them smoke, only 25 per cent of babies are still breastfed at six weeks and 25 per cent of women are obese. The figures for the top occupational groups are 5 per cent, 12 per cent, 75 per cent and 14 per cent respectively. Women from households in social class V are four times more likely to smoke in pregnancy than are women in social class I (Stationery Office, 1998: 15, 16, 22, 23, 72). If the IVs and the Vs live differently from the Is and the IIs, it is only logical that they will end up with different health outcomes.

It is not clear if the demand for a national health culture is in effect the demand for equality at the expense of tolerance. One can encourage expectant mothers to give up the tobacco and the amphetamines. One can call upon the Indians to go easy on the *ghee*. One can invite the Chinese to forego the *char kway teow*. One can encourage the British IVs and Vs to do as much sport and aerobics as the British Is and IIs. When all is said and done, however, if the Brazilians like their giant steaks and the Russians make a ritual of their vodka, there is only a limited amount a democratic society can do apart from making sure they are aware of the risks and subsidising swimming pools which will help them to burn off the fat. A National Health Service may be necessary but it is not sufficient. The British experience proves the point that low or no payment at the point of use has a relatively limited ability to level up the outcomes.

Attitudes and conventions are resistant to change. A society which is determined to level up the health outcomes must nonetheless venture into a controversial realm which to some will smack of cultural imperialism. The two most important risk factors for cervical cancer are early age at first intercourse and the number of sexual partners (Eddy, 1990: 214): does a tolerant society really want to censure permissive lifestyles where they are the norm merely because monogamous subcultures are much less likely to be a drain? Yet the techniques are there and the reconditioning is an option.

Regulation is one tool: here the State refuses to pay maternity benefit to a woman who has not attended her antenatal and well-baby clinics or shown that she has been to a talk on contraception. Prohibition is a second tool: people's reflexes change when licensing hours are shortened, drink-driving is comprehensively breath-tested, public houses are inconveniently situated, smoking in offices and public places is banned, commercial advertising of high-tar tobacco goes off the air. Information spreads the message: explaining why only 19 per cent of Americans smoke as opposed to 27 per cent of the French or English,

35 per cent of the Germans and 38 per cent of the Greeks. Cutler and Glaeser calculate that up to one half of the difference between America and Europe can be explained by belief-shaping paternalism that in America has pushed hard the message that cigarettes are extremely harmful (Cutler and Glaeser, 2006). Subsidies over time persuade rational consumers to substitute healthy bran for tooth-rotting sugar and to attend low cost tai chi sessions that keep moodiness, stiffness, colon cancer and cardiovascular disease under control. Taxes, for the same reason, get people used to rationing their consumption of utilities that make them ill. Wants that are negative needs effectively get priced away.

Taxes on sins are especially educational since, as Grossman says, they discourage most the impressionable young: 'We find that teenage price elasticities of demand for cigarettes are substantial and much larger than the corresponding adult price elasticities.... It follows that, if future reductions in youth smoking are desired, an increase in the federal excise tax is a potent policy to accomplish this goal' (Grossman, 1982: 194). It is less troublesome to condition the price-sensitive, the malleable and the inexperienced than it is to reacculturate the addicted. Taxes that discourage young people when they have little spending power are likely over time to produce a healthy pool of non-smoking adults. Such conservatives will not smoke because they were kept out of the smoking culture until they became set in their ways. Few people take up regular smoking over the age of 20. That is the strong argument in support of brainwashing through tax. It is, of course, easier to tax cigarettes than it is to tax illicit drug taking, multiple sexual partners and unprotected adolescent intercourse.

In the United Kingdom more cancer deaths are the result of tobacco than of any other single risk factor: 'In 1995, smoking was estimated to account for more than 30,000 deaths from lung cancer, and a further 16,000 deaths from cancer of other sites, notably the oesophagus, stomach, mouth and throat.... Smoking is also an important cause of chronic obstructive lung disease, coronary heart disease, stroke and aortic aneurysm. Furthermore... passive smoking causes lung cancer and coronary heart disease in adult non-smokers, and respiratory disease, sudden infant death syndrome, middle ear disease and asthmatic attacks in children' (Stationery Office, 1998: 83). Since there is a higher incidence of smoking among the lower income groups, a high price of tobacco is likely to be a step in the direction of more equal outcomes.

The opposite is, however, possible as well. British households in the lowest disposable income decile spend six times as much of their income on tobacco as do households in the highest decile. Such people might cut back on food, clothing, heating and other basic necessities in order to feed their nicotine dependence, augmented by drink: 'Deaths from diseases caused by alcohol show a clear gradient with socioeconomic position, with an almost fourfold higher rate in unskilled working men compared to those from professional groups. In addition, alcohol is a contributory factor to deaths from accidents, which also show a pronounced socioeconomic gradient' (Stationery Office, 1998: 85). About 37.8 per cent of households in the North East of England are economically deprived. In the South East it is only 5.1 per cent. Yet 25.1 per cent in the North East indulge in binge drinking, 25 per cent are obese, and 888 per 100 000 of the population are receiving treatment for drug abuse: the figures for the South East are 15.5 per cent, 20.4 per cent and 385 respectively (Department of Health, 2006: 9, 10). Drugs are already regulated and alcohol is already taxed. The prohibitions and taxes have evidently not eliminated the gap. Nor are they easy to enforce. Something like 16 per cent of cigarettes and 55 per cent of hand rolled tobacco enters Britain illicitly and in that way escapes the tax.

Vice is the stuff of which careers in social philosophy are made. Can a democracy really refuse income support to the 55 per cent of welfare single mothers in severe hardship who smoke to ease their distress? They get through, on average, five packets of cigarettes a week. They are price-insensitive to a rise in tax.

9.4. NARROWING THE GAP: MEDICAL CARE

There is more to good health than the formal health care inputs. Yet that is no reason to be complacent about the unequal absorption of scarce health care resources. Nor is it right to neglect the policy measures that could be taken to reverse the tendency towards inverse care.

The doctor–patient relationship, as was suggested in chapter 3, is normally initiated by the patient. Since the lower-income groups have less knowledge of the workings of the body than do the better educated clusters, they are less likely to seek early diagnosis and treatment for asymptomatic or semi-asymptomatic conditions like anaemia, pancreatic cancer, high blood pressure, high blood sugar, anal-retentive obsessiveness. They are less likely to recognise the dangers in sudden weight loss or breathlessness while climbing stairs. They are less likely to know about preventive injections or to demand a specific drug about which they have read. They are less likely to ask probing questions, to want longer consultations, to stand up to a middle class professional, to call for a second opinion or to insist upon a test or service which they have been denied. A stratified community, in short, can produce a segregated demand function in the area of health. Different groups make different requests. They end up with different services and impose different costs as a result.

Educational upgrading will help to equalise the knowledge stock. The spread of white collar employment and middle class culture will narrow the gap between those who ask questions and those who do what they are told. Evolution is on the side of levelling up. Even so, there will be a need for the medical system sometimes to take the lead if *de jure* access is to be translated into *de facto* utilisation. The British experience shows that the suppression of the price deterrent may be a necessary but that it cannot be a sufficient condition.

That is why it might be desirable for proactive doctors to call in at-risk occupational groups like coalminers for an X-ray; or to invite all females aged between 50 to 64 for a smear or a triennial mammogram; or to see all old people living alone at least once every six months. Medical and dental examinations can be offered to all children at school. Computerised records can be used to identify those patients most likely to benefit from preventive and not just curative care. So long as the attention is not compulsory, however, so long as the patient does not receive a *quid pro quo* (such as priority points for a favoured school or a council flat) in exchange for a blood test or a Pap smear, it will probably be the least health conscious, the most health deprived, who will continue to fall through the net. A well-intentioned health policy might raise the average standard of health but still not reduce health-related inequalities. The gap might actually be widened.

Access to women doctors, doctors who were born working class and doctors from ethnic or religious minorities is a further way of tapping into latent demand. Such pluralisation can ensure that patients have the chance to consult a practitioner who has personal experience of their situation, their diet, their expectations, their interpretations of the sick role and their subcultural baggage. Practice auxiliaries and health visitors from a diversity of backgrounds can provide support and counsel to a general practitioner who cannot be expected to know all the conventions of the whole rich tapestry. Respect for persons suggests nonetheless that all doctors in a multicultural society should know at least the basics about the exceptions.

All doctors in a mixed community should have some knowledge of minority conditions. These will include sickle cell anaemia (which targets ethnic Africans including black Americans and West Indians but not whites), thalassaemia (which is most frequent among Mediterraneans such as Greeks, Egyptians, Italians, Lebanese and Cypriots) and Tay-Sachs disease (a fatal inherited disease of the central nervous system to which Ashkenazi Jews, possibly as many as 1 in 25, are disproportionately exposed). The doctor should be able to empathise with the isolation and confusion of a new-immigrant wife: the problem is made worse where the patient cannot speak English or is embarrassed to be examined by a Western professional. The doctor should know enough about chapattis and tea to be able to counsel Indian lactovegetarians that phytates and tannins can inhibit the absorption of vitamin D in children as well as pointing the way to iron-deficiency anaemia in the adult years. Intellectual ambidextrousness, 'cultural competency', is a good thing in its own right. It is especially valuable in the health care sector lest a patient be falsely labelled as mentally ill or a referral to hospital be delayed because of an inability to sense an unspoken fear.

Social workers and district nurses have a valuable contribution to make. Visiting the hard-to-reach in their homes, they are well placed to recognise undetected pathologies simply by hearing about the symptoms, observing the baby-battering and spotting the rats. Self-help groups and voluntary organisations fill in still more of the gaps. A wider welfare net can complement the medical professionals. It can play a part in assisting the self-effacing to get the medical services that they need.

Education and culture explain why equal citizens with equal needs end up with unequal shares even in a National Health Service pool. Yet economics too can build barriers that keep equal citizens out. Insurance cover is not available to all. Where people do qualify, the expense can be a deterrent. Co-payments, deductibles, prescription charges and straightforward fees are most likely to price the less affluent out of the demand curve. That, as Beck established in his study of a small change in charges in Saskatchewan, is in itself a reason for not increasing the out-of-pocket hurdle: 'The impact upon the poor ... is considerably greater than the reduction of service experienced by the entire population, which has been estimated at 6 to 7 per cent' (Beck, 1974: 140). The impact overall was 6 to 7 per cent. The impact on those below the national poverty line was 18 per cent. Even a very low charge of $1.50 for office visits led to a reduction of 14 per cent in the use the poor made of their general practitioners.

While there may have been some overutilisation before the charge, and maybe even some malingering through bogus requests for sickness notes, it is not a pleasant thought that some tuberculosis and perhaps even some cancer should have escaped timely detection because of a price disincentive that the have-nots will have found disproportionately discouraging. No one welcomes the premature death from diphtheria or typhoid of a child whose parents could not afford to pay for care. At the very least means-tested exemptions and earmarked income maintenance would ensure that no one was denied basic care because of the expense. The free marketeer's caveat would be that the basic standard should mean the irreducible minimum. The tax burden is a disincentive to effort. Free services are a disincentive to upward mobility. Too much generosity, the free marketeer will say, might be as ill advised as too little.

Redistribution can be brought about in a market system through price discrimination. Charging different prices to different income groups, waiving payment where the patient is obviously down-at-heel, the doctor or hospital is in effect performing its own cross-subsidisation of the needy. While pharmaceuticals and appliances are the exception, most medical services have the advantage that they do not lend themselves to transfer, resale or arbitrage. Income in cash is often ranked above benefits in kind by those who say that even the poverty-stricken know their own utility best. Health care vouchers, earmarked for health but encashable at any approved outlet of the consumer's choice, are a compromise between exchange and command. So is non-discriminatory health insurance and across-the-board community rating which mandate the insurers to admit into the pool even the high risk subgroups most likely to cause a drain.

Equalisation at the national level can be effected through public finance. Progressive income tax shares out the burdens on the basis that the rich pay more. This would be the argument for national health insurance funded through general direct taxation, earmarked direct levies and earnings-related health care contributions. It would be a reason for tax-foregone exemptions (*de facto* a subsidy) for old age pensioners, the unemployed, the disabled and other statistically low-income groups. It would, negatively speaking, also be an argument against regressive sales and excise duties and for the suppression of tax relief granted to private health insurance. Especially will this phasing out tend to make society more equal where the 'fiscal welfare' on insurance would otherwise have been offered at the beneficiary's highest marginal rate.

Income-related payment tends to have a levelling function. Contributory social insurance need not. A regressive bias must be expected where national insurance is financed by a flat-rate stamp paid non-judgmentally by all, or where there is a ceiling level beyond which income-related payments cut off, or where high earners are allowed to opt out of (or to supplement) the common scheme, or where the coinsurance element is great enough to drive away the deprived. Even so, biased cover is better than no cover at all. The rising cost of health insurance may be causing a rising percentage of the American population to be voluntarily uninsured.

In the United States, millions of the needy are said to be unable to pay for private insurance. Costing upwards of $8000 for a family and $3000 for an individual, the financial burden is a major obstacle. Many Americans are passed over for tax-deductible occupational plans. Often this will be because the firm is small, on tight margins and squeezed by competition: 'A significant proportion of uninsured households, 54 per cent, are headed by a full-time worker; another 31 per cent of uninsured households are headed by a part-time worker.... Those uninsured workers are concentrated in small businesses: over half of all workers not offered insurance are employed in firms with fewer than 10 employees; 70 per cent are in firms with fewer than 25 employees' (Feldman, Dowd, Leitz and Blewett, 1997: 635–6). The excluded do not have any guarantee of prenatal care, inpatient services or even a family doctor. Yet they are not old enough for Medicare and not impoverished enough for Medicaid. The Medicaid eligibility level has been low. In some states it is not far above the federal poverty line. Historically at least, it has sometimes been as much as 40 per cent below. The lower-middle and the working class have been sandwiched out.

About 46 million Americans (approximately 15 to 20 per cent of the population) do not have health insurance on any given day. About one American in three is without health insurance at least once in a space of three years. Dispro-

portionate numbers of the unprotected are less educated, black or part-time.
Every 30 seconds in the United States someone files for bankruptcy because a
medical emergency has exhausted his funds. Many Americans are known to
economise on food and heating in order to pay for care. In spite of that Bundorf
and Pauly warn that it would be a mistake to exaggerate the hurdle. As few as
0.36 per cent of all Americans are genuinely uninsurable; while as many as 30
per cent of uninsured adults are in families with incomes at least 300 per cent
above the poverty line. Lack of cover can be a deliberate choice, particularly
since the United States has never made health insurance compulsory for all.
Affordability is not always the barrier that it appears. Between 25 per cent and
75 per cent of the uninsured could have paid for health insurance had they
wanted to do so (Bundorf and Pauly, 2006: 664).

The opposite point of view is that the 75 per cent and even the 25 per cent is
grossly out of touch. Rising living standards mean that the uninsured will one
day have more money to put in. Economic growth in the future is, however, little
comfort to the here-and-now left out. Many of the excluded simply cannot pay.
Assuming that they lack the funds, universal medical insurance, subsidised for
the poor, would fill the gap.

It would cost the American government about $20 billion dollars to guarantee
the medical services the uninsured would need if blanketed in. This might,
Cutler calculates, be money well spent. The economic value of the life-years
saved sums up to $33 billion, and the quality of life would make the figure
greater still. In other words: 'For every dollar spent, the benefits would be $1.50.
There is thus an economic, as well as moral, case for universal insurance coverage' (Cutler, 2004: 65, 66). It is important to remember, however, that the
sacrifice will not be an equal one. Unless the health budget is to go up because
the education budget simultaneously goes down, unless exceptional cost savings
can be made through a more efficient system of care, the answer will have to
be tax. Even if the economy is growing rapidly, the higher income bands will
have to pay for the transfers. The lower income deciles will pocket the gain.
Redistribution would be not just from the healthy to the sick but across the income levels as well. Politicisation of health insurance is moderate socialism as
well.

There may, therefore, be a cultural objection. One study established that only
23 per cent of Americans agreed with the statement 'It is the responsibility of
the government to take care of the very poor people who can't take care of
themselves'. The numbers in other countries were higher: 50 per cent of Germans agreed with the statement, as did 56 per cent of Poles, 62 per cent of
British and French, 66 per cent of Italians and 71 per cent of Spaniards. Commenting on these figures, Rice says that they 'graphically illustrate the very
different social ethics that exist in the US vs. elsewhere. In a country like the
US in which communitarian values are weak and markets are relied upon to

distribute so-called "merit goods" like health care, enacting reform like universal coverage is extraordinarily difficult. To do so it probably will be necessary for there to be a change in the prevailing social ethic, or – and this is perhaps the more likely route – to elect officials with this ethic who have the ability to pull the populace along with them' (Rice, 1991: 32). It was not Attlee but the British social ethic that was responsible for the health care collectivism of the post-Dunkirk 1940s. In America the actualisation of Galbraithian social democracy would have to wait upon the charisma of a Kennedy or the leaderliness of a Lee Kwan Yew.

Public clinics do exist in the United States. They (and many private hospitals) do not turn away the urgent cases. Charities and the ethnic groups provide a safety net, just as mission hospitals look after the lepers and the haemophiliacs in the Third World because no one else will. Maybe some Americans choose not to buy private plans for the economical reason that the emergency room is always there. There is certainly a temptation to make the last resort into the first. Yet the attraction of uncompensated care should not be exaggerated. Charity carries a stigma. The treatment room can have a naked light bulb. The seats might be torn because that is part of the message. Often the consequence is that the uninsured simply do without medical attention until it is too late. It is estimated that 20 000 non-elderly Americans die each year because they are uninsured. This is equal to the total number of deaths from diabetes and strokes (age-adjusted). It is about the same as the total number of deaths among infants (Cutler, 2004: x, 65).

Nor is the quality of care necessarily the same. Cost shifting is not absolute. The uninsured have fewer and shorter hospital stays. They see a physician less frequently. The uninsured are less likely to be diagnosed with depression or to have their hypertension controlled. The uninsured are less likely to be given advice on a low-cholesterol diet or to be prescribed preventive medication in time. Hadley and his colleagues (studying five high-cost discretionary interventions) showed that the uninsured in the United States were from 29 per cent (coronary artery bypass surgery) to 75 per cent (total knee replacement) less likely than the insured to receive expensive medical procedures: the uninsured were more likely to run up bad debt that the supplier would have to absorb. The uninsured were also 44 to 124 per cent more likely to die in hospital. It is not clear if this was due to an under-provision of necessary care or to their lower health capital at the time of admission (Hadley, Steinberg and Feder, 1991: 374, 377). Their health capital certainly cannot be said to have been in good repair: 'The uninsured are significantly less likely to receive prevention and screening services than the insured; serious diseases are detected at a later stage' (Cutler, 2004: 64).

Wenneker found that privately insured patients were 28 per cent (angioplasty), 40 per cent (bypass grafting) and 80 per cent (angiography) more likely to receive intensive treatment after a heart attack. It is possible the uninsured were seen by less experienced doctors or by doctors with less satisfactory paper qualifications (Wenneker, Weissman and Epstein 1990: 1258). As for the outcomes, Currie and Gruber established that more Medicaid leads to better child health (Currie and Gruber, 1996). The RAND health insurance study compared the differences in health status that were associated with plans with high co-payments and plans that were essentially free at the point of use. They found that the disparity in outcomes was not very great (Newhouse and the Insurance Experiment Group, 1993). The RAND study does not, however, permit a comparison with Currie and Gruber's sample who without Medicaid would not have had any plan at all.

In the United States, single people under 65 (unless seriously disabled) and adult couples without dependent children are ineligible for Medicaid. This means that most of the unemployed are left without protection and many of the working poor are not asset-poor enough to qualify for welfare. Some free marketeers treat this as an incentive to the left-behind not to retire prematurely into homemaking but instead to price themselves back into jobs. Tough love is seen by such ideologues as a bulwark against State welfare that encourages irresponsible scrounging, escalates costs, promotes voluntary unemployment and crowds out personal prudence. Access to Medicaid, however, complicates the issue. It is often said that welfare recipients are afraid to take a job since they will then lose their Medicaid entitlement along with their food stamps. This concern at least could be addressed by a sliding scale such that not all of the public subsidy would disappear at once. It is arguably the bottleneck of either/or eligibility and not the fact of social payment per se that is the real disincentive to seek employment. So, of course, is an existing condition. Legislation prohibiting exclusion even for chronic illness would help Medicaid recipients to earn life and insurance for themselves.

Markets are economically inadequate where they fail to capture the social spillovers. The interdependence and the feel-good are lost where some people fail to reach the social minimum that decent and altruistic fellow citizens treat as a social need. Fiscal collectivism, comprehensive and citizen based, is economically more effective. It moves both the donors and the beneficiaries to a higher level of satisfaction, self-perceived. It can also create budget deficits, lead to cuts in non-health programmes and push up the tax.

Money costs are not the only costs. Time is a further disincentive. The price is especially high for people who are on piecework and not a guaranteed salary. Consultations in the working day can mean a loss of earnings (together with the promotion-sensitive stigma of absenteeism and sickness) even if the doctoring itself is free. The affluent are better placed to avoid the queue by paying for private care. There is much to be said for fixed appointments, conveniently situated treatment centres, home visits for the housebound, evening and weekend opening, widespread publicity so that local people can be made aware of what is available.

Travel too is a problem. Because of the spatial concentration of supply, and because poor people are less likely to have a private motorcar, the fares and the timings can prove an especial deterrent to the less well-off. Access costs ration the demand. This is an argument for a minibus shuttle, mobile clinics in rural areas, flying paramedics when the next big town is simply too far. It is also an argument for cheap public transport in order to give lower income people (including retired people) more choices in shopping, leisure and networking as well as health. Subsidised (and/or concessionary) public transport has still further benefits. It would reduce road congestion, air pollution and traffic accidents. It would in these ways too be conducive to good health.

There is also a case for local treatment centres even where the concentration of services on a single site would deliver worthwhile economies of scale and scope. Buchmueller studied access to medical attention in Los Angeles County between 1997 and 2002 when funding forced more than 10 per cent of 131 hospitals providing trauma and emergency care services to close. What he found was that the well-insured secured cost-effective treatment in doctors' offices but that the most vulnerable, relying heavily on the cheaper option of the emergency room, experienced genuine inconvenience: 'Increased distance to the nearest hospital is associated with higher mortality counts from emergent conditions, such as heart attacks and possibly from unintentional injuries.... The results for heart attacks and injuries reflect a real effect of hospital closures' (Buchmueller, Jacobson and Wold, 2006: 759). Even if public transport is cheap, old people find it difficult to travel very far for care.

As with many central-city children who fall through the net, the adults on the margins will do without until it is too late. Their heart will fail: 'A 1 mile increase in distance leads to a nearly 6.5% increase in the number of deaths.... This result is consistent with the American Heart Association (2003) claim that the survival probability after cardiac arrest decreases by 7–10% for every minute without treatment' (Buchmueller, Jacobson and Wold, 2006: 755). Their accidents will turn into domestic tragedies: 'A 1 mile increase in distance to the nearest hospital is associated with an 11–20% increase in the number of deaths from unintentional injuries' (Buchmueller, Jacobson and Wold, 2006: 755). Distance matters. Sometimes buses are not enough.

Where doctors, both primary care and specialist, are employed by the State, differential capitations, tax exemptions and higher salaries can be offered to attract them into under-doctored areas of neglect. The number of doctors in the British National Health Service varies five-fold, from 2.6 for every 1000 admissions in some hospitals to 14.1 in others (Audit Commission, 2002). In 2001 the number of general and acute beds per 10 000 of the population varied from 315 in the North West to 222 in the South East. The number of hospital medical staff per 10000 of the population was 112 in the East. It was 200 in London (Ham, 2005: 206). There seems to be no clinical need for the dispersion. Manpower planning is an administrative solution. Local pay scales proportioned to demand and supply is another. It would certainly not make sense to pay doctors by fee for service to attend their private patients but by less lucrative salary or capitation where the patients are publicly assisted.

The establishment of a prestigious medical school or teaching hospital in an under-provided area will increase the number of local professionals with a knowledge of the turf. It will attract doctors who welcome the contact with colleagues, the Saturday lectures, the chance to participate in research. Medical students on scholarships and grants can be bonded to spend a part of their careers in the villages or the slums. Existing communities can be revitalised through investment in infrastructure and subsidies to industry. Bringing work to the workers will have a health status payoff where the alternative would be resettlement and the breakdown of social networks that are known to be making a contribution to mutual support and good health.

Selective discrimination within a broadly universalist system is a way of targeting the care-deprived while not reducing the resources that reward and protect the healthy. It would be unkind to close down hospitals in the suburbs in order to ship the bricks and mortar into the neglected inner city. It would be intolerant to deny the willing-to-pay the option of a private room, a named consultant, a convenient time, a shorter wait, a special drug that the national system cannot afford to provide. Even the health conscious have the right to be treated with respect. Spiteful levelling down is seldom a good way of making equal citizens equally healthy. Constructive levelling up is, however, a different matter. There is at the margin a strong case for a National Health Service or a national insurance plan that would treat everyone well but nonetheless give the relatively deprived disproportionately more of any increment.

The targeting can be based on patient categories. Worthy beneficiaries could be the under-fives, the over-65s, the partially sighted, the registered disabled, the one-parent families, the institutionalised, the unemployed. People falling into broad groupings like these are more likely to be on low incomes and probably also to have an unmet need. Alternatively, the fine-tuning can proceed by geographical area. This would concentrate the greatest increment on laggard districts where under-provision is conspicuous and health status significantly below the norm. The neglected areas once flagged up on the map, a funding formula could be introduced that would bias the health care increment in such a way as to put the most into their uncorrected backlog of need.

Points would be given for crude numbers, indicators of illness and death, the dispersion or concentration of the population, difficulty of access to medical care in neighbouring regions. Additional points would be given for above-average costs in the capital, a higher percentage of retired persons on the Coast, the local difficulty of upward referral due to unacceptable journeys, the absence or availability of private sector provision, the extent of local support services such as meals-on-wheels, home helps and day centres. Geographical location in such an approach is used as an indicator of social distance. It is a blunt instrument but at least it does away with the shame of the personal means-test. Even poor people do not want to declare that they have failed the market test of a livelihood for themselves and their loved ones.

The bias would equalise upwards the most in need. Such a policy would not make sense if the commodity were pins. Health care is different. The market alone cannot close the gap. The community through the State must get involved if health care is to be allocated by need rather than distributed like pins on the basis of the ability and the willingness to pay.

10. Cost

The share of medical care is rising. It is rising as a share of the national product, a share of government spending and a share of the household budget. The phenomenon is across-the-board. It is happening in all countries, developed and developing alike. The unit price times the quantity supplied tends to escalate. Medical care, in real terms, is costing more and more.

In 1950 the average American spent only $500. Average expenditure, cost-of-living adjusted, has gone up considerably since then: 'The average person in the United States uses nearly $5,000 in medical resources each year. That is more than the total spent on automobiles, TVs, and computers combined' (Cutler, 2004: x). The consequence is as unattractive as families priced out of insurance and old people forced to economise on food. The rise is a problem for the typical family: $5000 is a large slice of the average income, approximately $35 000. It is also a problem for the health care policymakers. They want to see people get well. They also want to leave sufficient resources for the other good things in life.

The concern is a general one. James Buchanan is speaking for many when he writes that the sorcerer's apprentice is becoming a real danger to social balance: 'In the United States, a large and ever-increasing share of total economic value is directed toward outlay on medical or health care services.... It becomes relatively easy to think of a share of one-quarter of the total value produced in the economy being devoted to medical and health care services.... The finitude of the resource base, the labor force and its complement of accumulated and natural capital, guarantees that the share of total value directed into medical services cannot continue to grow without limit' (Buchanan, 1990: 3, 10). Health care spending in the United States, costing between $5000 and $6280 per person ($1.9 trillion in aggregate), accounted in 2006 for 16 per cent of the gross domestic product. It is rising at a rate of almost 8 per cent per annum. This is about three times the rate of inflation (Smith, Cowan, Heffler and Catlin, 2006). As much market failure as need satisfaction, health care spending cannot continue forever to increase at this pace. It must be the task of public policy to keep the rise within the limits that the society believes to be appropriate.

This chapter is concerned with cost. It provides the foundation for chapter 11 on cost containment. The first two sections, 'Payment' and then 'Social and Medical Change', give the reasons for the rise. The third section, 'Countervailing Forces', is a reminder that some services are becoming more affordable even as others are threatening to break the bank.

10.1. PAYMENT

Chapter 2 presented evidence to show that the countries with the best morbidity and mortality indicators were not the countries that put the most money per capita into care. It showed that some observers now believe the causal relationship between spending and outcomes, at least for the richer countries, to be loose, uncertain and possibly even flat-of-the-curve. But that is not the way that ordinary consumers see things. The vast majority of citizens see the rise in the share of care not as a drain but as a characteristic of a culture that is getting its priorities right.

In a poor country people use their disposable income for food and shelter. Instead of seeing the doctor they rely on bedrest, herbs, traditional healers and over-the-counter medication. The body is known very often to heal itself given time. Where it does not, death is accepted as a fact of life. A higher level of pain is tolerated than would be the norm in a more developed society. Psychoanalysis is not widely practised. Tranquillisers are not the first line of defence.

As the society becomes richer, people become better placed both to pay directly for care and to pay for health insurance that makes medical attention more affordable. Rather than seeing the doctor in an emergency only, anxious healthholders can satisfy a taste for reassurance and early diagnosis as well. There is a precautionary demand for expert advice. Even if corrective treatment will probably not be needed, people want to be told that they are in good health. Learning the worst, higher incomes mean that individuals and their societies will be better able to afford the cost of the sequence that comes next. They will also be able to chance a gamble. The speculative demand kicks in where the likelihood of success is low but the last-resort procedure is all the hope that is left.

Ability to pay shifts the demand curve out. Yet the argument should not be pressed too far. Between 1950 and 1984 real medical expenditures in the United States rose seven-fold. Insurance, Manning and his associates calculate, explains no more than a tenth of the change: 'Nor can changes in real income (around a factor of 3 during this period) directly account for much of the rise. Income elasticities ... are at most 0.2 – much too small to account for anything like a factor of 7 change' (Manning, Newhouse, Duan, Keeler, Leibowitz and Marquis, 1987: 269). Health care at least for the individual should probably be seen as a necessity and not a luxury. Even poorer people sense that they have limited discretion. Comparing income elasticities over a cross-section of nations, Newhouse concludes that growing prosperity is unlikely to account for more than a quarter of the total increase (Newhouse, 1992: 8).

Higher incomes mean that more people can afford to pay for insurance and not just for care. It is a smoking volcano. The price deterrent per intervention becomes the excess only and not the full marginal cost. If the co-payment is 10 per cent, it is the 10 per cent and not the 100 per cent that influences the quantity demanded. The demand curve is not the true willingness to pay. Out-of-pocket spending on health care in 2006 accounted for only 15 per cent of total health care expenditure in the United States. Out-of-pocket payments for hospital care, at around 3 per cent, were negligible. Prepayment means peace of mind. It also means that consumers are under less pressure to question whether the marginal utility is truly proportional to the full extra cost.

Affluence makes private insurance affordable. It has at the same time a strong historical association with public payment and non-commercial provision. Because of the humanitarian and material externalities, richer countries have decided that adequacy must not lie where it falls. Health planning has the beneficial spillover that it keeps the size of the sector under control. Centralised decision-making makes it possible for the State to balance medical care against other claims on the nation's resources. Yet politicisation is a double-edged sword. Democracy is about elections. Health care is popular. Voters push out governments who do not satisfy their appetite for more.

Britain has socialised payment through the National Health Service. Even free-market America has opted, since 1966, for Medicare (for the aged and chronically disabled) and Medicaid (for the poor and their dependent children). Both schemes are funded mainly by taxes rather than contributions. The State is the largest health insurer in the United States: 13 per cent of the population is covered under the Medicare system and a further 10 per cent under Medicaid. Unlike the United Kingdom, the target group in both cases is the disadvantaged, economically as well as medically in need. The government in America accounts for almost half (44 per cent) of total spending on health care: businesses pay about a quarter, households about a third. About 29 per cent of federal, state and local revenues are spent on health care (Cutler, 1994: 13, 21). In the UK public expenditure on health in 2003 accounted for 83 per cent of the total. In Japan it was 81 per cent, in Sweden 85 per cent. America's 44 per cent is just below Mexico's 46 per cent (Organisation for Economic Cooperation and Development, 2005).

Pooling is in the air. Government is one part of the new collectivism but insurance companies are the other. Together, in the USA, these two risk-sharing mechanisms spend four times as much on medical care as do individuals and families (Cutler, 2004: x). Commercial insurance and the State umbrella operate side by side in both Britain and America. The choice of the sector need not be a rational one. Many people, aware of information asymmetry, are more comfortable with a non-profit insurer and more comfortable still with the State. Talking economics rather than psychology, the State sector has the further attraction that it is subsidised. It cannot be very easy for private insurers to deliver a cost-effective product if they are obliged to compete with a shop that is sponsored out of tax.

Cutler and Gruber studied the extension of Medicaid eligibility to pregnant women and to children from non-deprived families. Non-deprived families were defined to be households with resources above 185 per cent of the official poverty line. Focusing on the period from 1987 to 1992, the authors discovered that approximately 50 per cent of the increase in free or subsidised care in the United States had been at the expense of the private sector: 'We estimate a net crowd-out from the Medicaid expansions of one-half of the coverage increase' (Cutler and Gruber, 1996: 426). It was not just the uninsured who were being sucked up into Medicaid. It was the already-insured as well. Employees had less of an incentive to continue their employer-based cover: Medicaid provided an acceptable package for adults and even middle-income children were becoming eligible for the State-provided programme. The employers contributed less: the inference is that some or all of the savings they made were passed back to the workers in the form of higher pay. The community as a whole contributed more. The *net* increase in the population covered was more modest than had been intended. It is an indicator of society's generosity that applicants who declined private insurance were not excluded altogether from the public sector scheme.

Blumberg, Dubay and Norton, also studying Medicaid, found that significantly fewer subscribers had dropped private insurance for the public subsidy. They calculated that only about 23 per cent of the children newly enrolled when Medicaid eligibility became more comprehensive had actually migrated into it from the commercial sector. The balance of the new enrollees had been uninsured before the widening of the Medicaid catchment. Such entrants signed up for Medicaid without having had any exposure to the private sector at all. The net result was small. Insurance status switching was not Cutler and Gruber's 50 per cent nor even Yazici and Kaestner's 18.9 per cent (Yazici and Kaestner, 2000: 30) but only 4 per cent. The authors concluded that the simple replacement of one sector by another was very limited indeed: 'We find no evidence that the Medicaid expansions encouraged families with uninsured children to enroll their children in Medicaid rather than take up private coverage. These results imply that the primary impact of the Medicaid expansions was to prevent low-income children from becoming or remaining uninsured, not to crowd-out private insurance' (Blumberg, Dubay and Norton, 2000: 57). The results imply, in other words, that Medicaid cover was *new* cover and that it represented a *new* cost. The future may be less socialistic. As incomes rise and workers become better educated, the family is more likely to qualify for private insurance through work. Such insurance will raise the total cost to society but possibly relieve the Medicaid burden on the State.

Medicaid is not a perfect substitute. The payments it makes to doctors are lower than comparable rates offered by private companies. The risk is that doctors will devote less time to their public patients or (where there is excess demand) refuse to see them at all. The economic solution would entail a rise in cost. Baker and Royalty (sampling pregnant women) showed that a 10 per cent increase in Medicaid fees was associated with a 3.4 per cent increase in Medicaid consultations in the public sector clinics and hospitals. Office-based consultations were not affected. An increase in eligibility seems not to have increased poor people's access to non-institutional procedures. Overall, more Medicaid patients were being seen when fees went up, but not proportionately more (Baker and Royalty, 2000: 494).

Health status is more important than access per se. The rising cost of Medicaid is an economic concern. It is for all that a social benefit if it purchases a worthwhile fall in death and disease. Bradley Gray demonstrated that much remains to be done. About 10.84 per cent of births among Medicaid-insured women are low birth weight. In the non-Medicaid population it is only 5.73 per cent. About 1.12 per cent of children born to Medicaid-insured women do not survive twelve months. In the non-Medicaid population it is 0.52 per cent (Gray, 2001: 571). While deprivation is more than doctoring alone, and while in the absence of Medicaid the survival rates would probably have been worse, Gray drew the conclusion that more money would go some way towards closing the gap. An illustration would be increased and improved physician consultations in the crucial first trimester of pregnancy. Medicaid-insured women were 30 per cent less likely to have had a prenatal doctor visit in that trimester.

The relationship between consultations and costs is not what it seems. A 10 per cent higher-than-average Medicaid fee will increase the prenatal visits on which overworked doctors would otherwise have had to economise. Yet it is also associated with a 0.074 per cent lower absolute risk of an infant being born low birth weight. For very low birth weight babies the risk was reduced by 0.035 per cent. In the case of women in the lowest decile of family incomes, the improvement was greater still (Gray, 2001: 583). Total cost will fall as a result of the higher-than-average fees. Low birth weight is a greater financial burden than infant mortality. Cost savings accrue when the number of low birth weight infants requiring expensive neonatal and ongoing interventions goes down. As much as $16 800 per healthy child could be saved. Paying Medicaid doctors a competitive fee is cost-effective as well as equitable and just. The proposition is reversible. Lower-than-average Medicaid fees are a false economy. In the long-run the result is an increase in total cost.

Apart from subsidies to public patients and construction grants for selected hospitals, the State also offers tax relief on occupational premiums. The tax exemption has itself contributed to the rise in cost. Where health insurance is treated as a legitimate business expense, employers offer tax deductible fringe benefits in excess of the medical care that the employee would have bought had he been offered the equivalent value in taxable pay. The tax free concession means that the good is supplied at a price below its unengineered equilibrium. If the downward sloping demand curve exists, artificial cheapening must be expected to lead to an expansion in the quantity consumed. The distortion means too much insurance, too much coverage, too much care and too much cost. A merit good beyond an optimal point ceases to have much merit. In Germany being an *ewiger Student* (eternal student) used to be a reasonable option. Later the Germans decided that by the time the student reaches 40 he ought to be thinking about a job.

Overconsumption would be reduced if insurance were to be taxed as income in kind or if the tax exemption were to be restricted to basic cover only. Employees and unions would not be enthusiastic about the loss. Their resistance will be particularly strong if rates of personal income tax are high and health insurance as a consequence a valuable loophole. For individuals who pay their own premiums, the fiscal welfare clearly rises as they progress into the higher tax brackets. It is not the very poor who get the lion's share of the tax subsidy. Be that as it may, the rise in cost would have been less had health cover been treated as a commodity like any other.

Social as well as fiscal welfare puts up the cost of care. Social workers make sure that the isolated and the confused find out what is available: the disadvantaged, no longer neglected, acquire a claim to scarce resources. The comfortable support the defenceless because the future is hidden behind a veil: the life they save might be their own. The definition of decency is being upgraded over time: even a poor person nowadays expects a tolerable waiting time and an air conditioned ward. The job function of the professional has been broadened and socialised: the medical services are nowadays being asked to help drug addicts, alcoholic unemployables and lifetime misfits who in a less caring society would have been left to the Charity Organisation Societies, the police and the morgue.

Private or State, third-party protection releases the genie of expense. Rights having been bought or granted, rational consumers want to make the most of their entitlements. Moral hazard, as Mark Pauly points out, is not a moral failing but another name for *homo economicus*: 'The response of seeking more medical care with insurance than in its absence is a result not of moral perfidy, but of rational economic behavior' (Pauly, 1968: 535). The textbooks teach that marginal utilisation expands to the point where marginal utility is proportional to marginal sacrifice. That is just the problem. Where there is no cost sharing or when the annual out-of-pocket ceiling has been reached, the price at the point of use is zero. The last unit will be free. Being free, it will therefore be the unit that yields no more than zero marginal benefit.

The consumer faces no personal deterrent or hurdle where access to the buffet continues unrestricted. Even if the cost to the system is high, even if the medical effectiveness is low, still the service will be demanded. Areas of the economy that are not subsidised in this way will bear the economic burden of the twisted signals. The insured commodity will be overconsumed relative to other goods and services that are not prepaid. Non-merit goods will have to stand on their own two feet.

The consumer has an incentive to shop around for insurance. He has less of an incentive to shop around for the care that the insurance makes possible. There is no reason to search, monitor and bargain where it is third-parties who will pay. It is moral hazard again. Providers have an incentive to exploit the lack of resistance by expanding quantity and putting up the charge. They know that the patient at least will not be out-of-pocket. In the long-run the premiums will go up. There is no way that the single face in the crowd can keep the streets litter-free or prevent the village commons from being tragically overgrazed. It is the dilemma of collective action. What all can do, one cannot. One consumer's search for best-possible information, one consumer's decision to do without the marginal test proposed, would have an insignificant impact on the next renewal. One consumer's gains, if any, would be shared with the crowd.

Like the consumer, the doctor is the victim of his incentive structure. Supplier-induced demand and unneeded, unwanted appendectomies are the horror stories that dramatise the ubiquitous bias of the mundane. Easy reimbursement is a temptation to err on the side of more rather than less. Fee for service is an invitation to bleed the effective demand. Consider the burden of health care expenditure (HCE) in Germany: 'Gross earnings for private doctors and some specialists (e.g. radiologists) are twice or three times those of salaried hospital doctors. Physician expenditures in Germany amount to about 25 percent of total HCE, the highest share in Europe' (Culyer, 1989: 30). Consider the cost-cutting capitations and salaries elsewhere in Europe: 'It is striking that the four countries that do not use fee for service as the principal means of payment (Denmark, Italy, Sweden, and the United Kingdom) have the four lowest ratios of average doctor income to GDP per capita' (Culyer, 1989: 30).

Capitation and salary can keep the total cost down: they give the indolent the freedom to be inactive. Fee for service is more likely to put the total cost up: it offers the avaricious a sitting target. Yet personal gain is not the only reason why doctors supply the services that they do. Compassionate practitioners, knowing that there will be no financial burden on a patient who enjoys third-party protection, will supply tests and treatments in line with their professional ethic.

The professional ethic is a mixed blessing. Flat-of-the-curve medicine is made possible by a tap that is never turned off. In Europe, Cutler estimates, up to one-third of all care is inappropriate or ineffective (Cutler, 1994: 14). There is no reason for doctors to find out the true cost. There is no reward for selecting a procedure which is economical as well as effective. There is no mechanism for standardising the practice variations. There is no incentive to incorporate the social as well as the private cost. A competitive market presupposes a determined search for information about relative prices. Insurance which automatically rubber stamps the bill provides no motive for the doctor to invest time and money in such disinterested search. Not only that, prepayment also occasions the sterile waste of transactions and administrative costs. In America this overhead is equal to about 15 per cent of the claims that are made (Cutler, 1994: 14). The loading alone represents 34 per cent of the cost of a group insurance policy, 43 per cent of single and family contracts (Pauly and Percy, 2000: 20). Part of the paper-processing (such as utilisation reviews or the streaming of good risks from bad) keeps total health care costs down. Part, however, is a deadweight burden for which no status increment is secured in return.

More insurance means higher cost. Higher cost means more insurance. Martin Feldstein describes the vicious circle of defence and self-defence in the following way: 'For the community as a whole ... the spread of insurance causes higher prices and more sophisticated services which in turn cause a further increase in insurance. People spend more on health because they are insured and buy more insurance because of the high cost of health care' (Feldstein, 1973: 252). The higher cost of care produces higher premiums when the policies are renewed. Higher premiums, however, do not seem to be the barking dog that is required. The premium elasticity of demand is low. The commodity is seen as a relative necessity. Besides that, it is often the company and not the individual that pays.

The premium in an occupational plan is disproportionately funded by the employer. Households in the United States cover slightly less than 30 per cent of private health insurance premiums (Smith, Cowan, Heffler and Catlin, 2006). The amounts are not small. In 2005 the annual premium that a health insurer charged an employer for covering a family of four averaged $10 800. Of that sum the worker contributed $2713, 143 per cent more than in 2000. For purposes of comparison, the gross earnings of an American worker on the minimum wage in 2005 were $10 712. It is not cheap to join the club. Once insured, however, the individual need not ration his demands. It is then the others who pay: 'The larger the price-elasticity, the greater the welfare loss resulting from more generous health insurance' (Manning and Marquis, 1996: 610).

Welfare loss refers to the slippage that exists where the social cost of the service exceeds the out-of-pocket share that is borne by the patient. Manning and his colleagues recognised that the welfare loss from excess insurance would be less if the coinsurance rate were to be higher. The welfare cost of moving from 95 per cent coinsurance to free medical care was, they estimated, of the order of $37 billion to $60 billion (Manning, Newhouse, Duan, Keeler, Leibowitz and Marquis, 1987: 270). Feldman and Dowd also used data from the RAND Health Insurance Experiment to quantify the loss. They found it to be even greater: from $33.4 billion to $109.3 billion (Feldman and Dowd, 1991: 300).

Manning and Marquis calculated that the price elasticity of demand for health insurance was –0.54. The income elasticity was 0.07. The former figure is surprisingly price-sensitive for what the commodity is: when the price goes up by $1, the quantity demanded goes down by a rather large $0.54. The latter figure is all but a constant: when income goes up by $1, the purchase of cover goes up by a meagre seven cents. They then worked out that the optimal coinsurance rate would be 45 per cent. Holding the ring as 'the rate at which the marginal gain from increased risk pooling equals the marginal loss from increased moral hazard' (Manning and Marquis, 1996: 629), their 45 per cent would keep down marginal waste but ensure that marginal contingencies enjoyed adequate protection. Their rate would in that way bring into line the *ex ante* demand for health insurance with the *ex post* demand for medical care.

The effect of moving from a coinsurance rate of 95 per cent to an average rate of zero would be, they calculated, to cause something like a 50 per cent increase in demand. The same thing would happen in reverse if the co-payments were to be increased. The saving of resources would have no measurable impact upon the health status of the mean citizen: only vision and blood pressure in the RAND study were affected by the move away from free care, and then only slightly. The resources freed up could be targeted on the members of the community most likely to be in need (Manning, Newhouse, Duan, Keeler, Leibowitz and Marquis, 1987: 258, 265).

Feldstein sees the insurance-care nexus as a minus-sum game: 'American families are in general overinsured against health expenses. If insurance coverage were reduced, the utility loss from increased risk would be more than outweighed by the gain due to lower costs and the reduced purchase of excess care. Moreover, the estimated net gain from even a one-third reduction in insurance is quite large, probably exceeding several billion dollars per year' (Feldstein, 1973: 251). A lower level of cover would mean more risk and more anxiety. It could, on the other hand, encourage people to invest in prophylactic aerobics, or to search more intensively for better products and prices. The market mechanism in the area of health might become more competitive and more efficient. Economic welfare, in other words, might go up if health care were to be less comprehensively reimbursed.

Yet philosophy is not on the side of the economists. The conviction that health care is an inviolable human right works against the idea that corners can be cut and the poor made to pay. Equality is frequently taken to mean equal quality irrespective of cost. The fact that the deprived and the elderly are being left uninsured and exposed when premiums become unaffordable is not regarded as an acceptable way of reducing pressure on scarce endowments. Comprehensive, first-dollar insurance is one response. Universalist social medicine is another. Cost explosion is the result of good intentions at variance with supply-constrained demand.

10.2. SOCIAL AND MEDICAL CHANGE

Economic growth, commercial insurance and State co-payment are important changes that have contributed to the rise in cost. They have been complemented by changes in culture and technology which have an impact of their own.

A significant development has been the upgrading in expectations. This societal ratchet has been the medical-care concommitant of *embourgeoisement* and upward convergence. Early policymakers in the United Kingdom felt that there had to be a big push to clear the backlog of ill health. They predicted that once the policy of 'universalising the best' had definitively integrated the marginalised into the mainstream, the push would come to an end. Their assumptions proved unrealistic. Spending on health care in Britain has gone up six-fold in real terms since the National Health Service came into being. The cholera eradicated and the polio on the way to extinction, new demands took the place of the old ones. People requested more tests and referrals. They sought consultations even for minor aches that in the past they had accepted as a fact of life. They topped up their NHS entitlements with private health care spending to the tune of £4.5 billion in 2005 alone. People, in short, began to demand the marginal services and the standard of excellence that they identified with a better quality of life. They were reluctant to put up with the bare minimum. The result was a financial escalation which Bevan and the founders of the Health Service in 1948 had not anticipated.

Improvements in education contributed both to middle class job opportunities and to an understanding of disease and its treatment. Occupational upgrading made society culturally more homogeneous. More and more people regarded health care as an entitlement and convinced themselves that it was a right. Education itself made them more aware, more articulate and more critical. They were able to read health-related articles and to understand the media broadcasts. No longer willing to take what they were given without a word, their new-found status of consumer rather than supplicant itself levelled up the cost of care.

More health-specific information as well as more general knowledge seems to mean more medical services demanded. While one could also hypothesise that better educated people will consume less formal care because they will be more likely to use vitamins and jogging to head off the threat, Kenkel's data-set suggests the opposite: 'More informed consumers are significantly more likely to visit a physician.... Poorly informed consumers tend to underestimate the marginal product of medical care' (Kenkel, 1990: 590). Hsieh and Lin found some support for this result in Taiwan. Elderly people with better schooling, higher incomes and, crucially, personal experience in a health-related occupation were more likely than were the less educated to know when and where to go for appropriate attention: 'Lack of information can become an access barrier to preventive care' (Hsieh and Lin, 1997: 326).

Money was evidently not the only reason why the poorly informed among the over-60s in Taiwan were slipping up on early detection. It was a false economy: 'Most chronic diseases can be avoided if individuals can change their lifestyle.... The consequences of chronic diseases could be reduced by seeking preventive care' (Hsieh and Lin, 1997: 309). Urine checks identify diabetes in its pre-symptomatic stages. Blood pressure picks up the warning signs of heart or kidney disease. The more educated will have their tests and their follow-ups. Invoking Grossman's (1972) theory, one could even say that the productivity of the care will itself be greater since the more educated will be in a better position to convert the doctoring into health capital. As for the less educated, they are less likely to find the 'silent killers' before the 'silent killers' find them. In the long-run the economic cost to society will more than offset the short-term gain.

Demography too has an influence on cost. As agricultural societies move into manufacturing industry and high-value services, the birth rate tends to go down. In most developed countries it fails even to reach the replacement ratio of 2.1. The result is a saving: there are fewer dependent young people to put pressure on the doctors and the nurses. The dependent elderly are another matter. Rising life-expectancy means that there will be a greater burden on limited budgets in the later years of life. The old (especially the very old) are more prone to chronic health failings like melanoma and stroke. Their hospital episodes are likely to last longer. There is a greater probability that they will require long-stay residential treatment as well as in-and-out cure. The old impose an above-average cost. It is a demographic time-bomb that social trends do nothing to defuse. Industrialisation, urbanisation, the two-career couple, the preference for privacy, the financial deadweight of aged parents, all reduce the willingness of the multigenerational family to act as the primary carer. Unpaid relatives do not have the time to look after the retired and the frail. Old-people's homes and paid professionals fill the social void.

In poorer countries a death from malaria is a cheap way to go. In more developed countries, the epidemiological transition from acute to chronic is also an economic transition and a financial strain. As Derek Walker-Smith says: 'If one is less likely to die of diphtheria as a child, or from pneumonia as an adult, one has a greater chance of succumbing later to coronary disease or cancer.... By increasing the expectation of life, we put greater emphasis on the malignant and degenerative diseases which are characteristic of the later years' (quoted in Klein, 1983: 31–2). A fall in infant and productive-adult mortality feeds through into survivals in the high-cost golden years. More must be treated who in poorer countries would already have died.

The point is an important one. Berk and Monheit report that 27 per cent of health care expenditures in the United States were concentrated in 1996 on only 1 per cent of the resident population (46.3 per cent of them elderly). About 55 per cent of total spending was absorbed by the top 5 per cent, 69 per cent by the top 10 per cent. The bottom 50 per cent of the (civilian, non-institutionalised) population took up only 3 per cent of the health care allocations. The distribution had not changed radically since 1970. The rapid growth of managed care organisations with their gatekeeper function seems not to have altered the percentages. The inequality is striking. Healthy consumers in the bottom 50 per cent occasioned average annual medical spending of only $122 per person per year. For unhealthy consumers in the top 1 per cent the figure was $56459 (Berk and Monheit, 2001: 12, 13). Small savings, clearly, will not contain the $56459. Shorter inpatient stays and the use of generics will have at most a modest contribution to make. It is the minority and not the majority who are unbalancing the books.

Sick people cost more money. A disproportionate share goes to the irreversibly ill, unlikely to regain a satisfactory quality of life. Often they will be cared for not in hospices or in their supportive family home but in expensive hospital beds. Berk and Monheit say that the bed-blocking is simply not fair: 'A highly concentrated spending distribution may indicate that some population groups are obtaining excessive care with benefits not commensurate with costs, that other groups may be underusing medical care, and that overall social welfare might be enhanced through a reallocation of resources from the former group to the latter' (Berk and Monheit, 2001: 10). This does not mean that the feeding tube should be disconnected. What it might mean, however, is that patients who have not yet had their 'fair innings' should be given priority when blockbuster services cannot realistically be provided for all.

Some consumers pay for themselves. Most are covered by private insurance or by the safety-net State. Welfare ensures that even the impoverished have a share. As was shown in chapter 9, the amount of the reimbursement is by no means the same. Medical spending on the insured as compared with the uninsured is, in the United States, in the ratio of 3:1: 'Even the very sickest of the uninsured receive only a small fraction of the care that can be obtained by those with private insurance' (Berk and Monheit, 2001: 16). Private insurers pick the peaches who have the fewest flaws. The State and its subsidised services give the residuals a home. Whether it is spending too much or spending too little, the economic position at least is clear. In including the excluded, the warm-hearted community is putting up the total cost of care.

The bisectoral system makes it difficult for the State to cap the totals. Even if experimental treatments, magnetic resonance imaging, wonder drugs, heart, liver and bone marrow transplants could be ruled out for public patients, a very strong social consensus would be necessary if the State were to proscribe such expensive therapies in the private sector as well. Liberal democracy is favourable to demand-led supply. Going private is, however, a loophole and an open door. Both cost saving and equity presuppose that the private sector be subject to the same restrictions as the State.

Expectations, education, demography and inclusion are pushing up the cost of care. So is the relentless evolution in medical technology. A one-period model that abstracts from novelty and change gives a misleading impression of how science forever builds upon itself. Kidney dialysis, the coronary bypass, the joint replacement, the balloon angioplasty, the pace maker implant, genetic engineering, electronic foetal monitoring, radiation therapy, the computerised scan, the 'smart drug' for colon cancer that costs £130 000 for a two-year course – advances in medical technique such as these are more expensive per case than the routine management that was the best on offer before the discovery of open-heart surgery or the life-prolonging AIDS cocktail. The equipment manu-facturers and the pharmaceutical majors look to research and development for lucrative breakthroughs that will increase their profits. Doctors and academics become caught up in the momentum of medical research. Inventions and in-novations multiply faster than the ability of the community to pay for them. The knowledge that so many new treatments are not being taken up must be a source of frustration to the citizen who wants to be well. That frustration, in a tax-financed health care system, expresses itself in pressure on the political leadership to increase the funding that goes to health.

Some new developments do lead to better medical outcomes. It is hard to fault technology that increases the cures and reduces the costs: 'There may … be no need to worry about long-term cost growth, if the new health spending is more valuable than spending in other areas' (Cutler, 1994: 18). Not every change is, however, a change for the better. It is important, economically speaking, to work out the cost-effectiveness ratios and to make an impartial estimate of the comparative returns.

Sometimes the benefits will more than repay the private and/or the social costs. The problem arises where they do not: 'The marginal value of some in-tensive cardiac procedures is close to zero…. Many medical technologies may be used excessively, inadequately, or inappropriately' (McClellan and Noguchi, 1998: 90, 95). Want and need, as is so often the case, can go their separate ways. Patients tend to judge quality in part by newness and capital intensity. Shopping around for a clinic, a patient in a competitive market will want the hospital to have the latest equipment. He will not know or perhaps not even care that it is under-employed capacity, idle capacity that pushes up the cost. In a more liter-ate, more urbanised society, consumers are more likely to become aware of the state-of-the-art facilities that are coming on stream. Concentration of population makes expensive new technology more easily accessible. So does insurance. The most expensive is also the cheapest where the consumer does not have to pay.

New techniques often dispense with an inpatient stay. Where they make pos-sible day case treatment in place of hospital admissions, they economise on an especially costly part of the medical package. The reverse is true where domiciliary nursing has to give way to capital and wards. In some countries the insurers actually promote the more expensive scenario. They specify that they will pay for (more costly) inpatient but not for (less costly) outpatient care. Hospitals are not adverse to this discrimination. A built bed is a billed bed. Uneconomical overbuilding is the result.

Public policy has unintentionally contributed to hospital-cost inflation. Tax exemptions and capital grants have encouraged overbedding in not-for-profit institutions. They have also meant that profit-seeking competitors do not face a level playing field. Restrictions on new entry enable existing hospitals to retain their windfall profits. Rules that limit advertising make it difficult for cost-cutters to publicise their creative destruction. The hospital industry has been excused the spur of rivalry. The need to struggle might have led to the elimination of wasteful duplication. It might have been the trigger for the more efficient exploitation of economies of scale.

As with all bureaucratic organisations, there is slippage into 'x-inefficiency' or internal slack: 'The presumed formal contract cannot by itself tell us what it is that we want to know about intraorganizational behavior' (Leibenstein, 1987: 4). Competition might arguably make the medical and the managerial staff more amenable to economical calculativeness. The restriction of competition might be a reason for sluggishness and the rise in cost. The not-for-profit orientation of the service supply is less obviously so. The unit cost in for-profit and not-for-profit hospitals seems not to be very different: 'It is not self-evident that private sector bureaucracies are better controlled than public sector ones.... The case for privatization as a method of cost control or an agent for the promotion of efficiency is thus uneasy' (Culyer, 1989: 28).

Hospital administrators will often err on the side of expense. In a competitive market the management knows that expensive toys are status symbols that sell the product. The patients aside, the prestige associated with glamorous equipment and cutting edge science will make it easier for the fundraisers to bring in donations. There is a further consideration. A hospital known to adopt the latest innovations will be better placed to enlist consultants who value science and standing as a non-pecuniary plus. From the social point of view it would be preferable for cost-effectiveness to be put before conspicuous radicalisation. The problem is to convince the sick and their surgeons that newest will not always be best.

Capital increases the cost. Labour does so as well. The number of doctors is rising. The ratio of expensive specialists to general practitioners is rising. The doctor–patient ratio is rising. Supplier-induced intervention is a theoretical possibility. So is the overproduction of medical professionals where subsidised medical schools do not proportion places to employment opportunities.

Besides that, there is the physical inelasticity of the listening ear. Despite extensive mechanisation and ever-changing technology, health care remains a labour intensive industry. Newhouse is right to say that medical productivity can and does go up: 'The treatment of heart attacks has certainly changed more than haircuts or the performance of Mozart string quartets' (Newhouse, 1992: 9). The problem is that efficiency in the manufacturing sector goes up even faster. In services, because there is a person-to-person component, output per unit of input cannot increase beyond a point without debasing the quality of the product. The lightning consultation is simply not as effective as the appointment that explores the uniqueness of the patient's circumstances. The services sector is handicapped by its relative inability to cushion rising wages through rising throughput. Yet the pay it offers must be competitive and comparable if it is to be able to recruit and retain.

The medical market, moreover, is an imperfect one. Professional bodies such as the American Medical Association and the British Medical Association limit the supply of medical personnel. Entry barriers, protracted in-service internships and restrictions on the accreditation of medical schools (often presented as quality controls) lengthen the obstacle race. They restrict the supply of service even as growing demand is producing a bottleneck. Strict lines of demarcation between doctors, nurses, paramedical staff and medical auxiliaries reinforce the upward pressure on fees. In some countries doctors and nurses have even gone on strike in support of a claim. Logically speaking, there ought to be a rent or surplus.

The evidence, perhaps surprisingly, does not always bear out the expectation of ransom or booty. The earnings of doctors, at least in the United States, would seem to be broadly similar to those of other professionals, after allowing for the costs of training. Weeks and others calculated that the internal rate of return on investment in medical education for American general practitioners was 15.9 per cent. For dentists it was 20.7 per cent, for medical specialists 20.9 per cent. Business people reaped a return on their human capital of 29.0 per cent, lawyers of 25.4 per cent (Weeks, Wallace, Wallace and Welch, 1994: 1280). The comparisons (calculated over an hours-adjusted working lifetime) do not suggest that doctors inevitably have an extraordinary ability to secure a supernormal return.

The newsflash that striking professionals are letting their patients suffer and die, the saloon-bar imputation that fee-seekers are milking their punters for unnecessary treatments, is a threat to the doctor–patient relationship. The loss of confidence is reflected in a tendency to demand (and pay for) a second opinion, together with recourse to the malpractice action if something is believed to have gone wrong. The threat of a suit in turn forces the doctor into precautionary ('defensive') medicine of low cost-effectiveness or no clinical value. The excessive cautiousness imposes an avoidable burden on the system that resembles the very different phenomenon of supplier-induced demand. The fear of litigation sometimes causes medical professionals to refuse altogether certain kinds of business where the outcome is too uncertain, negligence a grey area and the probability of legal action too great. Gynaecology and obstetrics in the United States have often been neglected for this reason. Even 'frivolous litigation', with the associated publicity and time wasted in court, can damage a professional's reputation. As the payouts become larger, so the premiums paid by doctors for malpractice insurance become greater. The cost of care rises in a free-enterprise medical system when these liabilities are passed on to the final consumer.

Cutler comments that any saving in this area would be unlikely to have a major effect on cost since the actual sums involved are not large. Marginal tests and procedures amount to about three per cent of total health care spending in the United States. Malpractice actions add only another one per cent (Cutler, 1994: 16). Even so, there is clearly a gain to be made if the private cost could be made equal to the social. Kessler and McClellan, studying serious heart disease among elderly patients, found that malpractice reforms in the 1980s such as caps on compensation and the abolition of punitive damages had reduced hospital expenditures in the United States by 5 to 9 per cent: 'The estimated expenditure/benefit ratio associated with direct reforms is over $500,000 per additional one-year survivor' (Kessler and McClellan, 1996: 386). The reforms had not had an adverse impact on quality indicators like mortality or incidence of complications. Patients had not been harmed. Money had been saved. It could have been as much as $600 million per annum. Generalised to other conditions and age groups, the spending staved off could have been in excess of $50 billion.

10.3.   COUNTERVAILING FORCES

This chapter on the rise in cost should not end on a note of despair. There are countervailing forces which are working to reduce the economic deadweight per medical episode.

Thus drugs and counselling allow the domiciliary management of conditions such as schizophrenia and clinical depression which otherwise would have gone into the long-stay wards. Ulcers can be treated without surgery. Paramedics and nurses can perform low-level medical procedures. The polio vaccine has made curative treatment redundant. Low tech in the form of an aspirin, a thrombolytic, a low-cost statin, a low-salt diet all reduce the need for expensive high-tech later on. Beta-blockers prescribed after a heart attack cut the probability of a second heart attack by a quarter. Cataracts and hernias can be dealt with on an ambulatory basis. Inpatient days are going down: 'Admission rates are now barely above 1960 levels and age adjustment would wipe out the difference.... Length of stay has fallen' (Newhouse, 1992: 11). Pregnancies can be reduced via the birth control pill. Economies of scale have reduced the relative cost of manufactured inputs even if not the cost of face-to-face consultation. Techno-logical innovation has raised average productivity per diagnostician.

Better diagnosis and detection have made early treatment more likely before costly complications set in. Genetic decoding allows at-risk patients to demand a just-in-case mastectomy since cancer is worse. Capital equipment has reduced the rate of expensive recidivism: 'Though use of more high-tech procedures led to greater expenditure growth during the initial hospital admission, patients treated by these hospitals had relative declines in later hospital admissions, offsetting the more rapid growth in initial treatment expenditures' (McClellan and Noguchi, 1998: 95).

Improved managerial practices have made the health services more efficient. Better diet and housing have had a beneficial effect on the incidence of illness. Smoking cessation programmes leave the body after detox more robust. Internet technology makes it less time consuming to acquire information on price and quality. A table setting out the options makes it easier for consumers to select insurance plans that meet their needs. Cost-effectiveness studies identify the less expensive treatment. While a new drug or therapy might not reduce the total cost in absolute terms, cost-effectiveness makes it cost-saving relative to what would otherwise have been spent.

Reforms in primary care make the family doctor more productive. Group practices facilitate the division of labour. They encourage the efficient use of medical aides. Brown puts the improvement at 22 per cent (Brown, 1988: 354). Marder and Zuckerman felt that there were economies of scale in multi-physician practices. Making use of the 'survivor' approach to institutional competition pioneered by Stigler and others, they concluded that the decline in market share of solo and small practices showed that they could not have been very efficient. Scale economies continued to be reaped when there were as many as 100 doctors in a multispeciality group (Marder and Zuckerman, 1985: 173). Marder and Zuckerman correctly observe that there is no single output measure that can be called authoritative; and that health care inputs themselves are heterogeneous. Spillover social costs and benefits are not cap-tured by the focus on the practice rather than the nation. Even so, they conclude that there are cost savings that can still be made if the system moves further towards larger teams.

Concentration of third-party payment makes it easier to enforce approved medical compensation. A few giant insurers, especially if they are allowed to prespecify rates and quality standards in unison, are better placed to limit reim-bursement than would be a multiplicity of perfect competitors. Managed care through the health maintenance organisations holds down hospital stays and promotes the use of generics. Socialisation increases central control over fees. Over one-third of physician incomes and almost two-thirds of hospital revenues in the United States originate in the public sector. Government in America, while not a pure monopsony (nor even a near monopsony in the British sense), has more power over rates than it would in a pure market system.

A National Health Service has an even greater impact on prices. These, after all, become in-house parameters. Doctors on salary are more likely to be monitored. Their incentive structure is not conducive to supplier-induced demand. Hospitals are more likely to be profiled. Long waiting times and high death rates will stand out in the tables. The Opposition and the media are quick to ferret out the underperformance and the waste.

It is easy to point to shortcomings. The Healthcare Commission in 2006 found that 37 per cent of British NHS trusts (210 out of 570) had failed to manage their finances adequately and that a further 10 per cent were only 'fair'. Medically speaking, only 9 per cent were actually 'weak' in the quality of services they supplied but fully 51 per cent were no better than 'fair' (Healthcare Commission, 2006). On both measures, financial and medical, about half the NHS organisations in England and Wales were not achieving the standards the community had a right to expect. Yet the very fact that the data was published is a reason to be optimistic. Publicity will force the underachievers to raise their standards. Mid-Cheshire Hospitals or North Devon Healthcare cannot have been happy to see their lack of success highlighted in the national press. Besides that, a National Health Service is a single State-owned entity. The Minister has the right to ask the poor performers to produce action plans and to improve in time for the following audit. In this way the system has its own stabilisers that in the long-run are likely to grind out decent value for money.

Cutler and McClellan, noting the countervailing forces, say that the rise in cost should not be exaggerated. Rather than being an indicator of runaway inflation, the rise was mainly due to a rise in the quantity of treatments provided. As little as 33 per cent of the increase in spending in the United States, they say, was the result of a higher price tag per treatment supplied. If anything, the price could have gone down. Statisticians are notoriously slow to pick up improvements in quality over time. Adjusting official data for the upgrading, the outcome in terms of success rates and productivity may well have been an unexpected one. Sometimes at least, economics is on our side: 'Price indices for medical care are falling' (Cutler and McClellan, 2001: 26).

11. Conclusion: containing the cost

In spite of the countervailing forces, and in absolute terms, the total cost of care is going up. There is nothing wrong with that. If society wants better health, and if it is convinced that more care is the best means to the end, then it ought to welcome the rise. We do not cut or contain the cost of something that is doing us good. The share of foreign holidays, handphones, new cars, video games and owner-occupied housing has gone up as well. You get what you pay for. Every child knows that.

The debate is not about whether citizens in a liberal democracy should be denied access to a consumable that they crave. The debate is about whether extra care actually produces extra health. It is about whether an equivalent health status could be delivered at a lower cost. It is about whether health care at the margin is crowding out other consumption and investment opportunities that citizens if properly informed would have ranked more highly. The debate is also about the pressures on the State budget, the crisis in public finance and the threat to under-publicised areas of public expenditure. The debate, in other words, is about the optimum. What level of health care and what rate of growth are the targets at which the society ought to aim? It is not an easy question to answer. There is no consensus on what it is that medical spending actually does: 'The nature of the link between medical-care services and well-being is not well understood' (Newhouse, 1977: 115).

There is no real agreement on medical effectiveness, value for money, social ranking and political priority. Nor is there a general consensus on the target share of health care in national expenditure. What many people increasingly fear, however, is that automaticity has failed and cost escalation has got out of hand. In such circumstances there are three approaches to the containment of cost that can usefully be explored. The first is rationing by money and time. The second is demand-side guidelines on purchase and provision. The third is State intervention, either to constrain the market or to set it free.

11.1. RATIONING BY MONEY AND TIME

Economic theory posits a downward sloping demand curve. Consumers buy more of the commodity when the price is low than they do when the price is high. Increments in health care are subject to diminishing marginal productivity in respect of the health status that they confer. Improvements in health status yield diminishing marginal utility to the bodyholder who already has an adequate stock. The demand for health care is a derived demand. It is derived from the demand for health. The more care people have consumed, the less they will be willing to pay for a little bit more.

An excess of demand over supply can be choked off by allowing prices to rise to their market-clearing levels. Care provided free of charge at the point of use or fully reimbursed by a comprehensive insurance policy is, market-oriented thinkers say, an invitation to overconsumption and a cause of cost. The alternative is for the patient to put his money or his time where his mouth is. Wanting the attention, he would do without other things that fall within his choice set. Wavering, he would do without the care. His decision will not reduce but rather increase total cost where his penny-counting only leads in the long-run to an aggravation of his condition. In the short-run, however, the cost is not incurred since the treatments are not consumed.

11.1.1. Money Price

Pecuniary payment, out-of-pocket or out-of-savings, is a kaleidoscope of possibilities. The co-payment is a fixed amount such as a lump-sum prescription charge ('for the bottle') that the patient puts in towards the cost of his care. The deductible or excess is the threshold minimum that the patient must cover before the insurer becomes liable for any part of the cost. The coinsurance contribution is the agreed percentage of each bill that is paid by the insured party and cannot be claimed back from the fund.

The user charge can be general (an across-the-board deductible) or specific (the fee for an eye test, a dental check-up or an out-of-hours visit). It can be invariant (as where the entry ticket is a single, standard lump-sum). It can be pooled (as where the charges are subject to an annual cap not for the individual but for the family). It can be shaded by circumstance (as where the young, the pregnant, the retired are charged a reduced rate). It can reflect the ability to pay (as where a means test exempts the absolutely deprived). It can even be differentiated by the medical condition. An example would be a blood test provided free to intravenous drug addicts in order stem the spread of an externality.

A user charge can be a supply and demand price. Where there is no third-party subsidy or State-regulated ceiling, the fee would be the economics textbook's market-clearing sacrifice. A user charge can be an unpoliced border: once the client buys an insurance add-on that reimburses even the deductible, the co-pay would effectively have only a token or educative function. A user charge can be a deterrent barrier: whether without insurance at all or tragically exhausted at the insuring agency's annual or lifetime maximum, the client knows that he has to settle the whole bill on his own. Cost-sharing, in other words, can take a variety of forms. It would be a mistake to treat a user charge as if it were always the same.

(a) The empirical evidence

Price elasticity is the percentage change in quantity that results from a percentage change in price. It can be estimated as a global statistic for all medical expenditures. Manning and his colleagues found this figure to lie in the range from –0.17 to –0.22. A 10 per cent increase in price led to approximately a 2 per cent decrease in the quantity demanded. Since health care is a necessity, the coefficient is predictably low (Manning, Newhouse, Duan, Keeler, Leibowitz and Marquis, 1987: 268). Time, here as elsewhere, raises questions about the *ceteris paribus*. Are incomes also rising over time? Is the lower paid rural population contracting as a percentage of the whole? Is urbanisation reducing the complementary cost of journey times? The danger with a price–quantity relationship is that there are more relevant variables than price and quantity alone.

The global statistic ensures that expenditure does not disappear from the data where demand is not extinguished but is simply transferred across to a substitute. This would be the case where demand, responding to price, migrates from a specialist to a family doctor, from inpatient to outpatient care, from a Western-style clinic to a village midwife, from a full-body scan to a physical examination known to perform just as well. Less sensitive to cross-elasticity of this kind would be the microscopic approach that disaggregates by a single service demanded. Thus the Manning study showed the price elasticity of demand for hospital stays to be (as before) only –0.17 to –0.22 (Manning, Newhouse, Duan, Keeler, Leibowitz and Marquis, 1987: 268). Cromwell and Mitchell found a similar inelasticity in the demand for the services of surgeons: it was only –0.14 to –0.17 (Cromwell and Mitchell, 1986: 304). Rossett and Huang estimated the price sensitivities for doctoring and hospitalisation in the United States: they lay in the range from –0.35 to –1.50 (Rossett and Huang, 1973: 301). Wedig calculated the elasticity of demand for doctor consultations. It was –0.35 (where the patient believed his general health to be good) and –0.16 (where the patient was convinced that his general health was poor): 'Declines in health reduce the price elasticity of the original decision to seek care' (Wedig, 1988: 152, 159). Whether for the healthier or for the less-healthy, the price sensitivity was low. The commodity was something that consumers felt they had to have.

The price elasticity for an urgent appendectomy is zero. People must have the intervention or they will die. People in any case only have one appendix. They cannot multiply their purchases in response to a two-for-one discount. Emergencies, however, are the exception. More elective services show a stronger response. Cosmetic surgery, normally postponable and almost always a luxury, would be a world away from the cardiac arrest. Even dental check-ups can be price-sensitive: there is no guarantee that the patient will find them cost-effective. Chiswick, studying nursing homes for the elderly, established that the price elasticity of demand (the large figure reflecting the existence of good alternatives to the institutional setting) was –0.69 to –2.40 (Chiswick, 1976: 304). McCarthy, tracking office-visits to the doctor, discovered a very high sensitivity of –3.07 to –3.26 (McCarthy, 1985: 109). The responsiveness in McCarthy's figures might be due to the interchangeable attributes of a single doctor (perhaps regarded in the market as a perfect competitor with many near substitutes) or to the perceived low urgency of the complaint itself (repeat visits being taken to be an option and not a *sine qua non*). Reasons such as these (as well as different samples and statistical techniques) may explain the discrepancy between McCarthy's results and those of Wedig. It is also possible that McCarthy's respondents faced a higher deductible ceiling than did Wedig's. Price responsiveness becomes greater when the insurer pays less. Even so, McCarthy, Wedig and the other investigators all found a negative sign. When the unit price goes up, the units consumed go down. Charges imposed will depress the quantity demanded.

The long-term experimental investigation conducted (between 1974 and 1982) by the RAND Corporation gives an *ex post* insight into price and response. Approximately 2000 families in six localities were assigned at random to one of 14 different fee-for-service plans. All of the plans offered the same range of cover. Each plan had its own cost-sharing provisions. These ranged from zero to 95 per cent. Each imposed its own annual cap on out-of-pocket contributions. The highest maximum was $1000: price elasticity had no meaning beyond that point. All plans covered almost all core medical and dental services, together with prescription drugs. Participants had to be under 62 years of age at the time of enrolment. The relatively youthful cut-off served to exclude the cohort most vulnerable to multiple chronic conditions. It also screened out those about to qualify for subsidised Medicare (at age 65). Participants were expected to be on middle to low incomes. None had earnings in excess of $25 000 (in 1973 dollars). The RAND Health Insurance Experiment had the attraction that its database was not hypothetical but factual. It built on observed frequencies in preference to what-if questionnaires. What the study found was that the downward-sloping rationing mechanism was alive and well: 'All types of service – physician visits, hospital admissions, prescriptions, dental visits, and mental health service use – fell with cost sharing' (Newhouse and the Insurance Experiment Group, 1993: 338).

Where there was a coinsurance rate of 95 per cent, total spending on medical care was, for an average family, $679. Where medical care was free, the medical expenditures were $982 – almost half as much again. Outpatient costs per enrollee on the free plan were 68 per cent higher than those on the 95 per cent plan. Even hospitalisation proved to be price sensitive: allowing for the coinsurance ceiling of $1000, the distance from top to bottom (from $413 to $536) was about 30 per cent (Newhouse and the Insurance Experiment Group, 1993: 41). The study took care to ensure that the groups assigned to different reimbursement categories were comparable. Based as it was on co-payment categories, it was also able to identify not merely the gross price charged but, more importantly, the net price actually paid by the consumer. The RAND group found that the elasticity of demand in the coinsurance range from 25 per cent to 95 per cent was –0.14 to –0.21. Individuals in the 95 per cent coinsurance plan used only 15 per cent fewer services than individuals in the 25 per cent plan. The price sensitivity was not very great. Not much cost would be contained by increasing the coinsurance rate.

Using different data, Manning and Marquis were able to reach the following conclusion on the responsiveness of demand: 'Gross expenditures are 28% higher with a 25% plan than with no insurance, and the deadweight loss is 12% of the total expenditures' (Manning and Marquis, 1996: 629). Mueller and Monheit, in a (non-experimental) survey of their own, found that enrolling uninsured adults (aged under 65) in a plan with coinsurance not exceeding 10 per cent would increase the probability of dental treatment by 21 per cent. The loss of cover would result in a decrease of from 13 to 18 per cent (Mueller and Monheit, 1988: 70). The RAND results had been that enrollees in the free plan had 34 per cent more dental visits and 46 per cent higher dental expenses than enrollees in the 95 per cent coinsurance plan.

Charges matter: 'We estimate that with no cap on out-of-pocket spending, those with 100 percent coinsurance (that is, no insurance) would spend about half as much as those with free care, those with 50 percent coinsurance would spend about 63 percent as much as those with free care, and those with 25 percent coinsurance would spend about 71 percent as much. Variation in the size of a deductible has effects that are almost as large' (Newhouse and the Insurance Experiment Group, 1993: 82). In the work of Manning and Marquis, Mueller and Monheit, as in the RAND investigation, there is a strong inference that the price of care can effectively damp down the pressure on supply. It need not mean more sicknesses and more deaths: 'The reduced service use under the cost-sharing plans had little or no net adverse effect on health for the average person' (Newhouse and the Insurance Experiment Group, 1993: 339). Free care or 100 per cent coinsurance – rare conditions will be affected and the sick poor will underconsume if the costs are shared but at the end of the day most outcome measures are insensitive to the type of plan.

(b) Price as a deterrent

The empirical evidence confirms that fees restrict quantities. User charges force the consumer to think. They train the shopper in rational choice, focused search and the processing of information. Charges discourage triviality and indulgence. They ensure that wants approximate more closely to needs. Besides that, they are an incentive to keep scarce human capital in good repair. An apple a day keeps the doctor away. Prevention makes less economic sense if the subsequent cure is free. Both in limiting wasteful hypochondria and in discouraging moral hazard, user fees are an investment in market efficiency. They are an Adam Smithian incentive to keep down the discretionary costs of care.

Rationing by price squeezes effective demand into the constraints of supply. The British National Health Service, James Buchanan contends, does not: 'The inconsistency between demand-choice and supply-choice must be eliminated.... The individual, as the ultimate chooser, must be placed in positions where the two parts of what is really a single decision are not arbitrarily separated' (Buchanan, 1965: 16). The consumer in a free-on-demand system will rationally spend up to the point where the marginal benefit has fallen to zero. The voter as a taxpayer wants, however, to call a halt to the overexpansion and the imbalance. Pricing reunites the two sides of a single identity.

Charges encourage self-restraint. They price away the excess demand. Yet it would be a mistake to assume that they are all there is to economics. The truth is that they are a cactus. The juice is sweet but the spines are a reason to proceed with care.

Charges impose administrative costs. The household must schedule its expenditures in the light of its annual co-payment ceiling. The service providers must divert their energies from curing the sick to filling in the forms. The insuring agencies must keep track of who has paid whom when and for what. Where the transactions are numerous and the sums involved are small, the costs might actually exceed the deterrence. Free marketeering is not always cost-effective.

Charges, moreover, can be a threat to trust. Patients might feel more comfortable with a civil servant who is paid by the National Health Service than with a merchant who has a financial interest in their fee. They might go to the expense of extra tests and a second opinion exclusively because the price mechanism alters their perception of the doctor–patient relationship. Their anxiety will be matched by the embarrassment of the professional or hospital. Suppliers do not want to ask for an insurance policy or a credit card before they agree to examine a patient who is asking for their help.

Charges are a problem for the further reason that the signals are opaque. Search given the combinations and permutations will be expensive and incomplete. Lack of overview is a real obstacle to determining the best bargain or assessing the trade-off between bedside manner and quality of attention. One consequence is that monopoly rents will be approved without inspection. This knee-jerk pass-through is hardly what is meant by making sensitive market signals function well. It is, however, almost inevitable in monopolistic competition.

There are so many doctors and so many characteristics that a comprehensive sift is a daunting task.

Charges, again, are regressive and to that extent inequitable. The poor pay a greater percentage of their income than the rich. Cost-containing deterrence is clearly not across the board. An increase in charges can mean that the deprived drop out altogether while the prosperous consume no more and no less than before. Morally speaking, it would be easier to defend a price schedule if the quantity demanded by each market participant were to fall by the same percentage. It is more difficult to approve of a rationing system that prices the least healthy into low-quality care or into no care at all. It is a socially suboptimal demand curve that reduces quantity by bringing about the death of the most vulnerable, the most in need.

It might be more equitable to income-test the charges. Rather than an on-off either-or, it might be more appropriate to proportion payment to subjective sacrifice by means of a tapering scale. Selective discrimination might in the same spirit exempt high-risk users such as old people or subsidise high-risk areas such as neglected housing estates. A low deductible might be preferred to a high one. Even if co-payment above the tipping point is modest, the lower-income groups might still find initial expenditure a burden and a disincentive. Low user charges would price the poor back into care. This, however, would by definition be at the expense of deterrence. The curb on use is the economic justification for the rationing itself.

Charges ration. Insurance, however, reduces the bite. Where it is the third-party that pays, there is no pecuniary reason for the individual to search out the least-expensive supplier or to hold back on consumption. In the limit, where co-payments are zero, or become zero beyond an annual ceiling, or are made zero by a supplement or a rider, there is no downward-sloping demand curve at all. Cost containment through coinsurance is therefore an irrelevance in the natural heartland of insurance, where a medical emergency has occurred and the total sum protected is very large. Cutler points out that, in the United States, '82 percent of the population spends less than $5,000 on health care annually, but they account for only 29 percent of the dollars spent' (Cutler, 1994: 16). Eighteen per cent of the patients account for seventy-one per cent of the expenditure. Cost-sharing deters the majority who do not cost the system very much. It is especially hard on the fifth of Americans without insurance who have to pay for themselves. It does not have much effect on the big users who have already reached their maximum co-shares. At their level of spending, their cost-sharing will probably have run its course. The deterrent of price will have become very small.

Socialism is 'to each according to his need'. Capitalism is 'to each according to his want' – provided that he has bought full-cover insurance in advance. Capitalism, like the National Health Service, may be said to turn loose the demons of open-ended use and allocation by professional ethic. Where the doctors make all the decisions, the importance of price sensitivity becomes secondary and marginal. Insured user-charges and zero price at the point of access allow the individual to shift responsibility on to a collectivity or group. That, however, is just the point. Insurance is an economic tradeable which builds a wall against the price of care. It has no function or justification if it fails to protect fellow pool-members who have experienced a medical catastrophe. Only a very hard-hearted economiser would say that those afflicted by random vicissitudes should be denied the continuing benefits for which they had prepaid their premiums. Insurance exists to supply peace of mind. It is not bought and sold to contain medical cost.

(c) The income elasticity of demand

Rising incomes have an effect on consumption. A service that is regarded as discretionary at a low level of income might be demanded more readily when household incomes go up. The income elasticity to that extent can work against the disincentive of price.

The income elasticity of demand is the percentage change in quantity demanded that is brought about by a percentage change in disposable income. A number less than 1 suggests limited responsiveness: the good is a necessity that even poor people have to obtain. Chiswick found that in the case of nursing homes the elasticity was between 0.60 and 0.90: a 10 per cent increase in median family income was associated with an increase in nursing home use of about 8 per cent (Chiswick, 1976: 307). RAND investigators such as Manning have made the overall income elasticity approximately 0.2. Of the 700 per cent rise in the real cost of health in the United States since the Second World War, only one-fifth in Manning's estimation can be attributed to the increase in real incomes. Richer people value *good health* more highly. That does not mean that they are planning to commit proportionately more resources to *care*.

Other cross-national studies suggest, however, that the income elasticity is greater than 1. Culyer reports a figure of 1.3 for the OECD countries in the period 1975–1984. The totals, interestingly, conceal the microclimates: 2.6 in France and 2.1 in Spain but 0.7 in Austria and only 0.5 in the Netherlands (Culyer, 1989: 22). Culyer warns that his 1.3 might not mean what it says. If, for example, income elasticity is not the same for all social classes and if redistribution of income is taking place, then the pure elasticity will be distorted by the shifts. Also, there can be supply-side constraints: the US has 60 per cent more doctors than the UK but 27 per cent fewer hospital beds. There can be problems of aggregation: different countries have different levels of income. There can be differences in preferences (generalist versus specialist), in practice culture (in-patient versus outpatient), in insurance arrangements (including State sickness benefits), in administrative overheads (free-on-demand versus pay-as-you-go), in the population structure (notably the age pyramid). *Ceteris paribus* cannot be assumed.

As the heterogeneities are not endogenous to pure income elasticity, Culyer warns that the escalating Engel Curve in the data he cites might give an incomplete picture of the relationship between rising quantities and the ability to pay. Even so, the associations and the correlations do have a foundation in fact: 'The wealthier (per capita) a country is, the more it spends on health care per capita and the greater the proportion of its total income spent on health' (Culyer, 1989: 28). Health care is a necessity. It is also a luxury. There is no contradiction. The nation as a whole shows a high income elasticity, greater than 1: as national income rises, proportionately more of that income goes into care. The individual decision-maker, insured against all eventualities, has little or no need to take his income into account: whatever the service costs, someone else will pay. His income elasticity is that of a normal good. It is greater than zero but less than 1.

Culyer's estimate of 1.3 is in line with Newhouse's income-elasticity of 1.15–1.31. These elasticities are substantially greater than 1. Using a sample of 13 developed countries, Newhouse found that over 90 per cent of the variance in per capita medical expenditures could be explained by variation in per capita GDP. Since the increase could be in price or quantity, his calculations began with nominal values. He found that the average earnings of a doctor had increased at the same rate as wages in other lines of work: 'These data suggest that wealthier countries do not have higher relative factor prices for medical care resources, but are indeed devoting more real resources to medical care' (Newhouse, 1977: 117, 120–1). Parkin, McGuire and Yule confirm the general thrust of the result. They derive an income elasticity of 1.18. They also find that the income variable can explain 87 per cent of the variance (Parkin, McGuire and Yule, 1987: 113). These results are similar to those of Newhouse and Culyer.

11.1.2.   Time Price

Waiting times and waiting lists are an alternative to the pecuniary price. They guard the gate but do not require a monetary payment. They are unusual in economics in that the 'payment' made by the consumer is never actually remitted to the producer. As Alan Williams says: 'The time price that is "paid" by the demander is not "received" by the supplier, as it would be with a money price, so that the informational content of the "offer" is less accessible to suppliers' (Williams, 1978: 38–9). The information encoded in time is demand-side only. The supplier's resources are not augmented by the time that the consumer expends. The price 'paid' never enters into the producer's incentive structure. There is no link between the two sides of the circular flow.

No one likes to wait. That does not mean, however, that the inconvenience will be a strong-enough deterrent actually to stop patients from making the meter tick. Real-world investigation is necessary to put flesh on the conjectural *a priori*. Thus Acton found that the time–price elasticity of demand for outpatient visits was –0.14 (Acton, 1975: 607). Mueller and Monheit arrived at the same figure for dental care. At –0.14, the time–price elasticity (using travel time weighted by hourly wage as the measure of cost) was only slightly less than the money-price elasticity of –0.18 (Mueller and Monheit, 1988: 68). Coffey, concentrating on 960 low-income women, not all of them with jobs outside the home, found that the demand was restricted by time price but not very much: 'The effect is small: a 10 per increase in the time required to obtain care leads to about a 1 per cent decline in the probability of seeking care' (Coffey, 1983: 422).

Gravelle, Dusheiko and Sutton, studying the single procedure of cataract removal, found that elective (non-emergency) admissions in the National Health Service were a function of distance. The travel–time elasticity was –0.35. An increase in distance of 10 per cent reduced the hospital admissions demanded by –3.5 per cent. With respect to waiting times, the figure was –0.25 (Gravelle, Dusheiko and Sutton, 2001: 446). The figure of –0.25 is close to the range of –0.24 to –0.33 that was observed by Martin and Smith. The elasticity is low. It suggests there may have to be a long-run increase in capacity in order to satisfy a demand that refuses to go away: 'Substantial extra NHS resources may be needed to reduce waiting times' (Martin and Smith, 1999: 155, 160). The patient made no financial payment at the point of consumption. The fundholding practice responded differently when it allocated its referrals through the internal market. Since the practice had to pay, its incentive was the price, not the waits. The patients were different.

Even 'free' care is not free. Inconvenience and delay make the patient's schedule slope down. Allowance must be made for different types of care, number of visits required to complete a treatment regimen, different degrees of urgency and different income groups. Even so, there is considerable agreement that time prices can damp down the pressure of excess demand. They make markets clear in a manner which some regard as more equitable than the barrier of price.

Especially where it is felt that unequal incomes build unfairness into price, the willingness to wait at least alters the order in which the sick will be seen. The unemployed and the retired have little money but abundant time. For them the opportunity cost of having physically to queue is low. The men and women at the top, rewarded by results and not on a salary, are in a different position. For them, because time is money, and because health insurance enables them to jump the queue, a monetary *quid pro quo* would be the more convenient way of assuring their priority. Able to pay in a parallel market, the top executive does not need to weigh the frustration of a list against the diswelfare of dispensing altogether with the service. People on piecework will have no comparable insurance against having to wait.

Allocation by time is not, of course, the same as cost containment by time. For the delay to trim back the quantity, some applicants must not simply go private but rather abandon their search for good. Rationing by delay will only reduce the pressure on aggregate health care inputs when the discounted future marginal utility is diminishing so rapidly that the expected wait radically reduces the attractiveness of going on the list: 'If one wishes to return home today, a plane reservation today is worth a great deal more than a reservation tomorrow.... A person will join a waiting list if the present value of the good when delivered exceeds the cost of joining the queue' (Lindsay and Feigenbaum, 1984: 406).

A delay clears the market not just by rescheduling the treatments but by making the good or service subjectively less valuable to the patient. Besides that, a delay leads to attrition and natural wastage. Some people recover on their own, or move away, or even die. The effect can be appreciable. The wait-elasticity of joining a waiting list for a (non-emergency) hospital bed in the UK was found by Lindsay and Feigenbaum to be –0.55 to –0.64 for conditions like epilepsy or goitre which can be treated through drug or outpatient alternatives. It was from –0.65 to –0.70 for conditions like cataract and hernia for which there was no close substitute for inpatient care. No condition in their study was likely to become significantly worse if treatment was postponed. The preference revealed was exclusively the product of marginal discouragement when consumers felt they had waited long enough.

The poor in work are difficult to model. On the one hand, because their incomes are low, one could argue that the opportunity cost of spending deadweight time in doctors' waiting-rooms is comparatively low as well. On the other hand, because the marginal utility of low incomes is high, it is possible to say that the poor are precisely the people who can least afford to hold idle stocks of non-performing time. In the long-run, rising productivity and growing remuneration will mean that the less well-off will themselves find it ever more costly to take time off work. Higher incomes mean more expensive waits. Even in the short-run, however, there is no reason to think that the poor will necessarily prefer the queue to the price. In many countries the poor have the right to means-tested medical reimbursement. This subsidy allows them free access to the market sector. It is the independent and not the disadvantaged who have to pay.

Consumers often complain that the waits are too long. Impatient, anxious, sometimes in pain, they find it frustrating when their hernia repair or their precautionary scan is repeatedly put off. As sympathetic as one must be to their spoiled quality of life, still they have only limited grounds for complaint. If they have agreed to a system that rations by time and not by price, they cannot realistically insist that the waits should simultaneously be reduced to zero. Deterrence is needed where resources are not infinite. All that the members of the community can say is that the waits are excessive relative to what they were told they could expect.

One way of recognising an excessive wait might be in terms of the number of patients who opt out for the fast track instead. The fact that a large number of clients are seen to pay (or, if they have already subscribed to the allocation-by-wait system, to pay twice) is a signal that some customers at least are dissatisfied with the delay. If the cost is affordable and people are in a rush, it is not inevitably a shortcoming of rationing by time that patients have the safety valve of a market purchase that yields them greater satisfaction in their own estimation. It is, on the contrary, a good selling-point of the dual system that they have the opportunity to make the choice. Yet the fact that some passengers go by taxi when some busdrivers are down with flu does not mean that no wait can ever be called an excessive one. An excessive wait in the dual system may be defined as an overall groundswell of across-the-board discontentment. It is a wait where the numbers who desert have gone beyond the unrepresentative fringe that a tolerant society would regard as respect for minorities and their rights.

Another definition would be that an excessive wait is a wait that is regarded as unacceptable by the medical professionals. The doctor knows best. Sustained discomfort, deterioration of function, threat of contagion, risk of death are all variables that the doctors might take into consideration in ranking their patients and time-pricing their conditions. Where care is allocated by waits, it will often be professionals' judgment, *triage* by priorities and the administrators' budget that determine how many treatments are actually supplied. What the consumers want need not be what the consumers get. Supply-side paternalism regularly limits the overuse of the service even where there is no money price.

Society itself might want to register its view. Consensus might prefer that some patients and some conditions should be treated first. Where nice guys finish last and we as a We feel aggrieved, the wait is socially an excessive one even if the medical practitioners have a professional code which says that the wait in question is fine and good. A growth-minded community might say that an excessive wait is a delay that causes a greater loss of output to the community than would the marginal cost of treatment that returns the afflicted most rapidly to work. The interpretation focuses on human capital and the improvement in living-standards. A utility-maximising community might in contrast define the optimal wait in terms of the felt well-being of the geriatric and the chronically ill. Such an assessment would focus on quality of life, apprehension and inconvenience, rather than on productivity alone. There is no guarantee that it will contain the cost. There is no reason why it should.

11.2. PURCHASE AND PROVISION

Insurance, private or State, is countervailing power. The fund is obliged by the very nature of its limited resources to press for constrained utilisation and, hopefully, satisfactory health while discouraging the doctors and the hospitals from inflating the quantities and padding the prices. The individual does not have the time or expertise to recognise when his trust is misplaced. The insurer whom he pays to protect his health fills the market gap.

11.2.1. Information

The insuring agency has overview sufficient to identify the median standard. It is familiar with clinical studies of effectiveness and economic thinking on efficiency. It can advise the patient on the choice of doctor, hospital and treatment. It can provide free counselling on the relative cost, quality and riskiness of the medical alternatives. It has a private and personal incentive to keep the cost down. Assuming that the doctors and the hospitals have an incentive of their own to press for more and more, the net result might be that the biases will cancel out.

In some cases the insurer will offer advice but not specify a way forward. In other cases the insurer will proactively supply the care itself (the health maintenance organisation, the National Health Service) or will direct the patient to a preferred provider which it believes to be value for money. In coming to its decision it will make use of evidence-based evaluations, league tables, utilisation reviews and even second opinions for an estimation of the relevant success-indicators.

Thus, looking at doctors, the insurer will familiarise itself with differences in prescription patterns (including the use of tranquillisers, painkillers and generics) and in referral rates to consultants and clinics. In the case of hospitals, it will profile the doctor–patient ratio, average cost per standardised case, average length of inpatient stay. Where costs are out of step, unique circumstances such as an abnormally elderly local population must be recorded in extenuation. A hospital should be given the chance to say that its high cost per bed is not misallocation and slack but a welcome indication of its exceptional efficiency in reducing convalescent stays and maximising surgical turn-round.

Monitoring seems in practice to have had the desired effect. Feldstein, Wickizer and Wheeler found that utilisation review had reduced hospital admissions (per 1000 insured persons) by 12.3 per cent, hospital inpatient days (per 1000 insured persons) by 8.0 per cent, total hospital spending (per insured person) by 11.9 per cent and total medical spending (per insured person) by 8.3 per cent. At a discount rate of 5 per cent, this meant that a company plan covering 1000 employees would typically make a net saving of $633 000 over a five-year period (Feldstein, Wickizer and Wheeler, 1988: 1314). The effect the authors documented was one-shot. It is not clear if utilisation review would be as successful in reducing or limiting the rise in costs over time. Nor does the study address the possible effects on the enrollees' health.

Utilisation review must be complemented by medical audit lest poor workmanship be mistaken for value for money. Variance in survival rates per surgeon could be an indication of inexperience, incompetence or exhaustion. Sustained cross-infection might suggest that a particular hospital is economising on postoperative hygiene. Medical statistics such as these educate by means of comparison. League tables can shame underachievers into improving their performance. The fact that insurers make use of the success rates to identify over-treatment and over-compensation is an incentive for preferred providers, protecting their eligibility, to cleave to the mean and stick to the median. Doctors, it should be said, are in two minds about the publicity. While most are opposed to ineptitude and waste, many also feel that standard practice inhibits their clinical discretion to do the best for their own unique patient. Clinical trials and outcomes research mean that professional convergence itself must move with the times. Doctors will express the fear that the unthinking acceptance of the tried-and-tested is a vote against creative deviance that might in the long-run deliver a better product. Conservatism, however, pays the rent. Being excluded from the insurers' reimbursement is almost as bad for their economic survival as being struck off the medical register.

Data-collection clarifies what the peers are doing. Yet it also imposes an administrative cost. Duplicated collection imposes multiple burdens. Completeness and complexity mean additional overheads. It costs time and money to distinguish between marginal and average cost, or to separate out a ward with excess capacity from one that is always full, or to track patients' recovery in order to pick up relapses or readmissions should the original treatment happen later to fail.

Cost-effectiveness and cost-benefit analysis complement the medical evidence. They too harness rational choice to keep total cost in check. At the microeconomic level, new technologies are not introduced until it has been shown that they are worth the opportunity cost. Studies in that way not only contribute to cost containment but reveal why health care should be contained at all: because it is not paying its way. Macroeconomically, cross-country comparisons document expenditure shares, rates of growth and illness/death payoffs in a range of delivery systems. International comparisons do not prove that one system is better than another: the differences in data-sets, culture and material circumstances are often too great. They are, however, a shadow on the wall that gives an indication of what can and cannot be done.

It is easy to say that information will reduce the variance and that the convergence will mean a saving. Unfortunately for the cost-containers, the result might be a rise. In a paper entitled 'Is technological change in medicine worth it?', Cutler and McClellan reported that greater longevity, better quality of life, a reduction in time off work more than repaid the extra money spent on the new treatment scenarios: 'Technology often leads to more spending, but outcomes improve by even more' (Cutler and McClellan, 2001: 23). The authors conducted a cost-benefit study of medical advances in five common conditions: heart attacks, low birth weight infants, depression, cataracts and breast cancer. Except in the case of breast cancer (where the costs were equal to the benefits) they found that the gains far exceeded the expense. In the case of low birth weight infants, the present value of extra life-years to extra cost was in the ratio of $240000 : $40000, or 6 : 1 (Cutler and McClellan, 2001: 20).

Five conditions do not add up to medical spending as a whole (and other societal changes such as reduction in smoking should also be taken into account) but they are much more than a finger in the wind: 'The benefits from lower infant mortality and better treatment of heart attacks have been sufficiently great that they alone are about equal to the entire cost increase for medical care over time' (Cutler and McClellan, 2001: 12). Given a choice between spending more money on medical technology and spending more money on other investment goods in the choice set, the society should go for health. Why should its share in the GDP not rise?

Cutler and Richardson had shown the same. From 1970 to 1990 in the United States, the present value of lifetime health capital for a newborn child (discounting at 3 per cent) increased by $95 000. For the over-65s, who now live so much longer due to better treatment of cardiovascular and other kinds of later-life disease, the rise was greater, at $169 000. Yet the added cost of medical care was only $19 000 for infants and $34 000 for the elderly. The worth exceeded the cost: 'The increase in health capital is greater than the increase in medical spending; thus, the return to medical care could be very high' (Cutler and Richardson, 1998: 99).

11.2.2. Remuneration

Payment that is open-ended is a blank cheque. Providers can inflate the quantity or raise the price. In either way or through exploiting both loopholes at once, they can seek to maximise their returns. Where cost pass-through is permissive, they can push up their revenue. It is the task of the paying agencies to ensure that they do not shelter behind the medical mystique or abuse the trust of the public.

With respect to quantity, the paying agency might aim to limit the size of the package through preadmission certification for all but emergency inpatient stays. It might refuse its approval for a more expensive procedure if it felt that less costly (outpatient) management would meet the same clinical need. It might ask to see the X-rays and the reports before it accepted any liability. It might insist on a second opinion from its own doctor or its nurse-auxiliary in order to ensure that its budget was not being abused.

The patient once admitted, the purchasing agency might call for itemised billing. It might demand not only that medical attention, hotel facilities and pharmaceuticals be invoiced separately but that each test in a sequence be costed individually and that abnormal inputs be justified in words. In hospital, the insurer might keep the patient under constant and concurrent review to ensure that the next step is really the cost-effective one. Out of hospital, the insurer might check all the paperwork carefully to be certain that nothing had been supplied which had not been agreed. Administration, as always, entails expense. The policing overhead must be set against the cost-saving that results. There is no guarantee that good money thrown after bad will really be cost-effective. Yet a small number of large bills do, conveniently, account for the bulk of all expense. The agency might want to be selective in order to be economic. It might want to concentrate its attention on the greatest burdens and to spot-check the others through random sampling.

With respect to price, the insurers might substitute prospective for retrospective payment. Where the payment is not fixed in advance, the supplier has no financial incentive to be cost-efficient. Retrospective billing means that each doctor or hospital, paid with a blank cheque, will have no reason to pare the fees and limit the mark-ups. Prospective payment alters the nature of the game. Predetermined reimbursement is experience-rated and based on the average. The preannounced figure is not just a guideline ('usual, customary and reasonable') but a flat fee that is not open to further negotiation. The agreed-upon amount is the same whether the supplier makes a profit or a loss. Unexpected complications can occur and the costs can overrun. Where they do, the extra inputs or unanticipated surgery will be entirely at the charge of the supplier. The fixed rate, agreed in advance, shifts the burden of uncertainty not just from the patient to the insurer but then from the insurer to the provider. Prepublished payment in that way forces the supply-side and not just the demand-side to limit its extravagance. As Culyer writes: 'Any system that uses open-ended retrospective reimbursement for hospitals is likely to see a higher overall level of expenditure per capita and possibly a faster rate of health care cost inflation. Almost any form of prospective payment is likely to limit these tendencies by relating rewards to planned workload and encouraging awareness of cost per case' (Culyer, 1989: 29).

The evidence confirms the conjecture. Rosko and Broyles compared prospective with retrospective payment in 160 American hospitals. The cost per admission in the former case was 14.1 per cent lower than it was in the latter (Rosko and Broyles, 1987: 97–8). Yet cost per admission is not the same as total cost. Hospitals that had agreed prepayment determined by diagnostic-related group had an incentive to accelerate the admissions in order to maximise the sum of their fees. The day-case for haemorrhoids, hernia and abortion is only cheaper than the long-stay alternative where the income is not built up again through an increase in the day-cases seen. Rosko and Broyles found that the hospitals that were remunerated prospectively admitted 11.7 per cent more cases than those that were remunerated retrospectively. Where cost per admission goes down by 14.1 per cent but number of admissions goes up by 11.7 per cent, the cost containment is only 2.4 per cent. It is less than 14.1 per cent but it is a saving nonetheless.

Prospective payment will often simplify the administrative burden by classifying patients into diagnostic-related groups (DRGs). Each group is designed in such a way as to be 'clinically coherent'. Medicare in the United States introduced the system in 1983. It now encodes approximately 13 000 diagnoses and 5000 procedures into approximately 490 inpatient categories. The ten highest-volume Medicare DRGs represent about 30 per cent of total Medicare patients. DRG 127, Heart Failure and Shock, heads the list at 5.99 per cent of volume. Outpatient care is reimbursed according to a separate schedule of prospective payments. There are approximately 660 different ambulatory classifications on the list.

The logic of prospective payment based on the DRG is that the insurer has no need to inquire into the actual cost of the component services or of the bundle aggregate. It simply reimburses the supplier at the flat rate that was agreed upon for the Group. Economically substandard providers will make a loss per case unless and until they cut their costs. Economically efficient providers will be allowed to retain the surplus. Such discretion within the box is an incentive not to waste resources or to push up the cost of care. The maximum fee is also the minimum. All the provider can do to make money is to prune the cost.

A few big appetites can bankrupt the buffet. Where there is little dispersion in the severity of each complaint, no great threat may be expected from supernormal demands. Where there are high-cost risks, however, and where they can be spotted in advance, the provider paid prospectively will have an economic incentive to refuse the chronic cases that cost more than the norm. Prospective payment can starve out the most in-need. It keeps down the costs to turn away the supernormal pathologies. Yet it is not a good way to help the sick.

The political solution is for the State to prohibit such exclusion. Here the law would demand that savings made on the less complicated cases be used to cross-subsidise the more severe, more expensive ones. A more economic solution would be for the insuring agency (reinsured where appropriate by the State) to offer a special 'outlier' payment to providers which would otherwise have had to sponsor the exceptional drains on their own. There are very long stays, repeated blood transfusions, abnormally expensive drugs which could prove ruinous to a hospital that does not want the patient to die. These would qualify a hospital for prospective payment at a higher rate. So might context-driven heterogeneities such as higher than average wages, a disproportionate share of the financially indigent, involvement as a teaching centre, outreach medicine in isolated villages. The average DRG weight for the whole of a hospital's Medicare business is known as its casemix index. This index allows the severity of patient population to be compared between hospitals. Casemix may be used to assign an above-average entitlement to a hospital that, because of atypical patients or an atypical locality, is incurring legitimate expenses in excess of the rest. A large nation can encompass a multiplicity of variations. It would be inappropriate rigidly to impose a national norm when the whole is in truth a matrix of sub-markets.

The pragmatic adjustment may kick in at a low level of overhang. More commonly, the supplement will cover above-average costs only after a threshold of 10 per cent or more has been reached. This minimum is analogous to the deductible in a private contract. It forces the supplier to absorb some at least of the marginal burden. All 'outlier' invoices will have to be carefully scrutinised. It must be shown that it really is the intricacy of the bypass with haemophilia or the skyrocketing rents in Manhattan, not greed-driven quantity explosion, unwarranted practice variation or the internal inefficiency of thoroughly confused management, that is giving rise to the allowance. Defend itself as it might, the knowledge that the wall is also a door is an invitation to moral hazard. In the limit the earmarked extras might subvert altogether the end of cost containment. Too many exceptions can spell the end of the policy.

As with all fixed fee systems, prospective payment can potentially lead to under-treatment. Money can be saved by economising on the seniority or numbers of medical staff, lengthening the waiting times, simplifying the menus, reducing the battery of tests and prescriptions, making the inpatient stays dangerously brief. The relationship between the inputs and the outcomes is seldom clear-cut. Even so, the temptation to omit the fail-safes and the double checks is not reassuring to the patient who expects the clinical optimum and does not want a make-do. In the DRG system the providers and their professional bodies are seen continually to be pressing for the reimbursement targets to be raised. Patient confidence is undermined by so undignified a demonstration of avarice. The insurers' quality control and the prospect of repeat business are nonetheless reasons for thinking that abuse will not be widespread.

DRG might weed out over-treatment. Interestingly, there are several ways in which cost inflation would be the result instead. One is 'DRG creep', where a patient with several complaints is automatically put into the higher category that would maximise the hospital's income. Another is supplements and top-ups. While it is in line with respect for persons to allow differentiated patients to fine-tune their endowments, it nonetheless feeds cost inflation where the DRG is not given the final say.

DRG can increase total cost in another way as well. It may lead to faster throughput accompanied by more frequent surgery. Patients in operating theatres cost more than patients in beds. The cost per case might fall but the number of cases might escalate. The solution might be to impose volume controls. Ceilings to police ceilings make the system more unwieldy. There is a limit, moreover, beyond which the patients cannot be disappointed.

11.2.3.   Selective Incentives

Purchasing agencies are in a position to issue guidelines and to back them up with financial rewards. Hospitalisation will not be reimbursed where there is a domiciliary alternative. All tests must be performed in advance of admission. Surgery must occur within the first 24 hours of inpatient stay. Home visits must be restricted in favour of office turnover. Guidelines such as these force doctors who want to be paid to select the less-expensive option. There is no guarantee that this will be the outcome that would have been ground out either by medical efficacy or consumer's sovereignty. Minor surgery performed by a general practitioner supported by a local anaesthetic is an illustration of an intervention that many patients would prefer to have done with the backup and division of labour of a hospital. Cost containment is a valuable objective. It is not, however, the only test that a health care system is functioning well.

Incentives are a familiar means of encouraging doctors to perform certain tasks and phase out others. Additional payments have at times been offered to doctors who perform full annual check-ups, vaccinations, mammograms or cervical screening; who register the hard-to-reach in exchange for a finder's-fee capitation; who invest in preventive medicine through immunisation or the counselling of the obese; who visit the over-75s in their home to ensure that they are well; who attend refresher courses and volunteer for relicensing tests; who supervise trainee staff and are active in community care schemes; who provide out-of-hours services or form group practices with economies of scale. Bonuses for good patient feedback can encourage the doctors to invest in courtesy and attentiveness. Bonuses for antenatal care can reduce the long-term cost of low birth weight babies. Bonuses for the follow-up of prescription anti-depressants can cut the incidence of attempted suicide. Bonuses for below-average complications or above-average recoveries can stimulate the surgeons and the hospitals to race their counterparts for the prize. They would use only that technology which enabled them to perform.

These incentives have both clinical and economic objectives. For both reasons they have a tendency to keep health care cost affordable. As Cutler points out, the change in the rules would bring about a change in the game: 'Providers would think differently under such a system. If there were additional income to be earned by making sure cholesterol tests were performed, doctors would figure out how to increase testing' (Cutler, 2004: 101). They would send out reminders. They would programme their computers. They would trade at convenient times. The motive would be money but the endstate would be health. Adam Smith's herring men, subsidised by the State, set themselves the objective of 'catching, not the fish, but the bounty' (Smith, 1961 [1776]: II, 25). It was the bounty and not the fish that guided their endeavours. More fish and more boats were nonetheless the socially desirable outcome of the visible hand that refocused the incitement to interest.

Some incentives are targeted not at the supplier but at the patient. An insurer might, for example, promise to suspend the deductibles and the coinsurance (*de facto* passing on a share in the economies jointly made) if the patient agrees to same day surgery. It might quote a lower premium for an applicant who neither drinks nor drives (thereby providing a good reason for the rational healthholder to invest in his own health capital). An insurer might deny reimbursement to a patient who has not been referred via general practice (the family doctor in that way providing an initial assessment of underlying need). It might restrict the choice of supplier (a narrower panel making it easier for the insurer to monitor the treatments). Aware that prevention is cheaper than subsequent cure, the insurer might offer discounts on occupational plans where the employer sponsors gym memberships and runs stress management sessions. Aware that early detection is cheaper than the asymptomatic time bomb, the insurer out of self- interest might make annual check-ups compulsory and demand that all diabetics present for blood-sugar monitoring.

Business is business. Cost containment can be the result. Adam Smith said that bureaucrats on a salary were seldom known for their cost-conscious good husbandry: 'Public services are never better performed than when their reward comes only in consequence of their being performed, and is proportioned to the diligence employed in performing them' (Smith, 1961 [1776]: II, 241). Ultimately, as Cutler says, money talks: 'The medical system works the way the incentives steer it. Rather than fight the system or plead for it to be otherwise, we should instead line the incentives up right so the system gives us what we want' (Cutler, 2004: 46).

It is not very easy. Practitioners who get a bonus when cholesterol goes down will seek to register responsible patients who will take their drugs. Surgeons who are paid extra for above-average survivals will operate only on the healthiest specimens. The incentives can turn adverse. They can turn malign: 'These responses harm the system. It is the people who do not take good care of themselves or who are more difficult surgical candidates whom it is important to treat' (Cutler, 2004: 109). Payment systems that drive out the sick are no better than insurance plans that cream-skim the healthy. Since the poor are less healthy than the rich, the social gap could be widened and not narrowed by the bonuses. Cutler suggests, however, that the solution is to be found in risk-adjustment: 'The key is to give more credit to outcome improvements among harder-to-manage groups…. If the relative benchmarks are set correctly, insurers will not want to take the rich over the poor. Indeed, the poor could even be prized enrollees' (Cutler, 2004: 109). Money talks. It is the task of the paying agencies to design incentive structures that, eschewing adversarial confrontations, enlist self-interest in the service of both equity and efficiency at once.

11.2.4. Coordination

The paying partner might take the view that an integrated network is better placed to keep costs down than is a multiplicity of competitors. One inference might be that the purchaser and the provider functions should merge. The health maintenance organisation (HMO) and the National Health Service are illustrations of such a unification of finance with management. A multiplicity of agencies means that there is no concentration and no planning. Vertical integration means that the organisation that delivers the treatment is the organisation that insures and pays. That is why it is has a financial incentive to practise preventive medicine and to do without expensive surgery. Piecework fees paid to independent contractors have the opposite effect.

Manning in the United States compared a sample of HMO members with a control group receiving treatment under fee for service. He found that the patients covered by the prepaid plan experienced more well-child and gynaecological examinations but 40 per cent fewer hospital admissions and hospital days (Manning, Leibowitz, Goldberg, Rogers and Newhouse, 1984: 1508). Manning and his colleagues were aware that selection and self-selection could possibly have accounted for the lower cost per patient in the prepaid plan. They found, however, that the health-related characteristics (age, gender, percentage of women in the childbearing years) of the sample enrollees and of the control group were not significantly different. The reason for the cost-saving (and for an institutionalised awareness that standards of quality had to be maintained) had therefore to be rivalry between alternative providers. No business wants to lose its reputation or its customers. It is fair to say, however, that the HMOs do not need to cut their fees very far below the commercial carriers to obtain business. Only a small difference is all that is required.

The HMO can be large enough to plan. This would especially be the case where the HMO had its own delivery centres and did not contract out at all. The National Health Service is, however, the better illustration of a powerful near-monopoly that has enviable control over its own costs. The fact that there is a single payment arm makes clear to the single provision arm that the budget is fixed until the politicians readjust the ceilings. A single supplier with a single data-set makes utilisation review and internal comparison that much easier

(Miller and Luft, 2002). Disaggregated data and internal billing can provide a good map of the flow of funds.

A unified network with a single computer base makes the tracking of discharge and readmission more transparent. Follow-up data becomes available that in a multisupplier environment might have been lost into parallel files, all confidential. In-house accounting means that the relationship between inputs and outcomes can be estimated more easily. Information allows management to identify departments that are above-average in cost or below-average in medical effectiveness. It ensures that an allowance can be made for casemix, location or other salient circumstances. Only if they are in a position to make comparisons can the managers issue guidelines (say, to refer out-of-region to reduce a wait) or impose sanctions (in terms of salary, promotion, budget, bonuses). The management of a National Health Service can close uneconomic hospitals. It can transfer long-stay patients from wards to sheltered housing. It can manage the build-up or run-down of the nation's bedstock without the fear that the critical mass of beds will lie outside the national plan. It can liaise with social workers in order to provide a complete welfare package that prevents a relapse due to malnutrition or hypothermia. In ways such as these a single structure – a national *system* – can keep the costs down: 'Centralized control of health care budgets seems to result in lower spending levels than otherwise would be expected' (Culyer, 1989: 28).

A National Health Service can stimulate cooperation between public sector institutions. They can circulate over-ordered drugs that would otherwise go out of date. They can share expensive capital in order to minimise under-employment of plant and reap economies of size. They can offer joint contracts in order to keep specialised skills fresh through continuous exercise. Private hospitals can form a consortium but still their status as rivals is a disincentive to share. State hospitals are more likely to work together to contain cost: their budget does not depend on the paying business they can snatch from one another. The exception would be where the State imposes global budgeting and forces even State hospitals to compete.

The State can bargain as a single buyer for quantity discounts from pharmaceutical majors. It can negotiate with the unions for productivity-based pay. Countervailing power keeps the average costs down. The integrated web is not, however, the only possibility. A State system can also institute an internal market between publicly-owned institutions. Such competition is intended to facilitate choice and to make the costings keen. It does so without privatisation or the profit-maximising motive which many find incompatible with the ethos of care.

In terms of microeconomics, a single-payer system can get the unit costs down. In terms of macroeconomics, centralisation has the great advantage that it can impose cash limits. In the NHS as in the HMO and in Medicare, the total medical budget would not be demand-led but capped: 'The government would collect revenues dedicated for health care, and would pay for the care that people received. To ensure the system was affordable over time, the government would restrict the increase in medical costs to no more than the increase in national income – roughly equivalent to the increase in tax revenues' (Cutler, 2004: 62). Such a system incorporates an acknowledgement that much of uncapped care is not cost-effective. The single payer proclaims what services are to be provided and what remuneration can be claimed. It draws a line. In doing so, it frees up surplus resources for alternative uses that are better able to justify the inputs.

Yet there are pressures that work in the opposite direction. One is that the single payer might get the sums wrong. A ceiling that blocks out cost-effective benefits is a false economy. There is, besides that, the familiar lobbying from patients, doctors and other interest groups that politicises the budget. Consumer-citizens might want to pay more for more: 'If so, a binding cost ceiling might well impose a welfare loss, by preventing medical care consumers and providers from making mutually advantageous exchanges' (Newhouse, 1992: 19). Once private insurance has been suppressed, the result is a new source of pressure on the State. The vote motive can be a reason not to limit public spending but rather to increase it. The outcome can be total costs that rise and do not fall.

11.3. STATE INTERVENTION

Laws can shape markets. Alcohol, cigarettes, and noxious emissions are taxed. Positive externalities like medical research are subsidised. Prescription drugs are restricted. Recreational opiates are banned. Public goods are supplied. The beneficial spillovers, it is believed, outweigh the interference with the freedom of choice. A dying patient denied a kidney transplant because a market in human organs is against the law might not agree. Like the classic free marketeers from Mill to Friedman, he might say that the willing seller and the desperate patient are the better judge of what makes them feel better off.

Regulations to influence the price and quantity, like intervention to subsidise and ban, come under the same heading of the greater public good. It is sometimes argued that laws should be relied upon to contain costs. The first part of this section is about State controls because the market has failed to perform. The second part is about liberalisation and deregulation because market decentralisation has not been allowed to try.

11.3.1. Controls

Policies are needed to limit the polluting externality of the rising cost of care. One option is a regulatory board to fix the fees. Flexible prices are attractive because they respond to supply and demand. They identify local shortages. They set in motion the market-clearing equilibration. In the case of health care, however, demand tends always to outstrip supply. The argument for bill-capping and administered charges stems from the perception that quantity demanded and quantity supplied will never be the same. Never-satisfied demand cannot be encompassed within the textbook account of prices that gravitate and settle into rest.

The guideline proclaimed need not be a single fixed price. A formula like 'consumer price index minus x per cent' has the attraction that it forces suppliers to search out productivity-enhancing expedients that would combine profit-seeking with affordable care. In some cases it will not even be compulsory. Depending on the influence of the government, a 'guiding light' or statement of preference might be enough.

Yet there is a problem. A guideline can become a minimum and a target, not just a maximum beyond which the economy cannot go. Acting both as a ceiling and a floor, such a fixed price could breed allocative inefficiency due to the artificial narrowing of the spread. The non-competitive rate could be higher than the charge that the less-expensive suppliers would have made. In such circumstances the control would itself be inflationary. Besides that, cost is made up of quantity as well as price. Statutory controls imposed on the nominal magnitude can be circumvented through a compensating expansion of the real variable. Marginal tests and unneeded interventions will certainly respond to a reduction in price: that is the logic of supplier-induced demand. Looking on the bright side, Nguyen and Derrick, as was reported in chapter 3, found that the expansion was not in fact enough to cancel out the gains: 'With an expected 40 percent behavioral response for losing practices, physician price control can still bring about 60 cents for every dollar fee reduction' (Nguyen and Derrick, 1997: 294). Other studies, less optimistic, have found that the volume response was likely to be nearer to 100 per cent. Much seems to depend on whether the income incentive outweighs the substitution (price) effect; on the trigger point at which medical specialities will be shifted away from fee-regulated patients; on the extent to which the doctors are flexible enough to alter their standard practice; and on the reaction threshold at which even conservatives rethink their historic heuristics. These are empirical rather than theoretical issues. The answer will depend on time and place.

Price-fixing in the service sector is handicapped by the fact that, while one billet of steel is much like another, consultations, hospitals and operations are less standard and less homogeneous. Complexity makes it difficult to know what to decree. Also, medical technology is changing rapidly. Schedules tend to become out of date when new techniques come on to the market. There is in addition the costliness that results from non-price competition and low-return differentiation. Higher nurse–patient ratios can be advertised as a quality indicator. The service and the advertising of the service put up the cost. There is no evidence that the patient gets better more quickly as a result.

Price-fixing imposes an overhead cost to the extent that an administrative staff is required to police the limits. Invoices must be inspected. Quality must be monitored. Classification will invite avoidance: witness the DRG 'creep', considered before. Unregulated substitutes might expand into the vacuum. Where prices are capped in State hospitals but private hospitals can charge what they please, patients might pay more for more by seeking treatment in the commercial sector. Payments to private suppliers boost the total funds changing hands (the magnitude depends on the elasticity of demand) even if they reduce the burden on the State. There is no feasible way to plug all the loopholes and cover all the alternatives. If suppliers and demanders want to conclude mutually beneficial contracts at their own expense, it will be very difficult for the State to prohibit the add-ons. Named limits are difficult to enforce.

Since different hospitals face different unions, use different technologies and are differently placed in terms of their attractiveness to staff, the State could fix the rate per procedure on an institution-by-institution basis. The difficulty with a cost-based rule is that firms then have no incentive to reduce the cost: the markup allowed will always be the same. Another way of approaching the task would be to group hospitals by comparable characteristics (size, range of services, mode of ownership) and to set common prices for the pool as a whole. Here the problem will be to decide if rates should be geared to the least efficient (in which case the intramarginal will reap a windfall) or to the most efficient (in which case the great bulk might go out of business) or to the average (in which case the more efficient will not be under pressure to improve their performance).

A complement to specifying the price of final services will be to fix the cost of intermediate inputs. A prices and incomes policy can act on the factor incomes. Salaries of doctors and nurses can be regimented. Prices of drugs and equipment can be made subject to norms. To be successful, the input-price policy would have to be permanent: a short-term freeze will dent but will not deflect a long-term trend. Politically, the market-making may take a toll: the electorate will not warm to the news that young people are turning away from careers in health because the State is keeping remuneration below its competitive bid. The policy can be evaded. Consider what happens when a promotion is offered in place of a pay rise or a high-cost local hospital threatens to close down unless the community pays it a subsidy. The policy can be inequitable. Unless the low paid are given priority, the cleaners and the porters will find it difficult to improve their conditions of life. The policy can be subverted by special pleading. Vested interest has influence, power and name recognition. It is rumoured that in some countries incumbent rent-seekers even pay bribes. Regulators can be as ill informed and as money-minded as the rest of their fellow citizens. Public choice is not the same as public interest.

Prices of outputs and inputs can be regulated. No price controls are, however, likely to limit the spend where they are not accompanied by restrictions on quantity to keep the usage down. Otherwise the number of services could expand as soon as the price per service is frozen. Cost will not remain within the confines set by the State. That is why final output must be restricted or the supply of inputs braked. Control of inputs is often the best means for putting a lid on consumption. Even so, a word of caution is required. Price controls, whether of outputs or of inputs, can be made operative the moment they are promulgated. Quantity controls, operating through inputs, may have a longer fuse. Controls on the expansion of fixed inputs only take effect once additional care can no longer be squeezed from existing plant. Controls on variable costs operate more quickly as they do not wait upon the elimination of excess capacity. The more remote the threshold, the smaller the financial impact. The more immediate the margin, however, the easier it will be for the State planners to limit supply in order to keep down the cost.

Thus, in the case of medical personnel, long training periods might be required, foreign medical graduates kept out and the number of recognised medical schools kept down. Subsidies and training-grants might be cut back. Patients will complain of longer waits and lightning consultations but that is the price they must pay. More serious will be the concentration of the limited numbers of doctors in high-benefit areas, both occupational (surgery rather than general practice) and geographical (exclusive suburbs rather than deprived hilltops, jungles and deserts). The imbalance can be corrected by differential capitations, subsidised housing, compulsory posting and – for the patients – compensatory vouchers, income-related. As elsewhere, however, new solutions have continually to be found to correct the side-effects of the previous stopgaps. Citizens might reason that the better policy would be to do nothing at all.

As for hospitals, investment in staffed wards and in capital per bed might be refused a certificate of need in order to force patients into doctors' offices and ambulatory clinics. The policy could be counterproductive. Hospitals could be driven to an undesirably high point on their average cost curve. They could be underutilising their capital stock or falling short of their optimal factor-combinations. Meanwhile, the restrictions and licences have a qualitative as well as a quantitative dimension. Medicine stagnates where incumbent oligopolies are never challenged by ambitious interlopers with a radically differentiated new product. It is not easy to restrict entry while keeping novelty alive or to promote the survival of the fittest while keeping the fittest out.

Market structure is a real problem. Too many suppliers mean high average cost since the firms cannot spread their fixed overheads. Too few suppliers mean high retail price since each powerful business fights to gouge out the most the traffic will bear. A rule of reason is required to steer a middle course between the pro-competitive and the anti-competitive extremes. Monopolies and mergers policy must be pragmatic and it must be local.

One region might require a marriage broker to link up uneconomic producers. Horizontal integration eliminates the redundant slack. Vertical integration supports the specialist hospital with a rational network extending down to entry-point primary care. The government might say that minimum cost presupposes a single hospital. The cost-saving natural monopoly of that hospital might have to be protected from arms-race duplication and uneconomically idle capacity. Critics who complain of whole communities being held for ransom will have to be reassured that even a monopolist is seldom a *single* provider. Competition from day-case clinics and, indeed, from hospitals in neighbouring regions can be cited to show that alternatives are often adequate to prevent overcharging.

One region is tired of small shopkeepers who cannot afford to discount. Another region, however, might complain that combination and concentration have gone too far. It might say it is in need of antitrust intervention to break up a *de facto* conspiracy in restraint of trade. It might complain that oligopolistic collusion is fixing the rates, sharing out the territory and bargaining for inputs as a cartel. Such a region might accuse imperfect competitors of keeping out potential entry and of blocking mould-breaking innovations with the spurious justification that without market management all can so easily bankrupt each. If the former region is thinking of marriage, the latter region is in favour of divorce.

In the latter region, at the very least, the State might insist upon better disclosure of prices and outcomes in order where appropriate to name and shame. The State might offer financial support to assist new players to overcome the capital barriers. It might encourage multihospital chains on the assumption that overheads like advertising, research and practical know-how will be shared within the group while each local branch-hospital will have to compete with all the others in each locality. Tax holidays, investment subsidies and tariff-free importation of start-up equipment are prominent among the tools that a hands-on ministry can employ to ensure that the private sector performs well.

Certainly the State could lean against the prevailing winds by monitoring high-cost institutions. It could decertify incumbents that fail to satisfy patients' expectations. It could even allocate entry permits by auction in order to promote cost-conscious productive efficiency while transferring the monopoly rent to the State. Once again, an antidote must be found for an antidote. Citizens might not like the atmosphere of regulation that results. They might prefer a flexible system to one which freezes long-term entitlements in place. They might prefer local administration to national bureaucracies that seem alienating and remote. They might even want to scrap the intervention altogether in order to rely on Adam Smithian supply and demand.

11.3.2. Liberalisation

Controls have side-effects. They make the regulators dependent on the regulated for information. They lead to the regulatory capture of the policing panel by a regulated industry with a sad story to tell. All of this has led some observers to recommend policies which do not so much introduce new restrictions as get rid of old ones. Pro-competitive legislation might be able to arrest the rise in cost precisely because automaticity can be trusted to bring the economy back to health.

The market presupposes intelligent choices. The State can assist the consumers to make such choices by making public its utilisation reviews and its comparative audits. Tables and postings would reveal the age, gender and qualifications of local doctors, their prescription and referral patterns, their subsidiary expertise in non-standard treatments, their knowledge of minority languages. Such information would ensure that the patient became aware of a practice which could advise on diet, allergies and natural childbirth, which worked to a fixed roster of appointments, which saw patients in the evenings and on Sundays, which was well situated for public transport. As for hospitals, patients could be given full details of average charges, average length of stay, average waiting time, convenience of scheduling, hotel and catering facilities, nurse–patient ratios, availability of specialists and subspecialists, refresher courses attended by staff, documented rates of cross-infection, postoperative complications, readmission rates, age-adjusted survival rates per condition treated. Patients will want to have access to previous patients' opinions, to know how frequently the hospital has performed a particular intervention and to learn of any legal action or substantiated complaints. The bodyholder has a need to know if anyone does. There is no reason why the information should be confidential or transparency frustrated.

Commercial advertising could be of value in combatting supplier-induced ignorance. A market-friendly regulatory environment will be one where advertisers are not allowed to venture into manipulation, image creation, film-star endorsements, unrepresentative testimonials, exaggeration or fraud but are allowed nonetheless to state fully what they can do. Competition is predicated on a comparison of the alternatives. Salesmanship can supply some of the missing information.

Kwoka, writing of optometric services, showed that the removal of restrictions on advertising led to a decline of over 20 per cent in the prices of eye examinations and eyeglasses (Kwoka, 1984: 216). It was also associated with shorter consultations in the advertised sector. Non-advertisers gave higher quality examinations in the sense that they spent up to 11 minutes longer with the patient. While any erosion in standards can be seen as a threat, at least the customer was being given a choice. It should also be remembered that eyeglasses are not a once-in-a-lifetime buy. New entrants and new products arguably stand to gain the most from a hot line to the happening news. Later on the repeat purchases and the word-of-mouth of satisfied customers will prove that the initial outlay was worth the expense.

Publicity could lead to a greater spread of services and prices. Suppliers in the public eye know that their income is not guaranteed. The disadvantage is that the name-recognition of a trademark surgeon or an incumbent hospital might push the consumer ever deeper into the demand inelasticity of a habitual rut. The reliance on the tried-and-tested might be a defensive reaction to the information overload which makes people feel insecure and confused in an economic world where even time has a cost: 'In a market with complex information conditions ... advertising may inhibit rather than promote competition' (Rizzo and Zeckhauser, 1990: 498). Competence is a quality which by its very nature is difficult to make into a selling point. The proxy, an appeal to experience and the track record, is effectively an invitation to a conditioned knee-jerk that is itself anti-competitive. New entrants might not gain after all but rather lose. The barrier of differentiation could put up the cost of service.

Patients who rely on advertising might be cozened into buying glamorous services because of frequent repetition and an incomplete description. Telling the truth is not the same as telling the whole truth. An example would be a hospital which announces that it has up-to-the-minute equipment without mentioning that its scanner is only occasionally switched on and that its staff are forgetting how to operate it. If full disclosure reduces the total cost, then anecdotes and half-truths, perverse and anti-competitive, are just as likely to increase it. Besides that, where demand for the service is not easy to inflate, there is always the danger that advertising will simply reallocate the same pool of business. Such competition is minus sum. Costs rise for all players as each struggles to take the other's market share. It is a valid fear. Yet a good goose should not be overcooked. Laws against misrepresentation plus personal recommendations, practitioners' referrals, multiple sources of information, simple common sense are all checks and balances. They suggest that the last word after all might not go to ignorance and information asymmetry.

Rationality and competition can extend to medical schools and health care certification as well as to retail care. Differentiated institutions and demand-led qualifications make access easier and more pluralistic. They put teeth into the patient's choice. The move towards a spectrum of options, gateways and charges would be accelerated were the State to override the cautious traditionalism of the professional associations and challenge the artificial lines of demarcation. A nurse-practitioner could put in the stitches. A midwife could deliver a baby in hospital. A pharmacist could issue an anti-malarial without waiting for a prescription. It is wasteful for professionals to be over-trained when all that they are being asked to do is to clean up a graze. It is economic for consumers to accept treatment from less qualified suppliers if the price they have to pay is significantly less.

The reconsideration of conventional barriers would promote substitutability and availability at the margin. Such move towards *laissez-faire* would have the market-driven potential to reduce the average cost of care. It could also mean a greater supply of doctors and perhaps also of manufactured demand. It is never easy to know what would happen to total cost if the floodgates were opened. It is never easy to predict the final outcome if occupational licensure were relaxed to the point where it became simple registration without the paternalistic hurdle of professional self-certification on the part of the Royal Colleges and the Medical Associations. If entry ceased to be the joint product of cartel-validated examinations tied in with formal education, the quacks, charlatans, butchers, incompetents and opportunists might all rush in to make a fast buck. No one wants that. Rationing by price is suspect where the cut-price article is cheap because it is not very good.

Asymmetry of information could mean that the patient's health suffered, standards fell and contagious diseases raged unchecked. Overall cost could go up where the consumer, judging quality by price, travelled out along an upward-sloping demand curve in the direction of the more expensive treatments and professionals. Yet there is another side to the coin. There is already considerable variation in practice style and inpatient convalescence: '*necessary* hospital stay' and '*best-possible* treatment' do not mean what they say when all too often the doctors cannot articulate the reasons for their choice. Competition might actually shock the differentiated into convergence on the cost-effective option.

Besides that, free markets have correctives of their own. Malpractice lawsuits, interpersonal networks, multiperiod medical centres with a reputation to maintain, the opportunity cost to the individual doctor of being discredited and struck off, all might have the economic effect of making the healing business lean and mean. Where a capitalist corporation wants to maximise profits from its departmental-store clinic, it cannot afford to employ substandard doctors, however certified, who will frighten away its customers. Institutional signalling and the company's brand name could consign the irresponsible and the short-terming to the margins. As far as Milton Friedman is concerned, the most sensible course of action is to let the buyers and the sellers get on with the job: 'Licensure has reduced both the quantity and quality of medical practice.... Licensure should be eliminated as a requirement for the practice of medicine' (Friedman, 1962: 158).

Securing the trademark is costly of time and other resources. While special interest groups might welcome the narrow gateway, the public interest might be on the side of relaxation. A higher standard of quality than is needed for the job raises the cost of medical care. This was demonstrated by Kleiner and Kudrle in their study of dentistry in selected American states. Stricter occupational licensing did not improve the clinical outcomes (as measured directly by comparative rates of dental deterioration and indirectly by relative ratios of complaints and malpractice premiums). What it did was to restrict the number of new dentists, raise the price charged to the consumer and in the end boost the earnings of the dental professionals: 'Dentists in the most regulated states earn a statistically significant 12 percent more than practitioners in the least regulated states' (Kleiner and Kudrle, 2000: 573–4). A person in high-regulation California would pay $1630 more for a standardised correction than he would in low-regulation Kentucky. If Kleiner and Kudrle are correct in their diagnosis of overqualification, it is sound business logic that more liberal entry and exit should be relied upon to reduce windfall returns to the minimum. Competition might keep down the unit cost and raise the public's welfare.

Consumers lack medical knowledge. Yet it need not be the bodyholders themselves who decide what is good. As chapter 3 made clear, competition might operate through the agents who know best and not the principals who acknowledge their myopia. Competition in medicine might be competition at one remove. It might be the general practitioners and not their patients who log on to a computer, collect their data and shop around for a specialist or a hospital that will deliver the most cost-effective service. Disclosure is essential. In this respect the State can assist the referring doctor by insisting that all relevant information be in the public domain. Decision-making will still reflect quality. Hopefully, however, it will reflect economy as well. There is no reason why doctors ought not to be price-conscious. Financial health as well as physical health is in the best interest of the discrete humans being that the doctor is there to help.

The referring doctors need adequate information. Often they will also need a financial incentive of their own. Here again the State can promote a market-friendly environment by dictating that all family doctors, at least in a National Health Service, must hold their own cash-limited budgets. The doctors will then be obliged to search carefully for the best bargains. They will want to retain their patients and their capitations. They will also want to maximise the residual that falls to them once they have bought the services and settled the bills. Knowing that the practices are in the market, the competing providers will quote attractive prices in order to secure a steady stream of repeat business. Lower prices, unless quantities expand more than in proportion, mean a fall in the total amount of money that is spent on health.

As for the practice budget itself, the amount is determined by the funding authority. This body could be a health maintenance organisation or (as in the case of the National Health Service) the State. Either way, it will be cash-constrained by the membership fees or the taxes. The budget allocated to each practitioner will, particularly in the public sector, be broadly in line with the democratic consensus. It will reflect key medical and social variables such as the proportion of elderly or expensive patients on a doctor's list, local differences in medical costs, the incidence of absolute or relative deprivation in the geographical area where the practice is situated. The convention that the budget will be adjusted upward to accommodate the above-average drains is a source of reassurance to housebound disabled, the incurably schizophrenic, the infirm, the senile. Otherwise the primary care doctors might simply refuse to take them on. The criteria will be controversial and often politically sensitive. On the other hand, they are criteria and not random numbers. The knowledge that there is a ceiling focuses the mind on value for money. Budget caps put a lid on total cost. Search keeps down the average cost per case.

The money follows the patient. A comparison may be made with education vouchers, but with an obvious difference. In health it is the doctor (for the patient) and not the parent (for the child) who scans the options. The agent acts and the principal fits in. Allocative efficiency is the intended result of the internal market.

The hidden assumption is, however, that medical doctors have an MBA mindset. Some, no doubt, do. Alert and entrepreneurial, these are the doctors who attend the weekend seminars on unit trusts and invest speculatively in buy-to-rent. Many, however, do not. They are insistent that they see themselves as healers and helpers. They feel uncomfortable with the expectation that they should run a shop. Their professional image makes it difficult for them to economise at the margin or to make their money stretch. Such doctors complain that they face a conflict of loyalties where the practice budget forces them into a trade-off between high quality and low price. They say that cost-consciousness, let alone the profit-motive, can never be the proper maximand in the caring professions like health. A compromise might be for the agents to hire sub-agents of their own. Where there is a practice manager with a flair for computing and a feel for a deal, the labour of shopping and accounting may perhaps be delegated to someone who is not afraid to do business.

Cost containment is the great plus. As always, there is also a risk. Referrals might be dodged. Loss-makers might be dropped. The cost of convalescence might not be eliminated but cynically transferred from the medical services to a supportive family, meals-on-wheels, private taxis, community services and charity shelters. Even if no false economies actually make the news, the patient is not a fool. Especially if the budget-holder is allowed to retain his bottom line for himself, the patient will always suspect that his servant is acting on a private and personal agenda. This is antithetical to the bedrock of trust in the doctor–patient relationship. Economists put their faith in the Adam Smithian profit maximiser. Kidney patients might not.

Patients are, of course, free to change their general practitioner. In some cases they are allowed a say on the surgeon or hospital as well. Being ignorant of the success-rates and ill-informed about medical adequacy, they will probably not exercise their option. Competition is weighted against them.

No practice budget is ever infinite. It is a cause for concern. Where resources are cash-constrained, the doctor's financial plan can be wiped out by an unforeseen catastrophe. Even one patient, suddenly very ill, can command a disproportionate share in the resources needed for many others. The dilemma is a real one for a doctor whose patient might otherwise die. Public policy will in such exceptional circumstances often write in an escape clause that allows for piecemealism and supplementation. Long-term hospitalisation will be shifted altogether out of the practice budget. State grants to hospitals will cover the fixed costs in order to facilitate pricing by the marginal cost alone. New treatments, unmet needs and cost inflation itself will all cause the Government to top-up the practice budgets that have been agreed.

The safety valve is a serious door. While constitutionalism might cap total spending, special pleading can sweep the upper limits away. Moral philosophy is not much help. Is the subjective welfare of many citizens with small complaints greater than the felt utility of a minority of one who is at risk of death? Political theory is a broken reed. If all but one vote to deny the heart patient his life-saving drug, does that mean that his human rights are automatically extinguished because his neighbours do not want to share? Open-ended financing does not need to answer questions such as these. The strict practice budget does.

Competition within the framework of the practice budget ensures that the suppliers must satisfy their paying customers. There is still more that the State can do to liberalise the market. Restrictive practices such as monopoly and oligopoly should be scrutinised to discourage price-fixing and excessive profits. Hospital mergers without economies of scale or scope should be prevented lest they contribute to market imperfection. Free entry is more of a problem. More hospitals and more doctors mean more treatments, more capital and more expense. Competition, however, presupposes the weeding out of the complacent and their supersession by the dynamic. Cost containment in the circumstances points at once to restricted entry and to liberalised entry. The *just adequate* must be fired in order that the *rather promising* can take their seats. It is a challenge which will appeal strongly to policymakers who think that they have the skill to pick winners and identify the entrants most likely to outperform.

Competition can mean capitalist enterprise. In its most extreme form, the National Health Service would be privatised and so would the American not-for-profit sector. Public hospitals in the pure market homeostasis of Adam Smith are believed to have no financial incentive to be efficient. Only the gain-seeking and the grasping can be trusted, going for shareholders' profits, to keep down the cost of care. In that sense the internal market can be seen as a disequilibrium stage. It will one day have to be transcended by the full and State-free market that is as inevitable as evolution. Not all policymakers, however, see economic institutions as a simple either/or. Many observers would insist that there can be a halfway house. They would say that adequate competition can take the form of an internal market implanted within the non-Smithian parameters of a public-sector or a cooperative system. The property rights do not need to be reappraised. Claims and deeds do not need to be reallocated.

Enthoven, discussing rivalry and devolution even without the privatisation of the ownership title, calls such a healthcare system a form of 'market socialism' (Enthoven, 1985: 40). Competition between State-owned rivals would lead, if the market textbooks correctly describe the logic of supply and demand, to lower prices charged to consumers and higher wages paid to manpower. Competition can even lead to border-crossing despite the ownership line. This would be the case where the practice budget can be used for private consultants, scans and hospitals should the State alternative prove too costly or too slow. Hospitals, public and private alike, will arguably be more user-friendly if they have to earn their budget than if they receive an annual allocation irrespective of the services they deliver.

This, of course, assumes that the State will allow public hospitals to set their own prices. There will not be much real rivalry or price signalling so long as the State does not allow competing institutions, opted out of detailed directives, to determine their own markups and fix their own pay scales. It is, on the other hand, a misnomer to speak of a *national* health service where there is little or no democratic vetting of overcharging and overwork, fixed-term contracts versus tenured appointments. It is not clear what would happen if State-owned hospitals, managed independently, wanted to buy or sell land, or to segregate their wards by religious affiliation, or to close down a women-only subsidiary in order to centralise the business on a single site. A government system can insist that the local community be consulted on their emergency facilities or their psychiatric hospital. An opted-out system is less likely to be under any obligation to satisfy local people where it will then have to keep open a loss-making facility that is costing it money.

An internal market could be created *within* as well as *between* each treatment-centre. If budgets were devolved to the departments and if each had to buy and sell to the rest, such dealing could make each unit more sensitive to its prices and its second-bests foregone. Performance bonuses rather than the automatic *pro rata* of the previous year's rewards would give each department an incentive to be economical with inputs and to keep its patient stream up. This would keep the average cost under control.

Each department in an internal market would retain (except for shared overheads) all of the fee-income that it receives. It would then expand or contract in the light of its traffic. Cross-subsidisation of the loss-makers within the clinic or hospital would be a conscious choice. An economically unprofitable division might even be able to secure an earmarked grant from the central budget of the National Health Service. Such a subsidy would indicate that the State wanted certain services to survive but not where the funding had to come from other services within a single treatment centre.

The marketisation of health has implications for non-medical inputs. Hospitals supply surgery and treatments. They buy in pharmaceuticals, bed-linen and beds from private enterprise. Cleaning, catering and gardening can be provided directly. They can also be farmed out. It is a curious proposition that every input in a hospital must be treated as a medical input, every input in a National Health Service seen as a national responsibility. It might do much for cost-effectiveness if ancillary services were to be handed over to outside contractors who would tender regularly for the franchise and would lose their monopoly if quality and price were not right. As their workers are unskilled, ununionised, often less-educated, often inarticulate foreigners recruited abroad, some observers will object that bad pay and conditions will be the reason why a commercial firm can quote competitive rates. Buying in must be monitored if it is not to be an embarrassment. So must standards. Catering is nutrition. Nutrition is essential for recovery. Clearly, the kitchen is one area in which short-horizoned economies should not be made in order to succeed in the tendering process.

It is not easy to say what should be bought in and what should be produced in-house. Ideology breaks down in the face of applied economics. If catering can be subcontracted, can the same be said of intensive care? Should diagnostic tests and air-ambulances be put out for the keenest bid? The answer in terms of cures and in terms of costs need not be the same. As seen by the economist, however, it is all a question of what makes a market and what constitutes a firm: 'When we are considering how large a firm will be the principle of marginalism works smoothly. The question always is, will it pay to bring an extra exchange transaction under the organising authority?' (Coase, 1937: 404). Coase would say that he sees no difference in principle between the gift shop which is under franchise and the recovery room which is directly operated. Vertical integration saves on the search and the bargaining. Sequential contracting saves on the in-flexibilities of managerial overload and long-term locking in. As far as Coase is concerned, no decision can be made *a priori*. It all depends on the costs and benefits.

High Street pharmacists are Adam Smithian bakers and brewers. Hospital pharmacies are Bevanite socialism through and through. The distinction is far too simple. Coase would not be satisfied with an institutional *credo* that did not remain forever under review. It is not the pharmacy per se but the small increment and the rate of substitution that determine the charter. They fix the equilibrium for now. A decision once made will ultimately have to be made again.

There are no simple answers. This book has shown that health care must be responsive to the patient, the practitioner and the public. It must be medically effective and economically efficient. It must be resistant to any avoidable escalation in cost. It must be flexible and adaptable. Public policy must keep all the options under review. An obsession with single answers, like the quest for 'complete physical, mental and social well-being', is an uncompromising El Dorado that brings out the fanatic and the megalomaniac in us all. Titmuss was right to warn that there is 'something unhealthy about the perfection of the absolute'. The truth very often will be a mix. There is no panacea that will resolve for all time the tension between individual *and* society, consumption *and* investment, duty *and* preference, authority *and* exchange. Health care *and* public policy is an *and* and a compromise like all rest: 'The most important concept in political economy is the *and*. The most important asset in the study of the mixed economy is an open mind' (Reisman, 2005: 14). The student of social policy must adapt his tools to the *andness* which is all around.

Bibliography

Aaron, H.J. (1991), *Serious and Unstable Condition*, Washington, DC: The Brookings Institution.

Abel-Smith, B. (1959), 'Whose welfare state?', in N.I. Mackenzie, ed., *Conviction*, London: MacGibbon and Kee, 55–73.

Abelson, P. (2003), 'The value of life and health for public policy', *Economic Record*, 79, Special Issue, S2–S13.

Acton, J.P. (1973), *Evaluating Public Programs to Save Lives: The Case of Heart Attacks*, Research Report R-950-RC, Santa Monica, CA: Rand Corporation.

Acton, J.P. (1975), 'Nonmonetary factors in the demand for medical services: some empirical evidence', *Journal of Political Economy*, **83**, 595–614.

Akerlof, G.A. (1970), 'The market for "lemons": quality uncertainty and the market mechanism', *Quarterly Journal of Economics*, **84**, 488–500.

American Heart Association (2003), *Heart and Stroke Facts*, Dallas, TX: American Heart Association.

Andersen, T.F. and G.H. Mooney (1990), 'Medical practice variations: where are we?', in T.F. Andersen and G.H. Mooney, eds, *The Challenges of Medical Practice Variations*, London: Macmillan, 1–15.

Arrow, K.J. (1973 [1963]), 'The welfare economics of medical care', *American Economic Review*, **53**, reprinted in M.H. Cooper and A.J. Culyer, eds, *Health Economics*, Harmondsworth: Penguin Books, 13–48.

Association of Community Health Councils (1990), *Health and Wealth: A Review of Health Inequalities in the UK*, London: Association of Community Health Councils.

Audit Commission (2002), *Medical Staffing: Review of National Findings*, 30 August, www.audit-commission.gov.uk/Products/NATIONAL-REPORT/ D9C04946-ADD3-4fab-9374-OB691B81C6D1/AcuteHosp-Med-Staffing-06.pdf, accessed 1 February 2007.

Auster, R., I. Leveson and D. Sarachek (1969), 'The production of health: an exploratory study', *Journal of Human Resources*, **4**, 412–36.

Baker, L.C. and K.S. Corts (1996), 'HMO penetration and the cost of health care: market discipline or market segmentation?', *American Economic Review (Papers and Proceedings)*, **86**, 389–94.

Baker, L.C. and A.B. Royalty (2000), 'Medicaid policy, physician behavior, and health care for the low-income population', *Journal of Human Resources*, **35**, 480–502.

Beck, R.G. (1974), 'The effects of co-payment on the poor', *Journal of Human Resources*, **9**, 129–42.

Bergson, A. (1938), 'A reformulation of certain aspects of welfare economics', *Quarterly Journal of Economics*, **52**, 310–34.

Berk, M.L. and A.C. Monheit (2001), 'The concentration of health care expenditures, revisited', *Health Affairs*, **20** (2), 9–18.

Bevan, A. (1958), Speech in the House of Commons, 30 July, in *Parliamentary Debates (Hansard)*, Cols. 1382–98, London: HMSO.

Bevan, A. (1961 [1952]), *In Place of Fear*, London: MacGibbon & Kee.

Biddle, J.E. and G.A. Zarkin (1988), 'Worker preferences and market compensation for job risk', *Review of Economics and Statistics*, **70**, 660–67.

Blaxter, M. (1976), 'Social class and health inequalities', in C.O. Carter and J. Peel, eds, *Equalities and Inequalities in Health*, London: Academic Press, 111–25.

Blaxter, M. (1990), *Health and Lifestyles*, London: Routledge.

Blendon, R.J., M. Kim and J.M. Benson (2001), 'The public versus the World Health Organization on health system performance', *Health Affairs*, **20** (3), 10–20.

Blomquist, G. (1979), 'Value of life saving: implications of consumption activity', *Journal of Political Economy*, **87**, 540–58.

Blomquist, G. (1982), 'Estimating the value of life and safety: recent developments', in M.W. Jones-Lee, ed., *The Value of Life and Safety*, Amsterdam: North-Holland, 27–40.

Blumberg, L.J., L. Dubay and S.A. Norton (2000), 'Did the Medicaid expansions for children displace private insurance? An analysis using the SIPP', *Journal of Health Economics*, **19**, 33–60.

Boulding, K.E. (1966), 'The concept of need for health services', *Milbank Memorial Fund Quarterly*, **44**, 202–21.

Boulding, K.E. (1969), 'Economics as a moral science', *American Economic Review*, **59**, 1–12.

Boyle, M.H., G.W. Torrance, J.C. Sinclair and S.P. Horwood (1983), 'Economic evaluation of neonatal intensive care of very-low-birth-weight infants', *New England Journal of Medicine*, **308**, 1330–37.

Braybrooke, D. (1987), *Meeting Needs*, Princeton, NJ: Princeton University Press.

Brennan, H.G. and J.M. Buchanan (1980), *The Power to Tax*, Cambridge: Cambridge University Press.

Brennan, H.G. and J.M. Buchanan (1985), *The Reason of Rules*, Cambridge: Cambridge University Press.

Brent, R.J. (2003), *Cost-Benefit Analysis and Health Care Evaluations*, Cheltenham, UK and Northampton, MA, USA: Edward Elgar.

Brook, R.H., J.B. Kosecoff, R.E. Park, M.R. Chassin, C.M. Winslow and J.R.

Hampton (1988), 'Diagnosis and treatment of coronary disease: comparison of doctors' attitudes in the USA and the UK', *The Lancet*, 2 April, 750–53.

Broome, J. (1978), 'Trying to value a life', *Journal of Public Economics*, **9**, 91–100.

Broome, J. (1993), 'Qalys', *Journal of Public Economics*, **50**, 149–67.

Brown, D.M. (1988), 'Do physicians underutilize aides?', *Journal of Human Resources*, **23**, 342–55.

Brown, K. and C. Burrows (1990), 'The sixth stool guaiac test: $47 million that never was', *Journal of Health Economics*, **9**, 429–45.

Buchanan, J.M. (1965), *The Inconsistencies of the National Health Service*, London: Institute of Economic Affairs.

Buchanan, J.M. (1975), *The Limits of Liberty*, Chicago, IL: University of Chicago Press.

Buchanan, J.M. (1986), *Liberty, Market and State*, Brighton: Wheatsheaf.

Buchanan, J.M. (1990), *Technological Determinism Despite the Reality of Scarcity*, Little Rock, AR: University of Arkansas for Medical Sciences.

Buchanan, J.M. and R.L. Faith (1979), 'Trying again to value a life', *Journal of Public Economics*, **12**, 245–8.

Buchmueller, T.C., M. Jacobson and C. Wold (2006), 'How far to the hospital? The effect of hospital closures on access to care', *Journal of Health Economics*, **25**, 740–61.

Bundorf, M.K. and M.V. Pauly (2006), 'Is health insurance affordable for the uninsured?', *Journal of Health Economics*, **25**, 650–73.

Bunker, J.P. and B.W. Brown, Jr. (1974), 'The physician-patient as informed consumer of surgical services', *New England Journal of Medicine*, **290** (19), 1051–5.

Bunker, J.P., H.S. Frazier and F. Mosteller (1994), 'Improving health: measuring effects of medical care', *Milbank Quarterly*, **72**, 225–58.

Busschbach, J.J.V., D.J. Hessing and F.T. de Charro (1993), 'The utility of health at different stages in life: a quantitative approach', *Social Science and Medicine*, **37**, 153–8.

Buxton, M.J. and R.R. West (1975), 'Cost benefit analysis of long-term haemodialysis for chronic renal failure', *British Medical Journal*, **2**, 376–9.

Carlin, P.S. and R. Sandy (1991), 'Estimating the implicit value of a young child's life', *Southern Economic Journal*, **58**, 186–202.

Chaloupka, F. (1991), 'Rational addictive behavior and cigarette smoking', *Journal of Political Economy*, **99**, 722–42.

Chantler, J.K., A.J. Tingle and R.E. Petty (1985), 'Persistent rubella virus infection associated with chronic arthritis in children', *New England Journal of Medicine*, **313**, 1117–23.

Chassin, M.R., R.H. Brook, R.E. Park, J. Keesey, A. Fink, J. Kosecoff, K. Kahn, N. Merrick and D.H. Solomon (1986), 'Variations in the use of medical and surgical services by the Medicare population', *New England Journal of Medicine*, **314**, 285–90.

Chassin, M.R., J. Kosecoff, C.M. Winslow, K.L. Kahn, N.J. Merrick, J. Keesey, A. Fink, D.H. Solomon and R.H. Brook (1987), 'Does inappropriate use explain geographic variations in the use of health care services?', *Journal of the American Medical Association*, **258**, 2533–7.

Chiswick, B.R. (1976), 'The demand for nursing home care: an analysis of the substitution between institutional and noninstitutional care', *Journal of Human Resources*, **11**, 295–316.

Clarke, P.M. (1998), 'Cost–benefit analysis and mammographic screening: a travel cost approach', *Journal of Health Economics*, **17**, 767–87.

Coase, R.H. (1937), 'The nature of the firm', *Economica*, **16**, 386–405.

Cochrane, A.L. (1972), *Effectiveness and Efficiency*, London: Nuffield Provincial Hospitals Trust.

Cochrane, A.L., A.S. St Leger and F. Moore (1978), 'Health service "input" and mortality "output" in developed countries', *Journal of Epidemiology and Community Health*, **32**, 200–205.

Coffey, R.M. (1983), 'The effect of time price on the demand for medical-care services', *Journal of Human Resources*, **18**, 407–24.

Collard, D. (1978), *Altruism and Economy*, Oxford: Martin Robertson.

Colle, A.D. and M. Grossman (1978), 'Determinants of pediatric care utilization', *Journal of Human Resources*, **13**, 115–58.

Contoyiannis, P. and A.M. Jones (2004), 'Socio-economic status, health and lifestyle', *Journal of Health Economics*, **23**, 965–95.

Cook, J., J. Richardson and A. Street (1994), 'A cost utility analysis of treatment options for gallstone disease: methodological issues and results', *Health Economics*, **3**, 157–68.

Cooper, P.F. and A.C. Monheit (1993), 'Does employment-related health insurance inhibit job mobility?', *Inquiry*, **30**, 400–416.

Corman, H., T.J. Joyce and M. Grossman (1987), 'Birth outcome production function in the United States', *Journal of Human Resources*, **22**, 339–60.

Coulter, A., K. McPherson and M. Vesey (1988), 'Do British women undergo too many or too few hysterectomies?', *Social Science and Medicine*, **27**, 987–94.

Crandall, R.W. and J.D. Graham (1984), 'Automobile safety regulations and offsetting behavior: some new empirical estimates', *American Economic Review (Papers and Proceedings)*, **74**, 328–31.

Cromwell, J. and J.R. Mitchell (1986), 'Physician-induced demand for surgery', *Journal of Health Economics*, **5**, 293–313.

Cropper, M.L., N.B. Simon, A. Alberini, S. Arora and P.K. Sharma (1997), 'The health benefits of air pollution control in Delhi', *American Journal of Agricultural Economics*, **79**, 1625–9.

Crosland, C.A.R. (1974 [1971]), *A Social-Democratic Britain*, Fabian Tract 404, in his *Socialism Now*, London: Jonathan Cape.

Croxson, B., C. Propper and A. Perkins (2001), 'Do doctors respond to financial incentives? UK family doctors and the GP fundholder scheme', *Journal of Public Economics*, **79**, 375–98.

Culyer, A.J. (1971), 'The nature of the commodity "health care" and its efficient allocation', *Oxford Economic Papers*, **23**, 189–211.

Culyer, A.J. (1976), *Need and the National Health Service*, London: Martin Robertson.

Culyer, A.J. (1982), 'The NHS and the market: images and realities', in G. McLachlan and A. Maynard, eds, *The Public/Private Mix for Health: The Relevance and Effects of Change*, London: Nuffield Provincial Hospitals Trust, 25–55.

Culyer, A.J. (1989), 'Cost containment in Europe', *Health Care Financing Review*, **10**, Annual Supplement, 21–32.

Culyer, A.J. (2005), *The Dictionary of Health Economics*, Cheltenham, UK and Northampton, MA, USA: Edward Elgar.

Culyer, A.J., R.J. Lavers and A. Williams (1972), 'Health indicators', in A. Shonfield and S. Shaw, eds, *Social Indicators and Social Policy*, London: Heinemann Educational Books, 94–118.

Culyer, A.J. and A. Wagstaff (1993), 'Equity and equality in health and health care', *Journal of Health Economics*, **12**, 431–57.

Currie, J. and J. Gruber (1996), 'Saving babies: the efficacy and cost of recent changes in the Medicaid eligibility of pregnant women', *Journal of Political Economy*, **104**, 1263–96.

Currie, J. and E. Moretti (2003), 'Mother's education and the intergenerational transmission of human capital: evidence from college openings', *Quarterly Journal of Economics*, **118**, 1495–532.

Cutler, D.M. (1994), 'A guide to health care reform', *Journal of Economic Perspectives*, **8**, 13–29.

Cutler, D.M. (2004), *Your Money or Your Life: Strong Medicine for America's Health Care System*, New York: Oxford University Press.

Cutler, D.M. and E.L. Glaeser (2006), *Why Do Europeans Smoke More than Americans?*, Working Paper 12124, Cambridge, MA: National Bureau of Economic Research.

Cutler, D.M. and J. Gruber (1996), 'Does public insurance crowd out private insurance?', *Quarterly Journal of Economics*, **111**, 391–430.

Cutler, D.M. and M. McClellan (2001), 'Is technological change in medicine worth it?', *Health Affairs*, **20** (5), 11–29.

Cutler, D.M. and S.J. Reber (1998), 'Paying for health insurance: the trade-off between competition and adverse selection', *Quarterly Journal of Economics*, **113**, 433–66.

Cutler, D.M. and E. Richardson (1998), 'The value of health: 1970–1990', *American Economic Review (Papers and Proceedings)*, **88**, 97–100.

Daly, E., A. Gray, D. Barlow, K. McPherson, M. Roche and M. Vessey (1993), 'Measuring the impact of menopausal symptoms on quality of life', *British Medical Journal*, **307**, 836–40.

Daniels, N. (1985), *Just Health Care*, Cambridge: Cambridge University Press.

Dardis, R. (1980), 'The value of a life: new evidence from the marketplace', *American Economic Review*, **70**, 1077–82.

Davis, K. and R. Reynolds (1975), 'Medicare and the utilization of health care services by the elderly', *Journal of Human Resources*, **10**, 361–77.

De Cicca, P., D. Kenkel and A. Mathios (2002), 'Putting out the fires: will higher taxes reduce the onset of youth smoking?', *Journal of Political Economy*, **110**, 144–69.

Deaton, A. (2003), 'Health, inequality, and economic development', *Journal of Economic Literature*, **41**, 113–58.

Department of Health (2006), *The Health Profile of England*, London: Department of Health.

Detsky, A.S. (1995), 'Evidence of effectiveness: evaluating its quality', in F.A. Sloan, ed., *Valuing Health Care: Costs, Benefits, and Effectiveness of Pharmaceuticals and Other Medical Technologies*, Cambridge: Cambridge University Press, 15–29.

Dolan, P. (1996a), 'Modelling valuations for health states: the effect of duration', *Health Policy*, **38**, 189–203.

Dolan, P. (1996b), 'The effect of experience of illness on health state valuations', *Journal of Clinical Epidemiology*, **49**, 551–64.

Donaldson, C. (1990), 'Willingness to pay for publicly-provided goods: a possible measure of benefit?', *Journal of Health Economics*, **9**, 103–18.

Dowd, B. and R. Feldman (2006), 'Competition and health plan choice', in A.M. Jones, ed., *The Elgar Companion to Health Economics*, Cheltenham, UK and Northampton, MA, USA: Edward Elgar, 137–46.

Downs, A. (1957), *An Economic Theory of Democracy*, New York: Harper and Row.

Doyal, L. and I. Gough (1991), *A Theory of Human Need*, London: Macmillan.

Drummond, M., B. O'Brien, G.L. Stoddart, G.W. Torrance (1997), *Methods for the Economic Evaluation of Health Care Programmes*, 2nd edn, Oxford: Oxford University Press.

Drummond, M., G. Torrance and J. Mason (1993), 'Cost-effectiveness league tables: more harm than good?', *Social Science and Medicine*, **37**, 33–40.

Dublin, L.I. and A.J. Lotka (1930), *The Money Value of a Man*, New York: Ronald Press.

Dubos, R. (1959), *Mirage of Health*, New York: Harper and Row.

Durkheim, E. (1984 [1893]), *The Division of Labor in Society*, tr. by W.D. Halls, New York: The Free Press.

Eddy, D.M. (1989), 'Screening for breast cancer', *Annals of Internal Medicine*, **111**, 389–99.

Eddy, D.M. (1990), 'Screening for cervical cancer', *Annals of Internal Medicine*, **113**, 214–26.

Ellis, R.P. (1998), 'Creaming, skimping and dumping: provider competition on the intensive and extensive margins', *Journal of Health Economics*, **17**, 537–55.

Elo, I.T. and S.H. Preston (1996), 'Educational differentials in mortality: United States, 1979–85', *Social Science and Medicine*, **42**, 47–57.

Enthoven, A.C. (1980), *Health Plan*, Reading, MA: Addison-Wesley.

Enthoven, A.C. (1985), *Reflections on the Management of the National Health Service*, London: Nuffield Provincial Hospitals Trust.

Escarce, J.J. (1993), 'Would eliminating differences in physician practice style reduce geographic variations in cataract surgery rates?', *Medical Care*, **31**, 1106–18.

Evans, R.G. (1974), 'Supplier-induced demand: some empirical evidence and implications', in M. Perlman, ed., *The Economics of Health and Medical Care*, London: Macmillan, 162–73.

Evans, W.N. and J.D. Graham (1990), 'An estimate of the lifesaving benefit of child restraint use legislation', *Journal of Health Economics*, **9**, 121–42.

Evans, W.N. and J.S. Ringel (1999), 'Can higher cigarette taxes improve birth outcomes?', *Journal of Public Economics*, **72**, 135–54.

Feldman, R. and B. Dowd (1991), 'A new estimate of the welfare loss of excess health insurance', *American Economic Review*, **81**, 297–301.

Feldman, R., B. Dowd, S. Leitz and L.A. Blewett (1997), 'The effect of premiums on the small firm's decision to offer health insurance', *Journal of Human Resources*, **32**, 635–58.

Feldstein, M.S. (1973), 'The welfare loss of excess health insurance', *Journal of Political Economy*, **81**, 251–80.

Feldstein, P.J. (1988), *Health Care Economics*, 3rd edn, New York: Wiley.

Feldstein, P.J., T.M. Wickizer and J.R.C. Wheeler (1988), 'Private cost containment: the effects of utilization review programs on health care use and expenditures', *New England Journal of Medicine*, **318**, 1310–14.

Festinger, L. (1962 [1957]), *A Theory of Cognitive Dissonance*, London: Tavistock.

Fisher, E.S., D.E. Wennberg, T.A. Stukel, D.J. Gottlieb, F.L. Lucas and E.L. Pinder (2003a), 'The implications of regional variations in Medicare spending. Part 1: the content, quality, and accessibility of care', *Annals of Internal Medicine*, **138**, 273–88.

Fisher, E.S., D.E. Wennberg, T.A. Stukel, D.J. Gottlieb, F.L. Lucas and E.L. Pinder (2003b), 'The implications of regional variations in Medicare spending, Part 2: health outcomes and satisfaction with care', *Annals of Internal Medicine*, **138**, 288–99.

Folland, S., A.C. Goodman and M. Stano (2007), *The Economics of Health and Health Care*, 5th edn, Upper Saddle River, NJ: Pearson Prentice Hall.

Folland, S. and M. Stano (1989), 'Sources of small area variations in the use of medical care', *Journal of Health Economics*, **8**, 85–107.

Frederick, S., G. Loewenstein and T. O'Donoghue (2002), 'Time discounting and time preference: a critical review', *Journal of Economic Literature*, **40**, 351–401.

Friedman, M. (1962), *Capitalism and Freedom*, Chicago, IL: University of Chicago Press.

Friedman, M. and L.J. Savage (1948), 'The utility analysis of choices involving risk', *Journal of Political Economy*, **56**, 279–304.

Froberg, D.G. and R.L. Kane (1989), 'Methodology for measuring health-state preferences – IV: progress and a research agenda', *Journal of Clinical Epidemiology*, **42**, 675–85.

Fuchs, V.R. (1973 [1966]), 'The contribution of health services to the American economy', *Milbank Memorial Fund Quarterly*, **44**, reprinted in M.H. Cooper and A.J. Culyer, eds, *Health Economics*, Harmondsworth: Penguin Books, 135–71.

Fuchs, V.R. (1974a), *Who Shall Live?* New York: Basic Books.

Fuchs, V.R. (1974b), 'Some economic aspects of mortality in developed countries', in M. Perlman, ed., *The Economics of Health and Medical Care*, London: Macmillan, 174–93.

Fuchs, V.R. (1983), *How We Live*, Cambridge, MA: Harvard University Press.

Fuchs, V.R. (1986 [1978]), 'The supply of surgeons and the demand for operations', *Journal of Human Resources*, **13**, reprinted in his *The Health Economy*, Cambridge, MA: Harvard University Press, 126–47.

Fuchs, V.R. (1996), 'Economists, values, and health care reform', *American Economic Review*, **86**, 1–24.

Galbraith, J.K. (1958), *Journal to Poland and Yugoslavia*, Cambridge, MA: Harvard University Press.

Garber, A.M. and C.E. Phelps (1997), 'Economic foundations of cost-effectiveness analysis', *Journal of Health Economics*, **16**, 1–31.

Gardner, J. and A. Oswald (2004), 'How is mortality affected by money, marriage and stress?', *Journal of Health Economics*, **23**, 1181–207.

Geiser, E.G. and F.C. Menz (1976), 'The effectiveness of public dental care programs', *Medical Care*, **14**, 189–98.

Gerrard, K. and G. Mooney (1993), 'QALY league tables: handle with care', *Health Economics*, **2**, 59–64.

Gillon, R. (1985), *Philosophical Medical Ethics*, Chichester: Wiley.

Granovetter, M. (1985), 'Economic action and social structure: the problem of embeddedness', *American Journal of Sociology*, **91**, 481–510.

Gravelle, H., M. Dusheiko and M. Sutton (2001), 'The demand for elective surgery in a public system: time and money prices in the UK National Health Service', *Journal of Health Economics*, **21**, 423–49.

Gray, B. (2001), 'Do Medicaid physician fees for prenatal services affect birth outcomes?', *Journal of Health Economics*, **20**, 571–90.

Green, T.H. (1941 [1879]), *Lectures on the Principles of Political Obligation*, London: Longmans.

Greenspan, A.M., H.R. Kay, B.C. Berger, R.M. Greenberg, A.J. Greenspon and M.J. Spuhler (1988), 'Incidence of unwarranted implantation of permanent cardiac pacemakers in a large medical population', *New England Journal of Medicine*, **318**, 158–63.

Grossman, M. (1972), 'On the concept of health capital and the demand for health', *Journal of Political Economy*, **80**, 223–55.

Grossman, M. (1982), 'Government and health outcomes', *American Economic Review (Papers and Proceedings)*, **72**, 191–5.

Grossman, M. (1990), 'The human capital model', in A.J. Culyer and J.P. Newhouse, eds, *Handbook of Health Economics*, Amsterdam: Elsevier, **1A**, 347–408.

Gruber, J. and M. Owings (1996), 'Physician financial incentives and Cesarean section delivery', *Rand Journal of Economics*, **27**, 99–123.

Grytten, J. and R. Sørensen (2001), 'Type of contract and supplier-induced demand for primary physicians in Norway', *Journal of Health Economics*, **20**, 379–93.

Guralnik, J.M., K.C. Land, D. Blazer, G.G. Fillenbaum and L.G. Branch (1993), 'Educational status and active life expectancy among older blacks and whites', *New England Journal of Medicine*, **329**, 110–16.

Haas-Wilson, D. (1990), 'Consumer information and providers' reputations', *Journal of Health Economics*, **9**, 321–33.

Hadley, J., E. Steinberg and J. Feder (1991), 'Comparison of uninsured and privately insured hospital patients: condition on admission, resource use, and outcome', *Journal of the American Medical Association*, **265**, 374–9.

Ham, C. (1988), *Health Care Variations*, London: King's Fund Institute.

Ham, C. (2005), *Health Policy in Britain*, 5th edn, Basingstoke: Palgrave Macmillan.

Harris, J. (1985), *The Value of Life: An Introduction to Medical Ethics*, London: Routledge.

Harsanyi, J.C. (1982 [1977]), 'Morality and the theory of rational behaviour', in A. Sen and B. Williams, eds, *Utilitarianism and Beyond*, Cambridge: Cambridge University Press, 39–62.

Hatziandreu, E.I., J.P. Koplan, M.C. Weinstein, C.J. Caspersen and K.E. Warner (1988), 'A cost-effectiveness analysis of exercise as a health promotion activity', *American Journal of Public Health*, **78**, 1417–21.

Healthcare Commission (UK) (2006), *Annual Health Check*, http://annual-healthcheckratings.healthcarecommission.org.uk, accessed 1 February 2007.

Heasman, M.A. and V. Carstairs (1971), 'Inpatient management: variations in some aspects of practice in Scotland', *British Medical Journal*, **1**, 495–8.

Hirschman, A.O. (1982), *Shifting Involvements*, Oxford: Basil Blackwell.

Hirth, R.A., M.E. Chernew, E. Miller, M. Fendrick and W.G. Weissert (2000), 'Willingness to pay for a quality-adjusted life year', *Medical Decision Making*, **20**, 332–42.

His Majesty's Stationery Office (1942), *Social Insurance and Allied Services* (The Beveridge Report), Cmd. 6404, London: His Majesty's Stationery Office.

Holmer, M. (1984), 'Tax policy and the demand for health insurance', *Journal of Health Economics*, **3**, 203–21.

Hsieh, C.R. and S.J. Lin (1997), 'Health information and the demand for preventive care among the elderly in Taiwan', *Journal of Human Resources*, **32**, 308–33.

Hull, R., J. Hirsh, D.L. Sackett and G. Stoddart (1981), 'Cost effectiveness of clinical diagnosis, venography, and noninvasive testing in patients with symptomatic deep-vein thrombosis', *New England Journal of Medicine*, **304**, 1561–7.

Illich, I. (1977), *Limits to Medicine*, Harmondsworth: Penguin Books.

Jackson, L.A., A. Schuchat, R. Gorsky and J.D. Wenger (1995), 'Should college students be vaccinated against meningococcal disease? A cost–benefit analysis', *American Journal of Public Health*, **85**, 843–6.

Johannesson, M. and U.-G. Gerdtham (1996), 'A note on the estimation of the equity-efficiency trade-off for QALYs', *Journal of Health Economics*, **15**, 359–68.

Johannesson, M. and P.-O. Johansson (1997), 'Is the valuation of a QALY gained independent of age? Some empirical evidence', *Journal of Health Economics*, **16**, 589–99.

Johannesson, M. and D. Meltzer (1998), 'Some reflections on cost-effectiveness analysis', *Health Economics*, **7**, 1–7.

Johnson, M.L. (1977), 'Patients: receivers or participants?', in K. Barnard and K. Lee, eds, *Conflicts in the National Health Service*, London: Croom Helm, 72–98.

Jones, I.G. and D. Cameron (1984), 'Social class analysis: an embarrassment to epidemiology', *Community Medicine*, **6**, 37–46.

Jones-Lee, M.W. (1976), *The Value of Life*, London: Martin Robertson.

Jones-Lee, M.W. (1989), *The Economics of Safety and Physical Risk*, Oxford: Basil Blackwell.

Jones-Lee, M.W., M. Hammerton and P.R. Philips (1985), 'The value of safety: results of a national sample survey', *Economic Journal*, **95**, 49–72.

Joyce, T., A.D. Racine and N. Mocan (1992), 'The consequences and costs of maternal substance abuse in New York City', *Journal of Health Economics*, **11**, 297–314.

Kahn, M. (1998), 'Health and labor market performance: the case of diabetes', *Journal of Labor Economics*, **16**, 878–99.

Kant, I. (1961 [1785]), *Groundwork of the Metaphysic of Morals*, tr. by H.J. Paton, in H.J. Paton, ed., *The Moral Law*, London: Hutchinson.

Kaplan, R.M. (1995), 'Utility assessment for estimating quality-adjusted life years', in F.A. Sloan, ed., *Valuing Health Care: Costs, Benefits, and Effectiveness of Pharmaceuticals and Other Medical Technologies*, Cambridge: Cambridge University Press, 31–60.

Keeler, E.B. (2001), 'The value of remaining lifetime is close to estimated values of life', *Journal of Health Economics*, **20**, 141–3.

Kenkel, D. (1990), 'Consumer health information and the demand for medical care', *Review of Economics and Statistics*, **72**, 587–95.

Kessler, D. and M. McClellan (1996), 'Do doctors practice defensive medicine?', *Quarterly Journal of Economics*, **111**, 353–90.

Kind, P., P. Dolan, C. Gudex and A. Williams (1998), 'Variations in population health status: results from a United Kingdom national questionnaire survey', *British Medical Journal*, **316**, 736–41.

Kind, P., R.M. Rosser and A. Williams (1982), 'Valuation of quality of life: some psychometric evidence', in M.W. Jones-Lee, ed., *The Value of Life and Safety*, Amsterdam: North-Holland, 159–70.

Klarman, H.E. (1965), 'Syphilis control programs', in R. Dorfman, ed., *Measuring Benefits of Government Investments*, Washington, DC: The Brookings Institution, 367–414.

Klarman, H.E., J.O. Francis and G. Rosenthal (1973 [1968]), 'Cost effectiveness analysis applied to the treatment of chronic renal disease', *Medical Care*, **6**, reprinted in M.H. Cooper and A.J. Culyer, eds, *Health Economics: Selected Readings*, Harmondsworth, Penguin Books, 230–40.

Klein, R. (1983), *The Politics of the National Health Service*, London: Longmans.

Kleiner, M.M. and R.T. Kudrle (2000), 'Does regulation affect economic outcomes? The case of dentistry', *Journal of Law and Economics*, **43**, 547–82.

Knetsch, J.L. and J.A. Sinden (1984), 'Willingness to pay and compensation demanded: experimental evidence of an unexpected disparity in measures of value', *Quarterly Journal of Economics*, **99**, 507–21.

Kravdal, O. (2001), 'The impact of marital status on cancer survival', *Social Science and Medicine*, **52**, 357–68.

Kristiansen, I.S. and G. Mooney (2004), 'Evidence-based medicine: method, collaboration, movement or crusade?', in I.S. Kristiansen and G. Mooney, eds, *Evidence-Based Medicine: In Its Place*, London: Routledge, 1–19.

Kwoka, J.E. (1984), 'Advertising and the price and quality of optometric services', *American Economic Review*, **74**, 211–16.

Lakdawalla, D. and T.J. Philipson (2006), 'Economics of obesity', in A.M. Jones, ed., *The Elgar Companion to Health Economics*, Cheltenham, UK and Northampton, MA, USA: Edward Elgar, 72–82.

Le Grand, J. (1978), 'The distribution of public expenditure: the case of health care', *Economica*, **45**, 125–42.

Le Grand, J. (1982), *The Strategy of Equality*, London: George Allen & Unwin.

Le Grand, J. (1991), *Equity and Choice: An Essay in Economics and Applied Philosophy*, London: HarperCollins.

Le Grand, J. and M. Rabin (1986), 'Trends in British health inequality, 1931–1983', in A.J. Culyer and B. Jönsson, eds, *Private and Public Health Services: Complementarities and Conflicts*, Oxford: Basil Blackwell, 112–27.

Leibenstein, H. (1987), *Inside the Firm: The Inefficiencies of Hierarchy*, Cambridge, MA: Harvard University Press.

Lindsay, C.M. and B. Feigenbaum (1984), 'Rationing by waiting lists', *American Economic Review*, **74**, 404–17.

Lleras-Muney, A. (2002), *The Relationship between Education and Adult Mortality in the United States*, Working Paper 8986, Cambridge, MA: National Bureau of Economic Research.

Locke, J. (1993 [1689]), *Second Treatise on Civil Government*, in D. Wootton, ed., *John Locke: Political Writings*, Harmondsworth: Penguin Books.

Loomes, G. and L. McKenzie (1989), 'The use of QALYs in health care decision making', *Social Science and Medicine*, **28**, 299–308.

Lynch, J.W., G.A. Kaplan, E.R. Pamuk, R.D. Cohen, K.E. Heck, J.L. Balfour and I.H. Yen (1998), 'Income inequality and mortality in metropolitan areas of the United States', *American Journal of Public Health*, **88**, 1074–9.

Lynch, J.W., G.A. Kaplan and J.T. Salonen (1997), 'Why do poor people behave poorly? Variation in adult health behaviours and psychosocial characteristics by stages of the socioeconomic lifecourse', *Social Science and Medicine*, **44**, 809–19.

Madrian, B.C. (1994), 'Employment-based health insurance and job mobility: is there evidence of job-lock?', *Quarterly Journal of Economics*, **109**, 27–54.

Manning, W.G., A. Leibowitz, G.A. Goldberg, W.H. Rogers and J.P. Newhouse

(1984), 'A controlled trial of the effect of a prepaid group practice on the use of services', *New England Journal of Medicine*, **310** (23), 1505–10.

Manning, W.G. and M.S. Marquis (1996), 'Health insurance: the tradeoff between risk pooling and moral hazard', *Journal of Health Economics*, **15**, 609–39.

Manning, W.G., J.P. Newhouse, N. Duan, E.B. Keeler, A. Leibowitz and M.S. Marquis (1987), 'Health insurance and the demand for medical care: evidence from a randomized experiment', *American Economic Review*, **77**, 251–77.

Manor, O., Z. Eisenbach, A. Israeli and Y. Friedlander (2000), 'Mortality differentials among women: the Israel Longitudinal Mortality Study', *Social Science and Medicine*, **51**, 1175–88.

Marder, W.D. and S. Zuckerman (1985), 'Competition and medical groups: a survivor analysis', *Journal of Health Economics*, **4**, 167–76.

Marin, A. and G. Psacharopoulos (1982), 'The reward for risk in the labor market: evidence from the United Kingdom and a reconciliation with other studies', *Journal of Political Economy*, **90**, 827–53.

Marmot, M. and M. Bobak (2000), 'International comparators and poverty and health in Europe', *British Medical Journal*, **321**, 1124–8.

Marmot, M., C.D. Ryff, L.L. Bumpass, M. Shipley and N.F. Marks (1997), 'Social inequalities in health: next questions and converging evidence', *Social Science and Medicine*, **44**, 901–10.

Marmot, M. and T. Theorell (1988), 'Social class and cardiovascular disease: the contribution of work', *International Journal of Health Services*, **18**, 659–74.

Marquis, M.S. and S.H. Long (1995), 'Worker demand for health insurance in the non-group market', *Journal of Health Economics*, **14**, 47–63.

Marshall, A. (1949 [1890]), *Principles of Economics*, London: Macmillan.

Marshall, A. (1966 [1907]), 'Social possibilities of economic chivalry', in A.C. Pigou, ed., *Memorials of Alfred Marshall*, New York: Augustus M. Kelley, 323–46.

Marshall, T.H. (1981 [1965]), 'The right to welfare', *Sociological Review*, **13**, reprinted in his *The Right to Welfare and Other Essays*, London: Heinemann Educational Books, 83–94.

Marshall, T.H. (1992 [1950]), *Citizenship and Social Class*, London: Pluto Press.

Martin, S. and P.C. Smith (1996), 'Explaining variations in inpatient length of stay in the National Health Service', *Journal of Health Economics*, **15**, 279–304.

Martin, S. and P.C. Smith (1999), 'Rationing by waiting lists: an empirical investigation', *Journal of Public Economics*, **71**, 141–64.

Maslow, A.H. (1968 [1962]), *Toward a Psychology of Being*, 2nd edn, Princeton, NJ: Van Nostrand.

Maslow, A.H. (1970 [1954]), *Motivation and Personality*, 2nd edn, New York: Harper and Row.

Mather, H.G., N.G. Pearson, K.L.Q. Read, D.B. Shaw, G.R. Steed, M.G. Thorne, S. Jones, C.J. Guerrier, E.D. Erault, P.M. McHugh, N.R. Chowdhury, M.H. Jafary and T.J. Wallace (1971), 'Acute myocardial infarction: home and hospital treatment', *British Medical Journal*, **3**, 334–8.

Maxwell, R.J. (1981), *Health and Wealth: An International Study of Health-Care Spending*, Lexington, MA: Lexington Books.

McCarthy, T.R. (1985), 'The competitive nature of the primary-care physician services market', *Journal of Health Economics*, **4**, 93–117.

McClellan, M. and H. Noguchi (1998), 'Technological change in heart-disease treatment: does high tech mean low value?', *American Economic Review (Papers and Proceedings)*, **88**, 90–96.

McGuire, A., J. Henderson and G.H. Mooney (1988), *The Economics of Health Care*, London: Routledge & Kegan Paul.

McKeown, T. (1979), *The Role of Medicine*, 2nd edn, Oxford: Blackwell.

McKinlay, J.B. and S.M. McKinlay (1977), 'The questionable contribution of medical measures to the decline of mortality in the United States in the twentieth century', *Milbank Memorial Fund Quarterly*, **55**, 405–28.

Meltzer, D. (1997), 'Accounting for future costs in medical cost-effectiveness analysis', *Journal of Health Economics*, **16**, 33–64.

Menger, C. (1976 [1871]), *Principles of Economics*, tr. by J. Dingwall and B.F. Hoselitz, New York: New York University Press.

Meyerowitz, B. (1983), 'Postmastectomy coping strategies and quality of life', *Health Psychology*, **2**, 117–32.

Mill, J.S. (1974 [1859]), *On Liberty*, ed. by Gertrude Himmelfarb, Harmondsworth: Penguin Books.

Miller, R.H. and H.S. Luft (1997), 'Does managed care lead to better or worse quality of care?', *Health Affairs*, **16** (5), 7–25.

Miller, R.H. and H.S. Luft (2002), 'HMO plan performance update: an analysis of the literature, 1997–2001', *Health Affairs*, **21** (4), 63–96.

Ministry of Health (Great Britain) (1944), *A National Health Service*, Cmd 6502.

Mirrlees, J.A. (1982), 'The economic uses of Utilitarianism', in A. Sen and B. Williams, eds, *Utilitarianism and Beyond*, Cambridge: Cambridge University Press, 63–84.

Mishan, E.J. (1971), 'Evaluation of life and limb: a theoretical approach', *Journal of Political Economy*, **79**, 687–705.

Mooney, G.H. (1977), *The Valuation of Human Life*, London: Macmillan.

Mooney, G.H. (1982), 'Breast cancer screening: a study in cost-effectiveness analysis', *Social Science and Medicine*, **16**, 1277–82.

Mooney, G.H. (1991), 'Communitarianism and health economics', in J.B. Davis, ed., *The Social Economics of Health Care*, London: Routledge, 40–60.

Mooney, G.H. (2002), 'The Danish health care system: it ain't broke... so don't fix it', *Health Policy*, **59**, 161–71.

Mooney, G.H. and T.F. Andersen (1990), 'Challenges facing modern health care', in T.F. Andersen and G.H. Mooney, eds, *The Challenges of Medical Practice Variations*, London: Macmillan, 192–200.

Moore, M.J. and W.K. Viscusi (1988), 'Doubling the estimated value of life: results using new occupational fatality data', *Journal of Policy Analysis and Management*, **7**, 476–90.

Morris, S., M. Sutton and H. Gravelle (2005), 'Inequity and inequality in the use of health care in England: an empirical investigation', *Social Science and Medicine*, **60**, 1251–66.

Mueller, C.D. and A.C. Monheit (1988), 'Insurance coverage and the demand for dental care', *Journal of Health Economics*, **7**, 59–72.

Murray, C.J.L. (1996), 'Rethinking DALYs', in C.J.L. Murray and A.D. Lopez, eds, *The Global Burden of Disease*, Cambridge, MA: Harvard University Press, 1–98.

Murray, C.J.L. and A.K. Acharya (1997), 'Understanding DALYs', *Journal of Health Economics*, **16**, 703–30.

Musgrave, R.A. and P.B. Musgrave (1980), *Public Finance in Theory and Practice*, 3rd edn, New York: McGraw-Hill.

National Institute for Health and Clinical Excellence (2006), *Report on NICE Citizens Council Meeting: Inequalities in Health*, London: National Institute for Health and Clinical Excellence.

National Statistics (2006), *Life Expectancy at Age 65 Continues to Rise*, press release, London: National Statistics.

Needleman, L. (1980), 'The valuation of changes in the risk of death by those at risk', *Manchester School*, **48**, 229–54.

Neuberger, J., D. Adams, P. MacMaster, A. Maidment and M. Speed (1998), 'Assessing priorities for allocation of donor liver grafts: survey of public and clinicians', *British Medical Journal*, **317**, 172–5.

Neuhauser, D. and A.M. Lewicki (1975), 'What do we gain from the sixth stool guaiac?', *New England Journal of Medicine*, **293**, 226–8.

Neumann, John von and O. Morgenstern (1972 [1944]), *Theory of Games and Economic Behavior*, Princeton, NJ: Princeton University Press.

Newhouse, J.P. (1977), 'Medical-care expenditure: a cross-national survey', *Journal of Human Resources*, **12**, 115–25.

Newhouse, J.P. (1978), *The Economics of Medical Care*, Reading, MA: Addison-Wesley.

Newhouse, J.P. (1992), 'Medical care costs: how much welfare loss?', *Journal of Economic Perspectives*, **6**, 3–21.

Newhouse, J.P. and L.J. Friedlander (1980), 'The relationship between medical resources and measures of health: some additional evidence', *Journal of Human Resources*, **15**, 200–218.

Newhouse, J.P. and the Insurance Experiment Group (1993), *Free for All? Lessons from the RAND Health Insurance Experiment*, Cambridge, MA: Harvard University Press.

Nguyen, X.N. and F.W. Derrick (1997), 'Physician behavioral response to a Medicare price reduction', *Health Services Research*, **21**, 283–98.

Niskanen, W. (1971), *Bureaucracy and Representative Government*, Chicago, IL: Aldine.

Nozick, R. (1974), *Anarchy, State, and Utopia*, New York: Basic Books.

Nussbaum, M.C. (1993), 'Non-relative virtues: an Aristotelian approach', in M.C. Nussbaum and A.K. Sen, eds, *The Quality of Life*, Oxford: Clarendon Press.

Olsen, J.A. and C. Donaldson (1998), 'Helicopters, hearts and hips: using willingness to pay to set priorities for public sector health care programmes', *Social Science and Medicine*, **46**, 1–12.

Olson, C.A. (1981), 'An analysis of wage differentials received by workers on dangerous jobs', *Journal of Human Resources*, **16**, 167–85.

Organisation for Economic Co-operation and Development (2005), 'Health: spending and resources', in *OECD in Figures*, http://213.253.134.29/oecd/pdfs/browseit/0105061E.PDF, accessed 1 February 2007.

Parkin, D., A. McGuire and B. Yule (1987), 'Aggregate health care expenditures and national income: is health care a luxury good?', *Journal of Health Economics*, **6**, 109–27.

Pauly, M.V. (1968), 'The economics of moral hazard: comment', *American Economic Review*, **58**, 531–7.

Pauly, M.V. (1986), 'Taxation, health insurance, and market failure in the medical economy', *Journal of Economic Literature*, **24**, 629–75.

Pauly, M.V. (1988), 'A primer on competition in medical markets', in H.E. Frech III, ed., *Health Care in America: The Political Economy of Hospitals and Health Insurance*, San Francisco, CA: Pacific Research Institute for Public Policy, 27–71.

Pauly, M.V. (1994a), 'Editorial: a re-examination of the meaning and importance of supplier-induced demand', *Journal of Health Economics*, **13**, 369–72.

Pauly, M.V. (1994b), 'Universal health insurance in the Clinton Plan: coverage as a tax-financed public good', *Journal of Economic Perspectives*, **8**, 45–53.

Pauly, M.V. (1995), 'Valuing health care benefits in money terms', in F.A. Sloan, ed., *Valuing Health Care: Costs, Benefits, and Effectiveness of Pharmaceuticals and Other Medical Technologies*, Cambridge: Cambridge University Press, 99–124.

Pauly, M.V., A.L. Hillman, M.S. Kim and D.R. Brown (2002), 'Competitive behavior in the HMO marketplace', *Health Affairs*, **21** (1), 194–202.

Pauly, M.V. and A.M. Percy (2000), 'Cost and performance: a comparison of the individual and group health insurance markets', *Journal of Health Politics, Policy and Law*, **25**, 9–26.

Pearson, R.J.C., R. Smedby, R. Berfenstam, R.F. Logan, A.M. Burgess and O.L. Peterson (1968), 'Hospital caseloads in Liverpool, New England, and Uppsala: an international comparison', *The Lancet*, **2**, 7 September, 559–66.

Pechman, J.A. (1986), *The Rich, the Poor, and the Taxes they Pay*, Brighton: Wheatsheaf Books.

Pechman, J.A. and B.A. Okner (1974), *Who Bears the Tax Burden?*, Washington, DC: The Brookings Institution.

Peltzman, S. (1974), *Regulation of Pharmaceutical Innovation*, Washington, DC: American Enterprise Institute.

Peltzman, S. (1975), 'The effects of automobile safety regulation', *Journal of Political Economy*, **83**, 677–725.

Phelps, C.E. (1988), 'Death and taxes: an opportunity for substitution', *Journal of Health Economics*, **7**, 1–24.

Phelps Brown, H. (1988), *Egalitarianism and the Generation of Inequality*, Oxford: Clarendon Press.

Piachaud, D. and J.M. Weddell (1972), 'The economics of treating varicose veins', *International Journal of Epidemiology*, **1**, 287–94.

Pigou, A.C. (1932 [1920]), *The Economics of Welfare*, 4th edn, London: Macmillan.

Preston, S.H. (1975), 'The changing relation between mortality and level of economic development', *Population Studies*, **29**, 231–48.

Pritchett, L. and L.H. Summers (1996), 'Wealthier is healthier', *Journal of Human Resources*, **31**, 841–68.

Putnam, R.D. (1995), 'Bowling alone: America's declining social capital', *Journal of Democracy*, **6**, 65–78.

Rawls, J. (1972 [1971]), *A Theory of Justice*, Oxford: Clarendon Press.

Rawls, J. (1982), 'Social unity and primary goods', in A. Sen and B. Williams, eds, *Utilitarianism and Beyond*, Cambridge: Cambridge University Press, 159–85.

Reichman, N.E. and M.J. Florio (1996), 'The effects of enriched prenatal care services on Medicaid birth outcomes in New Jersey', *Journal of Health Economics*, **15**, 455–76.

Reisman, D.A. (1993), *Market and Health*, London: Macmillan.

Reisman, D.A. (2001), *Richard Titmuss: Welfare and Society*, 2nd edn, Basingstoke: Palgrave.

Reisman, D.A. (2005), 'Exchange and authority: the mixed economy', *American Review of Political Economy*, **3** (2), 1–15.

Reisman, D.A. (2006), 'Payment for health in Singapore', *International Journal of Social Economics*, **33** (2), 132–59.

Rice, T. (2001), 'Should consumer choice be encouraged in health care?', in J.B. Davis, ed., *The Social Economics of Health Care*, London: Routledge, 9–39.

Rich, G., N.J. Glass and J.B. Selkon (1976), 'Cost-effectiveness of two methods of screening for asymptomatic bacteriuria', *British Journal of Preventive and Social Medicine*, **30**, 54–9.

Richards, C. (1989), *The Health of Doctors*, London: King Edward's Hospital Fund.

Richardson, J. (1994), 'Cost utility analysis: what should be measured?', *Social Science and Medicine*, **39**, 7–21.

Richardson, J., J. Hall and G. Salkeld (1996), 'The measurement of utility in multiphase health states', *International Journal of Technology Assessment in Health Care*, **12**, 151–62.

Rizzo, J.A. and R.J. Zeckhauser (1990), 'Advertising and entry: the case of physician services', *Journal of Political Economy*, **98**, 476–500.

Roach, B. (2003), *Progressive and Regressive Taxation in the United States: Who's Really Paying (and Not Paying) their Fair Share?*, Working Paper No. 03-10, Medford, MA: Global Development and Environment Institute, Tufts University.

Roemer, M.I. (1961), 'Bed supply and hospital utilization', *Hospitals: Journal of the American Hospital Association*, **35**, November, 36–42.

Roos, N.P., L.L. Roos, Jr. and P.D. Henteleff (1977), 'Elective surgery rates – do high rates mean lower standards?', *New England Journal of Medicine*, **297**, 360–65.

Rosko, M.D. and R.W. Broyles (1987), 'Short-term responses of hospitals to the DRG prospective pricing mechanism in New Jersey', *Medical Care*, **25**, 88–99.

Rosser, R., M. Cottee, R. Rabin and C. Salai (1992), 'Index of health-related quality of life', in A. Hopkins, ed., *Measures of the Quality of Life*, London: Royal College of Physicians, 81–9.

Rosser, R.M. and P. Kind (1978), 'A scale of valuation of states of illness: is there a social consensus?', *International Journal of Epidemiology*, **7**, 347–58.

Rossett, R.N. and L.F. Huang (1973), 'The effect of health insurance on the demand for medical care', *Journal of Political Economy*, **81**, 281–305.

Ruhm, C.J. (2005), 'Healthy living in hard times', *Journal of Health Economics*, **24**, 341–63.

Russell, L.B. (1994), *Educated Guesses: Making Policy about Medical Screening Tests*, Berkeley, CA: University of California Press.

Sackett, D.L. and G.W. Torrance (1978), 'The utility of different health states as perceived by the general public', *Journal of Chronic Diseases*, **31**, 697–704.

Saffer, H. (1991), 'Alcohol advertising bans and alcohol abuse: an international perspective', *Journal of Health Economics*, **10**, 65–79.

Samuelson, P.A. (1954), 'The pure theory of public expenditure', *Review of Economics and Statistics*, **36**, 387–9.

Schelling, T.C. (1973 [1968]), 'The value of preventing death', in S.B. Chase, ed., *Problems in Public Expenditure Analysis*, reprinted in M.H. Cooper and A.J. Culyer, eds, *Health Economics*, Harmondsworth: Penguin Books, 295–321.

Schuster, M.A., E.A. McGlynn and R.H. Brook (1998), 'How good is the quality of health care in the United States?', *The Milbank Quarterly*, **76**, 517–63.

Schwartz, J. and D.W. Dockery (1992), 'Increased mortality in Philadelphia associated with daily air pollution concentrations', *American Review of Respiratory Diseases*, **145**, 600–604.

Sen, A. (1999), *Development as Freedom*, Oxford: Oxford University Press.

Simon, H.A. (1979), 'Rational decision making in business organizations', *American Economic Review*, **69**, 493–513.

Smith, A. (1961 [1776]), *The Wealth of Nations*, ed. by E. Cannan, London: Methuen.

Smith, A. (1966 [1759]), *The Theory of Moral Sentiments*, New York: Augustus M. Kelley.

Smith, C., C. Cowan, S. Heffler and A. Catlin (2006), 'National health spending in 2004', *Health Affairs*, **25** (1), 186–96.

Smith, J.P. (1999), 'Healthy bodies and thick wallets: the dual relation between health and economic status', *Journal of Economic Perspectives*, **13**, 145–66.

Starr, P. (1986), 'Health care for the poor: the past twenty years', in S.H. Danziger and D.H. Weinberg, eds, *Fighting Poverty: What Works and What Doesn't*, Cambridge, MA: Harvard University Press, 106–32.

Stationery Office (1998), *Independent Inquiry into Inequalities in Health: Report* (The Acheson Report), London: The Stationery Office.

Stewart, J.M., E. O'Shea, C. Donaldson and P. Shackley (2002), 'Do ordering effects matter in willingness-to-pay studies of health care?', *Journal of Health Economics,* **21**, 585–99.

Stigler, G.J. (1970), 'Director's Law of public income redistribution', *Journal of Law and Economics*, **13**, 1–10.

Strombom, B.A., T.C. Buchmueller and P.J. Feldstein (2002), 'Switching costs, price sensitivity and health plan choice', *Journal of Health Economics*, **21**, 89–116.

Sturm, R. (2002), 'The effect of obesity, smoking, and drinking on medical problems and costs', *Health Affairs*, **21** (2), 245–53.

Sutherland, H.J., H. Llewellyn-Thomas, N.F. Boyd and J.F. Till (1982), 'Attitudes toward quality of survival: the concept of "maximum endurable time"', *Medical Decision Making*, **2**, 299–308.

Szreter, S. and M. Woolcock (2004), 'Health by association? Social capital, social theory and the political economy of public health', *International Journal of Epidemiology*, **33**, 650–67.

Tawney, R.H. (1964 [1931]), *Equality*, London: George Allen and Unwin.

Tawney, R.H. (1966), *The Radical Tradition*, Harmondsworth: Penguin Books.

Thaler, R.H. (1991), *Quasi Rational Economics*, New York: Russell Sage Foundation.

Thompson, M.S. (1986), 'Willingness to pay and accept risks to cure chronic disease', *American Journal of Public Health*, **76**, 392–6.

Titmuss, R.M. (1950), *Problems of Social Policy*, London: His Majesty's Stationery Office and Longmans, Green and Co.

Titmuss, R.M. (1963), *Essays on 'The Welfare State'*, 2nd edn, London: George Allen and Unwin.

Titmuss, R.M. (1968), *Commitment to Welfare*, London: George Allen and Unwin.

Titmuss, R.M. (1970), *The Gift Relationship: From Human Blood to Social Policy*, London: George Allen and Unwin.

Titmuss, R.M. (1974), *Social Policy: An Introduction*, ed. by B. Abel-Smith and Kay Titmuss, London: George Allen and Unwin.

Titmuss, R.M. (n.d.), Unpublished lecture, in Papers of Richard Titmuss, British Library of Political and Economic Science, London School of Economics, Box 3/370. Cited by permission of Ann Oakley.

Titmuss, R.M. (with B. Abel-Smith, G. Macdonald, A. Williams and C. Ward) (1964) *The Health Services of Tanganyika*, London: Pitman Medical Publishing.

Tobin, J. (1970), 'On limiting the domain of inequality', *Journal of Law and Economics*, 13, 263–77.

Tönnies, F. (2001 [1887]), *Community and Civil Society*, tr. by J. Harris and M. Hollis, Cambridge: Cambridge University Press.

Torrance, G.W. (1986), 'Measurement of health state utilities for economic appraisal', *Journal of Health Economics*, **5**, 1–30.

Torrance, G.W., J.E. Siegel and B.R. Luce (1996), 'Framing and designing the cost-effectiveness analysis', in M.R. Gold, L.B. Russell, J.E. Siegel and M.C.

Weinstein, eds, *Cost-Effectiveness in Health and Medicine*, Oxford: Oxford University Press, 54–81.

Tosteson, A.N.A., D.I. Rosenthal, J. Melton III and M.C. Weinstein (1990), 'Cost effectiveness of screening perimenopausal white women for osteoporosis: bone densitometry and hormone replacement therapy', *Annals of Internal Medicine*, **113**, 594–603.

Townsend, P. (1979), *Poverty in the United Kingdom*, Harmondsworth: Penguin Books.

Townsend, P. (1987), 'The geography of poverty and ill-health', in A. Williams, ed., *Health and Economics*, London: Macmillan, 37–67.

Townsend, P. and N. Davidson (1982a), 'Introduction to the Pelican Edition', in P. Townsend and N. Davidson, eds, *Inequalities in Health: The Black Report*, Harmondsworth: Penguin Books, 13–34.

Townsend, P. and N. Davidson, eds (1982b), *Inequalities in Health: The Black Report*, Harmondsworth: Penguin Books.

Townsend, P., P. Phillimore and A. Beattie (1988), *Health and Deprivation*, Beckenham: Croom Helm.

Tu, J.V., D. Naylor, D. Kumar, B.A. DeBuono, B.J. McNeil and E.L. Hannan (1997), 'Coronary artery bypass graft surgery in Ontario and New York State: which rate is right?', *Annals of Internal Medicine*, **126**, 13–19.

Tudor Hart, J. (1971), 'The inverse care law', *The Lancet*, 27 February, 405–12.

Tullock, G. (1976), *The Vote Motive*, London: Institute of Economic Affairs.

Turner, R.J., B. Wheaton and D.A. Lloyd (1995), 'The epidemiology of social stress', *American Sociological Review*, **60**, 104–25.

Tversky, A. and D. Kahneman (1981), 'The framing of decisions and the psychology of choice', *Science*, **211**, 453–8.

Tversky, A., P. Slovic and D. Kahneman (1990), 'The causes of preference reversal', *American Economic Review*, **80**, 204–17.

Vayda, E. (1973), 'A comparison of surgical rates in Canada and in England and Wales', *New England Journal of Medicine*, **289**, 1224–9.

Viscusi, W. Kip (1992), *Fatal Tradeoffs: Public and Private Responsibilities for Health*, New York: Oxford University Press.

Viscusi, W. Kip (1993), 'The value of risks to life and health', *Journal of Economic Literature*, **31**, 1912–46.

Viscusi, W. Kip (1995), 'Discounting health effects for medical decisions', in F.A. Sloan, ed., *Valuing Health Care*, Cambridge: Cambridge University Press, 125–47.

Viscusi, W. Kip and J.E. Aldy (2003), 'The value of a statistical life: a critical review of market estimates throughout the world', *Journal of Risk and Uncertainty*, **27**, 5–76.

Wagstaff, A. (1991), 'QALYs and the equity-efficiency trade-off', *Journal of Health Economics*, **10**, 21–41.

Wagstaff, A. and E. van Doorslaer (2000), 'Equity in health care finance and delivery', in A.J. Culyer and J.P. Newhouse, eds, *Handbook of Health Economics*, Vol. 1B, Amsterdam: Elsevier, 1803–62.

Waldmann, R.J. (1992), 'Income distribution and infant mortality', *Quarterly Journal of Economics*, **107**, 1283–302.

Walzer, M. (1983), *Spheres of Justice: A Defence of Plurality and Equality*, Oxford: Martin Robertson.

Wasserman, J., W.G. Manning, J.P. Newhouse and J.D. Winkler (1991), 'The effects of excise duties and regulations on cigarette smoking', *Journal of Health Economics*, **10**, 43–64.

Wedig, G.J. (1988), 'Health status and the demand for health: results on price elasticities', *Journal of Health Economics*, **7**, 151–63.

Weeks, W.B., A.E. Wallace, M.M. Wallace and H.G. Welch (1994), 'A comparison of the educational costs and incomes of physicians and other professionals', *New England Journal of Medicine*, **330**, 1280–86.

Weinstein, M.C. (1995), 'From cost-effectiveness ratios to resource allocation', in F.A. Sloan, ed., *Valuing Health Care*, Cambridge: Cambridge University Press, 77–97.

Weisbrod, B.A. (1971), 'Costs and benefits of medical research: a case study of poliomyelitis', *Journal of Political Economy*, **79**, 527–44.

Weisbrod, B.A. (1991), 'The health care quadrilemma: an essay on technological change, insurance, quality of care, and cost containment', *Journal of Economic Literature*, **29**, 523–52.

Wennberg, J.E., B.A. Barnes and M. Zubkoff (1982), 'Professional uncertainty and the problem of supplier-induced demand', *Social Science and Medicine*, **16**, 811–24.

Wennberg, J.E., L. Blowers, R. Parker and A.M. Gittelsohn (1977), 'Changes in tonsillectomy rates associated with feedback and review', *Pediatrics*, **59**, 821–6.

Wennberg, J.E. and M. Cooper (1999), *The Quality of Medical Care in the United States: A Report on the Medicare Program (The Dartmouth Atlas of Health Care in the United States)*, Chicago, IL: American Health Association Press.

Wennberg, J.E., E.S. Fisher and J.S. Skinner (2002), 'Geography and the debate over Medicare reform', *Health Affairs*, 13 February, W96–W114.

Wennberg, J.E., J.L. Freeman and W.J. Culp (1987), 'Are hospital services rationed in New Haven or overutilised in Boston?', *The Lancet*, **1**, 23 May, 1185–8.

Wennberg, J.E. and A. Gittelsohn (1973), 'Small area variations in health care delivery', *Science*, **182**, 1102–8.

Wennberg, J.E. and A. Gittelsohn (1982), 'Variations in medical care among small areas', *Scientific American*, **246** (4), 100–111.

Wenneker, M., J.E. Weissman and A.M. Epstein (1990), 'The association of payer with utilization of cardiac procedures in Massachusetts', *Journal of the American Medical Association*, **264**, 1255–60.

Westert, G.P., A.P. Nieboer and P.P. Groenewegen (1993), 'Variation in duration of hospital stay between hospitals and between doctors within hospitals', *Social Science and Medicine*, **37**, 833–9.

Wilkinson, R.G. (1996), *Unhealthy Societies: The Afflictions of Inequality*, London: Routledge.

Williams, A. (1974), 'Measuring the effectiveness of health care systems', in M. Perlman, ed., *The Economics of Health and Medical Care*, London: Macmillan, 361–76.

Williams, A. (1978), '"Need" – an economic exegesis', in A.J. Culyer and K.G. Wright, eds, *Economic Aspects of Health Services*, London: Martin Robertson, 32–45.

Williams, A. (1987), 'Introduction', in A. Williams, ed., *Health and Economics*, London: Macmillan, xi–xiii.

Williams, A. (1997a [1985]), 'Economics of coronary artery bypass grafting', *British Medical Journal*, **291**, reprinted in A.J. Culyer and A. Maynard, eds, *Being Reasonable about the Economics of Health: Selected Essays by Alan Williams*, Cheltenham, UK and Northampton, MA, USA: Edward Elgar, 238–48.

Williams, A. (1997b), *Being Reasonable about the Economics of Health: Selected Essays by Alan Williams*, ed. by A. J. Culyer and A. Maynard, Cheltenham, UK and Northampton, MA, USA: Edward Elgar.

Williams, A. and R. Cookson (2000), 'Equity in health', in A.J. Culyer and J.P. Newhouse, eds, *Handbook of Health Economics*, Amsterdam: Elsevier, Vol. 1A, 1863–910.

Williams, B. (1973 [1962]), 'The idea of equality', in his *Problems of the Self: Philosophical Papers 1956–1972*, Cambridge: Cambridge University Press, 230–49.

Williamson, O.E. (1975), *Markets and Hierarchies*, New York: The Free Press.

Winslow, C.M., D.H. Solomon, M.R. Chassin, J. Kosecoff, N.J. Merrick and R.H. Brook (1988), 'The appropriateness of carotid endarterectomy', *New England Journal of Medicine*, **318**, 721–7.

World Health Organization (1962 [1946]), *Constitution of the World Health Organization*, in WHO, *Basic Documents*, Geneva: WHO, 1–18.

Yazici, E.Y. and R. Kaestner (2000), 'Medicaid expansions and the crowding out of private health insurance among children', *Inquiry*, **37**, 23–32.

Yip, W.C. (1998), 'Physician response to Medicare fee reductions: changes in the volume of coronary artery bypass graft (CABG) surgeries in the Medicare and private sectors', *Journal of Health Economics*, **17**, 675–99.

Yule, B.F., B.M. van Amerongen and M.C.M. van Schaik (1986), 'The economics and evaluation of dental care and treatment', *Social Science and Medicine*, **22**, 1131–9.

Index